ON A ROLL

A BAKER'S RECIPE TO REVITALIZE HISTORIC PENNSYLVANIA AVENUE

for my friend
Dr. Wanda McCoy
peace, blessings and love -
Margaret Powell
10.10.21

JAMES HAMLIN

December 31, 2015,

“James,
For many, experiencing their commitment and support for Baltimore has been a new phenomenon, but you have been a believer in Baltimore, and its people, long before it was fashionable. Thank you for your vision and commitment to our city. All the best to you in the new year! And whatever you do, don’t stop making those rolls!
Stephanie”

Stephanie Rawlings-Blake, Baltimore Mayor (2010 – 2016)

Photo credits:
Hamlin Family Collection
Medley Management and Prose, Inc.

Galley Book Cover Creation: *Dreamwurks Design*
Images of The Royal Theater used as background: *Historical Society of America*
Book Cover Design: Bob Cronan, *Lucidity Information Design, LLC*
Formats for Photo Inserts and The TRTCHC Impact Statement For The Royal Theater &
Community Heritage Center: *Visions That Transcend*

ISBN 978-0-578-63756-3 (Galley excerpt)
ISBN 978-0-578-96193-4 (Paperback)
ISBN 978-0-578-96194-1 (ebook)

In loving memory of Mattie Virginia Clemons Waymon, the single parent who made me what I am today and who inspired me to be me—and to give to others. You had so little, but you gave so much. I have been fortunate to have much—and I want to give.

****

"When we're dancing with the angels, the question we'll be asked: In 2019, what did we do to make sure we kept our democracy intact? Did we stand on the sidelines and say nothing?"

—The Honorable Elijah E. Cummings, United States Representative for Maryland's 7th Congressional District of Baltimore City and civil rights advocate.

(A life well lived: January 18, 1951 — October 17, 2019)

TABLE OF CONTENTS

ACKNOWLEDGMENTS

I noticed that in most memoirs, the author talks about all the people he or she would like to thank in their lives—those who got them to this point. So, I've shared a partial list here, and I've tried hard to demonstrate my gratitude by way of the events and flashbacks in my story. First, though, I must thank God for being there for me because He is always there when no one else is or can be. I thank Him for His unconditional love. Next, I would like to thank my mom for doing her best for me. While limited in education, she tried to add balance to my life. Yes, she often failed at her goal, but her love for me always fought its way to the surface—sooner or later.

My grandparents on my mother's side, in their caring—though sometimes strange—ways tried to live life the best way they knew how. My father's mother, Mother Hamlin (Essie), who loved me more than anyone during my formative years, instilled in me a faith in God. I had very little contact with my dad's father, James Hamlin. I guess it was because he ran his grocery store and spent little time at home. But I'm sure he loved me, too.

Then there was my Aunt Doris, who cared for us—my brothers Tony, Ricky, and me when no one else would. My stepfather, "Zeke" Harry Barron, was always there for me financially. I thank him for helping my mom take care of us.

I bet in every family there is a favorite uncle. In my family, it was Uncle Johnny, as we called him. He was like the older brother I never had. He was actually my mom's youngest brother. Out of all her siblings, he was the most down-to-earth, and he had a tendency to be blunt, telling it like it is. He was also a veteran of the Korean War. On occasion, he would talk about how the Japanese fought. Those stories intrigued me.

In my adult years, there is Brenda Taylor Hamlin, my loving wife. I am thankful to God for her. Brenda is the one person I have trusted longer than anyone. Brenda has always stood by me, even when she was not sure where I was taking our lives—or our relationship. I think she has always understood my love for her and that I would always fulfill my promise to her dad, which was to take care of her. The understanding between us first sowed its seed in our high school days.

I also need to thank all the educators I have admired down through the years. I was inspired by my eighth-grade art teacher, Mr. Apple. He was a short, average-sized White man, balding on the top of his head with light brownish blond hair around the sides. At Booker T. Washington Junior High School (as it was called back then), he was the only White teacher I had. He would give us a drawing assignment, and when I thought I was finished, I'd hand it to him, proud-like.

That's when he'd say, as he was handing it back to me, "Good. Better. Best. Never let it rest until the Good is better. And the better is the Best!"

A thank you goes out to Mr. Harris, my science teacher at Booker T., for always giving words of wisdom to both the boys and the girls in his charge. He was middle-aged and shared my complexion, chocolate brown. One of the best things I liked about him was that he was a cool cat. He talked to us on our level, but he didn't take any mess. And he was always down-to-earth like my favorite Uncle Johnny. Mr. Harris repeatedly reminded the girls that no man wants a dumb woman. To us boys, he preached respect for ourselves and for one another. Such respect showed up, he stressed, in how we dressed and in how we respected the women in our lives.

Pre-retirement and post, I have loved mentoring the students at Booker T. Washington Middle School as well as partnering with The Baltimore Ravens and others to do so. Thank you.

More recently, I'd like to thank The Ravens Football Hall of Famer Ed Reed for his support, for his friendship, and for calling *me* a father figure. Thank you to Glenn Younces and Courtney Aburn-Reisz of the Ed Reed Foundation. Thank you to the co-founders of my nonprofit, The Royal Theater & Community Heritage Corporation (TRTCHC): Alice Cole, Adrian Johnson, Charles Harrison, and the late Raymond V. Haysbert. Thank you, Kathleen Sherrill, Brian Grant, Dr. Brenda Brown, and Danny P. Henson, III. Thank you to Yvonne J. Medley of Medley Management and Prose, Inc., my writing coach and first-line editor, for being with me on this journey. And thank you to all my other fearless editors, Etoy Hamlin, Amy Davis, Alice Cole, Maggie Master, and John Kyle.

Okay, there are others, too many to name. But they will all find themselves in these chapters of my life.

PROLOGUE

Well, here I am, a retired UPSer, self-employed entrepreneur, community leader and activist, a baker, a youth advocate, a developer, a God-fearing man, and there's a host of other titles attached to who and what I am. I think it is safe for me to say that over the decades, I have earned the respect of many community leaders, political figures and supporters, and most of all, my family. Getting my journey down on paper has been an entire act of faith.

For years, I had been jotting down things that were occurring in my life. But I felt like I wasn't getting anywhere close to the makings of an honest-to-goodness memoir. Nothing was taking shape. Then I decided to take the approach, my wife, Brenda, suggested. Brenda Taylor Hamlin and I have been married for fifty-one years and counting.

She suggested, "Why don't you take a look at where you are today, then work backward."

So, I gave it a try. It got my engine started. And I decided to tell my story, mostly in real time occurrences. Thank you, Love of my Life.

So why did I title it, *On a Roll*? Well, when one sits down and looks back on his or her life, an important summation comes into play. Assessing my own playbook, I wondered if I've lived for myself or for all the people around me. Found in these pages will be portions chronicling my formative years: living in the midst of Jim Crow and witnessing its consequences and being a part of a fractured family with every member fighting to survive. It all happens in a time-stamped Baltimore of yesterday and today. What does history say? What do our current events reveal? I've tried to address these questions.

We make a lot of decisions in our lives, sometimes for ourselves and sometimes for the sake of others. Yes, there has been some pain for me. In fact, there's been a good measure of it. But there's also been the push to share the victories, the good things I've experienced in a community, long gone, as well as an overriding love for my family and the love my family gives back to me. So exactly where are the boundaries of balance for me? Well, the jury is still drawing up the District lines.

When I reflect on the components of The Avenue Bakery, I think of my wife, Brenda, and what she brought to the table. Yes, I was, and I still am *The Bakerman*, but she brought in the core Retail Operation Department. Her skills and knowledge of Point of Sale (POS) operations that she was required to have as a supervisor at Carroll County Public Library helped us structure our customer contact component.

My niece, Ashley Crawford, brought her expertise and knowledge to the business, too. In the beginning months, she was acquiring her degree in Hospitality from Morgan State University when she stepped up to apply her fresh skills at The Bakery. Ashley understood how to put together a Hazard Analysis Critical Control Points (HACCP) Plan that the Baltimore City Health Department required of us to earn our food license. It is a food safety management plan that creates and monitors food safety procedure.

That first day at The Avenue Bakery, back in August of 2011, my sister, Sandra Crawford, Ashley's mother, handled maintaining the cleanliness of the kitchen and facility during and after the operation. When Ashly and my son's mother-in-law, Susie Dezurn, handled the customers and our POS System the way Brenda had taught and trained them to do, we knew we were *On a Roll*!

At this moment, in the midst of 2021, I am not sure if anyone would care enough to read this account of my life except for my wife, children, and grandchildren. They may be a little curious about this sometimes-strange man who has always lived in their house or has lived in their sphere. They may want to better understand the things I say and do and have done. I am confident, however, that they are all clear on the things in which I believe: truth, integrity, and a refusal to understand why the powers-that-be can't understand why *all* Baltimoreans should have fair access to residential, societal, and economic equity. And I will live the rest of my life, working to create such equity and calling out those who fight against it. These are two of the main ingredients found in ***On a Roll: A Baker's Recipe to Revitalize Historic Pennsylvania Avenue***!

CHAPTER ONE

MY LIFE, ACCORDING TO BALTIMORE

My mother had ten children. She had ten children by five different fathers. And it gets a little more complicated than that because our respective fathers had children by women other than our mother. But be it inside the ten, birthed by our mother, or outside the ten; whether or not there was a half-blood bond or a whole-blood bond, we fought to remain a family. In fact, we all considered ourselves brothers and sisters, whole.

It's hard to remember everything that happened in my life, especially when I've had so many dramatic events occur. I truly believe that God has always been with me, though. And He's with me right now.

My earliest memory of life on this beautiful planet was the feeling of being so ugly that no one wanted me. No one except my mother and my father's parents—Mother Hamlin and Grandpop Hamlin. I lived periodically with my mother's parents, who were called Papa Burl James Clemons and Mama. I was not the only grandchild living with them. There was my cousin, Rosa, the oldest, and her brother, Herbert, a name he has always hated. Then there was my oldest sister, Dot. Sandra wasn't even thought of yet.

In my maternal grandmother's eyes, we were all bastard children who had been thrust upon her by her two youngest daughters, Mattie and Beulah. Mattie, my mom, who was the third from the youngest, and Beulah, the youngest girl, was next to the baby, Uncle Johnny. My sister, Dot, and I were conceived out of wedlock, and we had different fathers. Rosa and Herbert's situations were the same. Rosa and Dot inherited their mom's maiden name, which was Clemons. Herbert and I were given the last names of our respective fathers. So, Herbert's last name was Kelly, and that's what everyone called him until he passed away in 2014. If you didn't call him Kelly, you were asking for a fight. He hated his first name.

When people talk of prejudice today, most haven't experienced it in their home. You see, my cousin, Rosa, was a very fair-skinned little girl with pretty hair. Back-in-the-day, that was how we described a look that was as close to looking White as a Black person could get. My cousin, Kelly, owned a beautiful brown hue, the same as my sister, Dot. I was unfortunate, as was the thought back then because I was the darkest of the group. My hair was far from the *good* pretty, thick braids my cousin had. I had that sandy red hair that beaded up into little islands all over my head, somewhat like my African ancestors, I suppose. When company came, I was often sent to the small room in the attic, not to be seen by my grandmother, who referred to me as that black scamp. To this day, I have never looked up the word *scamp* to find out what I was in the eyes of my grandmother. One thing I did know; I was not a pretty sight, and there was not a lot of love for me in her heart.

My grandfather was different from my grandmother, though. He spent most of his time at Bethlehem Steel Mill, located in Sparrows Point, Maryland. During that time in my life, the only thing I remember about him was how hard he slept after working all night. He would snore so loudly; it seemed like the windows rattled because of it. Then he would get up and walk to the bathroom to prepare to go back to work. He was to me, at that time, a big burly Black man with a rumble in his voice when he spoke. He had jet-black eyebrows, a very thick mustache, and a Santa Claus-like round nose. I saw him walk to the bathroom one day, and I swore I would never wear long underwear. He wore the one-piece underwear that had an opening in the back for going to the bathroom. I remember seeing this huge man walking to the bathroom with his hairy butt hanging out this brown-stained opening. I said then, "Long underwear is not for me."

My grandfather, Papa Burl James Clemons, was the first man in my life whom I respected. For forty-nine years, he worked at Bethlehem Steel Mill. For one hundred and twenty years, Bethlehem Steel in Sparrows Point reigned in its industry. In the late 1950s, it employed upwards of 30,000 people. Its reign was designed not to go on forever. By 2012, the steel mill was dead due to several things, such as pricing itself out of its industry and its lack of innovation. And while the use of steel is still prevalent in the world, every time I rip a nice light sheet of aluminum foil from my Reynolds Wrap cylinder or see someone playfully crumpling up a light empty, flip-top soda can—I think, *Oooh, that's right, the next best thing, huh*. Both innovations signaled the Mill's demise. That said, in its day, it was formidable.

The work was hard, and the disdain and discrimination were commonplace for blacks. On the south side of Sparrows Point, homes were erected for White families. On the north side, homes for blacks were built, though they were not the same quality of the homes built for White families. But still, a sense of community, culture, faith, and even socializing among blacks grew strong. At the Mill, there were two mainstreams of employment, no matter one's qualifications.

There were White jobs and Black jobs. African American steelworkers were most likely assigned to perform the dirtiest and nastiest details. And if they had higher skills, they'd either hard-grind for years to be promoted, or they'd be assigned to train their less-qualified White counterparts who would soon become their bosses. These men, like my grandfather, fought hard to work hard. Still, for many, working at Bethlehem Steel was a ticket to the Black middle-class world. When I grew to manhood, well, almost manhood, I tried to get a job at Bethlehem Steel. But I wasn't hired—not because I was black, but because I was a lightweight. I didn't weigh enough. You had to be 140 pounds, and I was only 129 pounds.

Papa Burl James Clemons reared his family the best he could. He also served as a deacon and a pastor at the church in our small community. I remember listening to his powerful voice when he gave a sermon or started a hymn.

For years, I thought my grandfather was the only person in the family to own a car. He was always good to us kids. He would go to the market, bring fruit home, and tell us to eat all we wanted. He loved to see us eat. My grandmother never came out of the house except to go to church, hang up clothes, or to gossip with Mrs. Moore and Mrs. Collins in the backyard, or unless one of her daughters took her out clothes shopping. My grandfather did the marketing. Mama Clemons was hard to figure out. She seemed to have hated us. But I still loved her. She would hide the food all the time and dare us to go into it. She had very little education. She believed that the stories touted on the soap operas were real. And she faithfully watched them. My Aunt Doris would get upset with my grandfather because he wouldn't tell Grandma any different.

I was born in Sparrows Point, often referred to as *The Point*. I came into the world in a small two-story house located at 821 I Street. This was back in the day when doctors made house calls. From what I was told, my mother was in labor, and by the time the doctor got there, all he had to do was cut the umbilical cord. The circumstances of my birth became the one thing I took pride in, early on—I came into this world when I got good and ready. However, I do have a problem waiting for anything or anybody.

Sparrows Point was a small community that was on the grounds of Bethlehem Steel. As I mentioned, it was divided into two sections: the Black side and the White side. The stores were on the White side. Occasionally, we had to run from the White kids—*on the other side*—as we used to call it.

On our side, there were about three streets as I remember: two churches, a gas station, and the firehouse. The houses all seemed to have had a coating of red ash on them from the Mill, and cars were often covered in that red ash as well. The homes were small two-story houses with small backyards and small attic bedrooms. I remember our attic very well because I spent a lot of time up there peeping out the window while my cousin got to play with Wanda Moore. She was the granddaughter of Mrs. Moore, who lived next door. According to my grandmother, I was too black and ugly to play outside, least of all to play with Wanda. Wanda had a Ginger Snap brown complexion like my cousin, Herbert, or Kelly as he demanded to be called. And Mrs. Moore was light-and-bright like my cousin Rosa.

I am not sure why my grandmother hated my father so; perhaps it was his complexion. It appeared that whenever she looked at me, she saw him. I could see the hatred swell up in her eyes. I was unsure whether or not she hated him for not marrying my mother or because he gave her such an ugly grandchild. Or her anger could have been because she had reared her own children, and now she was stuck with us, her grands. Perhaps she feared the hard life that my dark skin would hand me—in her world as she knew it. In my grown years, I came to understand that fear almost always comes disguised as anger.

I was also taken to live with my father's mother when Mama Clemons got tired of looking at me. It used to be one vicious cycle. My mother would take me from Mother Hamlin's, back to her parents, and Mama Clemons would take me right back to Mother Hamlin. But there was the hint of a blessing hidden in all that back-and-forth because being pushed off to the Hamlins was the only opportunity my father, James Hamlin, got a chance to spend time with me. He worked all the time, and in my recollection, the time I spent with my father was very sketchy and brief.

I remember the days I spent with Mother Hamlin and Grandpa Hamlin; they used to have all kinds of toys there for me. Mother Hamlin had a snowball stand, and she also sold candy apples. I remember how pleasant it was when I used to go to church with them. Everybody loved Mother Hamlin and her grandkids. I also had another sister, Gertrude, who lived with Mother Hamlin. Gertrude and I shared the same father, but we had different mothers. These were the loving and caring sectors of my life, though brief. Gert used to take care of me as well. She was very loving.

My father did not live with Mother Hamlin but spent time with me there. He used to carry me around under his arm like a sack of potatoes. I remember him taking me to the house of his lady friend. I don't know or recall her name, but she was an attractive light-skinned lady, a buttercream. The one thing I do remember about her is that she would only look at the TV through a mirror instead of directly looking at it.

Until the day I die, I will always remember my father's hazel brown eyes, full of tears, when my mother would come to take me back to The Point. The two of us would cry for what seemed like hours. I don't know a lot about my father except that he loved me, and he was proud of me. I've heard a lot of stories about him. My mom told others and me that he was a good-looking man who looked sharp in his clothes. I know he was in World War II and that he drank a lot. His drink of choice was *Old Crow*, but he selectively called what he drank *Hadacol.*

Hadacol was a popular elixir, created in the 1940s on a whim, and it made its creator, Louisiana State Senator Dudley "Dud" LeBlanc, rich. To get around strict regulations for medicine, it was dubbed a dietary supplement with the claim to either cure or soothe just about whatever ailment a body could have. But its popularity was due to its main ingredient—twelve percent alcohol. In its day, songs were composed to tout and sometimes joke about its fame.

My mom had met James Willie Hamlin at my Uncle Wendel McLeod's tailor shop on Pearl Street in West Baltimore. The stories I heard often reminded me of the song, sung by The Temptations, titled *Papa Was A Rolling Stone.*

Visits with my father at Mother Hamlin's house faded away for no particularly expressed reason—at least not expressed to me, as a child. After losing track of him for many years, I tried to find him when I was in high school. I wanted to find out what he was all about. I wanted to put my arms around him and tell him how much I loved him despite the negative stories I'd heard about him. My mother drilled into my head, over and over, that he was no good and that he did not love me. In my heart, I knew better than that. To this day, I have not forgiven my mother for doing that. I guess that is the reason why I despise women who keep men from having a relationship with their kids, especially if their fathers are deserving of a relationship. I also think this has made a major negative impact on our community.

It is said, we are the result of what we have experienced. When I was a child, I hated how my mother would spew harsh negatives about my father. And she often used them as threats to make me behave. I remember her words as if she was saying it today.

She'd threaten, "If you don't do what I tell you, I will send you to your no-good father."

I swore to myself that if I had kids, they would know me and know how much I loved them. When I hear young women doing this to their children, it brings the hatred I have for this act to a boil. And nothing hurts me more than to see women use their children as pawns in a relationship.

Depriving children of their God-given and humane right to love and spend time with their fathers only to satisfy their vicious and vindictive quests is unjust. It is not the child's fault that his or her parents could not maintain the same satisfaction in the relationship they once enjoyed when they were pounding the flesh, and saying, "More, more, harder, faster," and screaming, "Oh God."

And, sadly, of course, there is the other side of the coin. My cousin, Rosa, was just a few years older than me. In her teen years, she became pregnant by a boy she loved. She believed with all her heart that they were going to get married. But it never happened, and she found herself a single parent, struggling to fill the void and love of an absent father who refused to participate in their child's upbringing. It was heartbreaking.

I imagine that both sides of that coin have shaped my manhood and my life as a husband and a father. Early on, I knew that I would be there for a child that I helped to bring into this world, no matter what. And even though I eventually married young, I knew that I would put in the work to make the union survive—even if I wasn't quite sure just what that would entail. Today, I am blessed that the one who vowed to love me also felt that very same way. Eventually, Brenda and I had a son and a daughter to love as well.

When I began searching for my father, I had not seen Mother Hamlin for more than fifteen years, but I remembered the church she attended. I was now attending Edmondson High School. The No. 23 bus ran up Edmondson Avenue just beyond the street on which the church was located. Finally, one day, I decided to go to the church and ask for her. I hoped that she could tell me how to find my dad.

Right away, when I got to the church, the woman I spoke to seemed to recognize me. I guess it was because I looked so much like my dad. She was very helpful. I was told that my grandmother lived at 2525 Edmondson Avenue., around the corner from the church. When I saw her, we both cried, first out of happiness, then out of sadness because she informed me that my father had died a month earlier.

In my young years, we bounced around a lot because of an array of difficult family and financial circumstances, not at all uncommon in our community. Mother Hamlin tried to find me, she said, but had no idea where to look. To this day, I have yet to go through a more painful experience. I try not to think about it because it brings tears to my eyes. Whenever I see a movie where a father and son share affection, it's painful for me.

Sometimes, I will look at pictures of my son and nearly cry grateful tears, hopeful I have been able to instill in him the love I missed out on—the love that my dad and I never got to experience fully. In my younger heart, I blamed my mother for this pain. And, yes, I must own up to the fact that my father shared some of that blame, but I also knew how vicious my mother could be. Sadly, from the only perspective I possessed, I knew how miserable she would have made his life if he had tried to establish a relationship with me.

Well, that's where my life started. From what I saw on television, I was living the life of a gypsy. Gypsies were people who moved from place to place. Everyone, including family, hated them, and they never trusted anyone. By the age of five, I owned all those traits.

In the summer of 1954, shortly before my sixth birthday, my mother brought me home to live with her and my stepfather, Zeke Harry Barron, and my little brother, Anthony "Tony" Waymon. I forgot to mention that I was born on August 24, 1948. Tony and I are four and one-half years apart. I remember him having to sit on the training pot for hours before going to bed. This period of time in my life was the loneliest because I did not have any other children my age to talk to.

We lived in a third-floor apartment located in the 600 block of Saratoga Street at the corner of Archer Street. At this address, I had my first encounter with the police, my biggest financial transaction of that time, and I'd met my first bully. During this time, I learned why an older cousin was interested in educating me about the facts of life. We'd never talk about that in our adult years. I had started school for the first time, which led to me getting lost for the first time. I remember it as being a traumatic experience. I also learned to see in the dark, and I developed a keen sense of hearing: superpowers I invoked at home.

Our apartment had two bedrooms, as I remember it. My mother and stepfather's bedroom had a coal stove not far from their bed. Tony and I slept in a bedroom right next to mom's, which was connected by French doors. Most of the time, the doors stayed open so that we could keep warm from the coal stove. It was the only heat we had.

The bathroom was down a long hallway that seemed to have been 100 feet long. The only time we used it was in the summertime or in the daytime. At night, we went to the bathroom in a small metal pail because the rest of the apartment felt as cold as the North Pole. The hallway was so cold that our sweaty feet, straight out of a warm bed, would stick to the floor before we could reach the bathroom. I always imagined that if either Tony or I ever made it to that freezing bathroom, and pulled our wieners out to take a leak, respectively, of course, we'd be found there the next morning, connected by a frozen yellow stream to a solid block of ice in the toilet bowl.

Our kitchen was about five feet down from the bathroom. It was always the center of activity when the gas was on. In other words, there were times when money was tight and the gas was turned off. In the mornings, mom ventured down to the kitchen, cut on the oven and all the top burners to warm up the room. She would then fill large pots of water on the stove for bathing. When the water got good and hot, she'd pour it in the large tin tubs to bathe us.

Downstairs lived a friend of my mother's, Mrs. Reola. We used to call her *Hot Dog* because she loved to eat them. Her son, Sammy, was about the same age as me. The mothers used to meet in our kitchen or in the bathroom to bathe us, kids, together. I remember the two of them commenting on how well I was endowed and how Sammy had some shortcomings in that department.

I clearly remember Mrs. Reola saying to my mother, referring to my anatomy, "That boy is going to grow up and kill some young girl with that thing."

Those mornings, getting the warm bath after walking down that long cold hallway used to get quite eventful. Like most moms, mine wanted to make sure I got a nice hot meal before going out to school in the morning. Her idea of a generous bowl of good ole Quaker Oats Oatmeal was certainly not my choice. This stuff was not like the new and improved oatmeal, and it was light-years before the apple cinnamon-flavored oatmeal with its friendly raisins.

This oatmeal was unfriendly. It had a job to do, and that's all it cared about. To me, it was thick as sludge, minus its dark coloring. I would pull up to the table, pick up my spoon, dig in the beige sludge and slowly bring it up to my mouth. As it got closer to my mouth, the smell always got to me. I would then open my mouth really quick and toss it in like throwing coals into a hot furnace fire. Next came the chore to swallow as quickly as I could. This would go on for about three more spoonsful, then my pace slowed.

The remaining bowl of oatmeal, now cold, had formed lumps as big as my fist. By this time, my impatient mother was growing as mad as a raging bull. Looking at me, snorting like a bull getting ready to charge, she'd shout, "You better eat that damn shit. So, you can get to school on time!"

Fear would give me the courage to pick up another spoonful. Now, the oatmeal was so thick and heavy; I could hardly pick up the spoon. With both hands, I'd work to get the heavy spoon to my lips and manage to get the paste off it and into my mouth. But the biggest task was to swallow it without choking to death. While sitting there, trying not to die from this stuff, I'd look over at my mom. The raging bull was breathing fire. Just as I'd get this huge lump to slide back to my throat and gag me, the bull would strike. She would fly around the table with the speed of Superman—faster-than-a-locomotive—to hit me in the middle of my back and deliver her famous line, "You better swallow that damn shit!"

I could not have agreed more with her description of what I was being forced to consume. My mother loved me but was a product of her upbringing and the limitations and threats that a Jim Crow world delivered to her on a daily basis. Later, my mother's yearning to provide for us would deliver us to our first experience with the law. I can't wait to share that later.

I learned to see in the dark, and I developed a keen sense of hearing. Ironically, as I think back, I was being trained for Vietnam because I had learned to do an excellent job at guerilla warfare. Let me explain myself a little.

For some reason, the only way I could get myself to sleep was to get on my knees and elbows and rock. Boy, did this keep my mother and stepfather, Zeke, up at night.

He would yell from the other room, "Stop that rocking and go to sleep."

I'd stop for a while and then start up again. He'd then sneak up to my bed and whack me on the rear. Although Mr. Zeke was dark as night, I learned to see him move in the darkest of night. I also learned to hear his every footstep as he tried to catch me rocking in the bed. I know I had to have pissed him off many a night after trying to sneak up on me only to have me quit rocking as he approached my bed. Over the years, thank God, I outgrew this method of getting myself to sleep. However, my wife thinks I am weird because I sometimes have to rock my leg to go to sleep. My son inherited the same habit as a child.

CHAPTER TWO

THE SIGNS AND WONDERS OF 2018

It's **Tuesday, December 18, 2018**, and the sixtieth birthday of my sister, Sandra Crawford. She had her birthday party on Saturday prior, and it was wonderful to see Sandra enjoy herself. My brother, Tony, flew up from Atlanta to surprise her. However, knowing how we all are, and all we've been through, I think she had a feeling he would be there for such a special occasion. My mother had ten kids, and now there are only four of us left: my older sister, Dot, Tony, Sandra, and me. My niece, Ashley, Sandra's daughter, coordinated the birthday party held at the Mingle Lounge on Woodlawn Drive in Gwynn Oak, Maryland. But all of us worked to make it happen.

These days, there's no fanfare in conducting daily life, business or celebrations in Gwynn Oak. It's located on Baltimore's northwest side and mostly African American now. But in 1963, the story was different. It was a tense scene, overrun with local protestors for equality, police arrests, and segregationists because Gwynn Oak Park, a privately owned amusement park, refused to allow African Americans through its gates. It was the only park of its kind in the area.

Not until a diverse group of folks, Black and White, clergy—preachers, priests and rabbis—several civil rights organizations, including CORE (the Congress of Racial Equality) and the NAACP (the National Association for the Advancement of Colored People), and politicians all worked together to right this wrong. What that meant was community leaders, citizens, and politicians came together to move a positive effort forward.

During several peaceful demonstrations to desegregate the park, angry mobs taunted and threw rocks at the protesters, and as many as four hundred of them, including activists and clergy, were arrested. About the arrests, the Baltimore County Police said it had no choice because of Maryland's No Trespassing Law. "I can't legislate," the then-police chief was quoted saying.

Before the struggle went national, local concerned citizens of color had been fighting for racial equality for as long as ten years. When the local demonstrations grew more organized, buses filled with protesters drove from New York, Philadelphia and Washington, D.C. to join the fight and apply pressure. And just as *The New York Times* was to shine a spotlight on the protest, the politicians stepped in to make things right. Then-County Executive Spiro T. Agnew, who went on to become the country's vice president—and would later resign in disgrace, like President Nixon—put an end to the segregation at the amusement park by working out a settlement with its owners. This happened on August 28, 1963. This was the same day as The March on Washington. Thousands flooded Washington's National Mall and heard Rev. Dr. Martin Luther King Jr. deliver his famous speech *I Have a Dream.*

The courtyard of my establishment, The Avenue Bakery, welcomes residents and visitors to West Baltimore's Historic Pennsylvania Avenue Corridor with a mural that celebrates and informs about civil rights pioneers and highlights America's Black historical legends from various sectors of life. In its center, a vibrant montage depicts Black protesters being dragged away by White police officers during a July 1963 protest demonstration at Gwynn Oak Amusement Park.

Today, the park is long gone, having succumbed to Tropical Storm Agnes in 1972. Neither the private owners nor the City that now owns the property chose to rebuild. However, the park's original wooden carousel was made famous when an eleven-month-old Black girl was lovingly hoisted upon it by her father, making the little girl the first of her race to ride it. The wooden carousel has been featured at Washington's National Mall since 1981.

On a grander scale, as a native son of the greatest historic African American community in the country—well, okay, that's how I feel about it—I want to see all of us—our state and city politicians, our business leaders, and our community activists of *Charm City*—work together to revitalize the community that encompasses the Historic Pennsylvania Avenue Corridor.

Baltimore Councilman Leon F. Pinkett III put it this way, and I agree, that the "West Baltimore Gateway is an organization that unifies many neighborhoods with a common vision. West Baltimore Gateway is a joint effort of the community associations of Penn North, Druid Heights, and Upton, along with the Pennsylvania Avenue Main Street program. West Baltimore Gateway seeks to foster prosperity, economic growth, and sustainable development to improve the lives of residents and the wellbeing of [Pennsylvania Avenue communities]. [It] embraces innovation, celebrates Afrocentric culture, and champions investment without displacement." What the councilman expresses is much like the function of the Pennsylvania Avenue Redevelopment Collaborative (PARC). Sadly, PARC was dismantled.

But I want us to make it happen. Let's bring back Pennsylvania Avenue's luster and its legacy to enrich the lives of Baltimoreans and restore its strong sense of community. And, yes, the residents will play a role in it, too. To do it will take economic development, a strategy not only fruitful for residents but also for Baltimore and the State of Maryland.

I have been working for decades on the rebuilding of Historic Pennsylvania Avenue, which *we* locals affectionately call *The Avenue*. This mission grew a bit more tangible for me when, in 2011, I came to build The Avenue Bakery, *Home of Poppay's Rolls*. I want to see the full resuscitation and empowerment of the residents of West Baltimore. Since 2011, The Avenue Bakery has become a cornerstone for The Avenue's redevelopment and the catalyst to rebuild Baltimore's famous Royal Theater.

Brenda Taylor Hamlin, my wife of fifty years, along with so many others and me down through the decades, have wonderful memories of that theater.

On Saturdays, The Royal Theater shows had matinees for kids in the community. To make the matinee, most of us kids and teens, got up early on Saturday mornings to run our errands and complete our chores, which for most of us included a good scrub down of the white marble steps leading up to the rowhouses we lived in.

"We would get to The Royal Theater by 12 noon. The show would start around 2 p.m.," Brenda recalled.

Brenda and I grew up in the same areas around Pennsylvania Avenue. And ran in the same circles. "The actual show, whether it would be James Brown or The Temptations—all those acts would put on a show for the kids. And then they would have a night show for the adults," Brenda added.

During this time, it wasn't unusual to walk up and down on The Avenue and run into some of the stars performing at The Royal Theater. On any given afternoon, one could see James Brown and the Famous Flames in the Boot Black Shops, getting their shoes shined for the show, or maybe see Marvin Gaye strolling The Avenue. These entertainers, soon-to-be icons, stayed at the homes of neighbors because there wasn't a hotel to put them up. They shopped, mingled, and drank on The Avenue. This brings me to the food and the rich flavor of various sub shops, which was long before the famous Subway chain. From nearly a block away, the fresh aroma of fried onions invaded your nostrils, your entire body and then led you right through the front door of a mom-and-pop sub shop to place an order.

Now, talk about clothes shopping. Well, there was some flavor to behold there, too. And if you were a young novice, trying to get a good deal, it would have behooved you to keep your eyes open. As a young teen, learning how to wisely spend my hard-earned money, I got an indelible lesson. There was a clothing store called Pop Kelly's. It was the place to go. Pop knew how to make a sale, and he sold everything you needed: High Boy shirts, pleated trousers, three-piece suits, and such. Especially popular at the time was Pop Kelly's assortment of mohair sweaters. I was a slim Jim, about 129 pounds dripping wet, which made me about a twenty-nine or thirty-inch waistline fit. Sometimes Pop Kelly or one of his unscrupulous salespeople would put a size forty suit on me then pull me in front of the mirror. And I'd have to admit; my reflection would be looking suave. I remember one suit in particular that I was purchasing around St. Patrick's Day. It was a dark green suit with a two-button jacket. The pant legs flared at the bottom, almost like a pair of bell bottoms. A young teen or a hardworking man, shopping for just the right Saturday night or Sunday-morning look, or both, could get woozy, standing there taking in the abundant good-looking-ness of it all, and I loved to dress.

So, I'm standing there in front of a floor-length mirror, looking good; but not realizing that Pop, or one of his salesmen, had snatched up a chunk of the suit's extra material in the back, giving the illusion of a perfect fit. And if I didn't have the extra money to get it tailored there—an added hustle stitched into their speedy sales pitch—I'd end up with a suit that made me look like I was wearing a sack. The entertainers, appearing at The Royal Theater, must have known that trick because they never performed or walked The Avenue in sacks.

The popular theater was unceremoniously ripped from our presence in 1971 by a cluster of small-thinking politicians and shortsighted community leaders, wanting to pronounce our community a lost cause. In my retirement years, I was moved to create a nonprofit dedicated to rebuilding The Royal Theater and revitalizing the economic strengths of our historic community with the guidance and support of several key players—about whom I'll talk later.

On April 20, 2005, The Royal Theater & Community Heritage Corporation (TRTCHC) was born. Since that time, our mission has seen a huge investment of time, energy, and retirement income from Brenda and me. This endeavor owns a huge part of our collective heart and history.

Back-in-the-day, on Friday or Saturday, folks would come home from a hard day's work, take a nap, and then get up refreshed and ready to hit the nightlife. From the 1920s to the mid-to-late1960s, the Pennsylvania Avenue community, its businesses, and its nightlife jumped. The Royal Theater hosted every well-known entertainer, Black or White, who made the best of it on The Chitlin' Circuit. Losing The Royal Theater signaled the downfall of Baltimore's thriving inner-city Black community. It was a history-making hub that fostered African American legacy.

The Chitlin' Circuit, prevalent during the civil rights era, was the collective name for a series of venues that straddled the southern states as well as certain northern and midwestern states that welcomed African American entertainers and catered to the mostly African American fans who loved them. They did so with dignity, minus color lines in audience seating and restrooms or the boasting of balcony-only restrictions for coloreds. The main venues on the Chitlin' Circuit consisted of the Apollo Theater in New York, The Howard Theatre in Washington, D.C., The Earle Theatre in Philadelphia, The Regal Theater in Chicago, and The Royal Theater in Baltimore. The Royal Theater is the *only one* that has been demolished.

As an African American entertainer, one had to first do well on the Chitlin' Circuit to be successful in the entertainment business overall. Like amateur night at the Apollo Theater, an entertainer had to cut his or her teeth on the Circuit. When one thinks of the Underground Railroad, consider that the Chitlin' Circuit served the same purpose for our arts and entertainment. The history of African Americans having to come up with innovative ways to accrue economic freedoms and cultural outlets as well as basic safety and survival rituals is not yet fully documented, considered, or adequately respected. I could go on.

Bringing things 2018-current, since my workdays at The Bakery begin at three a.m., hitting the nightlife comes few and far between for my loving wife and me. Brenda works right beside me, both at The Bakery and in our joint mission to revitalize Pennsylvania Avenue. And, of course, there are other major players dedicated to the mission as well. We have some formidable foes in the mix, too. Unfortunately, and some would say, surprisingly, our key foes reside in the government as well as within some of our community organizations. This is my Baltimore story, so I will be naming names.

Getting back to the birthday celebration, I left The Bakery early on Saturday to rest up for the party that night. You know, like folks used to do in the old days. And for the first time in years, fully rested, I was able to get my dance on at my sister's birthday surprise. I really enjoyed myself. In my younger life, when we used to party, I'd hit the floor and dance with every woman in the house, dancing until I was soaking wet. Normally, during the evening's prime, I'd have one hand dance with Brenda, and then she'd send me off to make my dance-floor rounds while she socialized. But the party always ended right, capped by a slow dance with my beloved Brenda. Saturday's party was a little different. I danced with some of the women in the house and worked up a sweat, but Brenda didn't get that final dance. She was a little tired from her busy day at The Bakery. I'm not sure if, prior to, she was able to get her nap in like I did.

The year 2018, had proven to be an unusual year because I had had several unexpected visitors throughout. The week before Christmas, I went in town to get bakery supplies rather than waiting until Wednesday, which is the beginning of our workweek. As I was leaving The Bakery, after putting everything away, and while the sun was also taking its leave, I noticed two older, casually dressed White gentlemen walking the neighborhood. The two men appeared to be walking along kind of surveying the area, which seemed unusual to me. As I looked closer, I realized that one of the men was Paul Graziano, the previous City Housing Commissioner and a resident of the Bolton Hill Community. Bolton Hill is a predominately White community here in West Baltimore, where the median cost of its brick brownstone homes goes for $500,000 and up. Just a few blocks away, in the African American communities of Druid Heights and Upton, the same type of homes are falling apart. A few have been converted into apartments, now dilapidated.

What in the world could they want? Was my thought.

A bit about the contemporary makeup of West Baltimore, my birthplace, the place of my formative years. West Baltimore is made up of several communities: Druid Heights, Sandtown-Winchester, Upton, Penn North, and the business district— The Pennsylvania Avenue Corridor.

For African Americans, born and bred in Baltimore, many still suffer from direct, "historical policies designed to 'quarantine blacks,' as Baltimore's mayor put it in 1911." Back then, "the city passed the nation's first racially restrictive voting law [that same year], which prevented residents of one race from buying a home in neighborhoods dominated by residents of another race. It also formed a Committee on Segregation to enforce racially restrictive covenants, which prohibited the sale of homes to Black buyers." [Excerpts are taken from a 2017 study, titled, *The Racial Wealth Divide in Baltimore,* and part of the *Racial Wealth Divide Initiative.* The Initiative is the product of a nonprofit called *Prosperity Now*, formerly known as the *Corporation for Enterprise Development* (CFED)]

And to this day, decades later, we still suffer recurrent blows and aftershocks. Even in our recent history, if an African American managed to acquire real estate in certain parts of the city, he or she has managed it under the wires of historical stopgap overseers—based on race.

To combat all this, licensed community development corporations and community associations were formed. And so we have The Druid Heights Community Development Corporation (CDC), The Sandtown-Winchester Community Development Corporation (CDC), The Penn North Community Association, The Upton Planning Committee (UPC), and not to be left out, representing the business district—The Pennsylvania Avenue Merchants Association. These CDCs and associations are manned by concerned citizens and work very closely with whatever political administration is in place at the time. I was, and still am, a part of the UPC. In 2003, I retired from the United Parcel Service (UPS) after thirty-five years of service. And, as I mentioned, in my retirement years, I set out to do more. So, I founded the TRTCHC.

A bit about Graziano, who served three Baltimore City mayors: Martin O'Malley (1999-2007) and served Maryland as governor from 2007-2015; Sheila Dixon (2007-2010), who left the post amid scandal; and Stephanie Rawlings-Blake (2010-2016). When the current mayor, Ms. Catherine Pugh, came into office in 2016, she had vowed to make good on one of her campaign promises, which was to replace Graziano in his dual role as commissioner of both The Federal Housing Authority of Baltimore City and the city's Department of Housing and Community Development. In Baltimore, growing demands for his ouster had taken place, "over poor conditions at city public housing complexes and allegations that maintenance workers there demanded sex in return for repairs," reported *The Baltimore Sun* in 2016. The maintenance worker sex scandal gained national attention. The housing authority settled a class-action lawsuit for up to $8 million. Other complaints centered on alleged negligence to enforce housing codes or pay attention to lead paint or "refusing to pay millions of dollars in settlements and court judgments in cases alleging that children were poisoned by lead paint in public housing," also reported in *The Baltimore Sun*.

Dayvon Love, the co-founder of the activist group called *Leaders of a Beautiful Struggle*, commented in the same *Baltimore Sun* story that "He [Graziano] presided over a housing policy that seemed to be going in the direction of gentrification."

But Graziano, who had a salary of approximately $220,000 annually, and left his position with approximately $116,000 in severance pay, expressed that if he didn't care about the work he did—championing for the cause of affordable housing—that he wouldn't have dedicated two-thirds of his life to it. Also, it should be mentioned that there was a growing decline in federal funding for capital improvements in Baltimore's public housing. In 1993, funding was at $42 million. By 2016, Graziano commented that it had dropped to $15 million. Half that money went to paying down debt, which left the agency less than $7 million a year to spend on building improvements.

Two more things about Graziano:

In 2006, during the O'Malley Administration, the TRTCHC, my nonprofit, was included in a meeting designed to put together the Upton Master Plan for the community. Various city agencies were there. Community representatives such as the Upton Planning Committee, the departments of Housing and Planning, the Baltimore Development Corporation, and others were in attendance. I made a presentation to the Upton Master Plan Committee that included all the above-mentioned. My presentation was in reference to The Royal Theater Project. As a result of my presentation, representatives from the Department of Planning suggested that we place the project in the 1500 block of Pennsylvania Avenue. It also provided TRTCHC with a map of the 1500 block and an acquisition cost analysis of site control, which means not only did they suggest the 1500 block but also gave me all the information that I needed to take possession of.

We later scheduled a meeting with Department of Housing Commissioner Paul Graziano to convince Housing to sell us the forty percent of the 1500 block of Pennsylvania Avenue that the city owned. Then we would be ready to pursue the acquisition of the remaining properties needed to build The Royal Theater Project in that block.

Graziano pulled the 1500 block's designated availability off the table of options without explanation. The news was a blindside and a planning setback because before that meeting, so many of us had come to the table to give further input and to move forward: property owners, community representatives, representatives of Planning and developers—all considering and evaluating property in the 1500 block of Pennsylvania Avenue as a go.

Hindsight, and a couple of post conversations with others who were in that meeting, led me to believe that principals such as George

Gilliam of the Pennsylvania Avenue Redevelopment Collaborative (PARC) and others in attendance that day already knew the meeting's outcome. All knew except me. And this is my summation of things: It seemed that the TRTCHC Project, set to happen in the 1500 block of Pennsylvania Avenue, was stepping on the toes of their vision and process for redeveloping The Avenue. At the time, Graziano may have been in support of other businesses already in place. For example, there was the African American-owned Chopper's Lounge, a club, and a popular barbershop, already located in the 1500 block of Pennsylvania Avenue, and its owner was thinking of expansion. There ain't no shame in that game because it was another way to boost economic strengths in the area. And I could get with that.

There was at least one other commercial landmark, The Casino Lounge, in that area as well. It was a part of the multi-million-dollar empire created by Little Willie Adams, who lived from 1914 to 2011. His life became a legend in our community. Journalist Mark R. Cheshire wrote a book about his life, titled *They Call Me Little Willie: The Life Story of William L. Adams*, published in 2016.

Willie Adams was short in physical stature but a giant in the community. He was a dynamo with little formal education but loaded with the courage and ingenuity it took to push beyond the barriers of Jim Crow to become an entrepreneur. Adams was a high school dropout who later returned to school to earn his diploma at the age of thirty-six. His success was well-documented. And he gave back to the community. Once he amassed his wealth, he mentored and often bankrolled up-and-coming African American businesses such as Super Pride supermarkets and Park Sausage. As a teen, Willie Adams began earning his business acumen and economic fortune as a runner in The Numbers racket. He kept his eyes open and his mouth shut, and he studied how things got done.

The Numbers, an illegal betting game of chance based on the outcomes of horse racing, was the forerunner to today's Lottery games that are prevalent throughout the United States. Yes, the government decided it wanted, and that it would get, a piece of the action.

Objectively, I believe that Graziano and others, such as George Gilliam of PARC, sitting around the table during that infamous meeting, had their minds in the right place. And I don't believe that the seemingly impromptu move to pull the 1500 block's availability off the table was all for personal gain. That said, the construction of new housing, which is often publicly touted as a community-growth alternative in lieu of commerce, can sometimes carry with it the placement of high-profile feathers in the political caps of others. It also offers a benevolent mirage for low-income residents—who in actuality will never be able to afford to reside in such spanking-new housing. And there's the potential financial padding of developers' pockets due to the assurance of city and/or state funding. Lastly, while housing is important, communities must also have commercial districts and development to provide stability and resource.

But I digress. Perhaps there is more than one way to do good for the community. I understand that. I respect that. And such a thing should always be acknowledged and addressed. But what ticks me off is the lack of testicular fortitude, among men and women, to tell me that—straight up.

Perhaps, the 2006 meeting was just a formality of bragging rights to show that at least a meeting had taken place on the matter. It would not be the last time for such a thing to happen—especially during the Catherine Pugh mayoral administration.

During the last two and a half years of Rawlings-Blake's administration (2010-2016), Graziano turned supportive of the plans and the new location that TRTCHC had proposed, which was the 1300 block of Pennsylvania Avenue. Ironically, I think that my project may have helped him hang on to his job just a little while longer.

Back to coming upon Graziano's evening stroll to The Avenue Bakery, I decided to pull my truck over to the curb and command their attention to see what was going on. The former Commissioner walked over to my passenger side. I rolled down the window, and both guys greeted me with a smile.

Graziano said, "We were just talking about you and The Bakery."

He also indicated the need to stop by to purchase some of what we provide, which was not unusual. The Avenue Bakery has long since become a routine stop for locals and tourists. I'm mighty grateful to God for that.

We went on to talk about the need for commercial development on Pennsylvania Avenue. He encouraged me not to give up on our plans, and he agreed that the plans were a holistic approach to changing Baltimore for the better. He encouraged me to "take a closer look at the new *Opportunity Zone* program that President Trump signed this week," indicating that the program encourages developers to invest in low-income areas. Graziano added how in his estimation, "The initiative addresses commercial and residential development."

Hmmm, was my thought.

It was ironic and refreshing to get this encouragement from Graziano after his public rejection, without explanation, of my attempts to acquire the 1500 block of Pennsylvania Avenue for the project. Perhaps this is a prophecy of major production in 2019 and beyond.

CHAPTER THREE

THE HUMAN EQUATION

On December 13, 2018, The Bakery hosted a meeting with Maryland's State Comptroller Peter Franchot. It was a meeting that he'd requested. Franchot wanted me to invite other stakeholders to discuss the future of Pennsylvania Avenue. Attending the meeting, upon my invite were: Tony Pressley, Druid Heights Community Development Corporation (CDC); Wanda Best, Upton Planning Committee; Annie Hall, Penn North Community Association; Janet Allen, Heritage Crossing; Tod Marcus, executive director of Martha's Place; Mariam Blackwell, Main Street; Van Anderson, Arch Social Club; Brion Gill, Pennsylvania Avenue Arts District. I also invited, but they could not attend, Rick Sussman, president of the Pennsylvania Avenue Merchants Association. Sussman also owns the Northwestern Loan & Pawnbroker at 1701 Pennsylvania Avenue, a family business since 1919; and Derwood Bush, president of Penn North Merchants Association.

Pennsylvania Avenue runs from Martin Luther King Jr. Blvd to Fulton Avenue. Pennsylvania Avenue plays a vital and physical part in each of the communities you'll see mentioned here. Each one of these communities has a section of The Avenue. And that's why these associations needed to be a part of this and in all discussions involving The Avenue.

As I understand it, the Comptroller is limited to what resources he can actually bring to the community. In my mind, to put it bluntly, he is the taxman who is responsible for sucking the money out of you after legislators decide to take it. However, I do understand that he has a close relationship with our reelected Governor Larry Hogan and that Franchot may be on a fact-finding mission. Other than providing funds to demolish decaying properties, Mr. Hogan has done very little to help Historic West Baltimore thus far.

When Mr. Hogan was elected to his first term, I invited him to The Avenue Bakery to discuss The Royal Theater project and the revitalization of Historic Pennsylvania Avenue. I sent a copy of my letter to Lt. Governor Boyd Kevin Rutherford and Kieffer Mitchell, the former District 11 councilman and advisor to Governor Hogan. My letter never garnered a response or an acknowledgment of receipt. Is that this Governor's style—not to respond to community requests? I pose such a question because, as the State Center Neighborhood Alliance co-chair, the Alliance and I have experienced the same thing.

Earlier in the Governor's first term, when we realized that he was not in support of the State Center Project, we tried to reach out to him for a meeting. We got no response. While he has been elected for a second term, I am much concerned about the decisions he will make, negatively impacting West Baltimore. Specifically, his abandonment of the Red Line Transportation Project halted the prospects of new job opportunities, right there at the transportation hub, and better public-transportation access to remote jobs. Such jobs to avail better employment opportunities to underserved communities, including its youth population. The State Center Project, by its design, would have created jobs in our communities as well. Certainly, our Royal Theater Project would create jobs and tax revenue for the city and state.

But still, there is hope, and interest, showing itself. Since Governor Hogan's second term, beginning in 2019, Peter Franchot's visit to The Avenue Bakery has given me the feeling that, perhaps, the Governor really wants to tap into the African American community and wants to make things change. I think Mr. Hogan understands that revitalizing Pennsylvania Avenue in Baltimore is a key component—however he can get that done. If Franchot and several local consultants to the city have correctly relayed the message, I think that now he's aware of my Royal Theater Project as well as the bigger picture of where I'm going to energize and support the entire area.

Still, there are bumps in the road. While the former mayor, Stephanie Rawlings-Blake, and former governor, Martin O'Malley, were on board with the project to rebuild The Royal Theater, the current mayor, Mayor Pugh, who took office in 2016, is not. It is my understanding that Mayor Pugh has conveyed to the community that she has a better plan or strategy to revitalize Pennsylvania Avenue and the funding to support it. She just hasn't let anyone know what that proposal or plan is, nor has Ms. Pugh shown that it is up-and-running. Mayor Pugh may have indicated to Governor Hogan that she's not interested in my project to revitalize Pennsylvania Avenue by way of commercial capital, citing that she has something better, or whatever the argument might be. But I'm sure that the Governor, with his background, understands that this project, already in the works, could be the catalyst to turn Baltimore City around.

Before The Avenue Bakery came to fruition in 2004, or quite honestly, before the notion was even conceived, I created a 501(c)(3) nonprofit dedicated to this mission. It was aptly named *The Royal Theater & Community Heritage Corporation* (TRTCHC). Those actively churning the wheels of the nonprofit, along with the success of The Avenue Bakery, comprise the reasons why city consultants, local politicians, and even local and regional developers are showing a growing interest in The Avenue and showing up at my door, surveying the overall mission. But such interest has taken years, going back to 2004 and beyond. The immediate short-term goal is to start off accomplishing small initiatives, like The Avenue Bakery success and enhancing the few other businesses existing in the vicinity. We will work to acquire properties in the area on which to rebuild The Royal Theater, which will create an anchor for a vital cultural, arts and entertainment complex. It will include museums, music and performing arts, thematic restaurants, businesses, and retailers. All this will provide a comprehensive cultural experience for Baltimoreans, boost tourism, resuscitate the community's economic growth, renaissance, and positive reputation, and enrich West Baltimore residents' lives.

But before we can get to the long-term vision, if we can make one block successful, then we can attract other developers to move us on to bigger things. The Governor is a business guy. I believe he understands all this. In an area overrun with depressed economics, crime, and residents struggling to survive, while living far below the poverty level at a median of $17,000 annually, a strong framework exists on The Avenue. There are three solid businesses on the block: a hardware store on the corner, a book distributor in the middle, and The Avenue Bakery, which pulls tourists from across the country. Together they cast a positive light into this currently stigmatized and abandoned community.

The Baltimore Sun reported on the systemic biases that prevent low-income areas from getting a seat at the economic table. "Commercial lending is concentrated in the central business district, industrial areas on the waterfront, and existing retail centers," revealed a 2019 report conducted by the Urban Institute. "Such commercial lending levels were five times higher per household in areas where fewer than half of the residents are black. It's the same for small business lending." But perhaps there is a small opening of hope. The report's findings featured in The Sun's story went on to state, "One exception was small business lending in high-poverty areas, which is a bit higher in low-poverty tracts." Perhaps we can capitalize and build on that.

The project aims to create economic opportunities for the community and let that light beam throughout Baltimore and beyond. It's about changing the African American community mindset. And instilling a sense of pride and dignity in its young and old to really change the landscape. You see, that's one of the things that I'm trying to get people to understand. This is not just about rebuilding The Royal Theater. But the theater is an important anchor. This project's totality translates into jobs, careers, economic opportunity, and community empowerment for its residents. I'm talking about the tangible consideration of the human equation—which has been lost.

CHAPTER FOUR

A TURNING POINT IN OUR COMMUNITY'S HISTORY

The depletion and some say the city's abandonment of Historic West Baltimore began not long after the race riots of 1968. The beginning of its troubles can also be tied to the ravages that most Black communities throughout the nation suffered due to the Vietnam War. Not only were we depleted of our communities' young male populations—the vital, the strong, and strong-willed—but also our communities were robbed of a potential resource of dedicated leaders. In the face of apathy and abandonment, such human resource was needed to seed and take root, to stand in defense of everything dear and vital to African American Baltimoreans.

So, let us backtrack a bit. The Vietnam War began around 1954-1955, but the Unites States' involvement began in 1961. The first arrival of U.S. combat troops came in 1965. You have to understand that during the Vietnam War, especially from the moment of U.S. tangible involvement, every African American young man around eighteen years of age had to sign up for the draft. Even today, when I look at my Edmondson High School graduating class of '68, I find that nearly seventy-five percent of us went to the Vietnam War. That happened in Baltimore. Our youngest, most vital resource was plucked from our struggling community at alarming rates and sent off to war. And when many of them returned, they came back in body bags, drugged-up from the poppy fields of Southeast Asia, or depressed or mentally debilitated, unable to function because they returned to a nation that scorned them.

I wasn't drafted. I enrolled in Coppin State College (now called Coppin State University) because I harbored dreams of escaping the dead-end employment paths that I watched strangle my grandfather's economic freedom and others in my family. As a child, I observed much. My grandfather was the first man I respected. For forty-nine years, he worked at Bethlehem Steel. That said, now, don't get me wrong, working at Bethlehem Steel was a great accomplishment. There's just so much to the story.

At the time, my family was living in The Point. My grandfather worked, and in between work and sleep, he managed to squeeze in a little time to let me know I was loved. His love was one of the ingredients mixed in the recipe that baked up enough courage in me to want to go to college. And while in college, I wound up marrying my high school sweetheart, Brenda. Not long after that, I became a father. I had not purposely chosen that particular life journey, but it turned out to be the only thing to keep me away from Vietnam. The government tagged me with a status called a 3-A classification, which meant I would be one of the last ones to be called up for the draft. It turned out to be a personal blessing for me, though I could have easily become a casualty of the '68 racial tensions.

In the midst of getting back and forth from the job I had at the time, I didn't realize the risky business of my nightly solitary walk to and from work. There I was, walking from the 1700 block of McCulloh

Street, crossing Jones Falls Expressway as well as the Jones Falls. There was a brick walkway across the Jones Falls, about three-and-a-half feet or four feet wide. Today, I think back to how I was crossing Jones Falls Road alone. You have to keep in mind that that was in 1968—the riots had taken place. There was racial tension everywhere. Anyone, Black or White, could have tried to attack me or knocked me off that bridge, or whatever the case could have been, and no one would have known the wiser about what could have happened to me. It was the dead of night; most of the city was asleep. That's just one of several instances that proves to me how God has looked out for me. During my times of weariness, battling the powers-that-be, I rest on the assurance that God has a plan for me. I'm so blessed. He has one for you, too.

I attended Coppin for only one year. Things got tough because I had to work to support my family. However, ironically, I lost my job because of school, which circled to cause me to drop out of school because I had to find a job to support my family, which had become my priority. Yes, I know, confusing. Perhaps I can explain.

Around six years old, the man who was my stepfather (for a brief time) was named Zeke Harry Barron. He instilled in me the value of work. From that point on, I've always held an honest hustle to keep money in my pocket. I used to babysit for my mom's friends, and she trained me well. At age thirteen, I worked for Archie Laden's grocery store on the corner of Druid Hill Avenue and Presstman Street. I worked every day after school and all day on Saturdays. I made seven dollars a week, enough money to buy my clothes and my Blue Tip Jack Purcell tennis shoes. At that time, Michael Jordan was a toddler, and Nike wasn't even born yet.

All through high school, I worked nights at a cotton factory that sat on the bank of the Jones Falls stream called Mt. Vernon Textile

Mill. It was located on Falls Road. The mill is long gone, but the building still stands today. I worked as a doffer, a job description that's also long gone. My responsibility was to monitor four thirty-foot-long machines. These machines turned cotton into thread. I'd take threaded bobbins off the machine, put empty bobbins on, restart the machine, and connect the threads that were broken. I'd do that every two to four hours.

On weekdays, I would come home from Edmondson High at three o'clock in the afternoon, go straight to bed, get up at 10 p.m. and walk to work. At night, during my meal break, I'd do my homework. I paid one of my coworkers, who had a car, to take me from work straight to Edmondson High School. When I got to Coppin, the Mill switched me from the night shift to its 3-to-11 p.m. evening shift. There was a class I had to take that began at 2 p.m.; I was due at work at three o'clock. And, so, the inevitable happened, I was late to work, too many times. That's why I lost my job.

Again, I believe that the Vietnam War's consequences played a pivotal role in the destruction of our community, and Historic West Baltimore in particular. The siphoning of its rich human resource stripped away our potential pool of strong, qualified, homespun leadership that could have put up a fight for economic and cultural survival. And perhaps by the 1990s, West Baltimore could have sustained itself with promises of growth. But instead, after years of neglect and vilification, in 2015, here came the civil unrest due to the Freddie Gray death that occurred while he was in the custody of the Baltimore City police. Corporate businesses moved out of The Pennsylvania Avenue Corridor. And then came the world's reaction to the murder of George Floyd by four Minnesota police officers in 2020. Its heartfelt connection also touched Baltimore's inner-city streets.

Over the decades, I have sensed an organized fear of economic competition between what West Baltimore could offer, pitted against The Harbor and Harbor East's economic prowess, built up from dirt and gravel. Why can't both coexist as beautiful facets of Baltimore? Who and/or what machine is at the helm of systemically paying off our local politicians to see that it never happens? And perhaps the phrase "paying off" is too strong, but there is certainly something in the air that fuels their inactions to create change.

CHAPTER FIVE

THE AVENUE BACKSTORY

Most African American Baltimoreans born in the 1950s or earlier can recall with fondness the cultural flavor, community spirit, entertainment hotspots, and the economic resourcefulness of The Pennsylvania Avenue Corridor that once was. Ironically, the natural order of all-things-positive on The Avenue between the 1920s to the mid-to-late 1960s was born out of segregation's unnatural circumstances. That said, for its encompassing West Baltimore communities, Pennsylvania Avenue wasn't yet the makings of a historical legacy that one day would sorely need economic revitalization and a historical renaissance. It was simply a life-sustaining anchor—for survival.

Visitors to the Corridor, nationwide and beyond, also enjoyed its rich and multilayered experiences. The communities threaded to Pennsylvania Avenue—Upton, Druid Heights, Sandtown-Winchester, and Penn North—were laced with big and small rowhouses that bustled with life, love, and promise. Their cleanly-swept sidewalks and polished white marble steps signaled community pride. Those steps were famous.

Part of one's responsibility as a kid was to go out and grab his or her supply of Ajax to scrub those front steps. On Saturday mornings, the goal was to get them polished, pearly-white. Most of the homes were single-family homes. Some were as large as the brownstones in New York that people talked about. Part of the fun for us kids, roaming on The Avenue, was a must-stop shop named *Tommy Tucker Five and Ten Cents Store*. We'd go in to buy the fun items and school supplies we needed and wanted. And we all used to venture down the street to the *Candy Kitchen*, a place that made all kinds of candies that we could buy. We didn't realize it back then, but what some of those Pennsylvania Avenue shops did was engrain in us the flavors of quality with its diverse offerings of goods and services. Much of what they passed on to us came from places that we had never even dreamed of visiting.

Residents and families that filled Pennsylvania Avenue's surrounding communities were folks of various economic statuses and backgrounds. The street sweepers, who were black, lived next door to the attorneys, the doctors, the principals, and the teachers. They were also intertwined with the factory workers, shipyard workers, and automotive workers too. The great African American migration, up from the deeper south that reportedly began back in 1917, placed us together, living in our neighborhoods. And we had the commonality of raising our families, making a living, and surviving Jim Crow. When a person walked up Pennsylvania Avenue, there were storefront businesses with apartments and housing above. The Avenue was also lined with theaters, restaurants, and nightclubs.

"At the turn of the century," reported the *Baltimore Sun*, March 20, 2014, "Baltimore's street sweepers were called White Wings because of the fancy white uniforms they wore, complete with coats and ties and matching pith helmets." The story continues, "In 1985, they were called hokey men—don't ask why; no one seems to remember how or when they got the name—and they wore whatever they wanted, usually under a bright yellow sweatshirt emblazoned with the logo of the city Bureau of Solid Waste."

A string of Black entrepreneurs called Arabbers (pronounced A-rabbers) was birthed out of the necessity of the times and a yearning for economic say-so. They sold everything from blocks of ice to vegetables, meat, seafood, and more. Residents who appeared at their front doors with money in hand, responded to the loud rhythmic call of an Arabber whenever he announced his wares. These men on horse-driven wagons angled up and down the streets. Residents had, down to a tee, their favorite Arabber's appearance in their respective neighborhoods.-

Sadly, just like what happened to The Pennsylvania Corridor, the powers-that-be are busy at work to let the tradition of Arabbers die. Yes, they are still in operation in West Baltimore. And residents still clamor for the sound of their horse-drawn wagons and the singsong catcall of Arabbers selling fresh wares. This community, as it stands now is, considered to be a food desert. For this reason, West Baltimore is probably the only community in the country that still has Arabbers. Supermarkets were a rarity in Black communities. The first market I can recall coming into the neighborhood was the A&P. It stood at the bottom of Linden Avenue.

Over the years, the city closed up many of the stables that housed the horses. And to this day, we only have about two or three stables left. And they are located in West Baltimore. We used to have hundreds of stables in and around Baltimore. By the 2000s, there were only a handful of Arabbers' stables left, and the city was trying to close them down completely. I became part of a nonprofit organization trying to find locations for the Arabbers during this period. One of the locations was on the property of the B&O Railroad Museum. Funds had been raised to build a stable there. And the mission was alive for a short period of time.

In February 2015, reporter Charles Cohen wrote about the Arabbers in Baltimore's *City Paper*. It appeared in the business section of Mobtown Beat. The full story was titled *Horse Sense.* Here is an excerpt: *"After almost two years of living as exiles in their own city, it looks like Baltimore's arabbers--African-American produce peddlers who for generations have sold their goods from horse-drawn carts--may finally be moving into a permanent home ("All the Pretty Horses," Mobtown Beat, Aug. 22, 2007; "Horse Nonsense," Mobtown Beat, Oct. 3, 2007; "Homeless Horses," Quick and Dirty, Mobtown Beat, April 23, 2008; "In-Stable-ility," Mobtown Beat, April 30, 2008).*

"According to city officials, a new stable for the community of arabbers removed from a city-owned building on Retreat Street in 2007 will be built on property owned by the B&O Railroad Museum just across the train tracks from Carroll Mansion in Southwest Baltimore. Right now, the arabbers and about 20 of their horses are operating out of temporary tent stables on a muddy lot next to the railroad tracks under the Monroe Street bridge in West Baltimore. Construction on a new stable, the arabbers hope, could begin by the end of 2009.

"I got my beliefs," says Donald "Manboy" Savoy, the elder of the community of displaced arabbers, who owns the majority of the horses with his son Donald Savoy Jr. "They promised they are going to do something. I believe them."

However, the funds designated to build or establish a new stable were depleted on the housing and the care of the horses at the B&O.

Back in 2008, the issue was addressed. And as representatives of Pennsylvania Avenue Redevelopment Collaborative (PARC), Executive Director George Gilliam and I tried to intervene with a strong letter to the then mayor, Sheila Dixon. In a letter, her administration responded, graciously promised to work to protect and "to preserve the Arabbers tradition of providing fresh produce to neighborhoods throughout the city." In favor of the tradition, not much happened after that.

Men and women shopped on The Avenue for groceries, furniture, collectible items, and their family's Sunday best. From dusk until dawn, lively, spry couples dressed to the nines floated from one nightclub or restaurant to another. A cultural and social anchor abounded The Arch Social Club. It stood stoically proud as it graced the corner of Pennsylvania and North avenues. The Arch Social Club, founded in 1905, which still stands today, has something in common with The Avenue Bakery, built in 2011.

On April 12, 2015, Freddie Carlos Gray, twenty-five, who lived only blocks away from The Avenue, was being chased, roughed up, arrested, and dragged off the front steps of what was thought to be his home in the impoverished neighborhood of Sandtown-Winchester. Allegedly he was in possession of a knife deemed illegal under a vague Baltimore law about knives. Reportedly (and there are conflicting reports and police testimonies), his screams of agony were ignored during the bumpy police van ride to the police station. On April 19, 2015, while in police custody, Gray died. His death came days after suffering a spinal cord injury. The officers involved in the case were indicted, but the charges were later dropped.

Pennsylvania and North avenues went aflame with hurt, anger, and frustration. Sadly, it was a déjà vu of the riots that occurred in 1968, a response to the same kinds of feelings of heartbreak, frustration, and anger in reaction to The Rev. Dr. King Jr.'s assassination.

However, in 2015, during the anger and civil unrest caused by the Freddie Gray tragedy, both institutions, The Arch Social Club and The Avenue Bakery, were unscathed. That fact so gratefully and tangibly demonstrated the respect and love that the community holds for them both.

The TRTCHC wants to build on that respect and love by calling up the economic support of development partners and Maryland's elected officials. It wants to create collaborations with Law Enforcement and Community Development Corporations (known as CDCs) to pull together the rebuilding and the rebranding of The Pennsylvania Avenue Corridor. It's ground zero. All the groundwork that we've done, and are trying to get done, has been done before—in Washington, D.C. on U Street and the community of Anacostia, and in Memphis on Beale Street. We, along with our community leaders and elected officials, should take some clues from their accomplishments.

The Chitlin' Circuit brought the greats to The Royal Theater, such as Duke Ellington, Nat King Cole, Louis Armstrong, Aretha Franklin, The Motown Sound, The King of Soul James Brown, and others. Pennsylvania Avenue provided the backdrop for performances by Thelonious Monk, Eubie Blake, and native Baltimoreans Ethel Ennis and The Dr. Phil Butts Band. One current concern is that a newly built Royal Theater might not, itself, be able to generate sustaining revenue because it would not attract top-level entertainers. Venues like *Maryland Live, The National Harbor,* or the 2300-seat Hippodrome Theatre, on North Eutaw Street in the Bromo Tower Arts & Entertainment District, would siphon off such talent. The original Royal Theater, in its prime, could seat only 1,349 patrons. We are planning to build a 3,500-seat theater, and the entire vision of The Royal Theater Project is designed to create the interest as well as the traffic to fill it.

Our goal is to build a theater in which top entertainers clamor to entertain and audiences flock to see. Right now, in 2019, we have proof of this becoming a tangible reality. When we began The TRTCHC Concert Series, held in The Bakery Courtyard, we never imagined that its popularity would grow so quickly. During the early days of the concert series, our area bands played pro bono because they knew what we were trying to accomplish—a safe and entertaining outlet for our community. These days, we now pay the musicians and vocalists who appear, and though we may not pay them a lot, according to the world of entertainment, we are overrun with requests from others to perform. We receive phone calls, musicians leave their business cards with us, and we receive emails from all the rich talent in Baltimore and beyond who want to perform in our concert series. And it's a blessing. By the same token, our audiences steadily grow as well.

One of the reasons why entertainers say that they want to play here is location. It's *Pennsylvania Avenue*. Musicians are well aware of the history and legacy of The Avenue. Musicians love the atmosphere we've created in the courtyard, made complete by murals that honor historic African American icons. Their stories have been colorfully etched into the 21st century. And then there's the clientele. Consistently, a diverse crowd, young and old, shows up for our concerts. We have white. We have black. We have various ethnic groups, sipping, eating, clapping, and jumping up to dance when the live music overtakes them. Then we have the back-in-the-day crowd, returning each summer because of the nostalgia factor. They come to honor what once was and to show their support for what could be—if we keep at it.

All this tells me is that if we build the jazz center at the same quality or better than what we have in The Avenue Bakery courtyard, we will have people flocking to Historic Pennsylvania Avenue. But this time, they will be coming from all over the country in great numbers. As the new east coast entertainment destination, it will also create that economic engine and opportunity for the community. That's the bottom line.

The summer concert series runs every first Saturday of the month from May to September. But if we had the capacity and the time, we could run it every week throughout the summer months. To me, it's simply the prelude to what could be when the TRTCHC project becomes a reality.

During the back-in-the-day glory days of The Avenue, I must acknowledge the illustrious Billie Holiday, nicknamed *Lady Day*, who is not only immortalized in our hearts but also in a statue that stands formidably on The Avenue. In 2015, Thomas Saunders, a Baltimore historian, told *The Baltimore Sun*, "Even though she was born in Philadelphia, we claim her."

Lady Day and I happen to have Fells Point in common. Saunders ran a Black History tour and production company in Baltimore until his death in 2018, called Renaissance Productions. He noted in *The Baltimore Sun*, "She grew up in Fells Point, and she would come back and sing at the Club Tijuana and Royal Theatre on Pennsylvania Avenue."

As mentioned earlier, many of yesteryear's African American icons in entertainment, civil rights, education, business, politics and religion as well as many who cross-pollinated their passions, talents, and efforts to make a difference in American life, are celebrated on the mural at The Avenue Bakery. Visitors to The Bakery, young and old, can engage in a fun-filled, fact-filled history lesson by taking the history quiz posted in The Bakery's lobby. And don't worry, panicky test-takers needn't fear. The answers to the quiz, along with informative mini-bios, are nearby. This is one quiz on which we want everyone to earn one hundred percent!

The Corridor and West Baltimore were rich with architectural history, much of which, like the Royal, was demolished under the umbrella of urban renewal. The term, urban renewal, is a misnomer for tearing down commercial structures to make room for affordable residential housing. But what happened instead was the destabilization of the West Baltimore housing market with certain developers growing rich and the construction of single-family homes and apartments at the expense of economic opportunities needed to support the community. The destruction of the commercial district halted economic stability for the community, our youth and left nothing to entice tourism.

A 2015 report produced by the Urban Land Institute (ULI) of Baltimore/Technical Assistance Panel, titled, *Pennsylvania Avenue Corridor: Restoring The Glory*, is still timely. About The Royal Theater, the report stated, "Its demolition was a crime. Its resurrection is a moral imperative." Surely it is a necessary anchor to the entire Royal Theater Project.

Now the fear is, at least for The Royal Theater, that while its former glory was partly due to the curse of Jim Crow; in today's world, it would not be able to compete with other area venues such as The Hippodrome or draw consistent high-profile talent and nationwide visitors like Harlem's Apollo Theater.

I grew up in this community. I came from this community. And, as I have said, back-in-the-day, if you wanted to experience good music and entertainment, good shopping, good food, and ambiance, you came to Pennsylvania Avenue. There, you were free to exercise full dignity, pride and mobility because Jim Crow didn't live within its parameters.

The Pennsylvania Corridor has been back in the national spotlight because of the Freddie Gray tragedy—and while we have that spotlight, we need to do something useful with it. The 1968 riots that gave license to the actions and inactions taken by our elected officials and business leaders at the time led to the Avenue's demise. Of course, naivete and failure to comprehend the value of what we had prevented us from pushing back.

But the buck still doesn't stop there. Yes, we blame the demise of a once-thriving business district on outside business leaders and our elected officials. But we, as African Americans living in the community, share some of that blame as well. Because of our concentrated focus on surviving Jim Crow's legacy, we failed to realize the value of what we had. We also lacked an appreciation of our community's impact in this Corridor had—and has—in Baltimore and this nation, ranging from politics to culture to economics to entertainment. We did not really value what we had prior to 1968. Because if we had, The Royal Theater would be standing just like the Apollo in New York, The Howard in Washington, DC, the Regal in Chicago, and the Earle in Philly.

THE BIRTH OF HARBORPLACE:

While this destruction was happening, our elected officials, spearheaded by then-mayor (1971-1987) and later governor (1987-1995), the late William Donald Schaefer, championed and won a hard-fought battle to build a retail and restaurant complex downtown. Mr. Schaefer and his developers christened it Harborplace. Today, we collectively refer to Harborplace, Camden Yards, the National Aquarium, the Convention Center, and even the light rail as The Inner Harbor. The land on which The Inner Harbor booms was once a stretch of rundown grassy fields accented by dilapidated piers rimming the Baltimore Harbor. Nearby residents used it for impromptu loitering and fishing.

The Inner Harbor was built up from little more than sticks and stones, and mud, and filthy water. It's ironic because, today, in the most historic African American community, we already have assets. We have the makings of strong economic development, i.e., The Avenue Bakery, which has become a welcomed tourism spot, and the three other businesses I mentioned earlier. We have strong and dedicated community development committees such as the Druid Heights CDC, the Upton Planning Committee, and the Penn North Community Association—these were briefly mentioned earlier. In the following chapters, they are further detailed, as is the mission of my nonprofit TRTCHC. Together we have a plan. All we have to do is come together to build the infrastructure. Compare that to Harborplace's beginnings that had nothing, no history, no legacy, no communities, and no fight for survival.

Its keys to success, you ask? The Harborplace mission had major politicians on board. It had major money people, like John Paterakis Sr., willing to invest time and capital to make it happen. When you chomp down on your next Big Mac, think of Paterakis. His H&S Bakery is one of the largest bakers on the east coast, and its subsidiary, Northeast Foods, Inc., is the largest supplier of hamburger buns for McDonald's. Paterakis came to former Mayor Schaefer's aid when he needed tons of dough to round out a section of the Harbor known as the Gold Coast.

REBUILD VS. REBOOT:

It should also be mentioned that from 1955 to 1971, Mr. Schaefer served three terms in the Baltimore City Council, eventually serving as its president (1967-1971). In 1971, an African American self-made politician, the late Clarence H. "Du" Burns, who had come to prominence through grass-roots involvement in his native East Baltimore, had run a successful race to become a Baltimore City Councilman for District 2. Early on, Burns was tagged with the nickname "Du" because, as *The Baltimore Sun* reported, "...in the 1940s ... he was knee-deep in local politics—always doing things for people." Like Mr. Schaefer, Mr. Burns also rose to become president of the City Council. Counting forward from 1971, *The Baltimore Sun* wrote that "for the next seventeen years he worked at City Hall, making urban renewal the centerpiece of his efforts."

In 1987, when Mr. Schaefer left his post as Baltimore City's mayor to serve as governor, "Du" Burns inherited the position to become Baltimore's first African American mayor. He served only eleven months, losing his primary race to Baltimore's first African American to be elected mayor—Mayor Kurt L. Schmoke.

Remember that it was in 1971 when The Royal Theater was unceremoniously torn down, void of political or community opposition; it happened just three years after the 1968 riots that erupted due to the assassination of The Rev. Dr. Martin Luther King Jr., White flight, of a middle class ethnic European variety that included Germans, Italians, and Jews, among others, went into full swing. It comprised the area's residents and shopkeepers, who had a stronghold on an ever-growing impoverished urban center, serving a Black majority. Baltimore was earning the reputation of a city that tourists did not want to visit. The corporate exodus that took place crippled any legitimate employment base left for its African American residents, who had no choice but to remain. As a result, some of those residents came up with alternative avenues of economic resources.

Once we had the riots and everybody abandoned Historic West Baltimore, the powers-that-be convinced the community that Pennsylvania Avenue had no need for cultural arts and entertainment or organized commerce. In other words, since it had been whittled down to a crime-ridden, lost cause, inhabited by second-class citizens, why inject any investment into it? Such thinking allowed The Royal Theater to be demolished.

As funds were coming to Baltimore City for redevelopment, some of that money was directed to Pennsylvania Avenue, but the money went for housing, making some people rich. No money was slated for the economic and cultural reboot that the area sorely needed. They tore down all the commercial establishments and cultural venues on Pennsylvania Avenue. While this was going on, a consensus took hold: *Let's build someplace else. Let's develop downtown.* From then on, any effort to revive economic stability on The Avenue wandered off into a rustic sunset.

The Royal Theater demolition earned a dubious distinction. It is the only major, historic African American-centered theater in the country that no longer stands. One can still enjoy The Apollo Theater in New York, the Earle Theater in Philadelphia, the Howard Theatre in Washington, D.C., and the Regal Theater in Chicago—all the other top venues of the legendary Chitlin' Circuit.

CHAPTER SIX

TALES OF THE NEIGHBORHOODS

It's Friday, January 11, 2019, and as usual, I'm up at 3:00 a.m. Now I have a lot on my mind while here on vacation at the house in Kissimmee, Florida. Brenda and I followed through with our plans to come down to the house on New Year's Day. Susie Dezurn, my son's mother-in-law, Etoy's mom, had asked if she could ride down with us. She wanted to spend some time with her favorite aunt, living in Orlando. We had already planned to pick up my sister, Gert, who lives in Petersburg, Virginia.

On the way down, we stopped in to see Jane, the sister of my good friend, Wyatt Arrington. He retired from UPS as well, and I was his first supervisor when he was hired. Arrington is a great guy. And he is truly enjoying his retirement. Brenda has often said that she loves the way he loves life. He has a bucket list of things that he's been mulling over and working on for years. He has tried to play the saxophone, a guitar and has taken voice lessons. He has purchased T-shirt printing equipment as well as studio recording equipment. He does hours of research on different things and then tries them out. He travels some, even though he's still hesitant when it comes to getting on planes. Here is a guy who used to jump out of planes when he was in the military.

But is afraid to fly. I could write an entire book on him and how he has been such a great supporter of what I am trying to make happen in Historic West Baltimore. He grew up in this community, too.

Right now, The Bakery is closed for our vacation. But while in Kissimmee, I'll be planning its reopening, scheduled for Wednesday, January 16. Brenda and I will get back to Baltimore on Sunday. And the grateful grind will begin. My truck needed an oil change down here, and the dealer indicated I would need new tires when I got back home. Yesterday I ordered them and made arrangements to have them delivered to York Automotive in Mt. Airy, Maryland to be installed on that coming Monday. This is a shop I have been using since 1980. When I find shops and services that I trust, I tend to stick with them. Ed York, the York Automotive owner, was an old-school, trustworthy guy who executed excellent service always at fair prices. Down through the years, as we got to know one another, if ever I had trouble with my vehicles, I could call him, and he would do whatever he had to do to oblige me.

I also had to reorder the flag banners that we use at The Bakery. The Bakery has a parking lot in front of it, which means the building itself, sits back about thirty feet from the sidewalk. To ensure that both pedestrians and folks driving by can still see us, I had specially designed flag banners made and posted at our sidewalk's entrance. It keeps us visible to everyone. One of the two banners reads:

The Avenue Bakery, Great Coffee. And the second banner proudly declares: *Join Us As We Rebuild The Royal,* One *Brick @ A Time, Our History, Our Legacy Our Destiny.*

It also has an image of The Royal Theater taken from the artwork in our garden at The Bakery. The purpose of the banner's message is to let people know why we are there and to garner support for our initiative.

Today is Friday, and I will reach out to Wanda Best, the Upton Community executive director, to determine if she can make the meeting I have scheduled with Al Hutchinson. Hutchinson is the President and

CEO of *Visit Baltimore*, the marketing arm of Baltimore's third-largest industry. I first met him in November of 2016, when he came to Baltimore. He was very impressed with The Avenue Bakery and what we have to offer tourists. He recognized, immediately, the value of the Pennsylvania Avenue community and the importance of what I am trying to make happen. Tourism is more than a $10 billion industry, and African American history and culture are major. In my heart, as well as in the many hearts of others, this community is the most historic African American community in the country. Yet, it remains absent from many annals that one could Google because of a multitude of injustices. But this is my tribute found on one of the panels of the brochures that visitors can pick up when they come to The Bakery:

ENTERTAINMENT

Pennsylvania Avenue's Jewels

Between World War I and II, Old West Baltimore's Pennsylvania Avenue came of age as an entertainment district and a "must play" venue for known and aspiring African American stars. It was a lively stretch of performance venues, department stores and specialty shops crowded with Baltimoreans and out-of-town shoppers. Parades were numerous as marching bands moved ahead of Elks and Masons. Thousands — both black and white — cheered them on along the way. At night the Avenue's clubs and cabarets pulsated from the sound of Jazz, Bee Bop, and Blues, as long lines of patrons waited to enter packed "houses" beneath brightly lit marquees. Theatres, taverns, dancehalls, and brothels were wedged between pawn shops and second hand stores at the southern end of the Avenue.

Royal Theatre, ca. 1949

Further north nightclubs, restaurants, theatres and hotels lined the Avenue. The Royal and the Regent theatres dominated the 1300 and 1600 blocks respectively. The Regent opened in 1916, and was rebuilt in 1920 as a vaudeville styled movie house. While the exact seating capacity varied, reaching as high as 2,200, there is no doubt that after the theatre was rebuilt it was one of the largest performing venues catering to African American performers on the East Coast.

The Douglas Theatre was renamed the Royal in 1926 and featured the City's first "talkie" movie, Hello Dixie. The Royal gained fame as part of the Chitlin' Circuit, a group of African American entertainment venues throughout the country. Patrons thronged the Royal to see stars including Ethel Waters, Pearl Bailey, Cab Calloway, Blanche Calloway, Louis Armstrong, Fats Waller, Earl "Fatha" Hines, the Temptations, James Brown, Stevie Wonder, Tommy Hunt, among others.

Regent Theatre, ca. 1950

The week before our vacation, Hutchinson stopped by the shop after calling me, days before. He indicated he wanted to take some time to discuss marketing with me. That's when he had suggested also inviting Best, of Upton Planning, to join us. My original view was to invite other members of the community to the possible meeting as well. My thought process was that all stakeholders needed to be involved with what happens to their community. I think the reason why West Baltimore has been neglected for so long is that it has been controlled by small groups, within the community, that have allowed politicians to control them.

We scheduled the meeting for January 16, 2019. But he asked if I could leave January,24, open for a possible hearing that was scheduled to take place at City Hall. That prompted me to—like in the words of Paul Harvey—understand *the rest of the story.*

For those of you, not familiar with the reference, Paul Harvey Aurandt, better known as Paul Harvey, was an American radio broadcaster for the ABC Radio Networks, beginning in the 1950s. He broadcasted news and commentary on weekday mornings, middays, and on Saturdays at noon as well as delivering his famous *The Rest of the Story* segments. From 1952 through 2008, his programs reached as many as twenty-four million people a week. Paul Harvey News was carried on twelve hundred radio stations, four hundred American Forces Network stations, and printed in three hundred newspapers.

Back to what Hutchinson was trying to clue me in on, I now realized that something was about to go down at the Town Hall Meeting, that not only would involve my overall mission but also it might reveal something that Hutchinson will need my assistance and/or input on.

I also must prepare myself for a January 21, 2019, meeting with Alexandria Mills. She emailed me to postpone the meeting to February 12, because she realized that Monday is a holiday, commemorating Dr.

Martin Luther King Jr.'s birthday. She is an impact investment associate for the Port Covington Impact Team, which is part of the Plank Industry. Kevin Plank is the founder and president of Under Armour. He is also the developer of Port Covington, the billion-dollar project to which the city has given major concessions.

When I met Alexandria Mills, I had no idea that she was African American. I was certainly pleasantly surprised to see someone like her, working in her capacity, and owning an understanding of the African American community. When I met her, she talked about her focus, which was to reach out to the communities around The Port Covington Project to ensure those communities were included and informed about what was happening around its residents. Then I shared with her about my project. Not only did she convey her excitement about it, but also she saw its relevance to The Port Covington Project.

"The representatives of The Port Covington project," she said, "would be interested [in the TRTCHC Project] as well."

Alexandria promised to inform one of those representatives, though I don't remember that person's name. He or she would be reaching out to me soon, she let me know. However, to this day, I have neither heard from that representative nor Alexandria Mills since. As I often say, it's like that old Temptations' song, "Like smoke from a cigarette and dreams that you soon forget, she faded away."

On September 19, 2016, Luke Broadwater of *The Baltimore Sun* reported that:

"The Baltimore City Council gave its final approval, Monday, [September 12, 2016]*, to a $660 million public financing package for Under Armour CEO Kevin Plank's massive Port Covington Project—a deal, supporters say will bring thousands of jobs to Baltimore, but critics say it's corporate welfare.*

City Council President Bernard C. "Jack" Young said the waterfront development proposed by Plank's Sagamore Development Co. was too good to pass up.

Young said the $5.5 billion project, which includes an expanded headquarters for Under Armour, shops, restaurants, housing, offices and manufacturing space, will spur economic growth in Baltimore.

"Under Armour is No. 2, next to Nike. We don't want Under Armour to move out of the city of Baltimore," Young said. "We've done what we could do. [Sagamore] is going to take care of the six neighborhoods surrounding Port Covington. I think we're making the right decision."

The council voted 12-1 to approve the subsidy. Councilman Warren Branch voted against the deal; council members Mary Pat Clarke and Bill Henry abstained."

I had scheduled a meeting with Mills, hopeful that Under Armour would get on board with my mission as a give-back to our community.

This meeting of the minds, comparing of notes and initiatives was triggered by Amy E. Pearl, director of Community Development for Seedpay, out of Washington State and Attorney, Brian Beckon of Cutting Edge Capital, out of California. I had met them at a seminar that was put on by Ron Hantz, founder and board president of Network for Developing Conscious Communities. He had asked me to be a presenter at his conference. I showcased Pennsylvania Avenue, its communities and The Royal Theater & Community Heritage Center Project (TRTCHC).

Pearl and Beckon were so impressed with the presentation, they scheduled a meeting with me at The Bakery. Both felt that my project would be an excellent project to take to the public, using crowdfunding. The expertise of Beckon's company, The Cutting Edge Capital, was to get projects to the crowdfunding platform. Pearl was a consultant for Seedpay and said that it could help to get adequate funding realized. Seedpay, as described on its website, "helps local merchants get more out of their day by delivering an easy and complete payment method. Our mobile payment solution enables quick and easy in-store, online, and business payments that focus on customer loyalty. Unlike other traditional payment methods, Seedpay has built a more reliable secure, and faster payment infrastructure that does not run on the legacy Visa/Mastercard."

However, we still don't have the $75-$80 thousand needed for the legal cost to make it happen. They also shared with me an organization out of Atlanta, the Tulsa Real Estate Fund. Jay Morrison is the real estate investor who put together the Tulsa Real Estate Fund that raised $10 million in a matter of months after going public due to pursuing crowdfunding.

I also received an email from Dr. Brenda Brown, indicating she had a couple of developers she wanted me to meet to share the details of our project. We first met in 2016, she was visiting Baltimore from New Jersey and was preparing for her attendance at the 50th-anniversary celebration for her graduating class at Morgan State University. She had stopped by The Bakery during that visit. She was so impressed with what she saw, and with our mission that she committed to helping. In January of 2017, Dr. Brown invited me to give a presentation to a development group in New York—WBG Property Advisors, LLC, located at 200 Park Avenue suite 1700.

My architect, Kathleen Sherrill, and I prepared our presentation and took a day trip to present on Friday, June 23, 2017. We met with Charles Wattley of WBG Property Advisors /Wattley Construction Company. After our meeting, Mr. Wattley asked me for a Memorandum of Understanding (MOU) or a Developers Agreement between his company and TRTCHC. He indicated that he was meeting with a group of bankers and his wealth management senior vice president regarding funds based on my project. It took a couple of weeks for me to produce an MOU because I had to get advice from my attorney, Emerson Dorsey of Tidings & Rosenberg, LLP, and have a joint meeting with Dorsey and my accountant, Arnold Williams, who is a partner of Abrahams, Foster Nile & Williams.

While we were trying to put together our agreement, I also had to show Upton Planning and Mayor Pugh that we had potential investors for the project because in January, the mayor had convinced Wanda Best and Jules Dunham to abandon our project—because *she* had better plans and better funding.

After the Graziano meeting of 2006, we went back to the research-drawing board to come up with a strategy to build our project in the 1300 block of Pennsylvania Avenue where The Royal Theater was originally located. However, we soon discovered that the city had designated it as Green Space, which initially meant that we couldn't build there. Thankfully, a compromise was in the air. We were told that we could use it, if we found another parcel of land that could be suitably deemed as Green Space in its place. With the help and suggestion of Joe Daniels of The Josa Group, LLC, his consulting firm, we did. I had met Joe in 2009, when he was with Verizon, ironically doing the same type of job, I was doing at UPS before I retired, which involved community relations outreach. In 2009, I was putting together The Pennsylvania Avenue Homecoming Festival. The former Governor Martin O'Malley really introduced us and convinced Verizon to become a sponsor for our festival. Joe was Verizon's Community Relations person. We met, and we jelled concerning the wealth of TRTCHC's mission.

And though that was accomplished, Mayor Pugh's eye remained fixed on the 1300 block of Pennsylvania Avenue, possibly to derail TRTCHC project. Reportedly, she may also have had plans for the future Green Space, for which her predecessor, Mayor Rawlings-Blake, had packaged funding.

In a January 2016 letter sent to me by Ms. Rawlings-Blake, she wrote, "Therefore, the Department of Housing and Community Development has recommended the appropriation of $1 million in its capital budget for land acquisition and site preparation to initiate the predevelopment steps necessary to construct a new ball field." Pre-packaged funding is very sellable as a lure to developers. Ms. Rawlings-Blake goes on to write in her letter, "We hope as you develop your proposal, you can use this letter to inform investors that the City is moving forward on a parallel path to make redevelopment on 1300 Pennsylvania Avenue possible."

Ms. Pugh could have something cooked up with housing developer Danny Henson because with monies already in the till for the future Green Space, half the finance battle is done, and there's easy money to be made. The 2017 meeting that Upton Planning set up, so that we could present our ideas and funding sources to Mayor Pugh—for The Royal Theater Project—turned out to be a sham. More on that later.

If Danny Henson's interest is to build housing, here's a word about that. One of the city's efforts that have been successful in the community is Workforce Housing. It is a program designed to help middle-class income households afford to rent or purchase newly constructed housing units. The building of Workforce Housing is not a problem. But for some elected officials, the work of building support to allocate funding for such a worthy cause is easy and a public relations boon. For developers, the gain of tax-credit dollars is lucrative. It's a win-win for everyone—except poor populations who are still left out in the elements. When one talks about true economic development to sustain a community and true social change, the move to simply build housing is lacking. And in this particular instance, there are plenty of other areas in the community that one could build Workforce Housing—places other than in the future Green Space, designated for the ballfield, located in the 1300 blocks of Argyle and Myrtle avenues between Lafayette Avenue and Dolphin Street.

This year, 2019, I must raise major capital or get major partners to possibly counter Mayor Pugh's mission to kill our project. She could harbor several motives, not wholly apparent to the naked eye, for wanting the land, located in the 1300 block of Pennsylvania Avenue, to be designated for a football field ballfield or handled by a well-known housing developer. Her motive could be that she has committed the land for her designated field, in the 1300 block of Pennsylvania Avenue, to a well-known housing developer, possibly Danny P. Henson, III, who, as I mentioned, once served as the Baltimore City Housing and Community Commissioner. Henson, who has known about me working on this project for quite a few years, also encouraged me to build The Bakery. Or maybe her actions are politically motivated—if The Avenue is fully revitalized, perhaps she would like to make sure that she can take full credit. The economic welfare of residents is at stake. Credit should not be anyone's motive.

Our goal is to raise at least $10 to $15 million to get us moving. When the community realizes we have the funding to make this happen, members and leaders in our community will actively get on board. Public awareness will increase and even mushroom across the nation. But I believe that right now, in the moment of real time, some of our community leaders have opposed it only because the Mayor has convinced them that: Number one: it is a pipe dream for which I will never be able to fund; and Number two: She has a better plan—an unstated plan—for getting there, first.

It's a déjà vu, back to when the political machine convinced the community to allow The Royal Theater to be torn down in 1971. We now have the political machine convincing them not to allow its rebuilding—at least by me. As I have repeatedly said, over and over, it is the political machine in Baltimore that is one of our major problems.

No, I don't have the money to make it happen, but my goal is to get the state and city to join my organization—to help convince developers and investors to come to the table. I commend former Governor Martin O' Malley and former Mayor Stephanie Rawlings-Blake for understanding the mission and contributing to our strides of success. People can say that they support, but these two put their support in writing and made provisions in their respective budgets (the last budgets before they left office) to make things happen. Our project is about changing the culture, environment, and economic future of the state's most neglected community.

While the nation's spotlight was on Baltimore City because of the civil unrest due to the Freddy Gray tragedy, a CNN Business report, dated April 29. 2015 was just one of many that painted the overall picture about African Americans in Baltimore City.

"Just over 63% of Baltimore's population is black and here are some of the stunning disparities they face.

[INCOMES] *Baltimore is located in the richest state in the country, Maryland, which makes comparing the incomes of blacks in Baltimore to the median income of the state overall particularly stark, with an almost $40,000 a year difference in earnings.*

But even if you compare the incomes of blacks versus whites living within the city of Baltimore, a large chasm still exists. White residents in the city make almost twice as much as black residents."

In a graphic, the story displays Median Household Income: Maryland, $73.538; Whites, $60, 550; Blacks, $33,610.

CNN dubbed its reporting on health disparities, *A Tale of Two Neighborhoods*. The report stated: "[HEALTH] *Baltimore is home to Johns Hopkins University, one of the nation's top medical schools and hospitals, but it is not the healthiest city.*

Life expectancy rates in the neighborhoods of Upton and Druid Heights -- where median income is well below the poverty line [which *is listed as $20,000 for a family of three] at $13,388 a year -- is only 63 years old. That's 20 years lower than the 83-year life expectancy for Roland Park, less than five miles away. In that neighborhood, the median income is $90,492."*

Once we returned from our vacation—or should I say working vacation, there would be a lot on my plate. But I was ready for it. The outcome of these meetings was going to be interesting, for sure, and it was also destined to be groundbreaking for what was to follow. I had also scheduled a meeting with my architect Kathleen Sherrill of SPARCH, Inc. I charged her to help me put a preliminary plan together in the event we could take possession of the property adjacent to the bakery. It is owned by the Druid Heights Community Development Corporation (CDC).

In 2004, I purchased a property from the Druid Heights CDC to build an office building. Instead, we ended up building The Avenue Bakery. Sherrill designed both concepts. The Druid Heights CDC also owns property adjacent to where The Avenue Bakery now stands. It is now 2019, and that property has been sitting undeveloped for more than ten years. The issue is that it sits on the corner of Pennsylvania Avenue and Baker Street. However, as I have strongly stated, The Avenue needs commercial development space. But the Druid Heights CDC project called the Bakers View housing project detracts from that need. That said, the property in question is not the only property that the CDC owns. It is also in possession of several lots on Baker and Division streets where it can build housing. To fulfill a goal to provide additional and affordable housing to residents in the community, the Druid Heights CDC does not need to take away vital commercial development space to do it.

The Druid Heights CDC is a powerful and successful organization that has been an asset to the community. And I commend it for what it has been able to accomplish. The description, below, was taken from its website:

The Druid Heights Community Development Corporation (DHCDC), a non-profit organization, was established in 1974. DHCDC is governed by an 18-member Board of Directors that include political, corporate, and community representation. Its mission is to promote and encourage areas of community development and empowerment through numerous initiatives. The overall goal is to accelerate the revitalization of the neighborhood with self-empowerment, employment and economic opportunities all while creating a stable and safe community environment.

Druid Heights is one of Baltimore's oldest neighborhoods with a rich historical background. The DHCDC's targeted geographic area is the Druid Heights Community located in central West Baltimore; the community is bordered to the South by Laurens Street, to the East by McCulloh Street, to the West by Pennsylvania Avenue and to the North by North Avenue. The community is predominately residential and its homes contain large interior design with three stories and as many as five bedrooms. Druid Heights also has a large population of African American families and inhabits roughly 10,000 residents according to the 2000 Census.

Druid Heights CDC has been the strongest and most successful CDC in West Baltimore. Again, I commend it for its success. However, it can't do it all, and its main focus is housing and community programs. When it comes to commercial development and creating jobs in the community, it has limited capacity or time to do it.

The Druid Heights CDC is not happy that I am interested in the property or that I have shared my interest with representatives of the State of Maryland's Department of Housing and Community Development. This has created problems for Druid Heights because the state is looking at its capacity to complete the Bakers View housing project, which, as I informed earlier, would sit on the empty adjacent lot next to The Avenue Bakery. The state representatives, who have contacted me, could not answer why the CDC has not followed through. The question in my mind is, where is the funding it received to build Bakers View? It appears the state wants to also contribute to Pennsylvania Avenue's development. One thing is clear about the current Maryland Governor's background. Mr. Hogan is a commercial guy. Gov. Hogan's biography notes: "Hogan is the founder and president of The Hogan Companies, which specialize in real estate brokerage, investment, and development. He took a leave of absence from the private sector from 2003 to 2007 to serve in the cabinet of former Gov. Robert Ehrlich (R)."

And I guess the rest is Maryland's history. However, my gut feeling is that the governor sees The Bakery as an anchor and that the rest of the block needs developing commercially. The Druid Heights CDC is standing in the way of Pennsylvania Avenue's progress. Then again, I am not sure if the state is trying to give me something—or putting it bluntly—to buy me off rather than support The Royal Theater Project. As I always say, "Time tells all."

And that's how the community has gotten into the position that it finds itself in today. The politicians would buy off the community leaders by offering something that amounted to personal gain, thereby abandoning the bigger, more holistic cause.

CHAPTER SEVEN

WHAT IS A POPPAY ROLL?

All I ever wanted to do in life was to be the father for my children that my dad could not be for me. After that, I guess I could never understand why we spend so much time complaining about our conditions and not enough time changing them.

I grew up in Historic West Baltimore as the walls of segregation were slowly crumbling. An understanding of slavery and the persecution of African Americans as a people—what was experienced—was absorbed into my being early on. I remember living in Sparrows Point as a little kid and having to be very careful not to get caught on the other side of town. The other side was an area past Sparrows Point where White people lived. The White kids would chase my friends and me and beat us up if we wandered over there—that's if they could catch us.

I remembered my parents and grandparents talking about the hangings and brutal beatings that took place on the Eastern Shore and in the South. I remember my mom and her friends talking about not being allowed to try on clothes before buying them when they shopped downtown. I remember watching TV and seeing the marches and reports of nonviolent protesters being attacked. I remember the riots and the torching of Pennsylvania Avenue when the Rev. Dr. Martin Luther King Jr. was assassinated. Pennsylvania Avenue was the heart of our community. I share this to say that I have an indelible mark branded into my soul and mind's eye as to what we've suffered as a people and the sacrifices those before us have made to set us free. I so admire their spirit and commitment to positive change.

Of those who've come before me, who decided to do something positive rather than to complain and/or accept their conditions and treatment, I decided, early on, to fight for change as well.

I also understand that slavery, segregation, and the systemic persecution of our people were and still are about economics. Although we were successful at getting laws on the books that freed us and provided opportunities for success, the war is not over. This war of which we have won many battles is about economics.

With that knowledge, what does one do? To me, once a person knows and understands the negative condition, he or she may find themselves in, that person should begin to formulate a plan to change it. I am not a scholar, a researcher, or a politician. I'm just one of those who believes that commitment and hard work hold the key to change. And it's not just about what I do for myself but how I can make a difference in others' lives to bring about positive change. I am not a very patient person; however, we need to draw a line in the sand and say, "Now is the time to do something to change the economic outlook in our community."

I also believe we need to develop a plan of our own, meaning African Americans and residents of West Baltimore, and not wait for the *something-out-there* to save us or change our economic status and future. Coming to this tangible way of thinking in my life, I came to understand how all the events that led me to this point played significant roles in my journey. Maybe you can see it, too. Our forefathers gave their lives to fight for a level playing field for us. I can, at least, do what I can to help win this on-going war.

I Had a Dream — of Entrepreneurship

As the owner, operator, and baker at *The Avenue Bakery* situated right on Historic Pennsylvania Avenue in Historic West Baltimore, my family and I enjoy much success. *The Avenue Bakery* is that one-of-a-kind place that someone dreams of having and waking up thinking *what a crazy dream. That could never happen.* Located in the country's most historic African American community, its full name is *The Avenue Bakery, Home of Poppay's Rolls.*

The question we often get is, "What is a Poppay Roll?" A Poppay roll is a yeast roll much like the rolls that folks say their grandmother or great aunt used to make back-in-the-day. However, *these* rolls are made only by Poppay. I'm a carbohydrate person, and I loved the yeast rolls that my mother used to make. But I never got her recipe. Early on in my adult life, I developed a recipe of my own and enhanced it over the years. Then there is the question, "Who is Poppay?"

Okay, now here's the answer to the question: Who is Poppay? Whenever I'm asked this, I always reply, "I am Poppay."

Let me share with you how I got that name. I grew up in the age where television shows came in black and white. There were three stations and a limited number of shows one could watch in prime time. There was the *shoot 'em- ups* as the old folks called them. Today, we call them Westerns. Then there were the entertainment shows like *The Ed Sullivan Show* and comedy shows like *The Red Skelton Show,* and *I Love Lucy.* Then there were the family shows like *My Three Sons, Leave It to Beaver,* and *Ozzie and Harriet.* These shows were supposed to have been about typical American families; however, there were no families in my neighborhood like any of them. One reason was that we lived in a segregated community, and a great number of our families were poor. As a matter of fact, only a few of us even had TVs in the first place.

To shorten the story a little, when my son, James, got married, and we were expecting our first grandchild, I came up with what I thought was a cool idea. I told my son and his beautiful wife, Etoy, "I want my first grandchild to address me as grandfather," like I had seen on the family shows on TV.

However, as fate would have it, my granddaughter Bria's first word for me was "Poppay."

I thought about it, and Poppay sounded cool, like French. I've been Poppay ever since. Again, in the words of conservative radio personality, Paul Harvey, "Now you have the rest of the story."

Besides The Bakery, I am involved with a host of organizations that ultimately focus on bringing about positive change in our community. I am a member of the *Baltimore Workforce Development Youth Council*, where I chaired the *Summer Job Youthworks* for eight years. I am a member of *Upton Planning Committee, Pennsylvania Avenue Redevelopment Collaborative.* I'm a member of *Black Professional Men*, an organization focusing on improving the lives of African American males. I can list quite a few more organizations that I am and/or have worked with over the years. Some of them will pop up as you continue to read the two cents I'm sharing.

At this point in my life, I believe I have the respect of thousands of individuals and organizations that I have worked with and/or supported down through the years. I truly believe many of them would say that I have made positive impacts in many lives. Personally, I feel there is much more I need to accomplish, and I'm hoping God maintains my health, resolve, and the precious time needed to reach my goals.

Now the question is, what are my goals? One of my goals is to be instrumental in redeveloping the most historic African American community in the country. I have this theory that as a community consumed in this economic struggle, we need to develop a mission that will bring us all together, moving forward on one agenda. Much like the struggle for the right to vote, including all the other changes brought about during the Civil Rights Movement, I have identified the mission. I have spent the past fifteen years (and counting) developing and nurturing it.

At-hand, the mission is the rebuilding of the famous Royal Theater, which was located in the 1300 block of Pennsylvania Avenue. As I've already mentioned, The Royal was one of the popular venues on what was known as the Chitlin' Circuit.

My dream of the future, hopefully, the near future, is to build or at least spearhead The Royal Theater and Community Heritage Center (TRTCHC), a state-of-the-art cultural and entertainment complex that will include a jazz museum and performing arts theaters. Thematic restaurants, businesses, and retailers will also occupy the facility, providing a comprehensive cultural experience while further resuscitating the community's economic growth.

As the focal point of the site and Pennsylvania Avenue, The Royal Theater will summon back local and national entertainers in genres including dance, voice, and instrumental music. Visitors will also experience classical and modern plays, musicals, and other theatrical performances in this uniquely historic venue. TRTCHC anticipates eighty percent utilization of the thirty-five hundred-seat theater, making it a viable and competitive venue in the southeast region.

Now that you have some idea of my focus for community redevelopment and my pursuit of an economic renaissance in this African American community, the question is, how did I arrive on this road?

I truly believe that entrepreneurship was in my blood even before I came to work in corporate America for more than thirty-five years at UPS, which paved the way. I say entrepreneurship was in my blood because Mother Hamlin, my dad's mom, had a snowball stand. She wanted to have as much say in her economic situation as she could. Even my dad worked for himself. And I took note of it all. I remember very little about just what my father did, although I do remember him owning a big truck. I think he did light hauling. Anyway, during my career days at UPS, I periodically had second jobs, and I explored photography. I even tried my hand as a *Kirby Vacuum Cleaners'* salesman. As a matter of fact, my first supervisor at UPS, Ed McClurkin, still owns the Kirby Vacuum cleaner; I sold him back in the '70s. Ed is one of my closest friends.

The Royal Theater Project hit my table full-scale in 2003. At that time, I was preparing for my final days in my UPS career. Besides holding down my job assignment as the UPS District Community Relations Manager and Training & Development Manager, I also held the position as the 2nd Vice President of Baltimore City Branch of the NAACP. I was its economic development chair as well as the chair of the Annual Business Breakfast Fundraiser. Part of my responsibility was also to be the point-person for the Home Buying Program partnership that the Branch had with Bank of America.

In 2001, the NAACP Baltimore Branch president, G.I. Johnson, had asked me to assume these positions after meeting at the NAACP National Convention, which had been held in New York. In case you're wondering, I have no idea what Johnson's first and second initials stand for. All I've ever heard him called is G.I. As the District Community Relations Manager for UPS, it was my responsibility to be the point-person for the event when it moved to Baltimore the following year, which was 2002. UPS has always been committed to communities, at-large, and especially to underserved communities. It also supports other organizations representing underserved communities, such as the NAACP, the Urban League, and the National Council of La Raza, which is the country's largest national constituency-based Hispanic organization.

The Business Breakfast Fundraiser was being held in the backroom of *Micah's Soul Food Restaurant* located on Reisterstown Road, and it normally raised around five hundred dollars. When we took it over the first year, we were able to negotiate with the then Wyndham Hotel to have it there, and our net proceeds for the event soared to sixteen thousand dollars. The following year our net was up to twenty-one thousand dollars. Now let me make the point that I did not accomplish this by myself; I had a super committee willing to follow me out on a limb to make things happen. There was Brad Redd, who ran the National Home Buying Program for the NAACP; Dave Palmer and Ken Westerly, who were from the School of Business at Morgan State University; Cynthia DeJesus and Omar Mohammad, who were with a Community Lending Fund Organization; Rahn Barnes, a VP at Provident Bank; and Louis Field, who owned his own tour company. Also, a committee member was Paul Taylor. He was the executive director for Baltimore City's Small Business Resource Center. This was the most dynamic, forward-thinking group of people with which I had ever had the pleasure to work. As far as this group was concerned, nothing was impossible.

In 2003, my committee decided we wanted to raise the bar. Previously, the keynote speakers had been local leaders such as Representative Elijah Cummings (D-MD 7th District). However, I had set my sites on Robert L. Johnson, the co-founder of Black Entertainment Television (BET). I felt he was the ultimate entrepreneur and that he could really draw the public and businesses. Also, I felt it would be a win/win for him and the NAACP because he was considering building a hotel in Baltimore. Call it reaching for the clouds, but it worked. He agreed to be our keynote speaker, and he made a contribution to the Branch as well. I was told that the National NAACP and President/CEO Kweisi Mfume also received a contribution to the National NAACP. Mfume held that position from 1996 to 2004.

This event turned out to be huge. It was the biggest business breakfast the branch had ever had, even to the date of this printing. With vendors and entrepreneurs from all over feeling that this was the place to be, we ended up commandeering all the convention space at the hotel, and just about every newspaper in the city covered us.

Basking in that success was great, but when things started to get a little competitive and political at the NAACP, I began to consider transitioning myself from its leadership. At this time, I also began planning my retirement from UPS. The work that we were able to accomplish with the support of President G.I. Johnson allowed us to make the Business Breakfast the leading fundraiser for the Branch. During our ongoing commitment to the Branch, we also lent our expertise and efforts to enable the success of The Freedom Fund Dinner, which was NAACP's signature event.

At the time this was going on, I had gotten into some conversations about our historical community and how we, as a people, let it die. Plain and simple, it was a shame that we allowed The Royal Theater to be torn down. In some of the conversations, folks condemned community leaders and politicians such as the former Mayor Clarence "Du" Burns and others for not stepping up to save it. "Du" Burns, who had been the city's first African American mayor, became so in 1987. He served eleven months until the second Black mayor, Mayor Kurt L. Schmoke, beat him in the primary race. The Royal Theater was torn down in 1971 as part of urban renewal. It was the same year "Du"

Burns had become a Baltimore City councilman. It is ironic that all the other venues on the Chitlin' Circuit are still standing and that the communities in which they thrive are much like the historic African American community of Baltimore.

Another thing that strikes me as strange is that Baltimore's Pennsylvania Avenue was also a thriving entertainment center. Whether you were black, white, Jewish, Catholic, or whatever, you came to Pennsylvania Avenue for the great food and entertainment—and The Royal Theater was the anchor. Now, the entertainment center is downtown, better known as The Inner Harbor. To make that happen, it took a direct initiative of Mayor Schaefer in the 1970s. The opening of Harborplace took place in the summer of 1980.

It should be noted that Pennsylvania Avenue is the only business district in the city that has two metro stops, which are the Upton Station and the Penn North Station. Then further up, you have a transportation hub located at Mondawmin Mall. All this would indicate that Pennsylvania Ave. would be an ideal site for transit-oriented development.

However, back in 2003, I had long since gotten tired of all the crying and whining about what could or should have been done to preserve such a landmark. What came to my mind was that the damage had been done; so, what were we going to do now. I asked around to ascertain if anyone had ever considered rebuilding the theater. Sadly, they hadn't. There was a resounding "no" hanging in the air. Then as fate would have it, I got a couple of messages from a gentleman named Bob Goetz. He indicated he had heard about the Business Breakfast and was sorry to have missed it. However, he said to me over the phone, "I'd like to meet with you to discuss a couple of projects."

I couldn't wait. A couple of weeks went by, but Bob and I finally met. He explained to me that he and a New York architect were in the business of rehabbing old theaters. Bob asked me if I had any ideas or knew of any theaters that were worth rehabbing. My response was clear and concise. "Yes," I said, "there are a couple of theaters still standing around the city that I suppose could be worked on. However, if you want to make a huge impact—rebuilding The Royal Theater would be the way to go." He seemed receptive to hear more, and I shared the history of Pennsylvania Avenue and the Royal. He, in turn, shared it with his architect, Craig Morrison, of New York. In 2004, Craig came, and we toured The Avenue and The Royal Theater site. He did a layout and a cost analysis for the project. I started working on doing what I could to make it a reality.

I knew I had to start putting a solid plan together, so I began sharing the idea with folks I knew and trusted. One of these people was Ann Mitchell, the wife of former Maryland Senator Michael Bowen Mitchell. The Mitchell family was and still is considered political royalty in Baltimore with a strong civil rights history. She and I met in our travels, working as public figures for our companies. I was the Community Relations Manager for UPS, and she did the same type of work for State Farm. We often found ourselves at various conventions and fundraising functions in the community. We both were involved with Druid Heights CDC, trying to bring resources to that community. In sharing our family stories, she had indicated her daughter, Micah, had graduated from law school and had passed the Bar exam. She gave me Micah's contact information in case I needed an attorney as I moved forward with the project.

I had also shared the concept with my accountant, Arnold Williams, who advised me to pursue the project through a nonprofit entity along with our for-profit company, BRIABRAN, LLC. His take on it was that the nonprofit would allow us to take advantage of grants and other forms of financing. At the time, Arnold Williams was a partner in the leading African American-base accounting firm, Abrams, Foster, Nole & Williams, P.A., in Baltimore and he was recognized at the

NAACP's Freedom Fund Dinner that our committee helped facilitate. That's how he came to my awareness. Based on his advice, I decided to hire Micah Mitchell as my attorney, and I believe I was her first client. Although she was new at it, I trusted her because she seemed to research everything before presenting me with options. I really enjoyed our attorney-client relationship because she was always there when I needed her help—and I didn't always get a huge bill.

As we moved forward, she introduced me to another attorney named Wallace May, who was a friend of her father's. May seemed to be a development attorney, Micah advised. "[And] I sincerely believe that he can help get the project off the ground," she let me know.

I worked with him for a short period of time, and I determined that he was more interested in compiling billable hours rather than delivering what was promised. I moved on. Also, later I got the impression that Micah had had a bad experience with him as well. She never shared the details, nor did I ask, but it was clear that she was not pleased with the results of our relationships with him. It cost me, and I realized that there are people who will take advantage of your passion.

With help from Micah, I began to put together The Royal Theater & Community Heritage Corporation, a 501(c)(3) charitable nonprofit, to move the project forward. She helped with filing the necessary corporation papers and advised me on the steps I needed to take.

As I mentioned before, I shared the project with people I trusted. Another such person was Ray Haysbert, a prominent African American businessman and a civil rights leader in Baltimore. And if that wasn't enough, Ray was also a veteran of World War II and a proud member of the historic Tuskegee Airmen. Ray Haysbert passed away in 2010. He was ninety years old. I met him years prior to creating the nonprofit when I helped the NAACP's Freedom Fund Committee put together its fundraiser. I had the privilege of visiting him at his home to inform him that we wanted to recognize him and another economically empowering individual (Arnold Williams). From that point on, he and I connected. I shared the project with him and asked if he would consider becoming one of our founding board members. He indicated the project was viable and agreed to join the board. Having Mr. Haysbert as a supporter was major since his reputation across the state and country for business and entrepreneurship was incredible. His strategic involvement with the Park Sausage Company and other economic projects was well-known as his being one of the Tuskegee Airmen.

From that point on, I worked to develop our board. The next person on the list was Alice Cole from the Office of Employment Development for Baltimore City. Alice and I had been working together for a few years at this point. She coordinated Baltimore's program, Youthworks' Summer Jobs. She and Skipp Sanders, who was the chair of Baltimore Workforce Development, recruited me to chair the program. Sanders became the director of the Reginald F. Lewis Museum of Maryland African American History & Culture (2011 - early 2016). My working association with both Cole and Sanders was all getting off the ground in 2001. I was also charged to help attract businesses to the program and increase the number of youths served. Cole accepted my invitation to join the board. She enthusiastically took on the task of secretary.

I continued to attract board members as I educated folks on the project. I scheduled a meeting with then-Mayor Martin O' Malley, who served in that position from 1999-2007. O'Malley served as Maryland's governor from 2007-2015, and he made a brief democratic candidacy bid in the 2016 presidential race. My scheduled meeting also included Baltimore's then Deputy Mayor Jean Hitchcock, whom O'Malley had appointed as such in 2000, to share the vision and the project. Both seemed to like the idea. They suggested that I reach out to the community to determine if it would support the project. Of course,

I had already been doing that. They mentioned a gentleman named George Gilliam, who was one of the community leaders who worked on Pennsylvania Avenue. O'Malley and Hitchcock also brought to my attention that the Upton Planning Committee was in the process of developing their community master plan.

This was all going on while I was forming my nonprofit, *The Royal Theater & Community Heritage Corporation* (TRTCHC). At this point, I had identified and confirmed all the board members. They were: Ray Haysbert; Alice Cole, secretary; Adrian Johnson, who was the vice president of Municipal Employees Credit Union of Baltimore (MECU); Joey Richards, owner of Charm City Signs; Art Varnado, vice president of T. Rowe Price; Edwin Avent, 21st Century Group; Charles Harrison of Harrison Associates, LLC; Thomas Kiefaber of The Senator Theater; Charles Sydnor, an attorney with the Enterprise Foundation; and George Gilliam, executive director of Pennsylvania Avenue Redevelopment Collaborative (PARC). In essence, these were the heavy hitters of the day.

Our board's first task was to put together the application for our 501(c)(3) nonprofit status. I was fortunate enough to meet Chester France of the C. Whitney Group, LLC, who was so excited about the project that he offered to take us through the application process, pro bono. Alice, our secretary, provided support and assistance by developing the operational documents (i.e., Conflict of Interest, Director Compensation Agreement Fundraising Policy& Procedures, Economic Development Policy and Procedures, Finance Policies and Procedures, etc.) and Board Member Responsibilities. That long process included everything from creating bylaws to adhering to IRS procedures and regulations, etc. In short, it was a complicated process that must be done right. As a result of his help and Alice's expertise, hard work and attention to detail, we submitted our application; we received no IRS questions, which was approved on the first round.

All-in-all, the newly founded nonprofit's mission was to make a newly built Royal Theater more than just the theater, but a destination that would give visitors to Baltimore a true African American experience. The project would create thousands of jobs, careers and recapture the economic engine that Pennsylvania Avenue had once been in the '40s, '50s, and early '60s.

I joined the Upton Planning Committee as they were developing their community master plan. When I introduced the project, it was overwhelmingly accepted. The consensus was that this project would be the anchor for the commercial district. There were City Planning people on the committee who researched the possibility of building the project on The Royal Theater's original site. However, their report indicated that such a possibility would not be viable because that particular parcel of land had been designated an *open space*. To build on the property, one would have to find comparable land in the neighborhood as a trade-off. They then went about the task of finding another site. The City Department of Planning came up with the 1500 block of Pennsylvania Avenue as the probable site for the TRTCHC project. The site was surrounded by Mosher Street on the south, McMechen Street on the north, and Division Street on the east.

The Planning Department completed an assessment of the cost to acquire the site, identifying the open lots owned by the city or occupied by businesses, or those lots simply deemed vacant properties. Looking at the cost, it seemed reasonable, so we adopted the recommendations. However, we didn't realize how difficult this site would be to obtain. In hindsight, we should have realized that one of the remaining club establishments, The Casino, still standing in this block was going to present an obstacle. The Casino was part of the Little Willie Adams Dynasty, as I call it. There was a barbershop owned by Raymond Nelson, who was also working on a plan to revitalize that block and bring some entertainment back to The Avenue.

As I was working with Upton Planning, I was also developing the scope of the project with Craig Morrison and Bob Goetz. We completed a layout of the project that would include The Royal Theater Marquee on the corner of Lafayette and Pennsylvania avenues. It would also consist of a five hundred-seat Jazz Center and a thirty-five hundred-seat Royal Theater. The cost of the project, according to Morrison's concept, would be around forty-two million dollars.

At this point, I felt as though I needed to get a sense of the present dynamics of Pennsylvania Avenue. I remembered what it was like when I lived in the community, but not much after. The last time I lived there was in 1968 when Rev. Dr. Martin Luther King Jr. was killed. I was there when all the riots took place. I was nineteen working at Mt. Vernon Textile Mills while finishing my senior year at Edmondson High School.

I will never forget the way I felt walking to work from the 1700 block of McCullough Street and noticing the National Guard policing the community. Streets glistening with hydrant water, smoldering burned-out businesses and residences that would later be either boarded up or torn down to the ground. The hollowed-out structures that remained, some to this day, are corpses of what was and reminders of how the powers-that-be abandoned the area.

The 2015 civil unrest, prompted by Freddie Gray's death while in police custody, brought those 1968 images back in 3-D.

Before the 2015 unrest, the only recent information I had sifted through came from the HBO television series titled *The Wire*. And in case you've never heard of it, to give you a brief point of reference, here is the show's proud pitch: *In the drug-ridden streets of West Baltimore, there are good guys and there are bad guys. Sometimes you need more than a badge to tell them apart. The Wire,* which was filmed in Baltimore and ran from 2002 to 2008, effectively put Baltimore on the nation's drama map of awareness for—in my opinion—all the wrong reasons. And except for becoming familiar with its existence and dramatic negative content, it was one show I never watched and hated with a passion. There are very few things I can say I hate, but this was on the top of my list.

The reason for my disdain was because of how the nation's most historic African American community was largely portrayed. Baltimore is not like New York. We have seen just about every kind of movie one can think of, being filmed in New York, from *King Kong* to mob movies, you name it. And yet, New York is still thought of as the greatest city in America. But the popularity of *The Wire* immediately branded Baltimore as a drug-infested, corrupt city. And we have yet to shake the stigma. During this timeframe, as we looked at Pennsylvania Avenue, we realized that even if I had the forty-two million dollars to build the project, the community was not ready. Walking up and down The Avenue, as it was nicknamed decades ago, open-air drug markets were in progress—visible and audible. Drug dealers could be heard yelling out red tops, blue tops, and other street-labels they used for their products. In the 1700 block of Pennsylvania Avenue, the ambitious dealers would stash their drugs and paraphernalia in the thresholds of various businesses. Boldly, they'd threaten the proprietors, letting them know that if the police were called, once the police vacated the scene, their fate would be in peril, once again. They had better remember who would be there, once the police vanished.

At this point, I had introduced myself to George Gilliam and explained why I was there. He seemed very interested and asked me to attend a couple of the PARC meetings. I had mentioned to a few people about what I was doing on The Avenue, and I was cautioned about dealing with George. He seemed to be an okay guy when I met him, and he seemed very passionate about making a positive difference in the community. I try to deal with folks based on how they deal with me. Certainly, I've known folks who didn't and don't particularly care for me in my career and travels. But I've never let that get in the way of my efforts to try to make a positive difference. I try to respect everyone whether or not we agree or disagree.

After attending a couple of PARC meetings, I understood the focus of the organization. PARC was formed in 2001 as an organization that would represent Pennsylvania Avenue, which crosses the boundaries of several communities. Those communities are Druid Heights, Upton, Sandtown-Winchester, and Penn North. The way I understood it, the communities focused on housing and other issues. PARC's primary focus was Pennsylvania Avenue, the commercial district. The Avenue was the economic centerpiece for all the communities mentioned.

From what I gather, there was a push to get Pennsylvania Avenue's participation in the citywide Main Street Program. This program provided resources to help revitalize community main streets across the country. Other communities such as Hampton, Federal Hill, and other areas in Baltimore were able to take advantage of these resources. However, because of the unique economic disadvantages of Pennsylvania Avenue, the program had to be customized.

With that said, the first step was to unify The Avenue under one umbrella, Pennsylvania Avenue Redevelopment Collaborative (PARC). With the help of Maryland State Senator Verna Jones-Rodwell (District 44, 2003-2015), who served as its vice president, the organization was formed. And The Pennsylvania Avenue Main Street Program came to The Avenue. Gilliam served as its executive director. The board of directors was made up of representatives from Druid Heights, Sandtown-Winchester, Upton, Penn North, and the business district.

There were business organizations that were a part of it as well. The organizations like the Associated Black Charities and Maryland General Hospital were on fire and in full support of PARC's agenda to strengthen our communities. Remember that PARC was busy putting together The Pennsylvania Avenue Main Street Program. The support of business organizations came in the form of providing resources that supplemented, in part, the salaries of George Gilliam and others. But when 9/11 took place, their interests scurried to other places, other causes. They abandoned PARC. In the aftermath, I helped PARC set up meetings with some of these organizations to try to get them back to the table. We were unsuccessful in our efforts. That loss put a financial strain on PARC's efforts.

I am sure many other factors played a role in such a dire consequence. However, I am sharing my understanding of the facts.

I knew that if we were going to economically revitalize The Avenue and bring back The Royal, I, and all the players who had shown interest thus far were going to have to change the negative perception of The Avenue as well as address the drug activity. We were going to have to give our community a reason to come back. It was so important to get all the involved players to realize that we had a diamond in the rough and that we needed to work to affect a tangible, positive change. I truly believed that we could do anything we put our minds to do. Nothing is more important than making life better for those who come behind us. If we don't work to make this a reality, then who will? If not now, then when? It's easy to say, "Somebody should do something." Now, I'm not altogether sure why, at that moment, I felt that I needed to be that *somebody*, but I did—and I still do. I guess I realized how God had blessed me, and how in some way, He had led me down this path. And still, today, if He leads me, I will follow.

After a few meetings with PARC board representative Jackie Cornish, who was also the executive director for Druid Heights CDC, Cornish asked me if I would consider taking the Economic Development Chair position for PARC.

As the Community Relations Manager for UPS, I had a working relationship with Cornish and the Druid Heights CDC to increase job opportunities for those living in the Druid Heights community of zip code 21217. UPS, The Enterprise Foundation, and The Baltimore Urban League formed a partnership. The Enterprise Foundation provided resources for job-readiness training, and The Urban League provided the training, while UPS provided the jobs. However, a problem arose for the program and for potential UPS employees. UPS had night jobs that it couldn't fill because individuals living in the zip code 21217, which encompasses Druid Heights, did not have public transportation to take advantage of available night-shift jobs. To overcome this obstacle, I pulled together Maryland Transit Authority (MTA), St. Agnes Hospital, and Retz Electronic School to come up with a solution. We convinced MTA to put in a temporary route for two years. UPS agreed to contribute $13,000 for those two years. And MTA committed to keeping the route in if the fares paid for its existence. To this day, if someone living in West Baltimore's 21217 zip code has to get to-and-from a night-shift job at the UPS Customer Center in Arbutus' 21227 zip code, he or she can still rely on the MTA bus route that I initiated.

I had also encouraged and assisted Druid Heights CDC to apply for a UPS Community Service Grant. The community was in the process of raising money for the rehab of its firehouse, which would later become Druid Heights CDC's new home. However, the community leaders did not receive the $100,000 grant. It did receive $25,000 to build a playground next to the firehouse.

With the ultimate mission in mind, I determined that I would take on that responsibility. In my mind, that is what's wrong in our community. Many of us have the expertise and skills to help turn our communities around but are reluctant to do so. Yet that doesn't stop us from complaining about what's wrong or commenting to anyone who will listen that someone should do something. I just don't understand the fact that we have more African American millionaires and politically affluent leaders than ever before, yet, they don't see the struggle or contribute to the mission. Sadly, I feel that their way of thinking could be, *I've got mine, I have reared my kids; they are successful. So, I have done my part.* Where would we be if those who died for our freedom thought that way? Okay, I will get off my soapbox and move on.

As I began to work with Gilliam at PARC, I realized that he was getting paid by The Pennsylvania Avenue Main Street Program, but it only amounted to about $19,000 a year, and he had to raise part of his salary. To help, I asked him to pull together a list of partners who were committed to the organization before 9/11. We scheduled meetings with those organizations, but we were unable to get any support financially or otherwise. George did a good job putting together the committees and following the Main Street requirements; however, paperwork was not his forte. We tried to find volunteers to help, but that was never consistent, either. Then there was the president of PARC, a gentleman named Ken Saunders who never seemed to attend any meeting yet handled the finances. These are some of the issues that the organization faced.

As part of the Economic Development Committee, my task was to attract new business to The Avenue. In that effort, I reviewed the Upton Master Plan to determine what businesses the community desired so that we could work on a strategy. Because of that review, it was determined that the commercial portion of the Master Plan had not been completed. Gilliam and I determined that we could do that with help from our Baltimore Development Corporation (BDC) representative, Cory Brown. We had several meetings, pulled together maps, identified properties, and completed the plan. We presented the plan to the Department of Planning, and a meeting was scheduled with BDC to review it. However, that meeting never took place because it appeared that BDC was not aware of the work—at least, that is what I was told. The bottom line is that we were able to complete the strategic plan for the redevelopment of the commercial district, which is Pennsylvania Avenue.

Moving forward, we knew we had to change the perception as well as the drug activity on The Avenue to attract new businesses. We held residential and business community meetings with the police department to review the stats and determine strategies. In our communications, and in working with then-Police Commissioner Leonard Hamm, as one of the initiatives, we shut down parking in the 1700-1800 blocks where the drug dealers were dealing out of businesses. This allowed the police department to better see what was taking place. In all, we were able to get the open-air drug market off The Avenue—over a period.

As we worked on the crime elements, we started implementing the commercial strategic plan we had developed for the Upton Master Plan. We worked on the committee to renovate Billie Holiday Park. When the park was originally constructed, the artist, James Earl Reid, designed a pedestal for her (her likeness statue) to be placed on. Back in the '80s, the political community felt the pedestal was too controversial and would not allow it to be put in place. The pedestal depicts graphics from Billie Holiday's work, *Strange Fruit*, which depicts images of Black men hanging from trees. However, the censorship of the work had been lifted, and the pedestal became part of the park's renovation.

We also worked on the Street Scape Project to bring new lighting, curb cuts, and signage. Legends Park, located in the 600 Block of Laurens Street, was also completed. This is an open-air park that could accommodate live entertainment as well as permanent seating for outdoor chess activities. This project resulted from a study and partnership with Morgan State University School of Architecture and Social Work.

While we were working on these things, we were trying to market The Avenue and make people feel comfortable coming back as well as attracting new businesses.

Cool Jazz on The Avenue, a Friday night concert series at the Lafayette Market, was one way to accomplish that during the 1990s. Rosa Pryor, an entertainment promoter for more than sixty years worked up and down the east coast, especially in Baltimore, commented that if something like The Market's Jazz concerts were to return then, the powers-that-be could see just how beneficial, and vital, the TRTCHC project is. The concerts used to bring folks to The Avenue and business to the merchants in the market. People felt safe and enjoyed the entertainment.

Gilliam informed me that John Paterakis Sr. had eliminated this practice. The multimillionaire businessman and Baltimore developer was known as *The Bread Man* because he owned and built the H&S Bakery empire and because he was known to give grand financial support to Maryland's political candidates. As mentioned earlier, he was one of Mayor Schaefer's biggest financiers and encouragers, helping him to invent The Inner Harbor. Paterakis, who died at age 87 in 2016, was well-seasoned in financial clout and political influence.

Around 1996, as reported on April 16, 1996, *Baltimore Sun* story, Mayor Schmoke dismantled the city's markets' bureaucracy in an effort to make the markets run smoother—but they did not. In bureaucracy's place, the nonprofit Baltimore Public Markets Corporation was born. A similar corporation had operated The Lexington Market since 1979. Paterakis was given oversight of some of the city's markets. His take on it was that the market was not in the entertainment business. That is so strange when you think about it because if that were true, why was there vibrant live entertainment at the Lexington Market every weekend, entertaining crowds?

Baltimore Public Markets Corporation states: *Baltimore's Public Markets are the oldest continuously operating public market system in the United States. In operation before the city's health department and even the mayor's office, the markets continue to maintain a tradition for which Baltimore is famous.*

Jazz concerts on Friday nights were fast becoming a staple for the area. "It was going well. People were looking forward to it," said Pryor. And if it were to return, it's her opinion that it would bring life back to The Pennsylvania Avenue Corridor and welcome a diverse crowd, "a place like The Royal Theater used to be," added Pryor. "And that's the vision that Jim is planning."

We held several meetings with Casper Jenco and Robert Thomas, the current managers of Baltimore's public markets, to suggest improvements. Although entertainment was not discussed, we talked about lighting and attracting new business there. As an attraction, we had suggested allowing the Baltimore Arabbers to place wagons in there to sell produce. The problem we had with that was that the market system had very strict leasing rules that made it difficult for any new business. We even discussed having a police officer stationed in the area that would eliminate the loitering of the drug dealers that would hang out there. This didn't go over well with Market's management as well. However, they did invest funds to put in a seafood stall, and it attracted a new tenant. I am not sure what happened, but the tenant didn't last six months. I believe the lease was too high, and the merchant could not grow the business fast enough. Plus, or minus, the only merchant that moved in and seemed to survive was Murry's Steak. It swooped in and took up about twenty-five percent of the space and eliminated the possibility of having any entertainment there in the future.

While working on all the things we needed to do to attract new business, there were organizational issues that were pressing. The year after I met Gilliam, his wife was killed. Apparently, from what I gather, she was shot by a senior citizen in one of the senior citizens' facilities that she managed. He said that it appeared she was going to survive, but suddenly, she passed. As it would be for anyone, this devastated him. She was his righthand and support, which allowed him to serve PARC and satisfy his passion for making a difference.

This negatively impacted his ability to financially and physically get his work done. There were many nights and evenings; I served as a sounding board for his grief. The board and I encouraged him to get help. He assured us that he had been reaching out to his pastor and to others to help him through this difficult time.

The next task at hand was the development of the Pennsylvania Heritage Trail. We were able to pull together historians and community leaders to form a committee to develop the Trail. It was funded by Baltimore Heritage and State Heritage dollars, which covered the trail, trail guides, and website. The committee came up with more than seventy-eight historical sites, and we had the task of reducing it to twenty-five, based on the funding and the desire and the need to make it a tight walking trail.

In the meantime, I continued to share the idea of the revitalization project with people I knew. One of those people was Danny P. Henson, III, who served as the Baltimore City Housing Commissioner under Mayor Schmoke. He served in that position for seven years. These days, Henson refers to himself as the "under-the-radar real estate developer." He is the owner of the Henson Development Company, Inc. Whenever I saw him at an event or press conference; we would get into a discussion on the revitalization of Pennsylvania Avenue. One time he mentioned U Street in Washington, D.C. and made a comparison to Baltimore's Pennsylvania Avenue. He spoke of U Street, now revitalized, having the unique restaurants and businesses that helped turn it around. He explained the secret to me.

"James, you must put something on Pennsylvania Avenue that you can't get anyplace else," Henson said.

With that in mind, coupled with the fact that people were coming back to The Avenue when the Jazz events were at the Lafayette Market, the only other event that brought people back was the annual Cadillac Parade. Gilliam had resurrected it nine years prior. After much discussion, Gilliam and I came up with the idea to have a concert series. This concert series would include R&B, Jazz, and gospel entertainment as well as comedy. We held them on Friday nights, much like the Friday Nights Jazz at the Market. But instead of the Market, the concerts were held on Lafayette Avenue, outdoors between Division Street and Pennsylvania Avenue. We were able to get the city to partner with us and to provide the stage and support we needed. We were able to get most of the entertainers to donate their time. We did have to provide the sound system for the event. In some cases, we were able to get some financial support.

The Royal Theater & Community Heritage Corporation (TRTCHC) provided funds for the sound system. This was also a marketing strategy for the nonprofit to get its name out there as well.

When the organization, TRTCHC, was supporting the concert series, we also became a sponsor for the Cadillac Parade to help keep it moving. The hope was also to attract bigger bands such as high school and college bands. Gilliam was able to get the Morgan State University Band to perform in the parade. He and bandleader Melvin Miles had agreed that the only fee that would be needed was for the band's transportation. Gilliam would raise the money through the vendors and any sponsorship he could accrue. However, one year, he was not able to raise the money, and Morgan stopped participating. From that point, only the community bands were left and the quality of the parade diminished. Then things got worse. While under Mayor

O'Malley's administration the city partnered with PARC to provide the cost of the stage, police coverage and equipment. But once his administration ended, the city no longer supported the event. That meant we had to come up with about $10,000 to pay the city to put on the event.

Gilliam was being bombarded with these issues, in addition to trying to cope with the death of his wife. Then I thought he had landed a deal of a lifetime. The now Governor O' Malley, from what I was told, appointed Gilliam to a position with the state. I believed it to be a community liaison position, working with communities around the state. I thought it was great because, as Gilliam explained it, sixty percent of his time could be spent working with Pennsylvania Avenue. It felt like we now had the inside track. However, the bottom fell out of that assumption pretty quickly. I am not sure what happened, but Gilliam resigned from that position.

When Gilliam took on this position, I tried to pick up the slack for what was needed to be done on The Avenue and The Pennsylvania Avenue Main Street Program. When he left PARC for the state position, it meant that BDC had to search for a new Pennsylvania Avenue Main Street Program manager, a position also held by Gilliam in addition to being the executive director of PARC. To this date, BDC or the community have never been able to hire the right manager for the job. There have been two since Gilliam's departure, and neither has been able to bring the community together the way he was able to do it, even after the Main Street Program was abruptly moved to Druid Heights CDC.

Troubles with one of The Pennsylvania Avenue Main Street Program managers, chosen after Gilliam, actually led to the demise of PARC. In search of a new manager, Baltimore Development Corporation (BDC) brought a young lady to the table. She was impressive, and the consensus was that she had promise. So, she got the position.

However, just like Gilliam, one of her main focuses was to raise part of her salary—in addition to what the Main Street Program provided. For the one or two years she was in that position, she was never able to do that. Becoming disgruntled about that arrangement and outcome, she began to charge that PARC owed her money. The young lady complained to Maryland State Senator Verna Jones-Rodwell, who was the vice president of PARC. The young woman alleged that PARC wasn't doing what it was supposed to do. The Senator's suggestion to PARC was to add new board members. Perhaps new blood could resolve the issue. New board members from Reservoir Hill, which is a community above North Avenue and close to Druid Hill Park, were added. These people ended up forming a coup and controlling everything, and as a result, rather than deal with the young lady's complaints; it controlled a vote to move the Main Street Program from PARC and move it to Druid Heights CDC. The young lady still was not able to raise her salary. Her ruckus got louder. And Senator Jones-Rodwell resigned from PARC altogether, figuring that she didn't need the negative publicity. She simply didn't want the dirt on her hands.

When Gilliam moved on from PARC/The Main Street Program to the state position, he was not able to continue organizing the Cadillac Parade. To help keep the tradition alive and improve upon the work that Gilliam accomplished, with Gilliam's blessing, TRTCHC and I took on the full responsibility. That meant raising funds, getting the sponsors and vendors, and marketing the event. In the process, a committee was formed, and we explored the idea of making it a weekend event starting with Friday Jazz Night, the Saturday Cadillac Parade and Concert, and an outdoor Gospel Concert on Sunday to get the churches involved.

The team was made up of the Cordy Group and me, which was the company that produced the trail guide and website for The Pennsylvania Avenue Heritage Trail. John Milton Wesley, Zack Germroth, and

Rick Lomonico comprised the Cordy Group's leadership. In the process, we tried to partner with the city because we felt it was a win/win that would make good advertising for the city and have a positive impact on tourism. The committee also included Baltimore Heritage and the current Mayor Stephanie Rawlings-Blake's faith-based coordinator to help bring the churches together for the Sunday event portion.

We were able to raise about $15,000. TRTCHC contributed around $10,000. We received a $5,000 contribution from Verizon. We believe that Verizon's contribution was encouraged by Mayor O'Malley. Gilliam came aboard to work on vendors and the entertainment part of the event. We could not convince or reach Melvin Miles to get Morgan back, but we were able, with help from Wanda Best of Upton, to get Lincoln University, out of Pennsylvania, to participate. With no success, we reached out to all the middle and high school bands as well.

Trying to pull off this event while Gilliam and I worked on different tracks was somewhat difficult. Of all that took place, it was my goal to improve it and to assure Gilliam and others that the parade was still his event. However, we got through it all, and the event was somewhat successful. *The Friday Night Jazz* went well, and the parade and concert, the core of the weekend, was great. The most disappointing day was Sunday. With all the city and our committee had done to bring the churches together, they did not do what they had promised. Instead of a four-hour event, it only lasted two hours, and the attendance was poor. After bringing together about ten churches to participate, actually, only two participated.

Now Gilliam had relinquished his position with the state and wanted to come back to The Avenue, but PARC as he left it, no longer existed and The Main Street Program had been moved. However, it was his goal and desire to retake control of the Cadillac Parade event. Certainly, this was an event he had orchestrated for about ten years, and I was not going to stand in his way. I explained to him how I had tried to keep it going while he was away and that I had no problem giving it back. However, I explained, I could no longer invest the same commitment of time, energy, and funds as I once had. I said, "But I will support you in any way I can, but only in a limited role. He understood.

Now, The Pennsylvania Avenue Main Street Program is handled by Upton Planning. When Mayor Catherine Pugh came into office, she moved the citywide Main Street Program from under the Baltimore Development Corporation (BDC) to the Mayor's Office. Understand that the BDC, although it is the development arm of the city, is not a part of the Mayor's office. But Ms. Pugh then assigned the former Senator Verna Jones-Rodwell to head up the citywide Main Street Program. And that's how the political machine operates in Baltimore.

CHAPTER EIGHT

THE BIRTH OF THE AVENUE BAKERY, AND ALL THAT JAZZ

At this point, I made the decision to move my energy in another direction. Back in 2004, Jacquelyn "Jackie" Cornish, the then executive director of the Druid Heights Community Development Corporation (CDC), mentioned that Druid Heights needed to sell the old Bakers Hardware property, located at 2229-2231 Pennsylvania Avenue. I was under the impression that the sale would include the building on the property and the adjacent property, but it was sold as one package. I decided to make the purchase and come up with a development plan.

We were trying to attract new businesses to The Avenue, so I decided that I would construct a complex that would have retail on the first level and offices above. To create the space for the 25,000 square foot building there were two additional lots I needed to purchase from the City. Normally it would only take about nine months to purchase the two properties, but in this case, it took nineteen. I think the problem was that one of the properties was under City Housing control, and the other was under the Comptroller's office. By the time I was able to take ownership, the economy had taken a nosedive with no end in sight. Certainly, getting tenants was not going to happen. My strategy for the office space was to possibly have space available for the transitioning of state agencies that may need space as the State Center Project, moved forward. With the lawsuit by Peter Angelos and his group slowing up and trying to stop the project, this was not an option. The sad part of it was that I had spent money coming up with the design and all the architecture components as well. I had even put it out for bid as well.

By the time 2010 rolled around, I had been sitting on this property for about six years. I kept remembering what Danny Henson had said, "James you need to put something on The Avenue you can't get anyplace else."

With that in my mind, I remembered how everyone who had tasted my rolls always urged me "to sell these things!" I had been baking dinner rolls for my family for more than twenty-five years. My mom used to do it when we were young but stopped. I never got her to share her recipe, but I worked at figuring it out on my own. Although I may not look like it, I am a carbohydrate man and can live off fresh bread.

For the last twenty years or so, Thanksgiving dinner has always been at our house. There are ten of us kids in the family, which meant Thanksgiving was a big deal. On top of that, my siblings always brought friends as well. This meant that I had to start baking rolls two weeks prior to Thanksgiving and store them in the freezer so that I would have enough for the holiday. Understanding the fact that I had this property, sitting, hearing Henson's advice swirling around in my head, I decided to put together pro forma for a bakery. Sitting down with Brad Redd, who is an entrepreneur from the heart, we started putting the numbers together. Redd, as you may remember, worked for National NAACP as its financial planner. He convinced me to let him manage one of my properties, and he did a great job. In order to get a better picture of what this project could look like, I partnered with Omar Mohammad of Morgan State University's School of Business, and I entrusted the project to students as an assignment. They came up with some interesting ideas and concepts that I was able to use. After all of this, I decided to give it a shot—make the bakery project a reality. Ashley Crawford, my niece, attending Morgan State University, pursuing a degree in Hospitality, would help develop a Hazard Analysis Critical Control Point plan (HACCP Plan). In a nutshell, the HACCP Plan states in writing how you safely produce and sell food to the public.

I made a drawing of the layout for the building. I hired an architect, Kathleen Sherrill, SPARCH, Inc.., to design the building. Kathleen had also designed the office complex that I had initially planned. I had met Sherrill at an affair that was hosted by *The Baltimore Business Journal* at the Center Club. It was a networking event, and we introduced ourselves to one another. When we began talking, I mentioned that I had retired from UPS.

And she said, "My father used to work there."

"Oh yeah," I responded, "What's his name?"

"Clarence Starghill."

What a coincidence: I had worked with her dad, and our offices were next door to each other! I was in Human Resource, and he was one of the Loss Prevention Managers. Everyone knew Clarence. He was about 6'2" tall, and he could have very well been a lineman for the Ravens, or any football team for that matter. He had hands that could palm a basketball and squeeze the air out of it as well. He was a fun guy who always had a story to tell. When Starghill passed away, it was a blow to me and other UPSers.

Sherrill and I discussed business that night. Shortly after, I contracted her to design the office building. Well, I gave her my little drawing, and she turned what used to be a community eyesore into a facility that continues to amaze everyone when they visit The Avenue Bakery. She's been working with me ever since. She also does work for The Royal Theater & Community Heritage Corporation (TRTCHC), pro-bono.

Finally, we were putting something on The Avenue that *you can't get anyplace else.* The Avenue Bakery is the *Home of Poppay's Rolls.*

To backtrack a bit, before we opened The Avenue Bakery, and before I even started the process of developing the business, when I met Henson, I had also met his buddy, Frank Coakley, at one of their watering holes in South Baltimore. For those youngsters who don't know what that is, it's a hangout where one frequents to socialize and maybe have a drink or two. Anyway, I delivered to them a half dozen of Poppay's Rolls to get their opinion of the product, and they both agreed, you couldn't get rolls like mine from anyplace—*else.*

On August 15, 2011, we had our grand opening at *The Avenue Bakery, Home of Poppay's Rolls.* All the press was there. Mayor Rawlings-Blake attended as did other political leaders as well as the community.

It was a momentous event and a day of promise for The Avenue. My family and I used our first anniversary year to celebrate Black History Month, 2012. We unveiled our first piece of artwork created by visual artist Cisco Davis. We also hosted a Job Shadow opportunity for the students of nearby Booker T. Washington Middle School. The school is also near and dear to my heart. It's my alma mater. Walking those halls decades ago, my strides were uncertain because of a challenging home life, childhood illness, and the undefined notion of success. But I had teachers there who encouraged me in the midst. I never forgot it. Back then, it was Booker T. Washington Junior High School. Now it's Booker T. Washington School of the Arts. This change came about as a result of the work of Camay Murphy, daughter of the famous musician Cab Calloway.

Organizing the Job Shadow event was a spinoff from what I used to do at UPS. As a District Community Relations Manager, I had developed relationships with different companies. So not only would I bring students to UPS, but also I was able to get UPS to furnish buses to take Booker T. Washington students to different companies to sample various career choices. I was able to convince UPS to sponsor a Junior Achievement Program called *The Economics of Staying in School*. The five-week program was a collaborative effort with the teachers at Booker T. And it took my Job Shadow Program steps further. And here's where life, for me, connects the dots. Decades earlier, *The Baltimore Sun's* apprenticeship program, if I had completed it, dangled before me the equivalent of a college education. Although the timing didn't work out, I never forgot what special programs could do for those not able to move forward by means of conventional routes. That's why at UPS, I wanted to do more.

The Economics of Staying in School program was facilitated by me and other UPSers. It was interactive and designed to motivate the students to stay in school. It gave them opportunities to openly discuss what they wanted to be when they grew up as well as what they needed to do to achieve those desires. And through a roleplay, students would discuss the perils of not staying in school. I will never forget one student when his classmate put the question to him, "What do you want to be when you grow up?"

The boy's response was, "I want to be an assassin." He said it, plain and simple, straight-faced. Prior to that, he had declared that he was indeed going to drop out of school.

Our mouths dropped—all of us, the students, teachers, facilitators, and me. Finally, I said to him, "Do you think that's really what you want to do?" There was silence on his part. I continued, "Let me give you an example," I said, "I'm an assassin." I gave that a minute, then asked the young man: "Do you love your mom? How many sisters do you have? Now *I'm* an assassin, and I've been assigned to take them out. How do you feel about that?"

I could see that the student was thinking, playing that out in his mind. And I felt like I could see the pain and discomfort he was having over such a dilemma. Finally, I added, "Maybe you should think about what kind of career you'd like to have other than that." The class moved on. But after that, I made sure that young man got an opportunity to come to UPS through the Job Shadow Program. I paired him up with one of the UPSers, a manager named Kenny Freeman, who was in our Technical Support Group (TSG). After spending time with Kenny in the TSG department, the young man decided that he wanted to be a computer programmer.

At the end of the *Junior Achievement Program* that consisted of *The Economics of Staying in School*, I realized that our students needed more. It's not like when I grew up—the teachers, the lawyers, the doctors—everyone lived in the same community. The children and the youth had opportunities to interact with professionals and emulate them. But that doesn't happen anymore. With the help of Booker T.'s teachers, I put together a curriculum for this program called *My Plan for My Future*.

When I'd come into the classroom, I'd give each student two of my business cards. On the back of one card, they would put their name and the career/job they desired. That business card, they'd return back to me. The other business card was for them to keep in case they wanted to reach out to me. I'd use the information they gave to me to find corresponding professionals of color willing to come in and address the students. It was a successful venture. And I am grateful. The curriculum's activity booklet, which I'd given them, had sections in which they could map out their plan for reaching their career goals. They were encouraged to research what high school and college they should attend, what classes they should take, and if they went to college, how they would pay for it, i.e., scholarships, financial aid, work-study, etc. All of it would be logged in and hopefully held dear between the pages of *My Plan for My Future*. We also brought in job applications for them to fill out and conducted mock job interviews. We did this because we determined that in some cases, students would have to work their way through college. With that being said, giving them job applications and interviewing skills was important. You can tell them that they can be anything and do anything. But if you don't give them the tools or a plan, such goals will never happen for them.

In addition to the *Economics of Staying in School Program*, as I mentioned, UPSers volunteered. They also volunteered to tutor math. The Booker T. Principal Ruth Bucketman and her staff identified students who were below grade levels in math. Some of the students were at a third-grade level in math. As a result of the efforts made by the UPS volunteers, their math skills elevated to eighth and ninth-grade levels.

When we opened The Bakery in 2011, we wanted Booker T. students to experience a sense of pride and even ownership about what was happening in their own community. We also wanted them to relate what their teachers were trying to teach them to the real world. I told them, "If you learn to read and learn math, then you could do almost do anything." So, they got an opportunity to read recipes, understand measurements, and understand the full product. We wanted them to understand entrepreneurship, not just the concept of working for someone else. We wanted them to think about creating jobs and careers for themselves—for which they would be at the helm.

Immediately, we knew that having young students visit The Bakery would not be a one-time thing. It would come to be what we do, on the regular.

When I was the District Community Relations Manager at UPS, we instituted *Take Your Child To Work Day*. One of our employees, Patricia Baxter, brought in her son, Parris. He was about eight or nine years old. Upon interacting with the children who spent the workday with us, I always emphasized how to shake hands and how to introduce themselves.

"The proper way to shake a hand," I'd say, "is to give a firm grip and always look a person in the eye."

"Parris was about nine or ten when I brought him to work with me for Shadow Day at UPS," Patricia Baxter recalled. "Mr. Hamlin came over to meet Parris and extended his hand to shake Parris's hand. When Parris shook his hand, he didn't have that firm grip. Jim took the time to explain what your handshake was supposed to feel like.

For years Parris' mom would tell me, "You know, Parris saw somebody, and he shook their hand, and every time he shakes somebody's hand, they're so impressed with him, and about how he always looks right at them." She said that whenever that happens, "We both look at each other and smile." Because they both know where it came from. Now they live in North Carolina. "He [Parris] is now a teacher and is passing the tradition on to the Next Generation," Baxter said.

Job Shadowing at The Bakery entails students coming to learn about recipes, producing and tasting products, and even taking samples home with them. When they arrive, we adorn them with chef hats and aprons, and they love it. And I love encouraging them in any way that I can to positively impact their lives. Number one, we're here to share the history and legacy of the community, and number two, instill in them a sense of pride and dignity—and let them know that they are loved, wanted, and needed.

In the years since our opening in 2011, we've hosted book signings, political-awareness events, and we started an outdoor Jazz Concert Series. But enjoying jazz on The Avenue didn't begin with us. As mentioned earlier, Pennsylvania Avenue was the entertainment center for Baltimore City during the 1920s, '30s, '40s, '50s, and early '60s.

Alluded to earlier, Rose "Rambling Rose" Pryor, an entertainer (vocalist and musician), a licensed entertainment promoter, and now a columnist for *The Baltimore Times*, has logged in all the changes on The Pennsylvania Avenue Corridor. Pryor has been at the forefront of The Pennsylvania Avenue scene for fifty to sixty years. In 2003, Pryor authored *African-American Entertainment in Baltimore,* and in 2013, she authored *African-American Community, History & Entertainment in Maryland: Remembering the Yesterdays, 1940-1980*. She's one of the go-to point-persons for digging up the fine points of The Avenue's past as well as the potential of its future. About her nickname, Rambling Rose, Pryor said it was a personal tribute from Nat King Cole.

Pryor is planning a sequel to her second book highlighting the world of African American entertainment in Maryland that's due out in February of 2021. In the 1990s, she was on the go-to list when Baltimore officials and outside investors wanted to be innovative on The Avenue.

In 1997, to breathe life back into the failing Lafayette Market, located at Pennsylvania Avenue and Lawrence Street, the city and state spent $3 million to renovate it and christen it The Avenue Market. Mayor Schmoke gave Housing and Community Development Commissioner Danny P. Henson, III, the task of making things better at the Market. He brought in Tessa Hill-Aston to liven up the effort. Hill-Aston went on to become the first female president for the Baltimore Branch NAACP in thirty years. Her active tenure stood from 2010-2017. But back in 1998, Hill-Aston created *Cool Jazz on The Avenue*. And it was a success. Pryor commented that when it all ended, she could see Hill-Aston's disappointment when she had to announce the last live concert.

"When I arrived," said Hill-Aston, "I found some empty stalls and several merchants on the brink of closing up shop," Hill-Aston commented. She organized Friday evening jazz and rhythm-and-blues concerts at the rechristened Avenue Market and persuaded merchants to stay open later. The concerts had drawn as many as two-thousand music-lovers to the market's stages, inside and outside.

This was going well until multimillionaire John Paterakis sought to deliver the last rites over the *Cool Jazz on The Avenue* at The Avenue Market by saying, "We [meaning the market] are not in the entertainment business." This was conveyed to me by George Gilliam, who was the executive director of PARC.

In an Oct. 16, 2016, Paterakis obit, reported in *The Baltimore Sun*, stated: "He [Paterakis] was also a behind-the-scenes heavyweight, The Sun said. He made donations to Governor and Vice President Spiro T. Agnew, a Republican, and Gov. Marvin Mandel, Sen. Paul Sarbanes, and Mayors William Donald Schaefer and Kurt Schmoke, all Democrats. He donated money during the current election cycle to state Sen. Catherine E. Pugh and former Mayor Sheila Dixon, both Democrats."

Critics leveled that such fiscal generosity afforded him favors when it came to making The Inner Harbor a reality.

"Paterakis' political contributions—he and his companies gave about $10,000 to Schmoke from 1994 to 1996—have also provided ammunition for critics of the Inner Harbor East project. They claim that Paterakis won favors in receiving more than $20 million in public subsidies and tax breaks for the project.

The history of the project stretches back to the early 1980s when the developer and former Mandel aide Michael Silver bought up what were then mostly weedy lots and railroad tracks to build what Silver hoped would be a suburban-style shopping mall." *The Baltimore Sun* reported July 23, 2000.

We are into our eighth year of business and have had customers come in from all over the country as well as international visitors. One year, I was delighted to meet a couple from Sweden. We have grown to become a Baltimore must-see-and-taste place for tourists. As a matter of fact, it is the beginning and/or ending for tourists who tour the Pennsylvania Avenue Heritage Trail, which is part of the nationally-recognized Star Spangle Trails.

Like I mentioned from the beginning of my story, as we have increased the reach of The Avenue Bakery, it has increasingly become the cornerstone for the redevelopment of Pennsylvania Avenue and the famous Royal Theater. The huge investment of our spare time, energy, and retirement income are worthwhile to me, my wife, Brenda, and our family.

Often, I get the statement from folks, "You have reached your goal. You have done it!" Again, I had no idea I would be doing what I am doing today. I think the desire to make a difference and somehow positively change lives is in my blood. The actions of my mom, Mattie Virginia Clemons Waymon, are a part of it as well. She was the mother of ten children and a single mother most of the time, but she was also a very kind and giving person. She always cooked as though she was feeding an army, much more than we could eat. Her reason for doing that was to make sure that those in our community, whom we knew might not have a meal to go home to, could come to us to satisfy a basic need. And the way she always handled that was also a way to share and treat folks with dignity. So, it was never unusual to have a guest at our table.

Looking back, I can track the occurrences in my life that got me here today. In each case, my path was carved due to the decisions that God allowed me to make. And He kept me safe throughout. This is God's work. And I truly believe that I am here where I am because He wants and puts me here. He created conditions in my life where I had to reach crossroads that could make or break me. And then He guided me and paved my way. Let me give you an example of what I mean.

CHAPTER NINE

SCHOOL DAYZ AND THE JAILHOUSE BLUES

I'll always remember my first day of school. The year was around 1954. My Aunt Mamie had a sister-in-law who lived across the street from us. Aunt Mamie was my mother's oldest sister. I will always remember that family because it had twenty-six kids and was the only family with a TV set. I used to go over there to see Davy Crockett, King of the Wild Frontier. Anyway, one of the twins was supposed to meet me at school and bring me home. My mother had taken me to school that morning. School Number 110 on Lexington Street was my first of many. Somehow, we missed each other, and I got lost. This girl, who had to have been in the fifth grade, picked me up. I was a little afraid of her at first because her face was severely scarred. She had apparently been burned. She was very nice to me. She took me to her house, where I was given some chocolate milk and a bologna sandwich. I still get cravings for that combination every once in a while. She took me back to the school where I met up with my cousin, who got me home. I guess that is why I look beyond what a person looks like. There is so much beauty in the hearts of people if we only give them a chance.

Now to talk about some of the tough issues of life with which I had to deal. Some people don't believe in temporary insanity, but I do. I experienced it twice in my life. After about three weeks of school, a bully decided he wanted my lunch money. My instincts told me to run, and that's exactly what I did. Well, the next day, he was waiting for me, and he decided to push me around a little. I still would not give up my money. He picked at me and taunted me all the way to school. The next day, I told my mom I did not want to go to school. Reluctantly, I explained that this boy was picking on me.

Somehow, I don't believe the label that's often given to women—*the weaker sex*. My mom's response to me was, "You are going to school, and if you see that boy, pick up something and hit him with it. He'll leave you alone."

My mom did not realize was that I knew how to follow instructions and that I liked to do things in a big way. She assumed I would use a stick of some kind to ward off my enemy. Instead, I confiscated a two-by-four and drug it along. I made it down the street, about a half-block, when my bully buddy stepped from behind a pair of steps to greet me with the daily whipping he'd planned to give me. All I can remember is raising the two-by-four once. Peering from the window, my mom insisted that I thrashed the young fellow so many times; she just knew the police would be visiting her, either to jail her or hire me. That afternoon, the bully came by our steps where we were sitting to ask my mom if he and I could be friends. Please don't get the wrong idea. Using a two-by-four is not the accepted means of obtaining friends. And I'm not saying that it's the acceptable way to handle enemies, either. I'm just letting you know what went down and how things came out.

Speaking of policemen, as a child, parents would always warn, "You better behave, or the *poll-lease* will get you." Like all kids, you don't believe everything your parents tell you. They'll say anything to scare you.

Well, at age six, a few months after moving to the big city, I had my first encounter with the *poll-lease* as the old people pronounced it. We lived on the corner of Saratoga and Arch streets, as I mentioned. Well, down Arch Street was the old Koesters Bakery. In the morning, we could smell the aroma of the freshly baked bread. We would see the delivery trucks roll out in the morning. In the afternoon, the drivers would return and park the trucks on the lot.

I will never forget that night. A friend of my mom's, Mrs. Mildred, had two sons, Tony, who was my age, and Bootsy, who was my brother's age. It was a hot night, and everybody was sitting out on the steps. Back then, that was where everyone sat and congregated in the evenings because it was too hot to be indoors.

My mom and Mrs. Mildred asked Tony and me to go down to the drugstore that was located on the corner of Lexington and Arch streets. We had to pass the bakery's lot, where the drivers parked their trucks, to get there. After being told not to take a shortcut through the lot, Tony and I decided to walk in and out of the parking lot's gates.

As we all know, as soon as you do something your mother tells you not to, you get caught. Just as Tony and I were leaving out the last gate, two policemen walked up to us. My heart almost popped out of my chest; it was beating so hard. Tony started crying, "We're going to jail for the rest of our lives!"

After what seemed to have been days, the officers finally got out of us where we lived. If we had a preference, we would have chosen a trip to jail—once we realized they were taking us home to our mothers. In our family, the mothers did the whipping and the tongue lashing that went along with it.

Well, we escaped a jail sentence. And I can't say this for Tony because I haven't seen him in years, but as for me, other than a parking ticket, every once in a while, the *poll-lease* haven't had to have much concern about me.

At the age of five or six, most kids begin to learn more about their relatives. It was also a time in my life where I began to meet more of them. I met my Uncle Jimmy, mom's older brother, and his wife, Aunt Edith, for the first time. I did not realize, at the time, that Uncle Jimmy would trigger a major change in my life.

Uncle Jimmy was a very responsible person. At one time, I think he worked at Bethlehem Steel. At this time, he was hustling—him and my aunt. In my eyes, he was a Robin Hood-type guy. He used to rob the rich and feed the poor. Their main hustle, from what I saw, was shoplifting. They would go downtown with a group of other thieves and return with clothes, food, and you name it. I believe a lot of my school clothes and Christmas toys were provided by my uncle and his merry men. I am not sure who the other guys were, but my cousin, Wendel McCleod, Jr., was one of them. Earlier, I mentioned my mom used to work at his dad's Dry Cleaners. By the way, his dad was also a Baptist minister.

Uncle Jimmy was a small man who I believe only weighed about 120 pounds if that much. He was always well dressed. He used to take pride in the fact that he wore $300 suits, $150 shoes, and $100 hats. In the fifties, when a pound of sugar cost five cents, believe me, he had a lot of money passing through his fingers. He always seemed kind of sickly, though. Little did I know at that time, I would, one day, be treated for tuberculosis, and it is possible that I may have contracted it from my Uncle Jimmy. It didn't matter because I loved my uncle. From him, I learned always to look my best.

My mom educated me a little. She informed me that shoplifting was not my uncle's only forte. He used to run numbers, too. Today's nationwide gambling games, collectively called, The Lottery, was, and still is, the nation's attempt to legally mimic and knock out the illegal game of gambling, called The Numbers. Uncle Jimmy also hauled and sold white lightning, otherwise known as moonshine, and among other things, he dabbled in prostitution. She said my grandparents visited him one day, and there were half-naked women all over his place in negligees. Certainly, this was not the type of career for the son of a preacher.

He and my aunt had a band of merry men who included a cousin of mine, Junior, who was my Aunt Mamie's son. Junior was a miracle man. I say that because, as a child, he used to hitchhike on the back of streetcars. From what I have been told, he was just about crushed to death while riding on the back of a streetcar. According to my mother, he was so badly crushed, he couldn't even pass water. But he recovered. He lived, got married, and had kids.

My Aunt Edith, at this point, was my favorite. I guess it was because she loved her Junior Boy—that's what they used to call me when I was a kid. She always made it clear to everybody that I was number one in her life. I remember she would stop by our house, sometimes, and give me hundreds of dollars to hide for her. I guess it was her mad money. Days later, she would ask me for her money, and I would go to my secret hiding places and get it for her. I always had hiding places where I knew no one would ever think of looking. She knew she could trust me not to tell anyone, not even my mother. She would sometimes talk to me about things that happened to her or how someone had abused her. I would listen to her and give her a hug. I guess that made her feel that someone really cared.

She never knew it, but she taught me how to listen and not judge. I learned that there was good in everyone, and we all are not able to take charge of our lives sometimes. I guess you could say she taught me compassion. Thinking about the past and writing it down gives me a better understanding of who I am. We all need someone in whom we can trust and confide. Today, I find myself being that for members of my family, friends, and even coworkers and subordinates. Now, I know why I am always willing to listen to someone who has a problem. I've always felt we all have something to give if nothing more than a little time to listen. Now, I think I know why.

While I lived on Saratoga Street, I got to know and meet relatives, friends of my mother and develop a relationship with my stepfather, Zeke. I have always been an observer of people. It is something I developed at an early age. I guess it came from the many days I spent in the attic bedroom, watching my cousins playing outside. Not good enough to play, I would watch and anticipate their actions.

My stepfather was a very reserved man, and he was that way until he passed away. I found him to be well informed with a good handle on the English language. He would return from work each day, clean up and have dinner. The rest of the afternoon he spent sitting at the front window and reading his daily newspaper. Occasionally peering over the top of his paper to look at some distraction on the streets. Depending on the day of the week or season of the year, there was always entertainment on the streets. Whether or not it was children fighting and/or playing, auto accidents, or the two men, up the street, who used to race their Harley-Davidson motorcycles up and down the street, there was never a dull moment.

I could always tell when he was deep into his newspaper because he had the habit of gritting his teeth. That used to run my mother crazy. Once in a while, my mother would yell at him, "Won't you stop gritting those damn teeth?"

He would look over at her for a moment, then look back down at his newspaper and return to gritting.

Mr. Zeke, as we had always called him, was a quiet man. He never bothered anyone and never seemed to have had friends. At six years old, to me, he was tall. But actually, he was a normal height. He was very dark, even darker than I was. He had very pretty big white teeth and was a very muscular man. I believe he was a pipe fitter with a construction company.

He was a very caring person. He used to drink, but he believed in drinking at home. He was not for hanging out at bars, and he hated it when my mother would go out drinking with her sisters and brothers. They would sometimes bring her home intoxicated and sick. He would clean up the mess she would make and try to assist her with her hangover while doing his best to ignore the verbal abuse that he received from her.

I remember him always asking her, "Why do you have to go out drinking all the time and come back raising hell?"

I learned a lot from him. Most of all, I learned to care for someone and love them despite themselves. He also taught me that the one thing, I wanted in my life was peace. He stressed to me the value of work. One thing he used to point out to me was a little girl, he would see, while looking out the window.

He would say to me, "See that little girl? Every evening, she goes to the store there and picks up the bags of coal for her family. I bet she gets an allowance for that. That's what you should be doing to earn money rather than always asking for money."

Since that day, I have always believed in working for what I get. I never ask for anything from anybody, and I never expect it. I've reared my kids to be the same way—and they are that way to this day. Now, I would be lying if I said they didn't hit dad up for a loan every now and then in the past. But they earn what they receive.

My Aunt Louise, her husband, Charles, son, Richard, and daughter, Virginia, were relocating to California because Uncle Charles' job was moving him out there. I got to know them when they stayed with us for about two weeks. Richard used to wear glasses but still had some difficulty seeing. I remember the day that someone was calling my mother's name from the street below, and Richard heard it. For some reason, he abruptly attempted to stick his head out the window to answer the call, but he failed to raise the window. He was lucky; he was not cut when he stuck his head through the glass. The person on the ground was lucky, too, because they were able to get out of the way of falling glass.

When my aunt's family spent the two weeks with us, the sleeping arrangements were very uncomfortable. I had the misfortune of having my aunt sleep in my bed with me. Like most of the women in my mother's family, she was big and round. For two weeks, I slept on the edge of my bed, an inch from falling on the floor. On top of that, I believed my aunt was a member of the porcupine family. She had prickly hairs on her butt that fought their way through her nightgown to scrape my back nightly. In the mornings, I would check my back for holes. I have recently informed my wife that if she ever grew hairs on her butt like that, we will be getting separate beds.

On the first floor lived two men, Mr. Clinton, an older gentleman with diabetes and an alcohol problem, and Mr. Clyde, an ex-soldier. They were very nice people and my first employers. I took Mr. Zeke's advice and ran errands for them. I used to run to the store for bread, cigarettes, milk, or whatever they needed when they were too drunk to go get it themselves. I also liked to watch them play checkers. Sometimes they would let me play also. When I look back, they were the only adults, other than my Aunt Doris, who played with us. Mr. Zeke and mama never played any games with us.

"Mr. Clyde is nutty in the head!" My mother used to say. That is because he always talked about the Army and would never wear anything but Army clothes. I didn't think he was nutty at all. He was a real nice person, and the Army was a big deal to him. It was like family to him. A blood family was something I never heard him speak of. Maybe the Army was all he had—and why take that away from him. It used to bother me when my mother would talk negatively about him.

During the time we spent at Saratoga Street, my brothers, Ricky and Maurice, were born. Maurice died at the age of two months. My mom said he died of gas gangrene that could have developed from a prior wound he might have had. I wasn't sure what that was or what all its symptoms entailed, but her explanation was that his bowels locked up and filled with gas. That was a sad time in our lives. He was the first of my siblings to die. I didn't understand death very much at that time. I just knew the next time I would see him would be in Heaven.

We moved from Saratoga Street to the 600 block of George Street. At this place, we had a whole house and a basement. The basement was dirt. So we couldn't play down there very much. But now we had a backyard in which we could play. Next door lived an old lady who had a dog by the name of Fluffy. I am not sure what kind of dog this was, but it was a medium-sized golden brown and white dog, possibly a cross between a Spaniel and a Schnauzer.

One day like a fairy tale, our dream came true. I don't remember why, but something happened to that old lady next door. I think she was moved to an elderly home, and she could not take Fluffy with her. She chose to give her to us, and boy, were we happy.

It was 1956. Ricky was a year old. Tony was three, and I was eight years old. My mom was also pregnant with my sister, Eldora. Just as the fairy tale dream-come-true arrived, so did one of the worst nightmares in our lives.

We were playing outside that Saturday afternoon. Mr. Zeke was at work or something, and mom was home. The police came to the house to speak to my mother, and she let them in.

They asked, "Ma'am, do you know what's in your basement?"

She gave them a blank look on purpose and responded with a simple, "No."

They must have considered it a rhetorical question. Because the next question they asked dripped with a commanding tone. "Can you unlock the basement, so we can take a look?" And when she moved slowly, they added, "If you don't unlock it, we'll gonna have to break the door, now."

She cooperated and opened the door. There they found thirty-six gallons of illegal corn whisky.

Looking up at her, one of the policemen asked, "Tell us how this got here?"

Blank-faced, again, she said, "I don't know. I have no idea how it got here."

"If you don't tell us, you're going to jail," they let her know.

At some time during this event, my Aunt Doris found out what was going on and stopped by. Once she determined that my mother was going to jail, she contacted my grandparents to let them know that they needed to come and get us. But they refused. Mr. Zeke came home later, and he was locked up, also. As a result of my mother and Mr. Zeke being arrested, Ricky was taken to a hospital because of his age. The police took Tony and me to the Children's Detention Center, located upstairs, above the Pine Street Police Station House.

The realization of two young boys, seeing their mother being taken away by police—against her will—set in stone, a lifelong fear and distrust of the police—is an understatement for me. And we thought that we were going to be locked up forever after we found out that our grandparents weren't coming for us.

When we got to the police station, they took us in through a side door. They walked us up what seemed like a huge staircase that was really wide. We were taken to a room that was located down a long hallway. They opened a door that was so thick; it looked like it could have weighed two hundred pounds. I was thinking that we would never get out of there. Inside there were two beds, but me and Tony huddled in the same bed. At first, I wanted to cry, but I knew I had to be brave because I was the oldest.

One of the policemen asked us, "Are you hungry?"

Together, we hobbled out a feeble, "Yes." We waited in the room for them to get us some food. But the next thing I remember was that we fell asleep. We were awakened several times by outbursts in the station house. By the time the police finally came in with something to eat, we could see the sun coming up. The eggs were soft and runny, and the only thing we could eat was the toast.

What seemed to be days, looking back on it, it was more like twenty or so hours. Finally, a policeman came in to let us know that someone had come to take us home. I had no idea who that person was going to be. At the time, I remember assuming that it would be my grandparents coming to get us. And, yes, there was relief in my soul because of it. But years later, in my adult life, reminiscing about that ordeal, I think about how sad it was that the assumption of my father coming to my rescue never crossed my young mind. I had become so removed from him and Mother Hamlin.

As the policeman opened that heavy door, I thought to myself, *I hope I never have to come back to this room again.* He led us back down that long hallway and down that wide staircase. At the bottom stood my Aunt Doris.

What a pleasant sight she was. With her arms extended and branding that pretty smile of hers, I still could see the tears in her eyes. She embraced us both with a warm and comforting hug. The only other time I ever felt this kind of welcome was when Mother Hamlin could hug me whenever I was dumped on her by my mother's parents.

I don't quite remember whether Ricky was in the car or what. I do remember the joy we felt, hugging each other when we arrived at my aunt's third-floor apartment at the corner of Argyle Avenue and Hoffman Street. After the welcoming, my aunt probably had to mop the floor for hours from all the tears we dropped.

The building that my Aunt Doris, the aunt who got us out of jail, lived in had three apartments. The entrance to her apartment was on the side of the building because there was a tailor shop at the front of the building. The back door to the tailor's shop was on the right, and her front door was on the left.

A man named Mr. Steptoe owned the shop. He was of average height and loved to play the trumpet. My aunt got annoyed when he played. But I loved it. He also owned two dogs, named Buster and Grinnell. Buster was a big white Boxer who was a very gentle dog. He always loved to be petted. Grinnell, on the other hand, was mean. Mr. Steptoe kept Grinnell away from people.

Once in a while, we used to see them in the backyard trying to mate. One time we saw the two dogs get stuck together. It was a sight for us, little boys, to see. Mr. Steptoe came running out, yelling at them, and he poured a bucket of water on them. We saw this long thing come out of Grinnell that seemed like it was three feet. Talking about two kids who thought they had seen a miracle, that's how we felt, minus any reasoning behind it. Tony and I looked at each other with our eyes as big as saucers.

We also saw the two dogs snatch a cat. That was another miracle of a totally different kind. The cat must have thought that it could tease the dogs by walking across the top of the wooden fence just slightly above them. It was the last miscalculation that cat would make. Buster and Grinnell grabbed that cat and tore it up in a matter of minutes. The cat didn't even have much time to scream. When they finished, there was nothing left that resembled a cat. We were amazed. And like kids, especially boys, do, we wanted to see that happen again.

For a short time, my two brothers, Tony and Ricky, and I had come to live with Aunt Doris. I'd considered it my opportunity to get to know my aunt and uncle. Before then, I had seen my Aunt Doris and Uncle Smiley when they visited us. Their visits were always short. Uncle Smiley's name was James Goudy. I also saw them having fun at their favorite bar on Pine Street, where my mom hung out as well. It was across from the Pine Street Police Station.

My aunt was a medium bronze-skinned lady about five feet five, up from the ground, which made her a little taller than my mother. I will always remember her saying that she had two left legs. That's because her legs looked like two large baseball bats. My sister, Eldora, has legs just like hers, only smaller. As a matter of fact, Eldora could be her daughter instead of her niece. Aunt Doris had a round face, a button nose, and beautiful white teeth of which she was very proud. I used to love to see her smile.

Aunt Doris was an immaculate and organized woman. She was the cleanest woman I have ever known. She believed the old saying *cleanliness is next to godliness*. She took it literally. No one ever caught dirty dishes in her sink. When we were given the chore of washing dishes, she came behind us to check every piece of dinnerware, including all the silverware. The clothes, sheets, and towels in her laundry were always whiter than when she purchased them. Her clothes were washed and soaked in the bathtub before being taken to the laundromat.

She kept a clean house, also. Everything had to be in its place and dusted. Aunt Doris was the only Black woman I had ever known who would hire someone to clean. She spent a lot of time socializing, so cleaning the house was not always on the schedule. But that house had to be clean. She knew a couple of alcoholics that she could trust to clean her house. And for a job, well-done, they only required a couple of dollars, which amounted to liquor money. Or, if she knew someone who needed to make a couple of dollars to help feed their kids, she would hire them as well.

Aunt Doris loved children. And I'm not sure why, but she couldn't have any. So, she lavished her love on us, along with every other child she met. She was loved by all the children in the neighborhood and their parents. If she saw or knew of someone abusing their children, she would threaten to call *Mrs. White* on them. In those days, *Mrs. White* was code for a social worker who earned a reputation for taking children from unfit parents.

Although she would never do anything that was considered too illegal, Aunt Doris had her hustles. One of which was loan sharking. She had certain clients, mostly males, who had good jobs. When they needed a loan, they would come to her, borrow, and pay it back at a rate of ten cents to twenty-five cents on the dollar. Keep in mind this was in the 1950s and '60s. Black people did not walk into a savings and loan institution or a bank to borrow money—at least not the Black folk at the bottom of the economic ladder. In my later formative years, *The Bottom*, where we lived, would come to be called, and discarded as, *The Ghetto*.

Uncle Smiley was a large man. He was heavyset, not fat. And he had a medium brown hue, crowned with a head of thick, curly black hair. His nickname came from his attractive smile that showed up every time he talked. He was a very kind person who would never hurt anyone.

Uncle Smiley worked construction jobs. He belonged to a local union that was located on Paca Street. I remember going over there with him one time. I have no idea just what type of job he did, exactly. But when he got home, every day, he'd head straight to the bathroom to take off his muddy clothes and bathe. My aunt was very particular about her house.

Life with my aunt and uncle was pleasant—and brief. They fed us well and did what they could to comfort us. They both loved us all, but Ricky was their favorite. I think it was the fact that he was always the entertainer. Ricky seemed to have the ability to sense what made people laugh, and he gave it to them. He was sort of an Eddie Murphy type. Ricky's favorite television show was the *Popeye* cartoons, and he loved to imitate the characters. My aunt and uncle got a kick out of his animated antics and comedic impersonations.

It was summertime, so I was not attending school. Still, most of our days were indoors. Aunt Doris got me to press our clothes to make sure we looked clean and neat. We had to pass her white glove test and always look our best, even in the summertime. In the evenings, we got to sit outside on the front steps with my aunt.

After about three weeks or so, my mom came home. We went back to the house on George Street. But things were not quite the same. Mr. Zeke was in jail. And from what I overheard, sitting around the grown folks, he took the blame for everything. He helped to get my mother released from jail, and he did not implicate my uncle. Everyone knew the alcohol in the basement was put there by my Uncle Jimmy.

I guess my mother needed help taking care of us and was pregnant with my sister, Eldora, at that time. This was when my second stepfather entered my life. I guess subliminally; I attached the term, stepfather to whatever man who started living in and sleeping in the same room with my mother. In my growing-up years, I witnessed a couple. My mom never married Mr. Zeke or Mr. James Crawford. Sometime before Tony was born and before I came to live with her, she married Henry Waymon.

At first, he was not staying in the house. I would see him walking down the street with my mom. He appeared to be what they called in those days a country boy. He had a buttercream hue, was about six-foot, three inches tall, and muscular. He had an odd sort of stride, though, as if he had one leg that was a tad shorter than the other. It was almost like that John Wayne walk.

Shortly after we moved back to the house, Mr. Zeke came out of jail. By this time, Mr. James, as we called him, and my mom were getting pretty close. For Mr. Zeke, who had cared for us and took the weight for the illegal alcohol possession charge, it had to have been painful to see her now pushing up on someone new. I am pretty sure he had heard something was going on before he came out of jail.

Needless to say, things got very busy at the house for a while. Mr. Zeke used to come by the house, casing it and stalking my mother. She would look out the front door and could spy him peeping around the corner. One day, he came by and threw something through the kitchen window. Mr. James went running after him. I don't remember if he caught Mr. Zeke or not. But I can still recall the feeling of pure chaos all around us and feeling anxious about it all.

One day, Mr. Zeke stepped right up to the front door, but my mom would not let him in. Instead, she threw his clothes out into the backyard. When witnessing all this as a child, my only thought was that I missed Mr. Zeke. And I felt that the way my mother was treating him was unfair.

Shortly after this, we moved in with Uncle Johnny on a small street off Pennsylvania Avenue. I don't remember the street name, but I know he was living with a lady who had two children. I will always remember sleeping in the same bedroom with those kids. It always had a rancid smell because they used to urinate in the bed all the time. Our dog, Fluffy, followed us there but was relegated to the basement. There she had two puppies. I had to walk through all the trash in the basement to feed them our table scraps after dinner. It must have been getting close to winter because I remember taking old sheets and covers down there to keep the puppies warm.

My mom and my cousin, Irene Colbert, were around the same age. They were very close and hung out together with my Aunt Doris, even though I think Aunt Doris didn't want them hanging around her all the time. To make a long story short, my mom and Irene decided to move in together in a big house in the 800 block of Harlem Avenue. Irene is the sister of my cousin, Junior, who used to hang out and hustle with my Uncle Jimmy. Irene, at this time, was married to Phillip Colbert. They had three children: Marie, the oldest; Jeannie and Phil, Jr., or Little Phil as we used to call him.

This time in my life was when I really began to develop my opinions and attitudes toward women. Or maybe, more specifically, it was my understanding of life, people, love, and sacrifices that was beginning to take shape. I also began to develop a sense of pride and self-respect that my Junior High School teacher would later help me drive home. I also gained some parameters about what I would come to believe and what I would and would not accept from a partner—enough of that. Let me go on to explaining this part of my life.

Phil was a hardworking man with big rough hands. Well-dressed and well-spoken, he was not. He was a country sort of person who seemed to be well-trained in the art of caring for people, especially children. Phil was a very patient man who took the time to listen to children and answer their insignificant questions, as most grown-ups often called them.

I remember the many Friday and Saturday nights Phil spent at home with us kids while Irene and my mother hung out for days. I studied him, seemingly choosing to stay home, change diapers, cook meals and watch television with us. He taught me how to pin diapers so when the toddlers pooped; the mess didn't run out on the floor. He taught me how to check the temperature of a baby's bottle by dripping the milk on the back of my hand instead of my palm.

It never failed. Irene would come home only to raise hell with him to justify her wrong. I saw him mentally and physically abused and disrespected as a human being. At the time, I could not understand why he took that abuse, but now I know. He loved her and his kids. He loved them more than he loved himself. Even though Phil knew for years that this wife of his was in love with, and seeing, another man, he sacrificed himself.

When school opened, I was registered in a new school. I believe it was Public School 118. I don't remember much about that school year, only that I did not go very often. No, I wasn't the kind of kid who would hook school. I loved school. I was registered not quite at the beginning of the year, and on occasion, I had to stay home due to family issues and uncertainties.

CHAPTER TEN

LED TO THE LIONS

It's 2:47 a.m., Saturday, February 2, 2019. I'm at The Bakery earlier than I need to be because I can't sleep. I have so much on my mind. Yesterday, there was a message on my phone from Darroll Cribb, president of the Upton Planning Committee. I thought it was rather strange to get a call from him. I called him back. Cribb wanted me to complete a Board training, and he wanted me to give him a few dates of my availability. As I have mentioned earlier, I'm a member of the Upton Planning Board of Directors, and I have been since 2009. I thought it was strange for him to make the call instead of Upton's executive director, Wanda Best. That's who I'm used to hearing from—when I *do* hear from Upton Planning.

Now my mind is wandering, again, and there's no time for that because I have critical decisions to make. For the past year, I have attended very few Upton Board meetings. One of my reasons for not attending many (routine) meetings is because of my hours at The Bakery. The board meetings start at 6:00 p.m. on Thursdays—when I am normally on my way to bed. However, when there are mandatory or critical meetings, I make sure that I'm there. But the most important reason that I haven't attended many meetings is that I no longer trust those running the organization.

My lack of trust began in January of 2017, when Wanda notified me, by phone, that Mayor Pugh had a plan to build a regulation football field or ballfield on the same site that the TRTCHC had planned to build The Royal Theater Project and cultural/entertainment venues; and that she had the funds to do it. Wanda called to inform me that Upton Planning was in support of the Mayor's plan. Before, it was in support of The Royal Theater Project. Apparently, there had been a meeting with Upton representatives and Mayor Pugh to which I was not invited. At that meeting, from what I gathered, she conveyed that she was not in support of The Royal Theater Project being constructed on that site.

I was shocked to hear Upton's sudden reversal, and the call blindsided me. Also, I didn't understand why I was being notified in a special phone call instead of being let in on the Mayor's special meeting in advance. I couldn't understand why there wasn't a board meeting to discuss the Mayor's plan. Such a big to-do because, surely, word would have been properly disseminated to all, assuring that all would be in attendance. Wanda's second phone call revealed that there was going to be a conference call and an official vote on the matter—whether or not the Upton Planning Committee would support The Royal Theater Project or support the Mayor's plan. I participated in that conference call and was questioned if I had the funds to make The Royal Theater Project a reality. Could I make the building of The Royal Theater happen? They asked.

Much to their surprise, my response was, "Yes, I have the means to move forward." They weren't expecting that answer. My statement negated the vote, and Best indicated that she would set up a meeting with the Mayor so that I could present my resources.

This course of occurrences pitted the Mayor and me in a tug of war for the same property—an empty lot in the coveted space of the 1300 block of Pennsylvania Avenue, which is Robert C. Marshall Field—that held the potential of being transformed into an invaluable stretch of real estate on which to create economic opportunities for the community.

Robert C. Marshall was an accomplished basketball and football coach who honed his career in Richmond, Virginia, Alabama, and Texas between the years 1918 to 1922. The question is: What is his connection to Historic West Baltimore and Pennsylvania Avenue? Also, why is the Upton leadership so protective of Robert C. Marshall Field to the point of not being willing to discuss the possibilities of moving the field to create a more functional venue for the community?

Mayor Pugh, who came into office in 2016, campaigned strongly on a platform to enhance and nurture Baltimore City's youth, particularly underserved youth. And on that account, I agree that there is a dire need to engage our youth. It also happens to be a pivotal part of my overall mission as well. But concerning this particular property, located in the Upton Community, owned by the City of Baltimore, when it comes to constructing a football field on the land, meaning erecting it on Robert C. Marshall Field. The Field encompasses both the 1200 block and 1300 block of Pennsylvania Avenue where The Royal Theater was located. However, there are a host of glitches when it comes to building a football field there. Serious glitches.

When the Mayor made her presentation to Upton Planning representatives, as I was told, she commented that plans to build The Royal Theater had been going on far too long. Adding to her opinion, reportedly, she commented, "James Hamlin doesn't have the money." She also threw in a jab about me not living in the community or Baltimore City. And I've got something to say about that.

"That James Hamlin, he doesn't live in the city of Baltimore," is what she reportedly said. It's a dig she's used quite a bit.

It's an attempt to decaffeinate and misdirect our major points to exploring and acting upon productive ways to revitalize The Pennsylvania Avenue Corridor. Many people who make major contributions to Baltimore City don't live within its city limits. Yes, I no longer live within the city limits, but it's my native home. I've invested three-quarters of a million dollars, thus far, and countless man-hours of sweat-equity in West Baltimore—dedicated to the revitalization and the renaissance of The Avenue. I go to work there six days a week—that's post my years at UPS in Baltimore. Certainly, *On a Roll* articulates that point as well as my love for Baltimore like a unique slice of Poppay's sweet potato pie; there's no denying my cultural stamp.

Ms. Pugh informed the board that she did have the funding to revitalize the area and that her project entailed building a regulation ballfield so that the area's youth could take full and awesome advantage of it.

The glitch? The characteristics of the property in question do not support the construction of a ballfield. Back in 2005 or 2006, the Pennsylvania Avenue Development Collaborative had a conversation with a representative of the NFL because it showed interest in putting a regulation football field on the Robert C Marshall site. That notion didn't grow legs. The property was surveyed and studied by architects, one of them being the architect working with me, Kathleen Sherrill, and the Department of Recreation and Parks to see if such a thing could be done. Troubling structural and design conflicts were revealed. Number one, there was a problem with the grade. The grade from Lafayette Avenue to Dolphin Street was to such a degree that a retaining wall would have had to be created. But by doing so, every time it rained or rained heavy, a river of water, streamed down Pennsylvania Avenue, would have been the consequence. Number two, there wasn't enough square footage to put a regulation field and a retaining wall in that same square footage. And there were other problems that, if done, amounted to a magnitude of unnecessary site cost.

As referenced earlier, in January of 2016, the findings were clear in a letter written by then-mayor, Ms. Rawlings-Blake. She explained how, clearly, such a mandate was physically impossible to achieve. The letter itself is featured on the back pages of this book. But the enclosure of her letter revealed this:

Redeveloping 1300 Pennsylvania Avenue Process:

Redevelopment of 1300 Pennsylvania Avenue would require relocation of the current ball field. A potential site for a new ball field is located between 1200 & 1300 blocks of Argyle and Myrtle Avenues. The City currently owns 90% of the properties located between these two blocks. The remaining 10% of privately owned properties would require acquisition. Implementation would require the following three phases:

Phase #1 - Appropriate 1 Million Dollars in HCD's Capital Budget for Land Acquisition Site Preparation.

Appropriation is contingent upon the Baltimore City Capital Improvement Program (CIP) process. If the appropriation is awarded then land acquisition, demolition, street and alley closure and lot consolidation will need to be completed to produce a developable parcel. There are 12 private properties that need to be acquired. Acquisition costs are estimated at $677,000. Site clearance (demolition), street & alley closure and lot consolidation will cost an additional $261,000. Acquisition and site preparation will take approximately 12-18 months. Once the parcel is consolidated, the ball field would be transferred from HCD's inventory to Rec & Parks inventory.

Phase #2 – Design & Construct New Ball Fields

A Landscape Master Plan would be developed for the new site, indicating the orientation and placement of the new athletic field and associated amenities, access points, landscaping and site servicing. Public consultation would be necessary to ensure local concerns are dealt with appropriately and there is support for the new facility. Taking between three and four months, this initial high level design process would be followed by preparation of detailed design construction documents by an on-call consulting firm of landscape architects and engineers.

Depending on the complexity of the design, especially site servicing and storm water management issues, the construction document package preparation could take between three and six months. Design costs could be expected to run approximately $105,000. An additional six to twelve months would be required for permitting, and six months for the procurement process. Depending on weather conditions, construction could be completed within six to eight months. Construction, assuming the placement of an irrigated natural turf football/multi-use field with overlapping ball field, restroom/utility building, pathways, landscaping and other amenities, and construction administration costs should be budgeted at $1,310,000. (This figure would be revisited once the initial Landscape Master Plan has been completed).

Additional funding would have to be identified and appropriated for the estimated $1,415,000 design and construction cost.

Phase # 3 **– Subdivide and Offer 1300 Pennsylvania Avenue, via a Request for Proposals Process**

The current zoning of 1300 Pennsylvania Ave is R-8 and the field would need to be rezoned through a City Council process (under the proposed TRANSFORM zoning rewrite the field is Open Space). The field is currently controlled by Rec & Parks. A Phase 1 test of the field to determine past historical uses would be prudent before initiating the redevelopment process.

To make the field available for redevelopment, Rec & Parks would initiate a subdivision. This requires survey work, preparing the plats for the subdivision, and Planning Commission approval (approximately 6 months). Once the property was subdivided, a recommendation would be made to assign it to the Baltimore Development Corporation. This would require an action by the Space Utilization Committee and the approval of the Board of Estimates (approximately 3 months).

The Upton URP is expired. Therefore once the parcel is subdivided, the City would establish the authority to sell the field through a City Council sales ordinance (approximately 2 months).

Once the property has been assigned and disposition authority has been granted, BDC would determine the RFP process. This may include drafting an RFP, publicly advertising the RFP, and awarding the property, which requires BDC Project Committee approval, BDC Board approval, and Mayoral approval (approximately 6 months).

BDC would then enter into an ENP, negotiate an LDA, and then enter into an LDA, which requires approval from the Board of Estimates.

Ironically, about four or five years ago, I had spoken with Ms. Pugh, then a Maryland State Senator for the 40th District, about The Royal Theater Project (building The Royal Theater). The theater would be built in the 40th District. Ms. Pugh, who also has the political background of being a state delegate and a former member of the Baltimore City Council, representing the 4th District, was in total support. At that time, she said to me, "We're gonna get that done." And on that very subject, Ms. Pugh took my meetings and took my calls until all of sudden; she turned radio silent. And just like that, I was out the door.

Before the mysterious evaporation of Ms. Pugh's support, I had been working with two men to create a pro forma for The Royal Theater Project: Danny Henson, III, and Zed Smith. Henson, who is mentioned in chapters one and two, owns The Henson Development Company. In 1993, Henson was appointed by former Mayor Kurt Schmoke to be the commissioner of Baltimore's Department of Housing and Community Development and the executive director of Housing Authority of Baltimore City (HABC). Zed Smith is the chief operating officer for Cordish Companies. Cordish is a global leader in commercial real estate, entertainment districts, co-working spaces, and more. To say that Henson and Smith were fully on board with The Royal Theater Project—for years—would be an understatement.

A bit of background about Smith: years prior, when I worked in the Human Resource Department of UPS, I hired young Smith when he was a Morgan State University student. It helped him fund his education. Today, Smith is notable for planning such projects as *Maryland Live*, *Live Resorts* in Madrid, Spain, and others. I imagine his work to help me was payback for the hiring and nurturing I had given to him so many years earlier. Henson is a Morgan State University graduate as well. And as mentioned in earlier chapters, Henson had always been a supporter of my efforts to revitalize Pennsylvania Avenue.

Back to the 2017 phone call from Upton Planning, telling me that, along with Ms. Pugh, it no longer supported The Royal Theater Project. While I was still churning over the possible series of coincidences that not only led to my absence at the biggest meeting, ever, featuring Ms. Pugh but also the absences of announcements, which I had grown accustomed to receiving up to that point—I got an unscheduled visit from Henson and Smith. The purpose of their meeting was to inform me that The Royal Theater Project would not work. At some point, my mind drowned out their reasoning as a result of the shock of their visit and what I was hearing. As another surprise to me, Joe Daniels, a gentleman, who had been working with me on the project, also came to dissuade me.

Back during Governor O'Malley's administration, when TRTCHC was working to put on the weekend festival, while the nonprofit had contributed $10,000 to the effort, Verizon donated $5,000. At the time, we believed that Gov. O'Malley had encouraged Verizon to give, for which we were grateful. As I mentioned earlier, Verizon's point-person was Joe Daniels. Like my UPS position in Community Relations, Joe was my equivalent at Verizon, and we had gotten to know one another. Joe would eventually work with me on The Royal Theater Project. He knew all the nuances, and he was totally on board. And when we found ourselves needing to swap out land suitable for Green Space so that we could continue to move forward with our project, designated for the 1300 block (which is the Robert C. Marshal Field), Joe Daniels helped to put together the plan.

I surmised to myself that the Mayor had come to shut the project down on several fronts. She sought to kill the support I had with Upton Planning, and through Henson, Smith, and Daniels, she sought to kill the very inner-workings of the strategic planning itself. Now, she was moving on to another slaughter. Next, Wanda contacted me to let me know that she was setting up a meeting with Ms. Pugh so that I could indeed present my funding resources to them both.

This latest development happened to occur around the time I met with executives from WBG Developers/Wattley Construction. That meeting took place in New York, and it centered on their funding commitment for The Royal Theater Project. To prepare and present at the meeting that Wanda was setting up, I notified Dr. Brenda Brown, who was a representative, and Charles Wattley, of Wattley Construction, to let them know that I needed them to be in attendance to prove that we had the means to move the project forward. I also explained what had been going on. We had not yet completed the Memorandum of Understanding (MOU) between TRTCHC and WBG Developers. However, thankfully, they still agreed to attend the meeting, set up by

Wanda Best (of Upton), with Ms. Pugh. It was the meeting I referred to earlier that was scheduled to take place in July of 2017.

When the meeting took place, immediately, I felt like my team, and I were innocent rabbits lured in a den of ravenous lions. All the city's agencies that I had met previously while developing the project were there. In attendance were representatives of Baltimore City Housing, Recreation and Parks, Department of Planning, Baltimore Development Corporate (BDC), and four other Upton's Board members.

Once everyone was introduced around the table, the Mayor's staff person opened the meeting and articulated the Mayor's plan. Then I passed around thé handouts that spelled out our plans, and I began to call on Dr. Brown and Mr. Wattley to share their financial commitment to the project. The meeting coordinator abruptly stated that they only wanted to hear from the community representatives, not from my team. It was at that point, the representatives of the Upton Planning indicated that they were in support of the Mayor's plan.

The Mayor was not in the meeting initially. She walked in later. Beyond cordial greetings, she kept her silence and took a seat. Her representative did all the work. I'm from corporate America. It's an arena where accountability means the utmost. In business, if you don't make the numbers or do what you're supposed to do or promised to do, you're grilled to prove it. So, I'm used to that, and I came to the meeting prepared. That's not a big deal. But the person who was running the meeting, in my estimation, was so rude and disrespectful that I honestly can't recall a meeting with such a negative atmosphere. Also, at that point, our city's image was damaged in the eyes of professionals/potential players, who had come from New York—wanting to help. For me, it was hurtful and embarrassing for the city to have others witness such inept, rude behavior. Dr. Brown shared with me later that she was appalled. We had both correctly assessed the anger and frustration brimming over in our eyes.

"I've never seen anything this unprofessional, ever," she expressed to me upon leaving City Hall.

I couldn't have agreed more. It was clear that the purpose of the meeting was to kill. Was it real, or was it Memorex?

At this point, I realized that this was not a decision-making meeting. The decisions had already been made. The purpose of this meeting was just to say that they had met with my group. The saddest part is that the representatives from Upton Planning had stated that the Upton community was in support of the Mayor's plan when there had neither been a board vote nor a community vote to indicate that.

There still has not been an opportunity for the community to voice an opinion or conduct a vote on the board's decision concerning The Royal Theater Project.

As a result of what transpired in 2017, I lost all respect and trust for those running the organization. Despite that, however, I have remained on its board because it's not my wish to hinder its overall progress in any way or to display any negativity to the community.

In 2018, I was picking up my sister, Gert, from Baltimore's Penn Train Station. As I mentioned earlier, Gert and I have the same father but not the same mother. She's an interior decorator and regularly travels for her business. Gert was heading to Baltimore from her home in Petersburg, Virginia, and I was picking her up. Gert was coming into town because I had hired her to work on my apartment building.

In 1985, in an effort to diversify my financial portfolio, I purchased a building in the Penn Station Community, which is now called The Station North Arts District. It's a historic building, more than 100 years old. It has three apartments, and I hired my sister to decorate the place from top to bottom. My apartment building is in an area that has become an overall part of the entertainment community in Baltimore, and it stands as a quiet testament to the very few African Americans, like me, being able to slip in and own property in that area. In Penn Station, property values have escalated over the years.

I parked and got out of the car, and soon after, I noticed one of the Upton Planning representatives, Jules Dunham, doing the exact same thing. We acknowledged one another, smiled, and I walked over to her car to exchange hellos. But we exchanged much more—it was confirmation for what had been burning my heart.

Well, the subject of how the Mayor's meeting with Upton Planning was not handled properly came up; how the Mayor's representative had rudely rejected all that had to do with The Royal Theater Project, and how the abrupt change of heart had transpired among everyone—when they were once in favor of working on and promoting the project.

She coined the summation in a simple phrase when she said, "It was political."

It should be mentioned that also in 2018, Ms. Pugh invited basketball legend and entrepreneur Magic Johnson to Baltimore for a meeting. As you know, Johnson is widely praised for the theaters he built in Maryland's suburbs. I'm not sure if anything concrete came of that meeting. What I do know is that it was another meeting to which I was not invited.

Now it's 2019, and I must make a critical decision about whether or not I am willing to take time out to attend the Upton Board training, or will I just resign from the board altogether. My thought process is that the board's training is probably tied to a requirement it needs to satisfy: a stipulation for a grant and/or an initiative it's working on—something of which I am not aware. I have not attended very many meetings, but I have not been getting minutes of the meetings either. Again, I don't want to do anything that would hurt the organization.

It's just that it's not in my nature to be comfortable around people I don't trust.

I have been a member of a lot of boards, and sometimes tough decisions have to be made. However, I had always been able to serve in a spirit of trust, respect, and adherence to proper procedures. For me, all that took place with Upton Planning remains hard to swallow. This lion-den experience, in my mind, is just another cog in the wheel of assaults—systemic, political, societal, and a lot of salt-throwing displaying a lack of cohesiveness that happens when underserved communities are pushed to the fringes of survival. It's one more assault that has kept *this* community in the state in which it has found itself for more than fifty years.

It's 4:00 a.m. I've got to get the kitchen, cooking.

CHAPTER ELEVEN

FOES AND BEDFELLOWS

It's Tuesday, April 20, 2019, and it's now 8:25 p.m., during spring break. We're on vacation with the grandkids here at the house in Florida. We just got in from the movies. The boys and I saw *Shazam!* Brenda and Bria saw *Little.* I opened Facebook on my phone and saw an entry that Bria had made.

It said, *20 years old plus and still treated like a kid.*

I think she is not completely happy with her spring vacation. I have a feeling this will be the last vacation we will have with all three of our grands. Brandon and LJ, I believe, still enjoy the time we spend together. However, I believe Bria has a different mindset.

It's 5:00 a.m., Easter morning, and I woke up from a dream where Adrian Johnson and I, our treasurer, were opening a bank account at Harbor Bank for the project. I guess it was in my subconscious because we were scheduled to meet with Joseph (Joe) Haskins, the bank president. Harbor Bank is the only African American Bank in Baltimore. I met Joe back in 2003 when he was one of the guests at that huge Baltimore Branch NAACP Business Breakfast that my committee put on. Over the years, he and I have communicated—and last year, he committed to help with the project in any way that he could. After waking up in a sweat, and my mind got busy, I got out of bed.

Although I am trying to relax my mind, get some rest and enjoy the grands, the task-at-hand keeps coming up. It's weird how things pop up out of left field with the power to keep one's focus, no matter what. Now up, I was flipping through YouTube on my phone, and there was a video titled *Baltimore: A Tale of Two Cities* by Michael Beach. This video highlighted the differences between Black Baltimore and White Baltimore income levels, investment, and crime. That YouTube video cleared from my head, and my heart, any second thoughts I had been experiencing about giving up on our project.

On Saturday, April 13, 2019, we had the family dinner I had planned for Brenda's seventieth birthday at The Rusty Scupper located in The Inner Harbor. At first, I was going to plan a birthday party, but I knew that was not her cup of tea. A nice dinner atmosphere with family was more to her liking. Lin, my partner in deeds, helped me out by visiting the restaurant in advance, making the reservation, and selecting the menu. We knew I couldn't afford to invite all the family, so we decided that the kids, grandkids, Brenda's siblings, and mine would make the cut. Lin completed the task of secretly inviting all the guests.

I had planned to tell Brenda on Friday, before, when we got home after work. However, I forgot to do that and realized it when I got up to get ready for work at 2:00 a.m. on Saturday. So, as I always do, I kissed her before I left and whispered in her ear, "Bring something nice to wear to work—because we're going out to dinner after work." As I left for work, I was thinking, I *hope she remembers what I said when she really wakes up*. I was hopeful that what I had whispered wouldn't get sucked up in one of her dreams. A couple of hours before I knew she would leave home, headed for work, I called her from The Bakery.

She tried to make me sweat for a moment before admitting that she'd heard me. "I'm looking for something to wear right now," she confessed.

Because it was Saturday, we had the full crew at The Bakery: me. Brenda; Susie, my daughter-in-law Etoy's mom; Brandon, Lin, and our newest employee, LJ, who works when he is not playing baseball. And let me add, here, that Susie has been working with us almost as long as we've had The Avenue Bakery. That's how cohesive this passion-business is. Susie is retired and puts in her hours of care part-time. At the end of the day, Lin took Brandon, LJ, and Susie home so they could get ready for the evening dinner. Brenda and I wrapped up what we had to do and got dressed at The Bakery. At this point, she only knew that she was going to dinner, but she didn't know where. She was surprised that we were only taking one vehicle and that I was leaving my truck in the parking lot. As we drove downtown and I began driving around The Inner Harbor, I think she realized we were going to The Rusty Scupper.

Now she knew where and that we were meeting the kids there. What she didn't know was that her brothers John, Larry, and Charles, my sisters Sandra, Dot, and niece Ashley, were there. Naturally, Charles brought his wife, Annett; Larry came with Wanda Best, whom he has been dating for a couple of years. As a matter of fact, I introduced them to one another. Dot and her husband, Paul Moore, were there. Her sister, Beverly, was away on vacation, and we were unable to reach her brother, Michael. My sister, Gert, could not make it because she had to stay home to take care of her husband, Bob, who has throat cancer.

Certainly, everyone greeted Brenda, and she gave me that smile and a look that declared *I am surprised and happy*. She commented, "This makes me happy to be with my family to celebrate my birthday."

I sometimes get a little emotional, but to make sure that all were in their proper places, and everything was going along as planned, I worked to suppress the joy that I was feeling about making my wife happy on her special day.

Of course, Wanda attends all the family functions with Larry. Although I have felt uncomfortable around Wanda since that call from her due to Mayor Pugh convincing her and Jules to abandon our project, including how it was handled, I don't let it interfere with family. I keep it outside of the family, and so does Brenda. Neither of us has mentioned it to Larry, either. This was Brenda's birthday celebration and certainly not the place to discuss community issues. However, I was compelled to ask Wanda if she and I could meet on that coming Monday. And she agreed. I wanted to settle things before vacation because I was hoping to meet with a former UPS partner to help raise money for the first phase.

On Sunday, she sent me a text saying that she would be out of town at a conference and would not be able to meet. She asked if we could meet after I returned from vacation. I am not sure if this was strategic on her part or if she was simply avoiding me as she has done in the past. *I'll see when I return from vacation*, I thought.

Well, it's 8:52 a.m., and we will be waking the kids up so that we can get ready for Easter Mass. I know Brandon will be ready to get up, but LJ is a different story. Although he is never difficult or complains, he is a little slow to move. When I peeped into his room around 7:30, I noticed he didn't clean out the dishes and soda cans as I had instructed him to do before going to bed. I will address that with him when I awaken the little gamer. He seems to use up a lot of his time playing games with a friend online. Yesterday, I had asked Brenda if we had a board game, we all could play together. She didn't give me the answer I was looking for.

Instead, she said, "The kids are in their rooms doing what they like to do."

I let my thought drop at that point.

As for the meeting, I anticipated, here in Florida, it didn't happen. Instead, my UPS partner asked me to send him the project's information, and I did. I am not expecting a positive response because his philanthropic endeavors are not quite aligned with what we are trying to do. I hope that he has friends or relationships that can bring support. When I return to Maryland next week, Brenda Brown and I plan to meet with a contact that heads up a nonprofit that may bring financial resources to the project. This year's focus is raising financial resources and making sure the community is on board; that is why I am trying to meet with Wanda; hopeful things have changed in our favor since the revelations of Mayor Pugh's unethical conduct have draped all the headlines, even nationally. It seems that Ms. Pugh may have used her position to coerce mighty book sales of her self-published children's book.

Well, we are back home from church, and Bria is quick to put her experience at Mass on Facebook. There was a moment in the Mass during which we offer each other peace with a handshake. Bria said that one of the White ladies was reluctant to shake her hand but did so and afterward sanitized her hands. Bria, I assume, viewed this as a sign of prejudice. I seem to think the woman would have done the same thing no matter whose hand she would have shaken. Some people have a thing about germs. However, Bria has vowed to only take her own trips from now on, and she is ready to go home. I love her very much, but that said, I do believe that she has control issues.

Now we are on our way to play miniature golf at LJ's request. Miniature golf was fun, and we all enjoyed it; I had two holes in one. Brandon, Bria, and LJ each had one. The scores were: Brandon 47, I had

48, LJ had 50, Brenda had 55, and Bria had 60. After miniature golf, we watched Bria feed the baby alligators. We then made the trip to the kids' favorite restaurant, Olive Garden. (Don't judge.) We came home stuffed, and everyone went to their favorite spots of the house.

Now I am planning our final two days of vacation. Tomorrow I will take the Kia in for service, a recall, and I need them to check the steering wheel's play. When I get back from the shop, I plan to get a load of mulch and have the boys help me lay it in the flower bed. Then I will exterminate around the perimeter of the house as well as the inside. My hope is that I get a chance to hit some golf balls at the range.

I had planned to take the boys to the golf course. The course that we normally go to is on Hoagland Blvd., right next to a small airport. But when we got there, the golf course was no longer there! We were able to find another course, close by, with a driving range. However, we couldn't use the driving range because they were wrapping up. But fortunately enough, the guy in the office allowed us to play a few holes for free. And I thought that that was very nice of him. I had a set of clubs with me and a couple of Brenda's clubs. We got started. I was a little rusty. Brandon and LJ were even rustier. We played three holes, and I worked with Brandon to help him swing his club correctly. But for the life of us both, I couldn't get LJ—my athlete—to absorb the difference between a baseball bat and a golf club. He just couldn't stop swinging that golf club like he wanted to make a homerun. Well, we got to three holes, and I got tired of giving him instructions. I got tired of chasing down balls, and I just got tired. In the words of Kenny Roger's song, *You got to know when to hold them, know when to fold them, know when to walk away, and know when to run*. So, we finally gave up, packed it in, and I resolved to know that I was not going to make a Tiger Woods kid out of LJ. We did, however, have a great time, hanging out together, just us three guys. It was about family, passion, and commitment.

CHAPTER TWELVE

A UPSer AT THE HEART OF THINGS

It's **Monday morning, February 11, 2019**. I am looking at the morning news, and the weather, freezing rain—and snow is making the lives of those traveling to work miserable. I am so fortunate to be retired, and The Bakery is closed on Mondays.

It has been a great weekend. Business seems to be picking up. The highlight of the weekend was my son's birthday party Friday night. Of course, I was able to get my dance on and show the young ones how it's done. The party was a celebration of his life, my pride, our family, the support of friends, and a reflection of the past, and of course, love.

As I looked at Ham greet family and friends who joined the party, I remembered the day I waited on his delivery at Sinai Hospital. I reflected on how proud I was to have a son and how determined I was to be a force in his life until the day I die. As I looked at the one hundred or so pictures of him, putting his life on display, it touched me because more than half of the pictures I had taken out of pride and love for my firstborn.

And a Hamlin birthday wouldn't be a Hamlin party without an Avenue Bakery cake. Our cake decorator, Sade Robinson, is just about the best there is when it comes to signature cakes. That girl is talented!

And the cake we dug into beheld an array of my son's pictures, ranging from babyhood right up 'til now, brandishing his big baldhead (that once was a cluster of dreads) and his big, bushy black beard. The room was packed with family and friends. And as I smiled at my wife, Brenda, she was smiling down at the cake that told the story of all our lives.

I must salute my daughter-in-law, Etoy, for pulling together a great celebration of her husband's life. I thanked her cousin, Nina Dow, as well. The party girl did a fantastic job, creating the décor that boosted a festive atmosphere. But that's her business, named, *The Original Party Girl* (OPG). She's a party coordinator. So, she's always spot-on for the occasion.

There were so many highlights at the party. My sister, Sandra, could not make the party because she was on her annual ski trip weekend. Sandra loves to get her dance like me. She had given her daughter, Ashley, specific instructions to represent her well. I have never seen Ashley dance like that ever; she really got it on. I was also shocked at seeing my granddaughter Bria's dance performance as well. She's twenty-two. I remembered how she was just a wallflower. At Sandra's party back in December, all she did was sit around and eat. But this time, she really showed her moves. And, of course, LJ, my grandson, did his thing as always. He's a true Hamlin.

As I have mentioned before, Brenda is not much of a dancer; so, I would always save the last slow dance for her. However, this night, after we had the cake presentation and formal celebration, I convinced her to stay on the dance floor—this amazed everyone. The song blasting the space couldn't have been more appropriate. It was Denroy Morgan's 1981 hit, *I'll Do Anything For You*. I mean it was made for us. Nearly everybody in the place got to snapping pictures and taking videos like the paparazzi, snapping away to capture a movie star. Her beautiful silvery crown and smile lit up their flashes.

While we were commanding that dance floor, a tall fellow was getting up from his seat at a nearby table. He fell into my side view. He was approaching the dance floor by himself. Maybe he was planning on tapping me on the shoulder so he could cut in on my dance partner and me. I don't know. I got busy ramping up a few moves, and evidently, it changed his mind. He retreated and stood by the wall. As the record began to fade, I began to leave the dance floor, wiping the sweat off my brow.

The big guy walked over to me and said, "Do you remember me? I am Rancy Tillery, and you hired me at UPS."

A bit stunned, I took a good look at him, then smiled and said, "Sure, I remember you." I asked him how he came to be at my son's party. He said something, but we both were struggling to hear one another over the music, so I didn't get all the connections. We were also excited at seeing one another.

Right there in the moment, Rancy had me thinking back to the early '80s when I managed the Rockville Delivery Center at our Burtonsville facility in Laurel, MD. Rancy was one of the fifty-five delivery drivers who were assigned to me. He delivered to the National Institutes of Health (NIH) building in Rockville.

As a manager, once a year, I tried to make sure I spent a day on the road with my drivers to get to know their areas and get to know them a little better. It made it easier to make operational decisions when they brought up concerns or when critical issues arose. On occasion, I rode with less-performing drivers to determine if they were following proper delivery and safety procedures as prescribed. My rides with Rancy were always interesting because the NIH building has an unusual floor plan and unique delivery requirements.

Back to my son's party. Rancy began to talk about how much he admired me, and he talked about the impact I had had on his life. He indicated to me how grateful he was that I had hired him.

"That opportunity helped make me the man I am today," he said candidly.

UPS has always been pro-active when it comes to attracting minorities and women, making sure that everybody gets an opportunity. During the '80s, UPS had this push to hire fresh pools of talent. And my job at that time was in Human Resources. So, my responsibility was to make sure that we hired for our evening operations and night work operations. I'm not sure why I was put in that position, but there I was. And I cultivated fruitful relationships with various colleges: the University of Maryland at Baltimore County, the University of Maryland at College Park, Community College of Baltimore City, Catonsville Community College, Coppin State College [University], Morgan State College [University], etc.

For the most part, I found that the kids who really needed job opportunities to help with their education and/or to fill in the gap came from our Historically Black Colleges and Universities (our HBCUs). Certainly, Coppin and Morgan were parts of that. I had developed a great relationship with a gentleman named Jim Roberts at Morgan State University, and I recruited lots of guys from Morgan. Out of that came Zed Smith.

Some of the guys I recruited stayed. Some took their learned skills and degrees and carved out careers with other companies. Back-in-the-day, my drill was to first discourage them from taking a job at UPS. Maybe they didn't have what it took to become a valued UPS employee. It was a motivational tactic. I wanted to see who was hungry and who wasn't. Those who stayed worked hard to prove me wrong. Some of them even excelled in management. And I know a couple of them who have retired. One of them was a guy named Vince Bailey. He recently retired from UPS after a career in Sales. He occasionally comes into The Bakery. His favorite item to purchase is our sweet potato muffins with raisins and walnuts. It gave me great joy to be able to give those young people an opportunity.

Rancy Tillery has now retired from UPS, and he's enjoying his life simply spending time with his grandkids. As the conversation was moving along to its end, we embraced one another the way real men do. I thanked him for his expression of gratitude.

And his final response as we departed was, "No, thank *you*."

This seemed to be a touching moment for him, and it was for me as well. You never know the impact you have on a person's life—positive or negative. But when you are faced with it, front-and-center, especially when you least expect it, boy, is it an eye-opener.

I tell you, "The Lord works in mysterious ways," that's what the old folks used to say.

We have no idea just how our interactions are going to impact their lives. It could be a word or a phrase that you utter. It could be a show of encouragement during a trying time. Or it could be an action, like me hiring all those guys that could have made a difference for decades to come. Certainly, the man who hired me made a difference in my life. In those moments, long gone, those guys I hired did their job, and I did mine. And in the moment, that was the long and the short of it.

But you're blessed when someone comes back to thank you. It goes to show what I would like people to understand. What you give—it's not always green and in your pocket that will stand the test of time—even if, in the long run, it could translate into monetary gain. Somehow or another, we have to understand that how we conduct ourselves and how we treat others or give advice encompasses the real gold.

Well, I was thinking that I would have to reschedule my session with my professional writing coach/editor, who's been helping me with *On a Roll*. Our Tuesday sessions begin at 11:00 a.m. However,

Dr. Brenda Brown wanted to meet with me when she got to Baltimore on the coming Tuesday morning. But wouldn't you know it, snow arrived today and promised to stick around until tomorrow. Dr. Brown was coming to town from New Jersey. The snow was coming from the north, too. So, she decided to postpone her trip and our meeting.

***

I had a great thirty-five and one-half-year career at United Parcel Service. It had its ups and downs like any career would have, but that's to be expected. I started working there on November 13, 1968. The weird thing, I was not looking for a job at the time. I was working for *The Baltimore Sun* in an apprenticeship program to become a printer. Like most jobs of this type, the new guys work at night. Working at night was not an issue for me because I worked nights at Mount Vernon Textile Mills for my three years of high school. Prior to that, as a child, I spent many nights changing diapers and feeding my infant brothers and sisters; that's another story.

However, while working at *The Baltimore Sun*, my best friend, Thomas Lewis, who lived across the street from me on McCulloh Street, stopped by the house to tell me there was a job that paid $3.45 an hour. He needed a ride so that he could apply.

"I need a ride out to the place. If you have the time," Lewis said.

Sounds strange now, but back then, the minimum wage was $1.25 an hour. And I was making a decent wage at $2.25. So, I wasn't looking for a job. At that time, Lewis didn't have a car, but I did. We were both nineteen.

I took him out to Moravia Park Drive to apply for a package handler job. Well, I got bored waiting for him and decided to fill out an application. This meant I would be interviewed, too. I will never forget that experience because that was the first time an African American interviewed me. And I'll never forget the interviewer: Willie Mann. Willie was a young guy about in his twenties, weighing around 170-175 pounds and stretching upward, past six feet tall or so. He was dressed in a suit and tie. But the biggest thing I noticed was that he wasn't, as we used to say, "light and bright." Sometimes for African Americans who moved forward in corporate America, looking closer to White was a factor. But Willie Mann was my complexion. In addition to how he was dressed, also impressive was the way he spoke, moving about in a company that had African Americans in management. The year was 1968. Rev. Dr. Martin Luther King Jr. was assassinated just months before my encounter with Willie Mann, and a lot of companies were not hiring Blacks. The next thing that impacted me was his assurance that there were advancement opportunities as well. And I had always wanted to have a job where I could wear a suit and tie.

This suit-and-tie thing came as a result of looking out the window of our second-floor apartment on Argyle Avenue, watching for my mom and stepfather, James Crawford, to come home from work. At the age of ten, it was my responsibility to babysit my brothers and sisters: Tony, Ricky, Eldora, and Sandra, and to have dinner on the stove by the time they got home. While looking out the window, I used to see people coming from work in construction-job attire; many of them had other labor jobs as well. But what most impressed me were those who came home looking sharp in suits and ties. And they weren't preachers. Keep in mind that I was living in a segregated community, so whether or not a person I observed was a doctor, lawyer, or a ditch digger, the major point to highlight is that we all lived in the same community. Of course, it's not like today. While you've heard of white-flight, there's also upper-affluent flight. As families of color began to do better financially, coupled with the ending of segregation, it was only natural for families to seek better places to live. Sadly, such a natural phenomenon means that the wealth of positive images vanishes before the eyes of those who are left without options. But as for the youth of yesteryear, we had plenty of positive images and examples to emulate. They were working folks we could aspire to be like.

The night after we completed our application and were interviewed, I received a call to start work. However, Lewis had not gotten a call at all. I felt pretty bad about that but decided that I would take the job. I gave my notice to *The Sun* and started my journey at UPS. I felt better about the whole thing when Lewis later landed a job at McCormick Spice Company. McCormick Spice paid well and had benefits. As a true friend, he had encouraged me to take the UPS job, and it did not affect our friendship. However, I tend to discourage young job seekers from taking their friends to job interviews, including my kids.

When I reported to work the first night, I became even more impressed with the company because my supervisor, Eddie McClurkin, was also African American. Having only his name, I had assumed otherwise. At the time, I had not heard of any African Americans named McClurkin.

My first night on the job was exciting. I was given safety instructions and training methods on how to unload trailers. This was not the suit-and-tie position, but I felt that one day, it could happen for me here. Making $3.45 an hour was like hitting the lottery. Mr. McClurkin, Ed, as he preferred to be called, was delighted with my work from Day One. It seemed I could unload trailers faster than what was required. As a matter of fact, in some cases, they had to tell me to slow down so that the persons sorting the packages could have time to read the labels. The pace of my work was derived from the experience I had gained on my very first job.

In 1961, we lived at 2000 Druid Hill Avenue on the third floor. The three-story rowhouse was across the street from Archie Laden's corner grocery store. Mr. Laden was a short, round Jewish man who always seemed to be gnawing on a big worn cigar that stuck out of the corner of his mouth, twenty-four/seven. He was heavyset and bald with a layer of hair around the sides of his head.

One day, at the age of thirteen, I asked him if he had a job I could do. At first, I was a little concerned because he had a big Boxer that I would often see him feed in the store's backyard. Although the dog didn't seem vicious, and I normally did well with animals, I cautiously decided not to let that deter me. I inquired, and he said, yes, he had a job for me.

"Report to Henry in the backroom," Mr. Laden said, chewing on his cigar and pointing the way.

Henry was an African American young man in his early twenties. Henry taught me how to clean fish, quarter chickens, and how to wrap products up for customers. Sweeping the floor and cleaning the place as well as occasionally helping the little old ladies in the community carry their groceries home was also a part of my job. Besides learning a strong sense of responsibility and a strong work ethic, Henry also taught me a sense of urgency. Whenever I had to cut up chickens or clean fish to fill a customer's order, Henry would always be there to say, "Hurry up, hurry up." Because of this, I got so good at cleaning fish; I could scale a fish, and throw him up in the air, cut off his head, and filet him before he hit the table. Now let me get back to the believable.

Well, needless to say, I've held on to that sense of urgency ever since, and it served me well at UPS. While I was working at UPS, I allowed myself to feel like I was finally accomplishing a firm financial footing of things. It really allowed me to take care of my family and move my family forward. After all, I was living in a whirlwind of life changes. In June of that year, I had graduated from high school. I graduated late because of the problems I had had as a child. That July, Brenda and I got married. And in September, I lost my job at the Mt. Vernon Textile Mill but was looking toward *The Baltimore Sun* apprenticeship program for financial and career redemption.

As I mentioned, I started working on November 13, 1968; but I was laid off once the Christmas season ended. It was something I had expected. Willie Mann had explained to me that I'd been hired on a temporary basis but that if I did well, the company would call me back for a permanent position. By this time, December of 1968, Brenda was pregnant with our firstborn and my namesake, who would eventually get nailed with the nickname Hammy. We were in our first apartment, a three-room penthouse in the attic of a house at 3719 Ferndale Avenue in the Forest Park area. Back then, the Forest Park community was considered an affluent community for upwardly-mobile Blacks. At first, I was not too worried about being laid off because it made me eligible for unemployment benefits. Our rent was manageable, we had little-to-no-debt, and Brenda was still working at Social Security—at least until the baby came. However, as time went on, I had yet to receive my unemployment benefits, and our rent came due. To bring in some money, I started hacking. Hacking was, and still is, a popular term for providing a cab service, picking up and dropping off fares around town. Hacking was illegal because it sidestepped the lengthy, complicated and expensive lawful requirements to operate a cab service mandated by the state. If you were a hacker, it basically meant that you could drive, knew the city well and that you had a car with four doors. For customers in the inner city, it meant that you were going to get a good deal for the car ride; and that you didn't have to depend on a legal but discriminating White cabbie, who would whiz by you—either afraid to pick you up or afraid to take you wherever you wanted to go in the community. On the downside of all this was number one: hackers irritated the legal cabbies and the state of Maryland because they didn't pay taxes. It produced unwanted competition, and number two: there were competition and rivalry among hackers and groups of hackers. Certain groups would claim certain areas around town as their domain—not willing to let new or sometimes-hackers in without paying a fee to the group.

Occasionally, I would go down to Mondawmin Mall and pick up fares. What I didn't know was that there was a group of guys that had claimed Mondawmin as their turf. These guys would run me and others off. And I'm certain that if they had caught us, they would have caused us bodily harm.

Hacking brought in a few dollars, but I soon realized that it could also be dangerous. So, for the first time in my life, I lowered my pride, which was motivated by Brenda's persuasion, and I asked her uncle, Norman Williams, for a loan to see us through. I promised to pay him back and did so the month I returned to work.

Uncle Norman and Aunt Gladys were the classiest people I had ever met. When Brenda and I were dating, they took us to The Keys Restaurant in Washington D.C., and that blew me away. In all my life, up until that point, I had never been to a sit-down restaurant, let alone a fancy place like that. I remember being very nervous and very careful how I ate. And I made sure I didn't eat too much. I was not, however, uncomfortable about was how to dress. I have always had a reputation as a well-dressed person who knew how to dress for any occasion. That's partly why I was able to capture the love of my life, Brenda Ann Taylor.

Anyway, Aunt Gladys was a beautiful woman who worked at the Pentagon, and Uncle Norman worked as a male nurse at Clifton T. Perkins Hospital Center, a psychiatric hospital. I can remember the time when a patient broke my uncle's jaw. They had fancy cars and always dressed well. They impressed me so because I didn't have anybody in my family like that. Sure, my Uncle Charles and Aunt Louise may have fallen into that category, but they lived in California. And maybe my Aunt Mamie and her pastor husband, Uncle Wendell McCleod, were like Brenda's uncle and aunt, but they lived in Boston.

Finally, on the first of February of 1969, Ed McClurkin called me back to UPS. He had indicated they would have called me sooner, but they had trouble contacting me. We didn't have a phone, and they had to mail me the callback letter.

Well, I was back at work, and Brenda was getting close to delivering the most important gift of life, my son. I was getting worried about leaving her at night, so I asked the one person I trusted to look out for her, and that was my brother, Tony (who also went by Waymon or Teddy or whatever name he was using at the time). Tony and I have come a long way growing up, and he knows better than anyone what I went through as a child. My return back to UPS included a new assignment: I became a sorter rather than an unloader. That meant I had to sort at the beginning of the belt and load four trucks at a time. Just so you know, UPS calls its trucks *package cars,* not trucks. I really enjoyed my job and the people with whom I worked daily. However, I had a couple of difficulties, my first year on the job.

Shortly after returning to work, we got a new supervisor, Walt Robinson, who was also African American. My hours at work were from 10:00 p.m. to 7:00 a.m. or until the job was complete. I also had a forty-five-minute lunch break. The problem I had, due to my speed of getting the job done, was that I could sort the belt, load my vehicles and eat my lunch all at the same time. I would set my food bag on the shelf of one of my package cars and take a bite periodically while loading. Then when our forty-five-minute lunch break began, I would lie down on one of the empty shelves to take a nap. When Robinson would call us back to work, I would get up and return to my station at the front of the conveyor belt. But these naps evidently weren't quality naps because, for some reason, I could not completely wake up, which caused me to fail to sort the belt properly. That meant the sorters behind me would miss their packages because they were not where they could get them. This produced complaints from my fellow workers about poor production. And I was reprimanded by my supervisor.

I will never forget the time Robinson called me in the office and said, "Jim, I don't understand how you do it. I have seen horses and all kinds of animals sleep on their feet, but you are the first human I've seen do that."

The other problem I had was making close to $4.00 an hour, twice as much as I had been making at *The Sun*—with overtime. I was meeting my financial responsibilities and felt as though I didn't need to work every day. So occasionally, I came up with excuses not to come to work. And I tell you, I got very creative at it. I am not sure what came over me. Soon, though, I began looking at that bundle of joy, our son; and I determined that I wanted to give him everything I'd never had. As I mentioned, Tony could tell you how he, I, and Ricky never had a bed of our own, let alone a bedroom to call our own. The three of us slept in the same bed for quite a few years. The apartments we lived in were always two-bedroom dwellings, which meant my mom had one bedroom, and the other was for us brothers.

I changed my evil ways and became a model employee. I was able to buy a new car, a Plymouth 383 Road Runner, probably not the ideal for a new family guy, but I fell in love with it. We quickly started looking for a better apartment so that we could move out of our three-room penthouse after Brenda had mentioned she saw a roach in the baby's crib.

We moved to 106 Diener Place, apt. # 101, which was in a brand-new development off Frederick Road near Edmondson High School. There, I was able to provide my son with his own room and plenty of space. I could also provide enough for my family so that Brenda would not have to work during my son's formative years. Things were going great at work as management began to encourage me to accept a supervisory position.

At that time, UPS had two facilities in Baltimore. It had one facility on York Road. And it had a facility where I worked, which was on Moravia Park Drive, off Pulaski Highway. Eventually, UPS built a brand-new facility, located at 3901 Vero Road, referred to as the Joh Avenue Facility, in Arbutus. When it closed the York Road and Moravia sites, everyone went to work at the Joh Avenue building. It happened to be so close to my home that I rode my ten-speed bike to work.

I declined the offer to enter the management ranks because I wanted to become a delivery driver. At the Joh Avenue facility, my job title was still *sorter*. I enjoyed the job, and the pay just kept getting better. My personality is such that whether or not it comes to work or my social life, my habit is not to have an entourage of friends. However, I do latch on to a few guys whom I deem as special. Having a lot of friends is not something that I need or crave. One of the people I befriended at the job was Larry McBride. He and I worked at the Moravia facility and seemed to share the same views. When we were at the other building, we bet on how long new hires would stay. McBride had recently come out of the military. He was a medic.

Brenda and I remained at Diener Place for a couple of years. During that time, I had decided that my road-runner days were over, and it was time to purchase a new luxury car. I enjoyed my Plymouth Road Runner, and I hated to give it up. However, I was peeling wheels too often, and I began to gain a few points on my driving record. I tell you, though, I had fun with that car and blew the doors off a few goats. In case you didn't know, the word, *goat*, was slang for a Pontiac GTO. As a matter of fact, McBride, who was driving a Mercury Cougar GT, often tried to outrun my Road Runner in a half-mile. We would race at night on Moravia Park Drive during the lunch break; this helped me keep myself awake. He may not admit it, but I beat him so badly and so often until he finally traded in his Cougar for a Road Runner.

In August of 1968, I had not long turned twenty years old. After saving up, I was enjoying my first car. Up to that point, nobody in my immediate family owned a car. I had learned to drive and enrolled in the Easy Method Driving School for a one-hour lesson. It was before the public schools had instituted Driver's Ed. My first car was a sweet burgundy 1963 Pontiac LeMans. But she had a sensitive gas pedal that I wasn't quite used to yet.

Well, I've got the car but hadn't quite advanced from Learning Permit status to card-carrying driver's license status. One night, my sister, Dot, asked me to take her out to my brother-in-law's job. It was her first husband, named Joe Knight. She needed to pick up something-or-the-other from him. I don't remember the direct task she had to do. But throwing to the wind, my regard to needing a licensed driver in the car with me, at all times, my response to her was, "Of course." And off we went. I just needed to make a stop at the gas station; I let her know. "I need to get some gas," I said.

I pulled into the gas station, and when I attempted to align myself properly by backing up—inching back, slowly, my foot pushed down on the gas pedal, and it was off to the races with nowhere to go. The car shot backward, sharply, and thank God (kinda), anchored me on a parking guardrail. And there I was, stuck. God is good because I could have hit the gas pump.

The next move was to call a tow truck amid the gathering onlookers, and with no driver's license to show, ask for help. My thoughts didn't get too far when the police showed up. My naivete allowed me the nerve to walk over to them for help. "My gas pedal is sensitive," I said to one of the two White police officers, "I hit it too hard and backed up on the guard there."

They looked, assessed the situation, and appeared to be tickled. My sister, Dot, evidently assumed that her best defense in all this was to stay in the car, silent. To the policeman, I said, "I got a tow truck coming to get me off."

The policeman said, "Well, as long as you're okay, everything is fine." And without asking me for my driver's license or registration or anything, the two got back into their patrol car and drove away. In 1968 and in 2019, such a situation could have gone a hundred different ways.

As time ticked along and as the old folks used to say that if "the good Lord blesses you and the creek don't rise," I got a little older and wiser. Also, when your wife says to you, "I have some news for you. I'm pregnant," you decide to focus more energy on buying that first home and put less focus on fancy cars and how fast they can burn rubber.

Although our two-bedroom apartment was comfortable, I wanted each of my children to have their own room and a backyard in which to play. We found a nice rowhouse in the Huntington area, which was not far from the apartment. It was well-kept, owned by an elderly White lady named Mrs. Schellberg. She was a widow and lived in the house by herself, who was its original owner. The house was located at 4647 Rokeby Road, and there was an elementary school right in the next block. The house even had a garage.

The buying process for the house seemed to be very simple. I remember the cost of the house being $16,000. And I think we put a down payment of roughly $1,500. And then we moved into the great neighborhood, nestled in the Huntington Community that was turning African American. It was just above Edmondson Village. We lived between two older families that nurtured us. One, the Demory Family, lived on the left side at 4645 Rokeby Road. Mr. and Mrs. Lansey, who had one daughter, lived on the other side of us. I really got to know the families very, very well.

Mr. Lansey was a retired shutterbug who was a photographer in the military. He gave me his photography books because I liked taking pictures as well and had a couple of cameras. His books taught me how to use darkroom equipment. Mr. Demory had been a police officer, and at one time, worked for the Department of Education. From him, I learned a lot about how to take care of a home. He gave me all kinds of tips on an array of things. He really educated me. And, unbeknownst to me, he got me ready for the next move in my life. My next residential move.

Life was good on Rokeby Road. But one of my coworkers, Pete Kearns, began telling me about a development out in Carroll County that was being built and about how reasonable the houses were. It caught my ear.

"There's a lot of open space," Pete said.

It started me thinking about how it would be nice for my kids to have a bigger backyard than the one we had on Rokeby Road. For me, growing up, my family never had a backyard. We moved from place to place. We never owned a home. It would be nice to see my children enjoy themselves in a spacious yard. In a house like my coworker described, we could be able to enjoy family and extended family. While we were at Rokeby Road, Brenda became pregnant with our daughter, Belinda. We call her Lin, for short. Our new expected addition was attaching our fate to a major move.

So, Pete showed me this development and where it was. I told Brenda about it, and she was only sort of open about it. But she was willing to hear me out, at least. Even though we loved where we were, we loved the neighbors and everything like that; it was just that I wanted a little bit more for my family.

We drove out to Sykesville, which is in Carroll County, Maryland. What we saw was dirt and wooded area, along with hints of promised housing construction. We brought Brenda's grandmother with us to survey the land. Nanny is from North Carolina, and she enjoyed farming and gardening. So perhaps, she was attracted to the dirt we saw. On the other hand, Brenda's facial expression was half smile, half thought, *where in the world is this man taking us?*

But we kept it moving. We picked out a lot, and we picked out a house. And before we knew it, the next task was to sell our old home. Well, we'd only been in that house two years. And occasionally, we would have parties at the house. One of my coworkers, named Roy Brown, had a lady friend who had visited us on Rokeby Road. She remarked to him and us that she really liked our home. When she found out that we were moving, she was interested in purchasing the house. We had purchased that house for $16,000. And we sold it for $26,000. This gave us the $10,000 we needed to have our new house built.

The way it turned out, the lot that we picked out and my neighbor's lot were the two biggest open lots in the community, and they were situated as such that the builder could not put a lot between us. It gave us an acre of space. And that's one of the reasons why we've lived here for forty-six years. We love the open space. Every year we have a cookout during one of the summer holidays, and we host about one hundred of our extended family members and friends.

Saying all that, my heart has not moved, not one iota, from Baltimore, the place of my birth, my formative years, UPS years, the place of my work-after-retirement years, and my mission to revitalize The Pennsylvania Avenue Corridor for residents living there now.

Living in Carroll County has presented my family with a strange set of circumstances; we are still the only African American family in our neighborhood. But we've never had a problem with race. Our children are well-rounded because while they lived and went to school with those who didn't necessarily look like them, on the weekends and other times, at random, they spent much of their time with relatives in the city. They have a healthy perspective about diversity—and can feel at home just about anywhere. Brenda has been a Scout leader and enjoyed being active in our children's school and extra-curricular activities. And, to this day, our children harbor no fear about branching out to new experiences. My son and daughter understand that we're all looking for the same outcome in life. They're well-adjusted adults.

My son is a supervisor at the VA Hospital in Baltimore. My daughter works at the administrative office of the Hilton Hotel. She used to work at the Wyndham Hotel, and the woman that once managed the Wyndham wanted to take her to Virginia with her. I'm grateful.

I don't know why God gave me this particular life experience except to say that perhaps living where I do, watching my family exist without incidents of racism, lets me know that racial and economic equity can be obtainable. Can't it?

Fast forward to my living for forty-some years in Carroll County; I continue to receive comments from different people about being there. *How are we getting along? Do we feel safe?* As a matter of fact, not far from us, roughly five or six miles away, there's a major farm that used to play host to Klu Klux Klan rallies and that sort of thing. However, my family has not had a problem here.

In our residential development, in the winter months, between my backyard and my neighbor's, we play host to all the children and teens, sledding. In the summer, we play host to friendly get-togethers. And I realize that our particular experience of living well, minus the experience of targeted community or individual racism, is unusual. Please let me interject, here, that it is sad to have to say that such a thing as living amicably among different races is unusual when it should be the norm.

So why have I had the privilege of these experiences? Some would call them near-misses of calamities or the ability to exist in a bold innocence to stay positive. I'm sure many have had their share of instances during which the balance of safety could have served up irrevocable harm but didn't. Perhaps, while standing in the midst, one was only able to correctly assess impending danger long after the fact—as I did about my solitary midnight walks across the Jones Fall Bridge to-and-from work at the Mt. Vernon Textile Mill. Could the reason for us still being around, be because God has something for us to do, to spearhead—something in which our active role is needed?

Perhaps, despite continuing news reports chronicling the luster and loss of The Pennsylvania Avenue Corridor due to systemic racism; despite reports such as The Urban Land Institute (ULI) 2015/16 report citing the need and calling for action to revitalize the area; despite the 2019 Urban Institute report, formally citing the economic and investment disparities in Baltimore's African American communities due to the legacy of, and ongoing racist policies; despite my blindsiding setbacks perpetrated by some of Baltimore's past and current political powers—pushed up against the genuine need for the success of The Royal Theater Project—perhaps, I have been protected because God knew I needed to hold on to my personal proof that a productive means of interaction could indeed become tangible. I'm prayerful He wants me to operate in the space of knowing what could be possible and persevere.

CHAPTER THIRTEEN

TEACHABLE MOMENTS/TEACHABLE MOVEMENTS

It's Wednesday, October 24, 2012, at 2:33 a.m., normally, I am on my way to work to get the baking started. This week we are on vacation in Florida, and as usual, I can't sleep. So, I guess I can write about my life, concerns, and goals.

After our long drive from Maryland, we slept most of Sunday and part of Monday; and we enjoyed a long leisurely dinner. Tuesday, we connected with Gertrude and Bob, my sister and brother-in-law, who were also vacationing in Florida. They had a timeshare. We enjoyed one another's company, took in a movie, dinner and called it a day.

But my mind was busy with all kinds of issues, plans, concerns, and obstacles. First, I was disappointed that I couldn't attend the funeral of Clarence Mitchell, III because we had already booked our vacation. I really wanted to offer my condolences to the family, especially to Michael Bowen Mitchell and his daughter, Micah. If you'll recall, I became Micah's first client after she passed the Bar exam to become an attorney in 2005 when she helped me to form my nonprofit, TRTCHC.

In the meantime, the artist Cisco Davis was working on completing the mural in our garden. The mural will highlight the Mitchell family and the role it played in the history of this country and in the Civil Rights Movement. There would be others to be commemorated in our mural as well. One of my concerns was trying to determine how and when we would unveil the completed mural to the public.

***

It's Monday, December 10, 2012, about 5:57 a.m., I got up, took the dogs out, and came back to the house to eat my Apple Jacks, the breakfast of champions. I am not looking forward to my visit at Chesapeake Urology with Dr. Sigmon. The week prior, I had a biopsy procedure, and this is the day I'm scheduled to learn the results. I don't understand the dilemma that I have found myself in. I feel healthier than ever, but my PSA numbers have been steadily rising. This morning, I'm wondering if this is going to be the day that my life will change, and not for the better. I'm wondering if the need for surgery will come up and/or just what else I'm going to have to make decisions about. Whatever is going to happen, I've made one decision, and that is—if the news is negative—if indeed I am looking at prostate cancer, I will make myself ready to accept it and move on to the next step.

I ended up having two biopsies. And both biopsies were without sedation. The first time, it was uncomfortable. The second time, it was a killer. So, let me tell you now that if I ever have to do one, again, they're gonna have to put me to sleep. Thankfully, both biopsies came back negative. So, the Good Lord blessed me. But what came out of this experience, though, was the importance of regular checkups and inquiries about my health. My doctor will be monitoring me every six months or so.

While I was waiting for the results, I was thinking that I needed to prepare Brenda and the kids. I knew I would need to make life changes if the worse results materialized. I would need to work with Brenda to get the house sold and get her into a smaller place, demanding less upkeep. Then I would start selling some of our properties so that she would have less to deal with. Continuing the mission to revitalize The Avenue would be another matter entirely. I'd have to figure out how the mission would continue to move forward—with or without me—in the flesh.

My message to everyone reading *On a Roll*—especially the men—is to get your PSA and all your bloodwork done every year. Follow up with your doctor, not only to maintain your life but also to maintain your quality of life.

***

This is my first Journal entry for 2013. I am sitting at Orlando International Airport, waiting on flight #606 back to Baltimore.

Back in 2003, when I was preparing for my retirement from UPS that next year, Brenda and I purchased a home in a Florida resort development called Terra Verde. Not only would it be our vacation home, equipped with a pool, but it was also part of my plan to diversify my financial portfolio. I wanted to purchase two additional homes, but Brenda convinced me to purchase the home and one townhouse in that same development. The strategy was to lease the townhouse on an annual basis, and that would pay for our second home. This year, we had leased it out to a couple of guys. Daniel Coombs, based in Florida, who works in the real estate and leasing business, finds us our rental clients. Before we prepared for our trip home and left for the airport, I was able to meet with Coombs to tour the townhouse and make sure he had the keys. The townhouse looked like it had been kept up well. The only main issue, according to Coombs, was general wear-and-tear. I took note that the stove and refrigerator were a mess. And it looked like we were going to have to get the backyard wall, separating us from the neighbors, repaired. Pondering my landlord to-do list and all I need to get done in Baltimore, I am thinking about putting the place on the market. But that's enough of house issues.

I came down here to Orlando to take care of the townhouse business and to get some rest. I was able to get some rest but not get rid of the pneumonia I brought down with me. A runny nose and phlegmy coughs continued to plague me. All in all, though, I knew I was blessed to be alive. During the vacation, one of the things I did was to take in a Tom Cruise movie titled *Jack Reacher*. It was okay, but I anticipated a little more action.

Throughout my time in Orlando, I remember my mind being flooded with the issues I considered pressing back home in Baltimore. The first thing was to get the supplies I needed and get The Bakery ready to open on that coming Wednesday in January. Then I needed to shore-up the plans for the Black History Month event that we were planning in conjunction with Booker T. Washington Middle School. I had a meeting set up with Stuart Hudgins. I'd contracted him to shoot a video for Black History Month. Hudgins is a historian and a talented graphic artist, among other things. As far as I know, he's always been an entrepreneur and has done excellent graphics work in New York and various other places. Whenever I need to come up with ideas about historic montages, he's my go-to guy, depicting the legacy of Pennsylvania Avenue immortalized in my murals, promotions, or videos. I don't remember just how I met him; I'm only glad that I did.

While in Orlando, I left a message for Larry Gibson, an attorney and currently a law professor at The University of Maryland School of Law. In 2012, he was pivotal on my list because that same year, he authored a book titled *Young Thurgood: The Making of a Supreme Court Justice*. I was hopeful that Gibson would render a presentation to the Booker T. Washington students we were inviting to The Bakery. Once I could seal the deal with Gibson, I could then commit to a solid event date.

I also needed to set up a meeting with Booker T.'s principal, Mrs. Debbie Thomas, to shore up a date feasible for the students' visit to The Bakery. Another meeting I needed to set up was one with Caprece Jackson-Garrett of Bonneau Caprece, who is a publicist and strategic marketing specialist. Caprece would be handling the promotions and marketing for the event. And all this was going on while artist, Cisco Davis, was creating a landmark mural on The Avenue Bakery Wall of Fame. I remained in contact with Davis to ensure that the mural would be completed on time. Complicating that fact was always the threat of inclement weather—after all, it was winter.

In the midst, I was also thinking and churning about the business, making it more profitable. So, one of the last meetings I set up to take place, once I got back to Baltimore, would be with a gentleman; I forget his name. He promised that he could promote my soon-to-be-famous sweet potato pies from Baltimore to Richmond. We talked about the different types of packaging. We determined what the packaging would be. We created a barcode label for the pies, and so on.

But as in the lyrics of The Temptations' song titled, Fading Away, *Like smoke from a cigarette ...* [and] *dreams that you soon forget...* that fella simply faded away.

***

It's Friday, August 9, 2013, three days before my brother Harold's birthday. He passed away on May 4, 1993. He had sickle cell and was on dialysis. He had gotten to the point of feeling that since he was being prescribed so many drugs at Johns Hopkins, adding a little marijuana didn't much matter. He was getting treatment at Johns Hopkins, and he worked there as well. In fact, so did my mother and my sister, Sandra. I miss Harold's super sense of humor and joy for life. He was the kind of guy who kept you laughing all the time. Harold was one of my younger brothers. And he had one of those great big smiles with great big front teeth that sparkled like the grill on a 1959 Cadillac.

But he was a late bloomer. He didn't date early. Finally, he did end up dating a young lady by the name of Rebecca Jones, and from that relationship, he had three children. He also had a son by a young lady named Patricia McNeill. If he were living today, even though he had to be a part-time dad, he'd be so proud of his children. One of his daughters, Marlene, graduated from college. She went into the military. I think she was in Iraq. Now, she's working toward getting her medical degree. Harold was the oldest of the Crawford children.

The family is here at Massanutten Resort for its annual vacation. I am in our room. Hammy; my new son-in-law, Blair Frederick; grandsons, Brandon; LJ, and his friend, Tre, are all at the water park. Brenda; Etoy; my daughter, Lin; and granddaughter Bria are all on their way to the spa. I figured I would take this time to get back to my story, *On a Roll.*

I am eager to get back home to move forward on a host of initiatives. In the process, I'm hoping to get out of the depressed mood I had found myself in for about three full weeks. I couldn't seem to shake it, no matter what I did. While on vacation, I had been able to get quite a bit of rest. But, still, I hadn't felt like doing much. I do remember one particularly good day, though. It was the day I had spent with the boys while the grown-ups stole away to visit the wine garden. The boys and I went to the Go-Cart track, played pat-pat golf—that's what LJ called miniature golf. We then visited the bungee tent after we first made an important stop at the refreshment counter for snowballs.

At the refreshment counter, something got us off-track but presented itself as a teachable moment. I stood at that counter for about ten minutes to treat my boys to snowballs. Four men, servers behind the counter, came in and out of view but never asked me what I'd like.

The longer I waited, the more agitated I became. It appeared I was being ignored. I got so angry I started to ask the question, "Is someone going to wait on me?" But instead, I walked over to the boys and explained to them, "Never beg anyone to take your money." I made sure that they understood just how long we had been waiting and that those servers had noticed us as soon as we had walked up to the counter. This was obviously a case of unfair treatment, at the least. And instead of getting a taste of snowballs, what they did get was a taste of discrimination. And I wanted them to feel and understand the uncomfortableness of it all. And to remember it. But the lesson would not end there. I would also show them how to take appropriate action as well. I explained to them that I would be filing a complaint with the resort's authorities.

LJ asked, "What will happen to the people?"

I explained, "They would get in trouble. And our complaint will make sure they don't treat anyone else like this."

***

It's Friday, November 1, 2013, at 1:30 a.m. And I am getting ready to go into The Bakery. I am wondering to myself who I am and who should I be, really. Let me share where I am going with this. I have been thinking about the fact that so many of our young Black men are behind bars. My thought is that too many of them didn't have that father figure in their lives to guide and help rear them. On the other hand, I believe they never knew who they really were or are.

I called my sister, Gert, yesterday, while on my way home from Orlando to say hello, and let her know how much I truly love her. I was also curious as to what our grandmother's maiden name was. Gert informed me that, while everyone knew our grandmother as Mother Hamlin, her maiden name was Duke. Her first name was Essie. She had two sisters and a brother. I went on to ask her did she know what our Dad's real name should have been. She said she believes it may have been Hite and Grandfather Hamlin adopted him when he married Mother Hamlin. There goes my point—who in the world am I?

Gert talked about how everything was always a secret back-in-the-day. Old people didn't tell you anything, and you better not ask, or you may get a backhand across the face and find your lips on the floor. We had a long conversation about how so many of our young men don't know who they are or who their birth fathers are. In my mind, so many women in our society have committed a disservice to our heritage, culture, and our future. That's how my heart bleeds due to my own personal experience. That said, let me say, here, that I am not negating the culpability of men, who seem to walk away from their families so easily.

I was thinking about the only brother I have left, Anthony Theodore Waymon, who has no clue as to who he really is. His last name was given to him by my mom. The name came from her husband, at the time, who was Henry Waymon. Mr. Henry and mom were only together for a short period of time. That's the information I got from what she shared with me. However, my brother was born after mom and Mr. Henry had parted. The sad part is that she went to her grave, never letting him know who his father was.

These kinds of things happen every day in our community, and for the most part, it is seldom talked about. I have this theory about sickle cell, as some of us know, occurs when both parents have the gene or trait. My theory is that those two parents who carry the gene are related and that relationships may have occurred possibly generations in the past.

I must get out of the house and get to work. I'll pick this conversation up a little later.

CHAPTER FOURTEEN

MAYORS, COME AND GO

It's Tuesday, March 12, 2019. It's 1:44 a.m. I have been up since 11:00 p.m., March 11. I am almost ready to go back to bed, but my mind is working overtime. I am thinking about Brenda's seventieth birthday celebration. She is not really a party girl, so I have decided a nice dinner with family would work for her. She loves crab cakes, so I am planning a family dinner at the Rusty Scupper located downtown at the Inner Harbor. Lin, my partner-in-crime is helping with the plans. Hopefully, we can wrap up the plans on Saturday.

I often tease Brenda about buying her a Three-wheel motorcycle for her seventieth, but I haven't done that—yet. I am thinking of how I can rent one for just her party, though. But I haven't figured it out yet. I will speak to my nephew, Andrew, who loves, and has a bike.

I am also thinking about this book, my memoir, and how it will impact the lives of many. I just saw the Mayor's State of the City speech, and I am sure she is doing what she believes is good for Baltimore. However, I keep thinking that no one has all the answers, and everyone makes mistakes. If you believe in something and are willing to make sacrifices to reach your goal—such as the goal of doing what's best for Baltimore—then you should. I think it is natural to second-guess one's decisions; however, having faith in God and where He leads you is important.

I know this year I must raise the money to move this project forward. It's now or never. I have decided to approach some of my retired UPS partners to sell them on our goals and hopefully get them to invest in the future of our young people and our community. I am not counting on anything. One thing I do know, my UPS partners understand the struggle, and we all have been fortunate to be successful. My hope is that they are wondering what it will take to positively change life in our urban communities. Hopefully, I can get them to realize the impact that our project will have.

I have tried to convince developers and investors to support this project. I have written letters and met with everyone I could think of that could help. My approach has always been that our project is about improving the future of our young people by changing the atmosphere and the economic outlook. It is not my nature to ask anyone for anything. With that said, I am not comfortable approaching my UPS family. I have had minimal contact with some of them, although I have worked with others and been around them ongoing. However, I must put my pride aside for the sake of positive change.

I am also feeling Paul Graziano's encouragement to continue to pursue the project. He mentioned the Opportunity Zone Program, which could raise funds for commercial projects. I investigated the program and realized it could be a selling point for my UPS partners. The program allows those who experience challenges with capital gains to benefit from what it offers. I will start this leg of my journey this week and see where God leads me.

On the direct Avenue Bakery front, I'm also planning out this year's Concert Series. We have set the dates, and I must find time to get the permits. I normally book the bands as well; however, I've decided to give that task to one of our board members, James Dow. James is more than a board member: he is my daughter-in-law's uncle. He's also a gifted musician. His band played during our very first concert, pro-bono.

When James Dow discovered that I dabbled in a little alto sax playing in high school, he convinced me to purchase a new sax and egged me on by giving me a few lessons. He got me as far as me playing *Mary Had a Little Lamb* seasoned with a few Miles Davis notes for added flavor. Well, I never really drummed up the time or the dedication to practice on a regular basis. But James, getting me to that modest accomplishment, signaled his love for music and our ability to work together—through thick and thin. However, I plan to add sax playing to my bucket list.

Upton Planning has its board meeting this Thursday, and I think I will adjust my schedule to attend. They have developed a Request for Proposal (RFP), and it's on the agenda. As a board member, I should already know what that is. But I don't. It's because I can't attend many of the meetings, and I don't receive copies of the minutes. But I should. I want to find out what that entails and if it has a bearing on TRTCHC's goals. I am sure they don't expect I will attend.

Needless to say, I have a lot on my plate, and time is moving fast. Well, it's 2:57 a.m.; I guess I will shut this down and turn off the TV. This Jason Bourne segment, I've seen a couple of times already.

***

It's 6:32 a.m., April 2, 2019, and I slept most of the night. I just woke up, very excited, from a very vivid dream. I was at an event that was being held by acting Mayor Jack Young after Mayor Pugh decided to remove herself from her dream job. I'm wondering if the dream was a premonition of facts or merely wishful thinking.

Somehow or another, the event was being held next to Robert C. Marshall Field, where we want to rebuild The Royal Theater. A group of us were there, consisting of community members, political figures, developers, and investors. As we looked to the sky, we saw the spotlight projection of a sign that boasted *Royal Theater Always A Good Show, Coming Soon.* It appears we just had a meeting where Jack publicly announced his support of The Royal Theater & Community Heritage Center. After seeing the image in the sky, I woke up with my heart beating fast and my mind running like Secretariat in The Preakness. I couldn't get to my computer fast enough to start writing before I forgot my dream. And here, I am, now. I got it on. The first time I have ever written down a dream on paper.

Yesterday, the first—April Fools' Day—was one of the happiest days of my life. The reason for my joy, excitement, and uncontrollable expression of my, *thank you to God*, was because my grandson, Brandon, passed his driving test and received his Maryland state driver's license. This was a huge accomplishment for him and a reflection of the confidence and support that Brenda and I have given him. Although cars have always been an interest to him, Brandon never seemed to push the issue of wanting to drive. And that was so, even though he had graduated from the Lincoln Technical Institute with an Auto Mechanic Certificate.

Brenda and I gave Brandon most of his driving lessons when he received his learner's permit. I believe my daughter, Lin, Brandon's mother did not have the temperament and calm demeanor that was needed to get him started. So, we stepped in. Once we were able to get him over his fear of driving, she was able to help. We were hopeful that when we bought Brandon his first car, his excitement would urge my son-in-law, Blair, to help teach him as well. Blair happens to be a commercial driver. I am not sure why Blair was reluctant to give him lessons, but I assume his illness, Sarcoidosis, was a factor.

All of that is not important now that Brandon has his driver's license. He can now move his life forward. He can now seek that job in the automotive field and gain full-time employment wherever he chooses. Since 2011, he has been an employee of The Avenue Bakery and has learned the business from the beginning. He knows more about the operation of the business than anyone other than Brenda and me. I would really hate to lose him, but I want him to pursue his dream and calling in life.

I have always been the father for him that Henry Sorrell, his biological father, and my first-in-law refused to be. When Brandon was a little guy, I would take him to community meetings when Lin was a single parent and had to work in the evenings. Lin and Blair have been married for six years and counting.

Getting back to that dream, I believe it was the result of my meeting with Dr. Brenda Brown and the mounting issues Mayor Pugh was facing. I met Dr. Brown, a graduate of Morgan State University, when she came to Baltimore to attend the 50th Anniversary of her class. She now lives in Newark, New Jersey.

Prior to founding the Urban Strategies Group, LTD, Dr. Brown was the first tenured and appointed District Administrator for Special Education with the Board of Education in New York City, and was responsible for the delivery of instructional and related services for children with special needs in one of the largest school districts in the State of New York.

Working within the inner-city, Dr. Brown recognized the need for improving the living and working conditions of underserved neighborhoods in cities. With more than 30 years' experience in administration, management, and program development, she focused her invaluable knowledge and finely-honed skills toward founding the Urban Strategies Group, LTD. And in doing so, she rededicated her life to helping the citizenry and civic leaders of neglected communities to rebuild their dreams and their futures through positive and strategic planning. Her expertise in the area of government and non-government systems, negotiating, troubleshooting and problem-solving have led to successful alliances in urban reconstruction and development.

Our meeting went well and began with Dr. Brown sharing the results of a meeting she and Brian Grant of the Grant Engineering and Construction Group, out of Newark, NJ, had attended earlier that morning pertaining to redevelopment and moving our project forward. Brian was also in the meeting that Dr. Brown and I had, here, in Baltimore. The key point she had learned was that Wanda Best and Jules Dunham were the two people controlling what takes place in the Upton community. She shared with me the importance of getting these two people's approval. I assured her that I would attempt to do that.

Brian followed up by reiterating the importance of getting the community's approval and accruing a possible written agreement. He advised that if I couldn't get these two people to support our project, getting hundreds of signatures of community residents to sign a petition of support for the project would be an option. He also laid out what he and his development group needed to proceed with the project along with a possible timeframe.

I shared what I was working on and my goal to raise the funding to move forward. We had to cut the meeting short because Brenda and Brian had to catch their train back to Newark. Since the meeting was at The Avenue Bakery, I made sure that Brenda went home with a dozen of Poppay's Rolls. We all departed from one another's presence, clear about what needed to be done, and most of it was on my table. It was also determined that the obstruction by Mayor Pugh might not be a factor since she had taken a leave of absence from her position. The immediate fill-in for her post was Baltimore City

Council President Jack Young, who was a supporter of the project early on.

Now you have the *Paul Harvey,* as he always finalized, "The rest of the story." All this was the root of my dream. I will never forget April Fools' Day, 2019.

CHAPTER FIFTEEN

RING THE BELL

It's 10:30 a.m., May 12, 2019, Mother's Day. We just got through our task of getting Rock and Bruno, our Miniature Pinschers (they call them min-pins for short), up for the day. I have the task of taking them out, and Brenda prepares their meals and cleans any mess they make. After that, I was heading to the kitchen to fix Brenda a Mother's Day breakfast. Walking through the living room, with the TV on, my favorite show was airing, *Sunday Morning on CBS.* It caught my attention. They were doing a story on Colonel William McRaven, who commanded the SEAL team that was able to get Osama bin Laden. He talked about his SEAL training and how there was a bell that you could ring if you wanted to get out. But, he said, "If you want to be successful, never ring the bell."

It's not often that I am inspired by television, but this was an inspiration for me because there are times when it crosses my mind to *ring the bell.*

Over my sixteen years of working in my home community, I have seen countless individuals come to our historic community, excited — wanting to help, and willing to engage their expertise and resources. But when those individuals arrive with such enthusiasm, only to be assaulted by distrust and opposition to whatever they want to bring to the table, I've seen these investors and developers grow weary and discouraged. They stand themselves up before our community leaders and politicians, for a time, to explain their good, viable strategies. But before long, they ring the bell, and they simply head elsewhere.

I yearn to make a difference. Yet, there have been times when ringing the bell moves into my spirit as well. In my mind, summations of giving up threaten to surface and take up space. It's because of the constant, unexplainable opposition I'm faced with from segments of the community. My frustration derives from my natural inclination not to deal with repeated stabs in the back, especially when those—key community leaders and some elected officials—fear that economic equality for all will take something away from them. And this represents a distrust of another kind—infighting. I wish to have no part of it.

Dealing with individuals who want to be in charge and run everything that happens in our community—causing its detriment—gives me an urge to ring the bell. But I am unlike those business-savvy do-gooders who have crossed my path—the ones who could see this as a solid investment—but leave because it just gets too hard. I have skin, and love, in this game.

With all that said, I just experienced a bell-ringing urge yesterday. May 11, 2019, was the anniversary of my mom's birth. Part of the day, while working at The Bakery, she was heavily on my mind. I thought of how she would feel about what I was doing. How she, if she were here, today, would spend her spare time helping me out in the kitchen and performing small duties, whatever she could still manage. As I am writing this and reflecting on her, the tears are forming. And it's getting difficult to see the computer screen through them. You see, regardless of the decisions she made, good or bad, she was always proud of me. I often overheard her brag about something I did for her sisters, friends, and other family members. She shared how I had prepared breakfast for her or took care of my siblings while enjoying her outings, which could last a couple of days. I love, miss, and thank her for creating the man I have become. Well, enough reflection, let me dry my eyes and continue with the present time.

Yesterday, I attended the meeting with Lady Brion. Brion Gill (Lady Brion is her stage name), mentioned earlier, is the young lady who's heading up the initiative, leading the charge to transform The Pennsylvania Corridor into an arts and entertainment district. Community leaders, including Councilman Leon Pinkett, were also a part of that meeting to discuss the application that she submitted to the State to designate Pennsylvania Avenue as the Black Arts and Entertainment District. The meeting was held at The Arch Social Club. Van Anderson, its president, was the host for the meeting. I decided to drive up from The Bakery, four blocks away. The meeting started at 5:00 p.m. The Bakery closed at 4:00 p.m., Brandon and I were cleaning up for the week since we were closing on Sunday for Mother's Day.

When I pulled up to park on North Avenue, I noticed Wanda Best getting out of her car in front of me. As she walked beyond my vehicle, I waved, and thought she would stop, so we could walk over to the Arch Social, together—through the layers of men, young teens, strung-out women, and substance abuse salesmen advertising their products, making themselves available to their clientele—along Pennsylvania Avenue. But that was not the case. Wanda walked ahead of me as if I wasn't there and as if she wanted nothing to do with me.

Walking into The Arch Social Club always summons the continuous vibe of African American legacy. The feel is thick and rich, like a thick, cold chocolate milkshake, one that you not only have to give an extra pull to get at but also because you want to. And you can't wait for that first taste of undeniable flavor. The very ambiance of The Arch announces pride. Its existence is intended to be that way and to go on that way. Coming into its main space bathes one in warm multicolored lighting, much of which looms over its huge bar area. Its chairs and tables, which show their age, also give a hint to the stories that only they could tell—if that were possible. There'd be tales of flashy parties, wedding receptions, retirement parties, and the coming-out parties of politicians. Those seasoned tables and chairs would also have stories to tell about neighborhood civic meetings like the one I'm waiting for right now. All of this is visited by the ghosts of celebrities, crowning our past as well as our present and our future. Today, walking into The Arch Social Club foreshadows the stories to come and the chapters destined to be written into this community's ledger.

We entered The Arch, and I sat in the bar area on a stool next to Councilman Leon Pinkett. It happened to be on the opposite side of where Wanda was sitting. Van Anderson was busy preparing seating for us in the hall area where they would later host a Mother's Day event that evening. When we filed into the meeting room, I sat next to Wanda.

Lady Brion indicated that the state required the Arts and Entertainment District to be housed, or perhaps a better term is, that it must be placed under a community 501(c)(3). There were two entities available: Druid Heights, represented by Tony Pressley; and Upton, represented by Wanda Best. Tony felt as though Druid Heights had too much on the table to take on the responsibility of the Arts and Entertainment District. At this point, Wanda Best volunteered Upton as the entity to temporarily house the Arts and Entertainment District.

I was the only Upton board member there, so I leaned over to Wanda and whispered, "Do we have to get board approval before making this commitment?"

Her response was a brisk, "No. I can make the decision."

We left the meeting, and I walked out with her. To be honest, it took some maneuvering to make it look like a congenial tag-along and a casual impromptu. With the flying white elephant circling over our heads, she tried to ignore my presence, first; then worked to create a conversation with Annie Hall, President of the Penn/North Community association, who also was in tow. Annie was walking with us because Wanda was giving her a ride home. Annie doesn't drive. When I got an opening, I asked Wanda, "When are we going to meet?"

"We will meet after Darroll Cribb returns."

Reaching my truck, stunned over the day's events, and dismayed over the backdrop of community despair, I said to myself, "Why am I dealing with this conflict, rejection, and total disrespect when Brenda and I could be traveling, playing golf, and enjoying our life as Snowbirds? Why, am I here, subjecting myself to this?" Those were rhetorical questions.

The question might also be asked: What has driven Wanda to this point? Her attitude and behavior stem from me reaching out to meet with our Board President, Darroll Cribb. At the same time, the president of The Marble Hill Association had submitted a letter to Darroll, asking him to call a special meeting of the Upton Board. He also gave Wanda a copy of the letter as well, and he emailed a copy of the letter to the entire board. So, it wasn't lost on me that Wanda's curt quip resulted from her still being upset about me, and another Upton board member, named Atiba Nkrumah, also going over her head to ask Darroll to call a meeting. But frankly, my thought in the moment was, *what were we to do?* The Upton Association had been turning into a Wanda monarchy. It was at this point when I was all-but-sure that I was about to *Ring the Bell.*

This, I believe, is very difficult for Wanda because she is used to doing things/running things her way without opposition of any kind. In a way, I understand her not wanting to meet at this point; she is supposed to pursue the board's wishes, although she does not operate in that way. Now that there are some questions from board members that must be resolved, she finds herself in an egotistical, even

Trump-like, quandary. However, we would not be at this juncture had we been able to meet and discuss things openly as respectful adults.

I hate conflict. But feel that I have to do something to resolve the issue that has created a feeling of distrust. As I've mentioned, it has materialized in various forms. This problem must be tackled and resolved so that we can all move forward as a unit to bring great outcomes to our community. I feel that the folks who oppose me fear that I'm trying to take over. But I am not taking over. The overall goal is just too big to allow anyone to take over because its completion requires the work of many hands. I'm trying to bring resources and help. And though I can clearly see this as an uphill obstacle course—perhaps much like those Navy SEALs that Colonel William McRaven talked about, I am somewhat optimistic. I'm also hopeful, at this writing, that Darroll and the rest of the board members will not be intimidated by the monarchy Wanda has created.

Wanda has done great things for Upton, and at her core, she is a good person, but that doesn't mean that our executive director should have the final word on what happens in our community. I am not sure what is going to happen at this point. It's a wait-and-see outcome. In the past, those who have had expressed opposition have been removed from the board, even in the slightest of ways.

I am in the process of crafting a letter to Wanda and will send it to her home. The letter will reflect on our past relationship, prior to the former Mayor Catherine Pugh's divisive message, action, and influence on the community. It is so sad that we allow politicians to control us. That is not their function. My letter is positive, and I'm hopeful it can heal us. Writing this memoir and revealing the inner workings of our community is very difficult. I don't like sharing our shortcomings. However, to make a change for the better, we all need to understand our problems. We all need to learn to trust one another and strive to be trustworthy. We also need to be open-minded enough to discuss and repair our relationships positively. I have hope.

The way things are going … things are moving so fast. And it's getting to the point where there's a lot of homework, and background work that I've gotta get done. Since Mayor Pugh has kind of moved out of our way, to a degree, now I've got to go back to reinstate the commitments from the community that she pulled away. With that being said, I have a letter of support from Councilman Jack Young. Once I get the community's support, meaning Wanda Best and Jules Dunham, and if I get a support letter from Upton, then I'll have to go back to my politicians and start fresh. Because Jack Young was the city council's president. Now he's the mayor.

On May 6, 2019, the new president of the Baltimore City Council, Brandon Scott, was just sworn in. I have met him once. So, I have to get a letter of support from him as well. I have to reach out to him, get him up to speed, and educate him on what I'm trying to accomplish. Then I'll have to go to the councilmen for the District, who are Eric Costello and Councilman Leon Pinkett, to get their letters of support. Once I have that, I can start moving with some of the developers and some of the investors who have come along to support or want to support. I'm hoping to get all the ducks in a row in the project. Also, with TRTCHC's board of directors, there's a couple of people who may be willing to join the board who can also bring resources to the table.

CHAPTER SIXTEEN

HAPPY MOTHER'S DAY AND DISCOVERIES

Today is Sunday, May 14, 1995. As everyone knows, it's Mother's Day. I have so many mixed emotions and feelings. The love I have for my mother is solid, but it is so difficult for me to drain my heart of the hurtful childhood memories of a fractured family. Sometimes they hover above my good intentions as a dutiful son. To manage, I call up the fact that my siblings and I have loved one another throughout. So today, I did all the expected things with Brenda's help. Mom had the gift cards and breakfast in bed and the loving greeting I worked to give.

From her expression of thanks, I know she was happy and enjoyed her day. But as hard as I try to forget those tough times as a child, they regurgitate in my mind. When she looks at me, I suspect she has no idea what is going through my head. I am doing my best to take care of her. Sometimes I study her face, now aged and innocent-looking, and what I see are scenes of me being the oldest person in the house. Figuratively, of course. I recall visions of having to take care of four or five kids, not knowing if or when my mother was coming home. That anxiety still resides in me. Having my mother tell me on a Friday that she is going to the market and would be back in a few hours, only to have those hours turn into days; well, it's hard to settle even at forty-seven years of age. Being told to clean the house and the kids, which I did. And being told to get myself dressed, so that we could all go to a movie—only not to see her, again, for three days—well, the disappointment and fear that perhaps, my life was going to change dramatically, which it often did, due to some unseen mishap—couldn't just let me enjoy a movie. That childhood fear is baked into my brain.

I keep thinking to myself, *forget about the past. Live for now; that's what counts.* Are we products of our past? What we are today is a total sum of our life experiences, be it positive or negative. It's a collection reel of both. Our life experiences can bring out of us the good or the bad. Hopefully, we can control our choices to choose good outlooks and behaviors over bad. But I'm sharing because I want you to understand why I have mind explosions.

Life was hardly peaceful with the conflict hovering in the atmosphere between my mother and my cousin, Irene, who was around the same age as my mom. Added to that would be the battles between Irene and Phil. I would sometimes think to myself, I *will never allow someone to treat me like this.* When our time with Irene and Phil ended abruptly. Due to one of their blowups, we moved into a second or third-floor apartment on West Fayette Street. It must have been after school was out because I don't remember traveling to school from there. Or it could have been one of those times in my life when my mom was slow to register me for school. What I do remember is looking out the window all the time, waiting for my mom to return from her nights out. These were also the days I spent looking out for Tony and Ricky.

We didn't stay there too long. My mother didn't like this area of the city. I think I remember seeing my sister, Gertrude, when we lived here. Mother Hamlin lived somewhere near West Fayette Street. Little did I realize that my father, whom I seldom saw, lived in the area, too.

Our next move was to an apartment on Argyle Avenue and Hoffman Street. This was on the second floor, below where my Aunt Doris and Uncle Smiley lived. This was a pleasant move for us because our Aunt Doris was a very loving person, and she was fun to be around.

Evidently, the relationship between Mr. James Crawford and my mother had taken a serious turn because she became pregnant with my sister, Sandra. Eldora, fathered by Mr. Zeke, was the baby at this time. They are eleven months apart.

As you may gather, he moved in with us. As much as I wanted a father figure, I refused to call him "dad," but I always showed him respect. We—those of us who were not his—called him Mr. James. And though we did, he still treated us, okay, and he never hit or punished us. My mother did that. Life, there on Argyle Avenue, was somewhat stable. Little did I know that would be as close as I would ever get to what many refer to as a family unit.

Maybe I have the wrong idea of what a family consists of. Certainly, today's family units can be a lot different than the traditional norm thought of in those days. The family that I dreamed of was owning a dad and a mom living together with their children in a home possessive of a peaceful and loving atmosphere. The children would enjoy a feeling of comfort and security, and stability. While I understood the premise of chores, I must have been doing a lot of hallucinating to believe I would ever be able to fill most of my day playing outside with other children. Gazing out our apartment's front window, looking at other children, I kept hope alive. But little did I know this dream of mine would never come true for me. I am a happy man, though, because I was able to provide that atmosphere for my own children.

Enough of feeling sorry for myself. Let me get back to this story. Living at this address was quite interesting, at least to me. I started up again at an elementary school on Argyle Avenue, Harriet Beecher Stowe Public School. I also remember transferring to a school on the corner of Pennsylvania Avenue and Dolphin Street. I think it was school number 125. I remember it was next door to the police station.

I remember some of the students who were in my class. The first person to come to mind was James McKinney. He was a light-skinned kid with what we called, back then, *good hair*. He lived further down Argyle Avenue and had two or three sisters. One of his sisters was a little older than we were, but I had a crush on her. I would have dreams about kissing her and *doing a little bit*. That's what we called whatever we thought having sex meant, which wasn't a clearly developed thought at all.

He and I used to play together. Sometimes, he used to visit my house. Sometimes, I'd visit his house. It was not often that I got the freedom to do so. But it was nice when I did. We used to have our little cowboy and Indian figurines to play with. It seemed to me he had the best family because he and his sisters all had the same last name, and they looked like brothers and sisters. They also had their mother and father living with them. He also had more neat toys than what I had. The only toy I had better than his was my Colt 45 toy gun. It was big and had a barrel that could be taken out.

The next person I remember is Reginald Everett. He was a big kid who looked like he should have been in junior high school. His legs didn't fit under the school desk very well. Reginald had something wrong with one of his eyes. It looked like it was cloudy. I think he could only see out of one of them. I will always remember when he told the teacher something that I shouldn't have done. It taught me never to trust him to keep a secret. And, quite frankly, that's how I am today. I trust you until I can't anymore.

For some reason, I was very aware of my body and all the things my body parts could do. One day, bored with whatever the teacher was talking about, I realized I had a hole in my right pants pocket. I then realized I could reach into my pocket and pull my penis up through my pocket. Well, this was a fantastic discovery for me. I was so excited that I could do this; I just had to share it with someone. So, I whispered to Reginald, "Do you want to see what I got in my pocket?"

The first thing he said was, "No." But curiosity soon got the best of him.

When I showed Reginald what I had in my pocket because he didn't have two good eyes, he couldn't make it out at first. But when he did, he immediately shot his hand in the air and told the teacher what I had done.

She called me up to the front of the class and asked, "James, did you really do what Reginald said you did?"

With the class staring and salivating due to the drama, I lied. "No." And I burst into tears. I never cried so hard in my life. Well, that was a lesson learned. Be careful, who you trust with revelations.

At home, life with Mr. James as my stepfather constituted a roller coaster ride. I could not figure out why he and my mom were together. Part of it was that he was her knight in shining armor, saving her when Mr. Zeke was not able to. The other reason was that she gave birth to my sister, Sandra, his first child.

James Hamlin delivers United Way documents to United Way of Central Maryland.

The Avenue Bakery being constructed, 2011.

The Avenue Bakery on the Pennsylvania Avenue Corridor, opens, 2011.

The photomontage of theaters that once existed on Pennsylvania Avenue in West Baltimore is unveiled by the mural's creator Graphic Artist and Historian Stuart Hudgins in The Avenue Bakery Courtyard, 2014.

The Civil Rights Photomontage is unveiled in The Avenue Bakery Courtyard, 2014.

Dignitaries enjoy The Civil Rights Photomontage celebration, 2014: Left to Right: Wanda Best, Baltimore's Former State Delegate Keith Haynes and State Senator Barbara Robinson, James Hamlin, Stuart Hudgins and a State Representative.

James Hamlin teaches his grandson, 14-year-old LJ (Little James) Hamlin, the bakery business.

***The Royal Theater & Community Heritage Corporation* (TRTCHC) Founding Board Members, Left to Right: Adrian Johnson, VP of MECU; George Gilliam, Ex. Dir. Of PARC; Tom A. Kiefaber, owner of the Senator Theater; Alice Cole, TRTCHC Board Secretary; Charles Sydnor, attorney; Arthur Varnado, VP at T. Rowe Price; The late Ray Haysbert, a Tuskegee Airman, member of The Baltimore Urban League and one of the founders of Park Sausage.**

TRTCHC's proposed site for the rebuild of The Royal Theater, which was its original site.

Taken in the early 2000s, Left to Right: James Hamlin, 2nd VP of Baltimore City Branch of the NAACP; Neil Duke, 1st VP of Baltimore City Branch; Kweisi Mfume, President of the National NAACP (now representing Baltimore's 7th Congressional District); G.I. Johnson, President of the Baltimore City Branch of the NAACP.

James Hamlin and Former Maryland Governor Martin O'Malley (picture was taken while still in office).

Former Mayor Stephanie Rawlings-Blake and James Hamlin's grandson Little James, a.k.a. LJ (picture was taken while still in office).

Former Baltimore City Mayor Bernard "Jack" Young and James Hamlin, 2019.

James Hamlin receives a community award from The Baltimore Times.

TRTCHC Board Member Alice Cole, James Hamlin, Baltimore City Council President, who became Baltimore City's Mayor Brandon Scott in 2020, and Ashley Crawford (Hamlin's niece), in The Avenue Bakery conference room.

During a museum exhibit unveiling at The Avenue Bakery, addressing the crowd are James Hamlin and Amy Davis, author of the *Flickering Treasures* book and original Smithsonian's National Building Museum exhibit, 2018.

James Hamlin receives a Citation from the Comptroller of Maryland Peter V. R. Franchot. Taken in front of The Avenue Bakery's Civil Rights Photomontage, 2014.

James Hamlin, Baltimore Ravens Safety and Pro Football Hall of Famer Ed Reed, and Yvonne J. Medley, editor, during the 2019 Pro Football Hall of Fame induction in Canton, Ohio.

Brenda Hamlin, James' wife, with Pro Football Hall of Famer Ed Reed in the front lobby/exhibit space of The Avenue Bakery.

James Hamlin poses with Ed Reed Foundation's Representative Glenn Younces during Ed Reed's Annual Fitness Program at Booker T. Washington Arts Academy for its middle school-age students, 2019.

Susie Dezurn, James Hamlin Jr.'s mother-in-law, and Brenda Hamlin model The Avenue Bakery's T-shirts for sale, depicting Black History themes.

James Hamlin with the late Rep. Elijah Cummings.

Roderick C. Willis and James Hamlin, co-hosting their radio program, titled, *Positive Black America Baltimore* on WOLB 1010-AM.

Essie Duke Hamlin, known as Mother Hamlin, James Hamlin's paternal grandmother.

James Hamlin's father, James Willie Hamlin, posing in his military uniform. He served in the Army Transportation Corps in World War II.

James Hamlin's father, James Willie Hamlin sharply dressed in New York.

Some of James Hamlin's siblings: (Top: Left to Right) Carl and Harold; (Bottom Left to Right) Sandra, and Marlene who died of Sickle Cell at 8 years old.

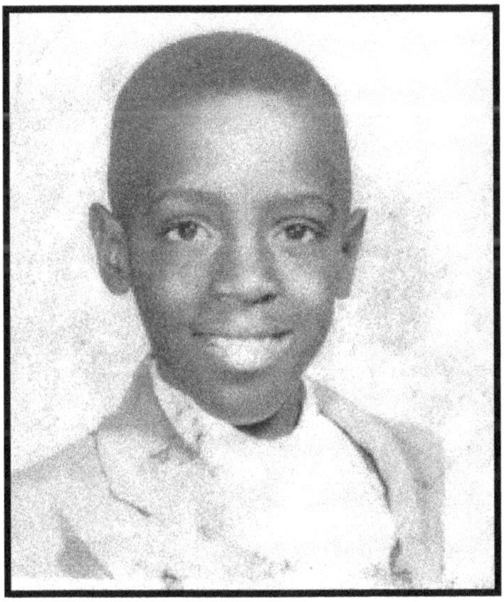

James Hamlin at age 10.

James Hamlin's ninth grade class at West Baltimore's Booker T. Washington Junior High School (renamed Booker T. Washington Arts Academy).

James Hamlin's yearbook picture, Baltimore's Edmondson High School, 1968.

Man wearing the hat is Jerome Clemons, a.k.a. Uncle Johnny, talking to a friend. He's Hamlin's Favorite uncle.

James and Brenda Hamlin's wedding reception at the Park Heights home of Brenda's parents, July 13,1968.

James and Brenda Hamlin celebrating their 50th Wedding Anniversary at Ruth Chris Steakhouse with children: James "Ham" Hamlin, Jr. and wife, Etoy; Belinda "Lin" and husband, Blair, 2018.

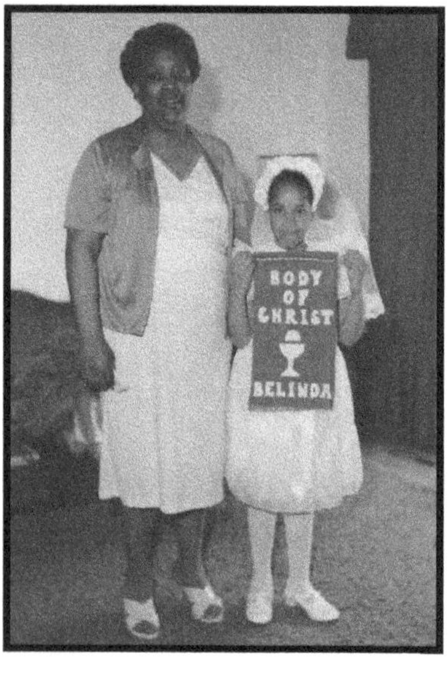

James Hamlin's mother, Mattie Virginia Clemons Waymon, and her granddaughter Lin Hamlin.

Lin, Grandmother Mattie and James Hamlin, Jr. in 1984.

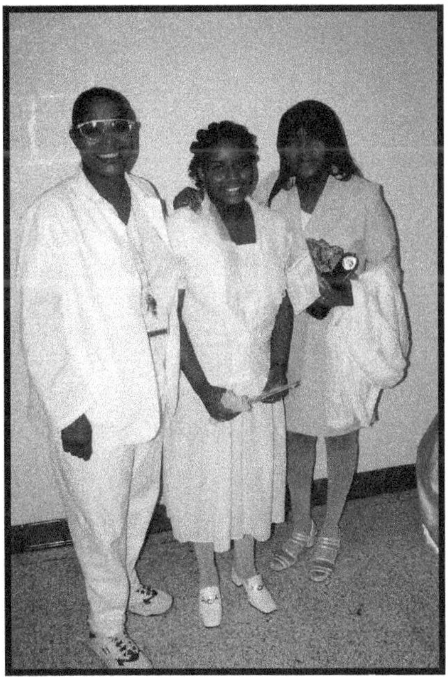

James Hamlin's sister Eldora Barron, niece Ashley Crawford and Ashley's mother, Sandra, also James' sister.

James "Ham" Hamlin, Jr. enjoying his fiftieth birthday party celebration.

Oldest grandson De'Angelo "Delo" Lewis (Ham's son) and James Hamlin.

James Hamlin holding grandson, one-year-old LJ. His Aunt Lin is in the background.

James Hamlin with 10-year-old grandson Brandon Sorrell.

The Three James': Grandfather Hamlin, son Hamlin and grandson Hamlin, enjoying vacation and golf.

Three of James Hamlin's four grands: Delo, Bria, LJ and pet Miniature Pinscher, Sonic.

James and Brenda's
Junior Prom.

Bria & Grandfathers
James Hamlin and
Wallace Laster.

Hamlin and Son, James.

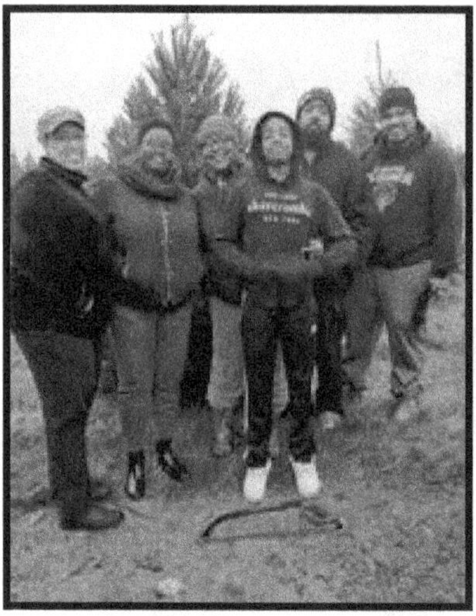

James Hamlin's daughter, Lin; granddaughter Bria; daughter-in-law, Etoy; grandson, LJ; son, Ham; and grandson, Brandon during their annual Christmas tree hunt.

Gertrude Hamlin Scott and James Hamlin, celebrating Gert's 60th Birthday in Long Island, NY. James and Gert share the same father.

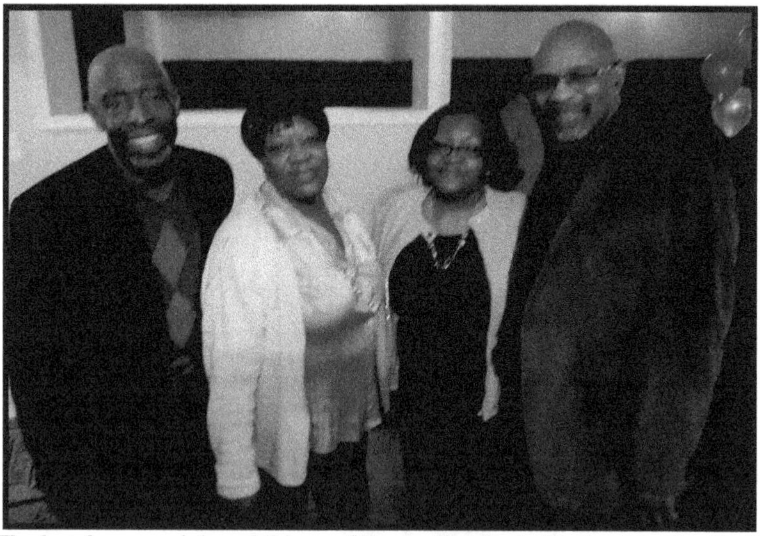

The last four surviving children of James Hamlin's Mother Mattie: (Left to Right) James, Dot, Sandra and Waymom-Theodore-Tony (all the names he likes to call himself), 2018.

Avenue Bakery Guest Book Excerpts

July 2013 - January 2019

Continental US

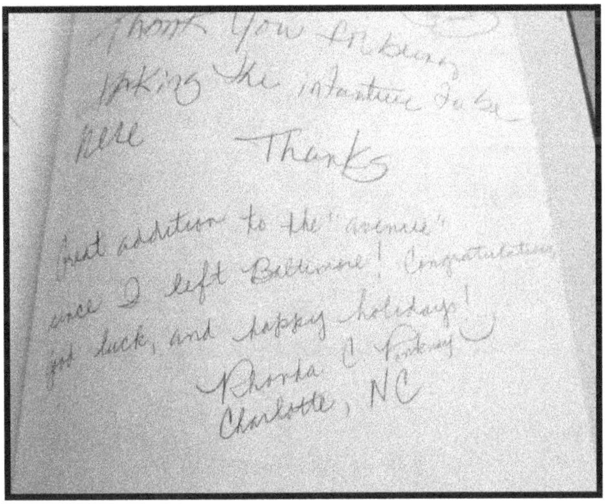

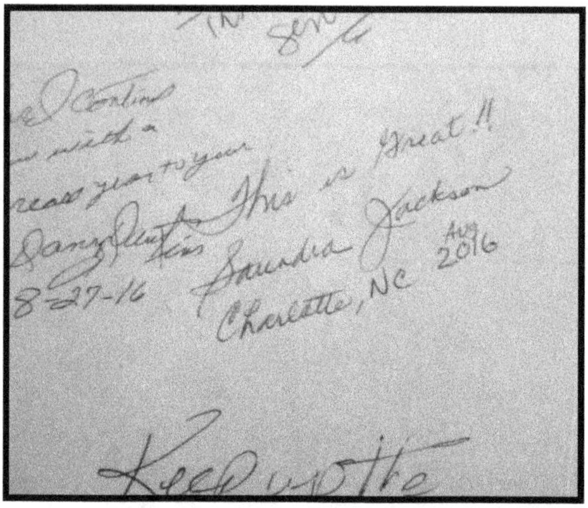
This is Great!!
Saundra Jackson
Charlotte, NC
Aug 2016
8-27-16

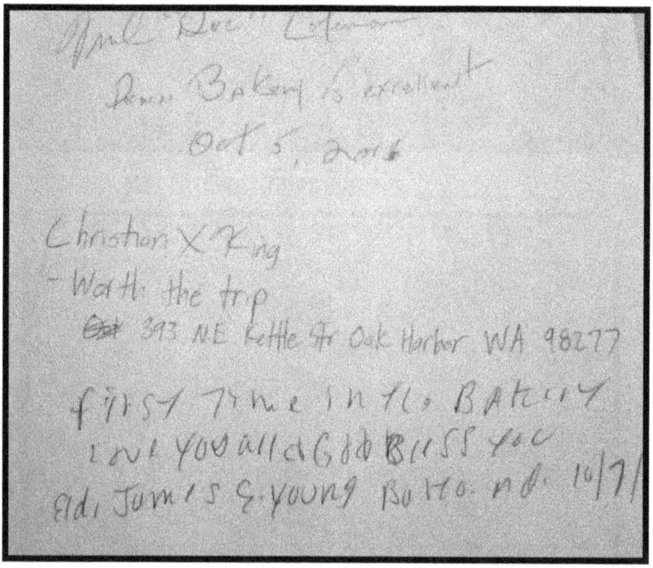
Bakery is excellent
Oct 5, 2016
Worth the trip
393 NE Kettle St Oak Harbor WA 98277
First Time in the Bakery
Love you all & God Bless you

friends & family
God Bless
You!
Brooklyn
NYC
5/27/17
B-more

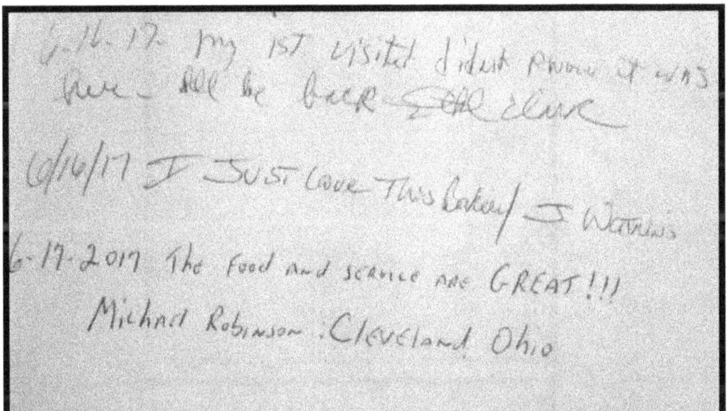
6/16/17 I JUST LOVE THIS BAKERY / J Watkins
6-17-2017 The food and service are GREAT!!!
Michael Robinson : Cleveland Ohio

Love YA!
PA 9-1-13
Christine J Brack 9-1-13
Thank God for the Baker
CJB

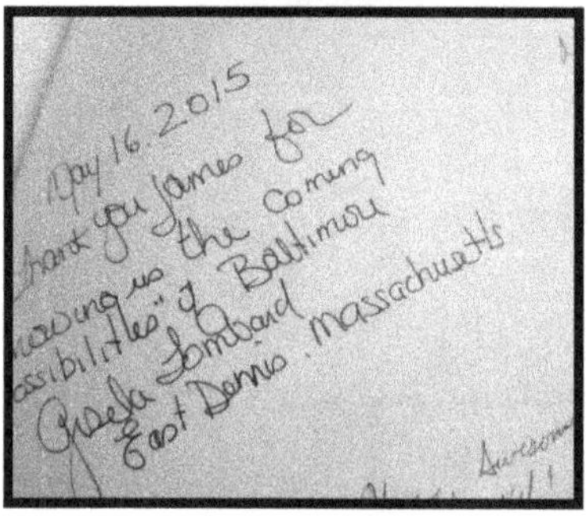
May 16, 2015
thank you James for
showing us the coming
possibilities of Baltimore
Gisela Lombard
East Dennis, Massachusetts

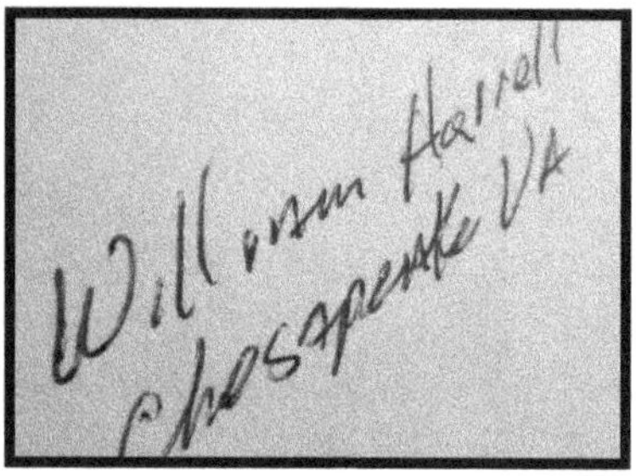
William Harrell
Chesapeake VA

Potatoe
Pie
& Apple
Eddie Campbell
Fort Laud., Fl. 33311

Hamilton Gobeh
Thank you

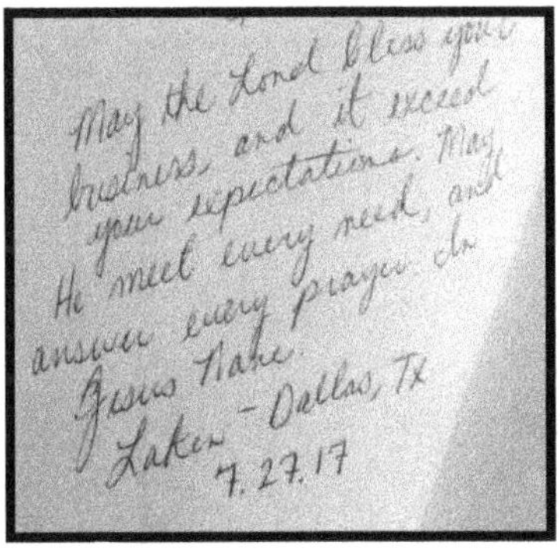
May the Lord bless your
business, and it exceed
your expectations. May
He meet every need, and
answer every prayer in
Jesus Name.
Laken - Dallas, TX
7.27.17

Best Wishes
From Catonsville MD
R Howell

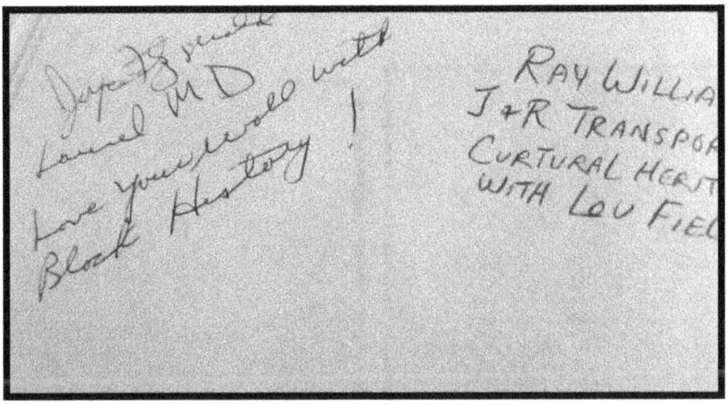
Laurel MD
Love your work with
Black History !
RAY WILLIA
J+R TRANSPOR
CURTURAL HERIT
WITH LOU FIEL

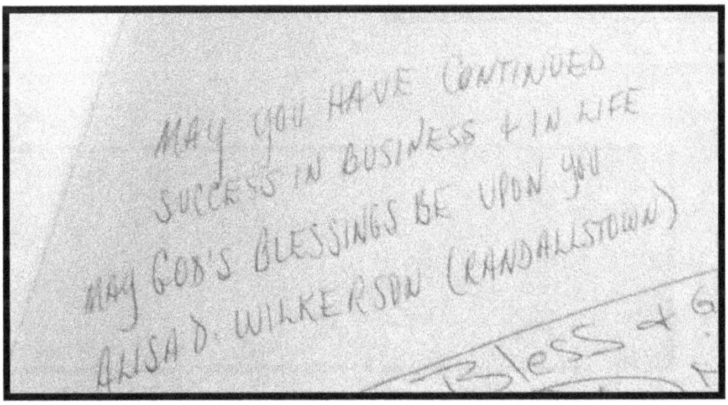
MAY YOU HAVE CONTINUED
SUCCESS IN BUSINESS + IN LIFE
MAY GOD'S BLESSINGS BE UPON YOU
ALISA D. WILKERSON (RANDALLSTOWN)

I was driving by and saw your store
Your Sweet Potato MUFFIN is WONDERFUL
Timothy Scurry
Overlea MD
Jim
Much Success!
you are great
i love your

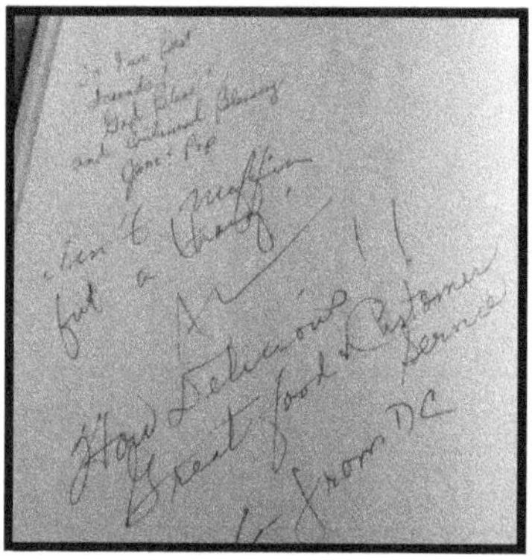
Great food & Customer Service
from DC

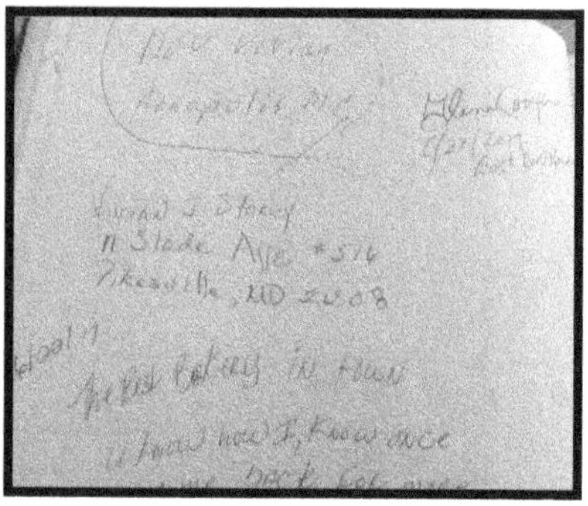
Pikesville, MD 21208

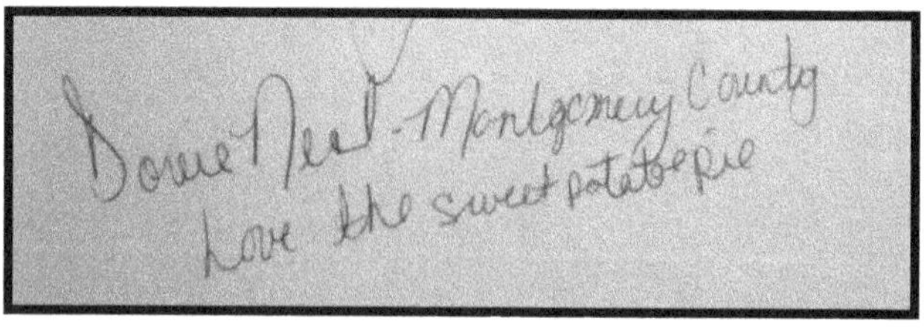
Montgomery County
Love the sweet potato pie

General Comments from Various Visitors

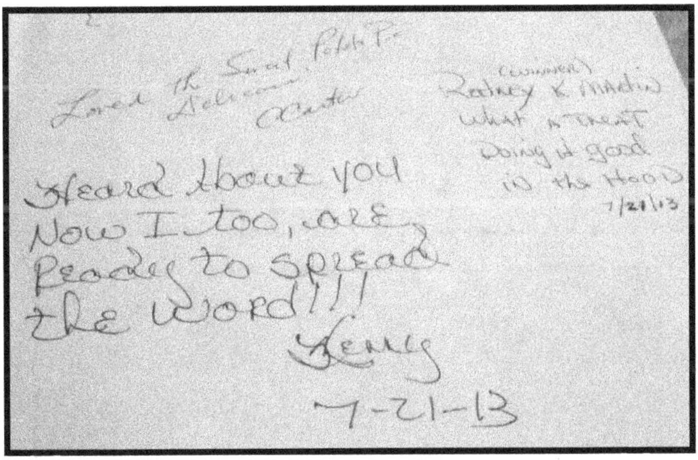

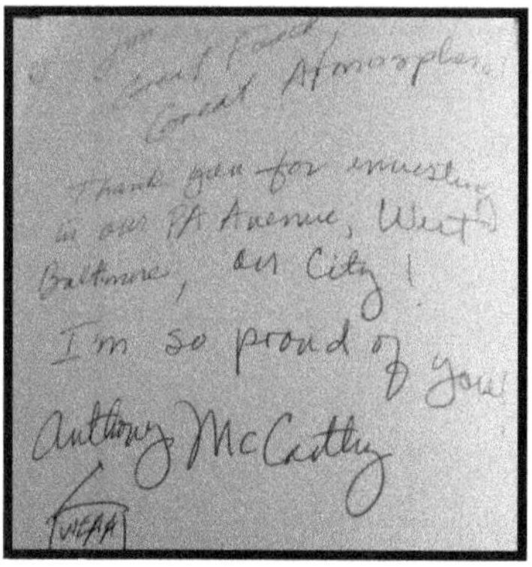
Great Atmosphere
Thank you for investing in our PA Avenue, West Baltimore, our City!
I'm so proud of you!
Anthony McCarthy

Peter Franchot
comptroller
State of Maryland
7/14/14

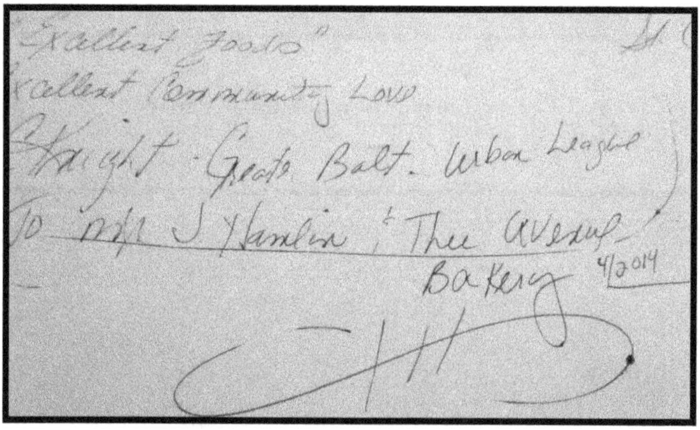
"Excellent Foods"
Excellent Community Love
Greater Balt. Urban League
To Mr J Hamlin, Thee Avenue Bakery
4/2014

RAY WILLIAMS
J+R TRANSPORTATION SERVICE
CURTURAL HERITAGE TOUR
WITH LOU FIELDS 11/7/14

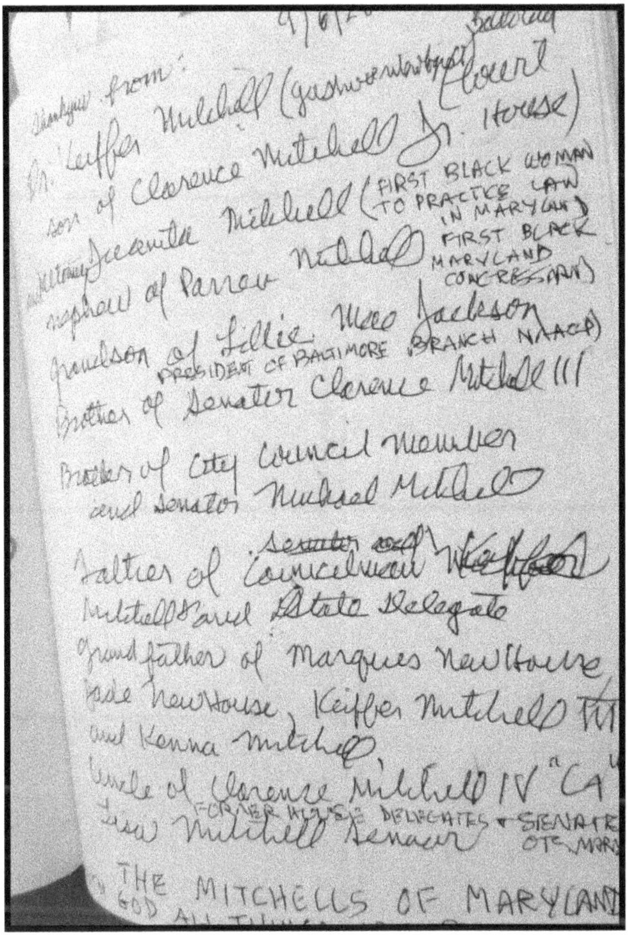
Thankyou from:
Dr. Keiffer Mitchell
son of Clarence Mitchell Jr.
Juanita Mitchell (FIRST BLACK WOMAN TO PRACTICE LAW IN MARYLAND)
nephew of Parren Mitchell FIRST BLACK MARYLAND CONGRESSMAN
grandson of Lillie Mae Jackson
PRESIDENT OF BALTIMORE BRANCH NAACP
Brother of Senator Clarence Mitchell III
Brother of City Council member and Senator Michael Mitchell
Father of Councilman
Mitchell and State Delegate
Grandfather of Marques NewHouse
Jade NewHouse, Keiffer Mitchell
and Kenna Mitchell,
Uncle of Clarence Mitchell IV
Lisa Mitchell
FORMER HOUSE DELEGATES + SENATOR
THE MITCHELLS OF MARYLAND

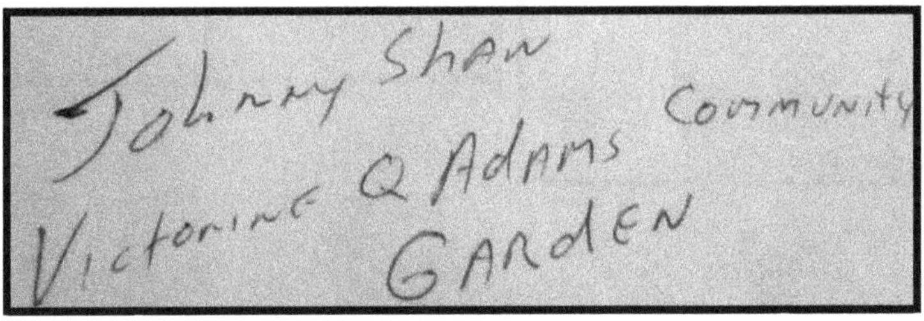
Johnny Shaw
Community
Victorine Q Adams
GARDEN

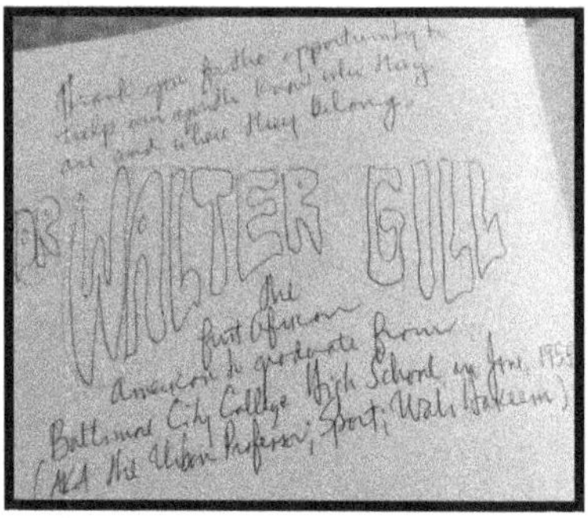
WALTER GILL

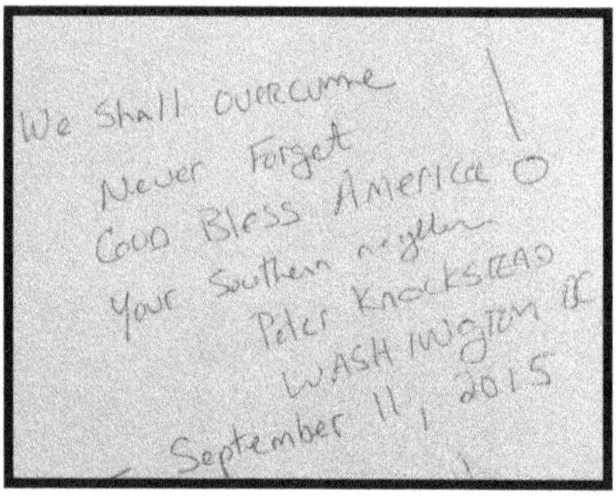
We Shall Overcome
Never Forget
God Bless America
Your Southern neighbor
Washington DC
September 11, 2015

Good Morning
Very very nice place.

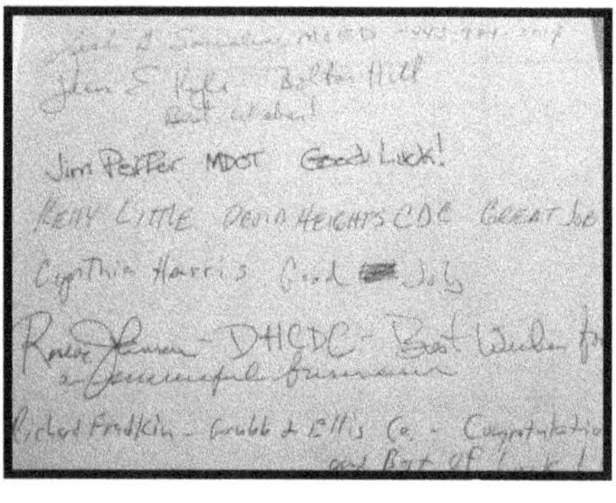
Jim Peffer MDOT Good Luck!
Cynthia Harris Good Job

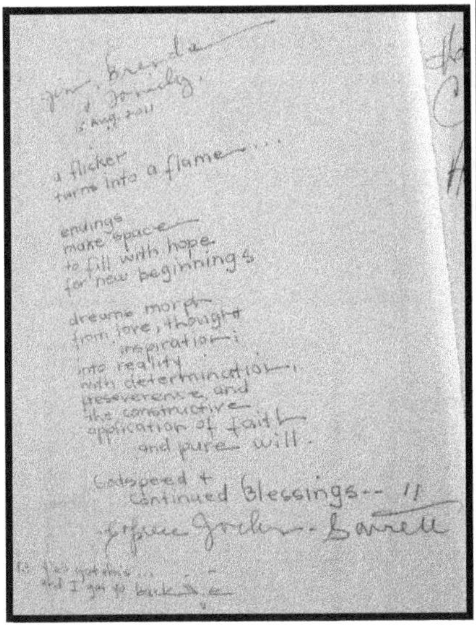
a flicker
turns into a flame...
endings
make space
to fill with hope
for new beginnings
dreams morph
from love, thought
inspiration
into reality
with determination,
perseverance and
the constructive
application of faith
and pure will.
Godspeed +
Continued Blessings -- !!

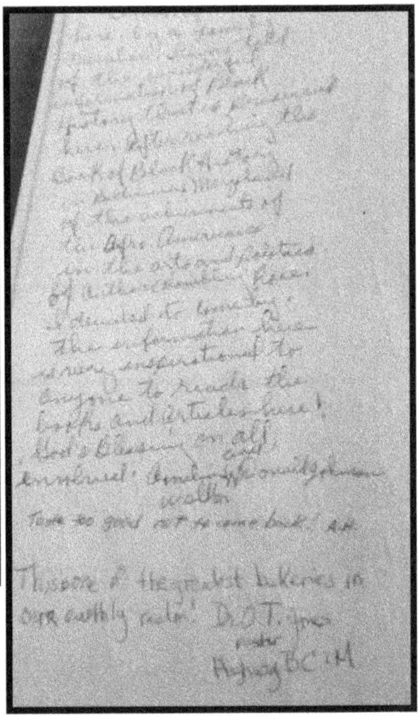
The information here
is very inspirational to
anyone to reads the
books and articles here!
God's Blessing on all
involved!
This one of the greatest bakeries in
our earthly realm!

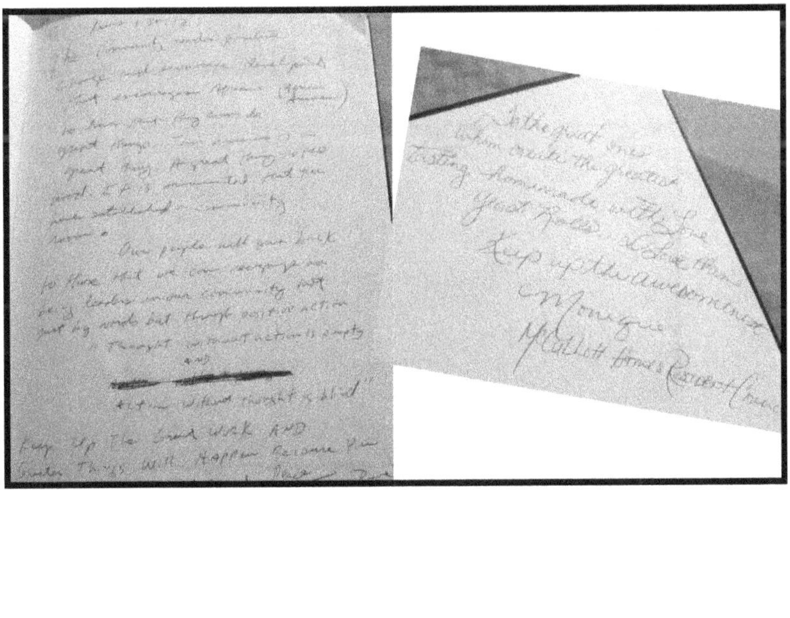
Keep Up The Good Work AND
Greater Things Will Happen
To the great ones
who create the greatest
tasting homemade with love
Yeast Rolls.
Keep up the awesomeness
Monique

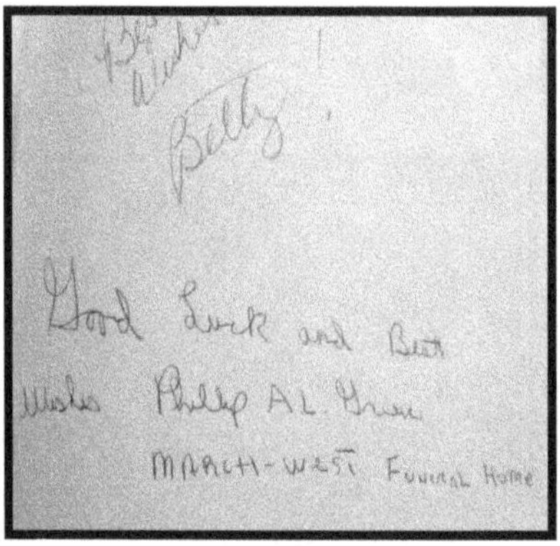
Good Luck and Best
MARCH-WEST Funeral Home

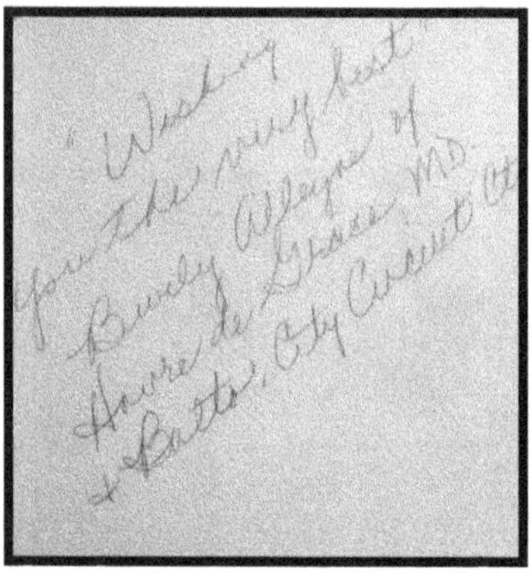
"Wishing you the very best

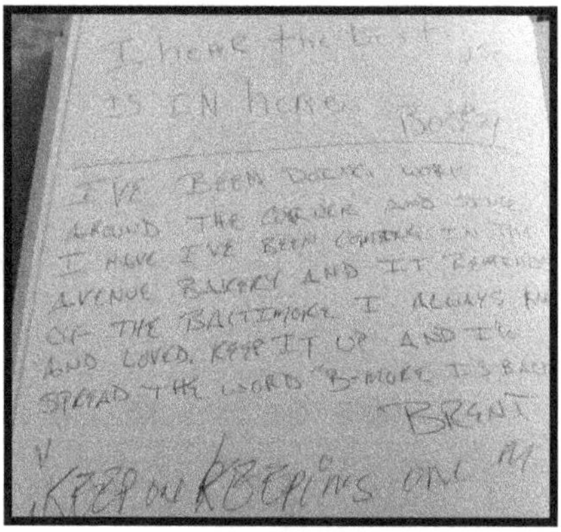
I hear the best
Keep on

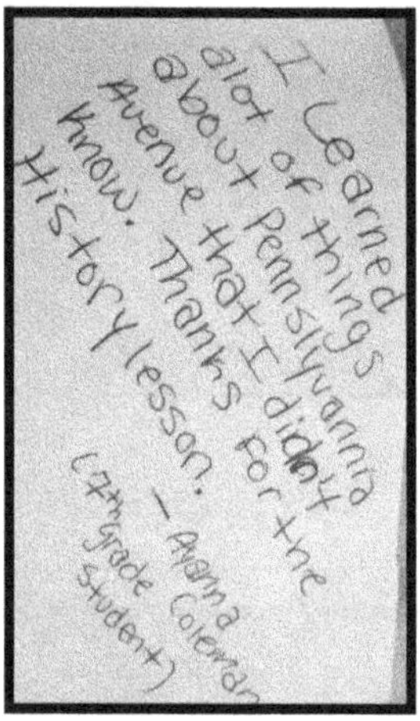
I Learned alot of things about Pennsylvania Avenue that I didn't know. Thanks for the History lesson.
(7th Grade Student)

I am so proud of you! I stopped to experience the vision!
Greatness at its BEST!
Thanks for being an inspiration.
Principal, Booker T. Washington MS

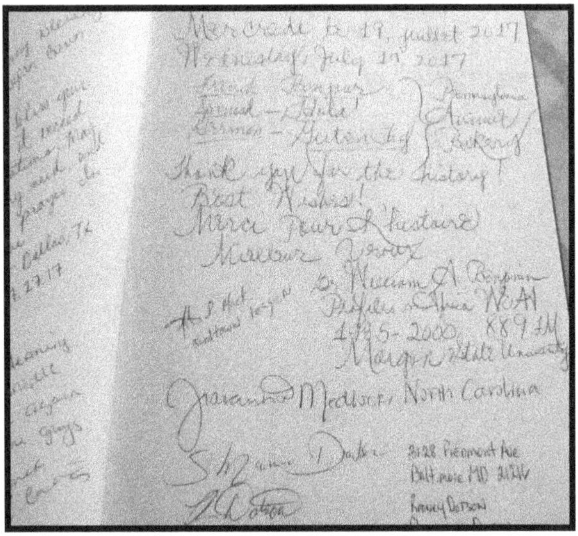
Mercredi le 19, juillet 2017
Wednesday, July 19 2017
Thank you for the history!
Best Wishes!
Merci Pour L'histoire
Meilleurs Voeux
North Carolina
3128 Piedmont Ave
Baltimore MD 21216

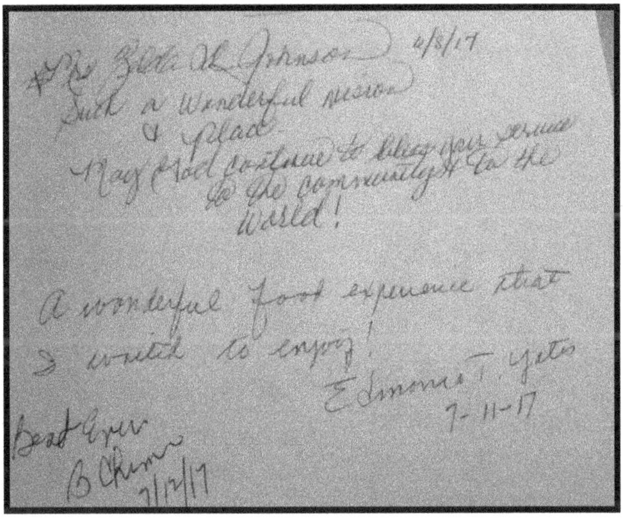
6/8/17
Such a Wonderful mission
& place
to the community & to the
World!
Edmond T. Yates
7-11-17
Best Ever
7/12/17

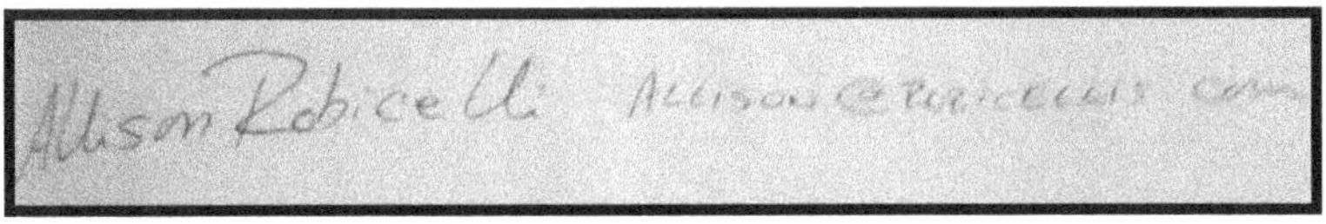
Allison Robicelli

Church Visitors

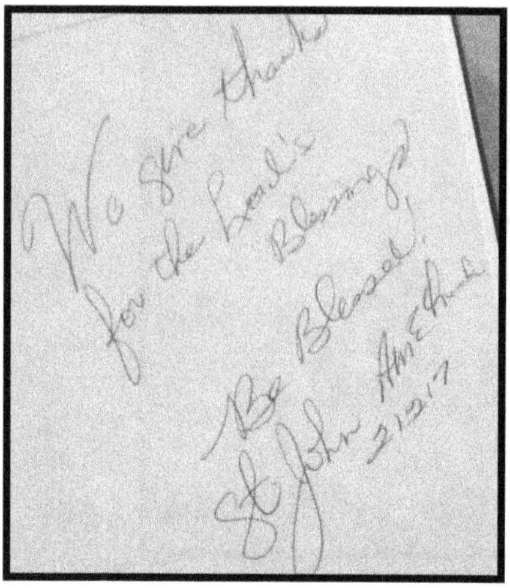
We give thanks
for the Lord's
Blessings!
Be Blessed!
St John AME Church
3/12/17

God Bless U all
from Kings Deliverance
Holiness Church 1200 N.
Fulton ave. 410-728-8040
Bishop John Jones

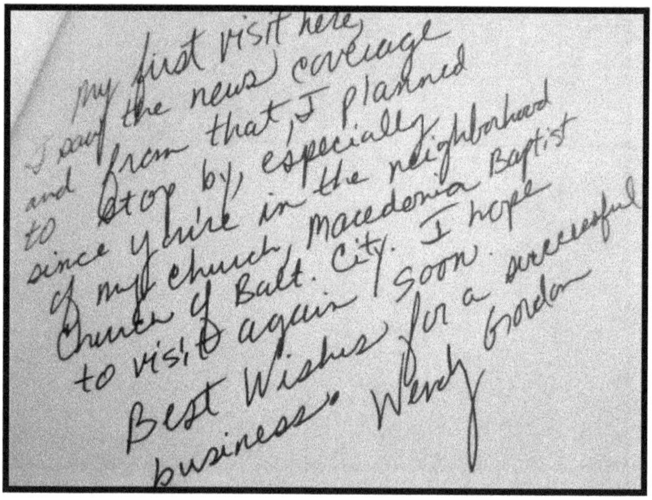
My first visit here.
I saw the news coverage
and from that, I planned
to stop by, especially
since you're in the neighborhood
of my church, Macedonia Baptist
Church of Balt. City. I hope
to visit again soon.
Best Wishes for a successful
business. Wendy Gordon

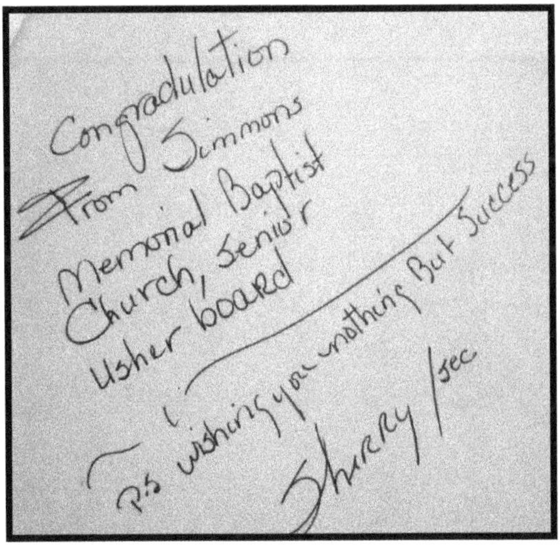

Congradulation
From Simmons
Memorial Baptist
Church, Senior
Usher board
P.S. wishing you nothing But Success
Sharry /sec

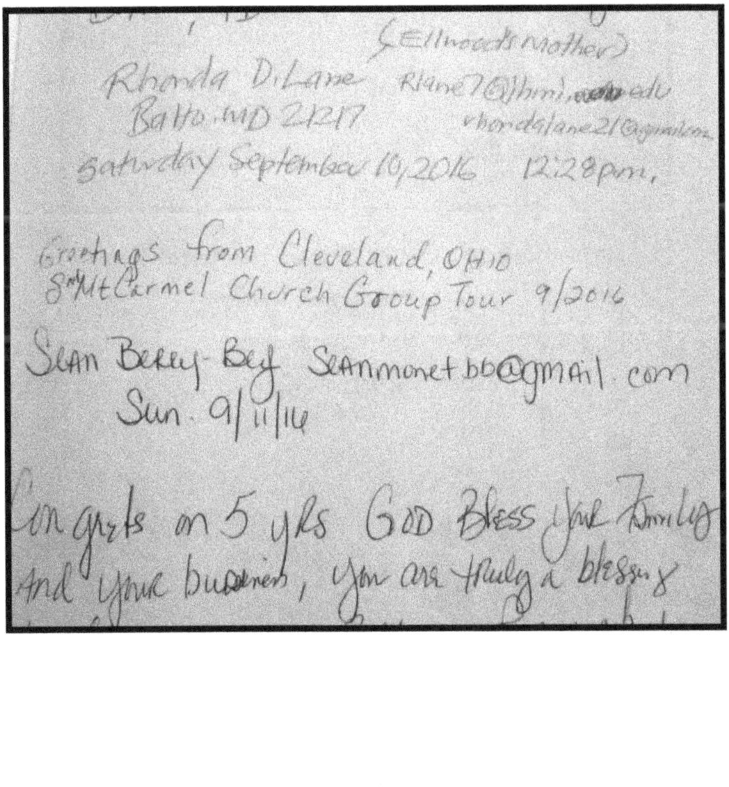

(Ellwood's mother)
Rhonda DiLane rlane7@jhmi.edu
Balto.MD 21217 rhondalane21@gmail.com
Saturday September 10, 2016 12:28pm.

Greetings from Cleveland, OHIO
St Mt Carmel Church Group Tour 9/2016

Sean Berry-Bey Seanmonetbb@gmail.com
Sun. 9/11/16

Congrats on 5 yrs GOD Bless your Family
and your business, you are truly a blessing

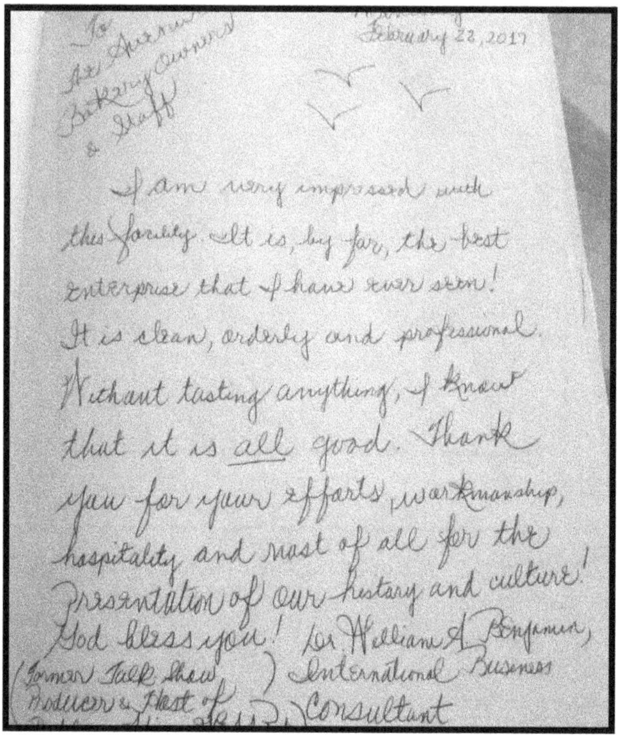

To
The Avenue
Bakery Owners
& Staff

February 22, 2017

I am very impressed with this facility. It is, by far, the best enterprise that I have ever seen! It is clean, orderly and professional. Without tasting anything, I know that it is all good. Thank you for your efforts, workmanship, hospitality and most of all for the presentation of our history and culture! God bless you! Dr. William A. Benjamin, International Business Consultant

(Former Talk Show Producer & Host of

Stop in to visit the TRTCHC Garden and Mini Museum

Located at the Avenue Bakery

2229 Pennsylvania Avenue

Baltimore, Maryland 21217

CHAPTER SEVENTEEN

TESTICULAR FORTITUDE IS GENDER NEUTRAL

It's **Tuesday, May 7, 2019**. I had a long day yesterday. I went to bed late but still couldn't sleep all night. So here I am, at 3:56 in the morning, and my mind is busy. It appears that things are moving rather fast at this point with the TRTCHC project, and I know I must keep up with everything.

Last Friday, May 3, I attended the Upton developers meeting for a couple of reasons. I wanted to get familiar with the developers coming to the table and familiarize myself with those graced with the approval of Wanda and Jules. I also wanted to schedule a meeting with them to discuss getting their support for The Royal Theater and Community Heritage Center Project—now that Catherine Pugh has resigned. We were supposed to have met before I went on vacation, but she put it off until after I returned. This was my first opportunity to touch bases since returning from my vacation.

The meeting had already started, and Wanda waved me upfront to sit next to her. I cautiously did so. I listened to the individual who had been approved by Upton and the City to rehab the 800 blocks of

Harlem and Edmondson Avenues. There had been a press event, featuring the new Mayor Jack Young, a couple of days past. While sitting next to her, I leaned over and mentioned to Wanda, "I have people coming to me who want to support the project. And I need the approval of Upton."

Her comeback was, "There's people coming to Upton as well." She also acknowledged, "The project makes contributions to the community."

Surprised to hear her plug, at least privately in our whispers to one another, I reminded her that, "The first phase of the project of roughly ten million dollars is an upfront contribution."

Acknowledging that, too, she said, "I'll schedule the meeting this week. Please just don't," she added, "meet with the City before we meet."

I didn't ask why; however, that feeling of distrust and a current of under-handed activity was either afoot or on the way. Still, I nodded my compliance.

While at the meeting, Mrs. Christine Blake of Christ Temple Church approached me with questions about the rehab of The Lenox Theater, of which their church has been a part for more than twenty years. It's also the last of the theater sites on Pennsylvania Avenue. The church no longer holds services in the building but recently received a grant to stabilize its structure. Since the pastor of the Church passed away, the building has decayed. Christine's question was whether or not she needed insurance on the building before she has a contractor come in and do the work on the building. She said, "I've received conflicting information, and I wanted to get some clarity."

I gave my opinion and mentioned that, "My insurance agent, Tony Ambush, could advise you. He'll be at our Jazz event on Saturday." The Jazz event, which was the first in The Avenue Bakery's 2019 Jazz series, was scheduled to take place on May 4. But she indicated she could not make the event and asked if I would connect them. I had her write her contact information on a piece of paper, and I stuck it in my pocket.

Saturday, May 4, 2019, I was running around greeting people and making sure the concert was running well. I met quite a few new people, and I touched bases with the folks who always come to our events. There was this heavy-set White lady, Shaiyel Seltzer, who approached me, looking for Wanda Best and any members of Upton Planning Committee. In fact, anyone who crossed her path, she intercepted them to ask, "Are you an Upton Member?"

When she came to me, I mentioned that Wanda was not there at that time, but I was curious as to what she needed. Apparently, she wanted to purchase property in the 1400 block of Myrtle Avenue and wanted to talk to Upton. To keep short the long story that she wanted to tell, I asked, "Give me your name, and I will forward it to Wanda." Wanda was in attendance at the Jazz Fest, but I didn't want to call her out or put her on the spot. This was another one of those instances when the two of us didn't mix business with pleasure or family. The atmosphere was hectic around us, but festive, and my individual attention was being pulled in a hundred different directions, but I was driving to keep my focus on the woman. She complied, and she wrote her name on a piece of paper. Now I had two white pieces of paper with names on them in my pocket.

Later, I sent Wanda an email and thought I had given her Mrs. Seltzer's information but instead gave her Mrs. Blake's information. When I spoke to Wanda on Monday about returning the chairs I had borrowed for Saturday's concert, she mentioned Mrs. Blake's request for insurance information. I explained how I was going to introduce Mrs. Blake to Tony Ambush, my insurance agent.

Wanda replied, "We are handling that. You can give me the insurance agent's number. And I will give him a call."

At that time, I was in the middle of cleaning out the grease trap at The Bakery, and I didn't have time to look up the number. While working, the thought came to me, *Mrs. Blake came to me because she was getting conflicting information, and I mistakenly shared it with Wanda.* So, when I got home, I immediately called Mrs. Blake with Tony Ambush's contact information, letting her know that, "I've already spoken to Tony about you during the concert." Mrs. Blake was thankful. My take is that Wanda is doing her best to control everything on The Avenue and in the community.

On May 2, I had met with Dr. Brenda Brown, and she brought Kyle McNair to the meeting. He is the comptroller for the Weinberg Foundation. Like always, I gave him a tour of The Bakery and my usual introduction-to-The-Avenue speech before we sat down to talk. I also gave him a warm Poppay's roll, which all of our first-time customers receive from us. He held it in his hand for the longest time before taking that first sumptuous bite. By this time, he was excited and enthusiastic about what I was trying to accomplish. I then gave him a breakdown of the project. It seemed as though the more I shared, the more excited he became. I could see in his face that his mind was busy formulating his strategy to become a part of and to bring his foundation on board. Inside I was thinking and feeling, *is this really happening.*

After giving my presentation, Dr. Brown gave her fire-and-brimstone articulation, stressing the importance of what needs to happen between Kyle and me. She brought us together, and in her authoritative, motherly demeanor, she expected us to make things happen. As I mentioned, Kyle enjoyed his sample of our rolls. In fact, it was to the point of him being anxious to purchase samples of our products to take back to his office. He left us with bags of what The Avenue Bakery has to offer. It was a good meeting, and I was excited to have met Kyle.

My hopes were riding high that something significant would happen soon.

Like I often do when I meet people who make commitments to help, I send them an email, thanking them for their time and indicating that I'm looking forward to developing the relationship. I did that at 1:45 a.m. on May 6, when I woke up as I usually do on Monday mornings. This is when it's quiet, and I have time to think and follow up. On that morning, I happened to have looked through my received emails to catch up on things, which is also my practice to do. I noticed a message from Kyle indicating he would like to present TRTCHC with a $20,000 grant. The unexpected happiness froze me. Once I could think, again, quite naturally, I went over in my mind all the processes of receiving grants. We will have to provide a list of documents, and either have an audit or find a fiduciary agent or organization. Associated Black Charities (ABC) came to mind immediately. I have known Diane Bell-McKoy, its president, for years and have been involved with ABC before she landed the job. I was thinking that Associated Black Charities could handle the fiduciary responsibilities for TRTCHC.

I have scheduled a meeting with my board of directors for next Monday, May 6, so that we can discuss and vote on our next move as well as our next task. Although we are moving forward, I won't feel comfortable until I get back the support of Upton, which Wanda and Jules are controlling at the moment.

***

It's Friday, May 31, 2019; it's 4:42 a.m. I am at The Bakery, and normally, I start getting the kitchen ready to begin the workday. The last two days have been very slow because it is our first week back after Memorial Day. But I'm a little ahead of the game because we didn't sell very much. Everything is still fresh. With that said, I have a little time to reflect on the issues I am dealing with and my concerns. I spent last week seeking a fiscal agent in case we needed one to secure a grant from the Weinberg Foundation. Kyle McNair, the comptroller of the Foundation, has chosen The Royal Theater & Community Heritage Corporation for a $20,000 grant; the stipulation is that we needed to submit the documents he requested by today, May 31, 2019.

He needed our IRS 501(c)(3) letter, copies of our last two 990 tax returns, our financial statement, and a copy of our most recent audit. If we had not received an audit, we needed to have a fiscal agent. However, due to the size and financial category that we are in, my accountant, Arnold Williams indicated that Compilation Reports should be enough.

I immediately submitted the 990's and the IRS letter. I was waiting on my accountant to complete the remaining documents submitted yesterday, May 30. I was unsuccessful at contacting Kyle yesterday to confirm if he received the documents that my accountant, Arnold Williams, prepared. I also wanted to make sure that he was satisfied or if I needed to have a fiscal agent. I had indicated in my emails and voicemail that I had a fiscal agent on standby if needed.

Last week, I contacted and visited Fusion Partnership, one of the possible fiscal agents that Alice Cole, our secretary, had researched. They seemed to be willing, and I was impressed because they had handled funds for the Annie E. Casey Foundation, which is an organization named after the UPS founder James Casey's mom. After talking with the representative, it appeared they could not decide to take us on in the timeframe we needed.

Then I visited Players Philanthropy Fund, located in Towson, and I met with Seth McDonnell. I shared with him our situation, and he indicated that Players could handle the transaction. When I indicated that we were to receive a grant from The Weinberg Foundation, his eyebrow raised, and he became a little curious and wanted to know how I was able to do that. In the moment, I had the feeling that my beautiful tan was at the crux of his question. I wanted to ask *what do you mean by that?* But what I did was sidestep his curiosity to inform him about our project and how our initiative aligned with his foundation's mission. Then I reached into my folder to pull out one of my business cards to hand him. When it became apparent to the both of us that I didn't have any left, he jumped in to say that he would have his assistant send me the documents I needed to sign for Players Philanthropy to become our fiscal agent.

"Thank you very much," I said, cosigning my appreciation for his time with a strong handshake. I finalized, "I thank you for your time. And I'll let you know if I need your services." Before leaving the parking lot, I pulled a business card from my truck and a copy of the one-page description of our project, and I brought it back to Seth's office. As I walked down the hall, I noticed his office was next door to the Weinberg Brokerage Firm. It raised my brow. I walked into his office, presented him with my business card and a two-sided page description that informed about the TRTCHC project. At that point, he looked at the first phase of the project, which has an eight-million-dollar price tag. Then he perused the second phase of the project, which has a fifty-two-million-dollar price tag on it. I noticed the wild expression on his face.

He said, "Fifty-two-million dollars? That's a pretty hefty project."

Directly, and with confidence, I said, "It's a holistic project to developing our community." We parted ways.

Quite naturally, after not being able to speak to Kyle McNair, I began to wonder if something had gone on to pose a setback for us. This grant is a step toward moving the project forward because these funds would be used to put together a professional presentation that could garner additional funding. So, today being May 31, I admit to myself that I am a little nervous. *However, it's in God's hands.* That's the thought I'm allowing to roll through my mind.

Yesterday, I reached out to Danny Henson to schedule a meeting to discuss the project and its move forward. I was expecting we would meet sometime next week; however, he suggested today. This afternoon, even. The last meeting, I had with Brenda Brown, Grant, and Kathleen, she suggested that Danny and I meet since his forte is housing, which we all knew. He was the one who suggested we seek a nonprofit status to bring resources for soft costs that we don't have to pay back. I also realize that there are gatekeepers in Baltimore who can make or break progress when it comes to development in this city. As a former housing commissioner, Danny is on that list.

Down through the years, various key would-be players, including out-of-towners, have shared with me that there needs to be a housing component to the project. And certainly, years ago, when Danny Henson, Zed Smith, and I worked to put the project's pro forma together; there was a housing component to that. But I hadn't asked Danny, arguably Baltimore's proclaimed Housing Guy, to spearhead and build for TRTCHC, what was obviously his bailiwick. It wasn't that I didn't appreciate his talent or recognize his wealth of experience; reaching out to him in that respect just hadn't come to me. Instead, I reached out to experts in New Jersey and New York, who very much licked their lips on the wealth of my proposals, and they wanted in. Oh…but for the grace of the gatekeepers!

When I brought the outsiders to the table—to Ms. Pugh's table—my hindsight-take on it is that perhaps, she may have coordinated with Danny Henson because of his strong background and focus in-housing. Perhaps that's why she and her henchmen kept pulling the plug on my progress, unexplained. Perhaps that's why I received a stunning about-face of support in that fateful meeting I had with Danny and Zed Smith. The meeting in which they both proclaimed that the project was not going to work. Perhaps they were really saying that the project would not work as long as Danny was not a part of it. And so, perhaps the former Mayor Pugh had decided to push me out, bring Danny in, and move forward with my project concept—without me. Perhaps the handwritten explanation had been written on the wall for all to see. Except for me, it was written in coded language and behavior. Hindsight is a beautiful thing, but I wish it could come in the midst, not in the hereafter.

However, these days, since Ms. Pugh's abrupt departure, the way things are turning, the project is benefitting from the longtime relationship between Brenda Brown and Danny Henson. They've known one another for years. He had suggested to her that TRTCHC should reach out to a nonprofit organization to seek a contribution or render a grant to our cause that we wouldn't have to pay back. She encouraged me to continue to work to bring the community on board. She also pulled my coat on, reaching out to Danny as well.

Thus, that good-ole hindsight has moved into my crystal clear rearview about this entire path that I've been traveling. Perhaps it could've been shortened if I had asked Danny Henson to be a part of the project's housing piece in the beginning. Perhaps I could have averted a lot of chasing one's tail.

On the other side of all that, I believe Dan and I have a good relationship. He's also one of my customers at The Bakery. Dan was one of the prime persons in my journey who motivated me to put The Avenue Bakery, here, on Pennsylvania Avenue. I am looking forward to our meeting today.

I am also reaching out to our new Baltimore City Mayor, Jack Young, as well as the new President of the City Council, Councilman Brandon Scott to make sure both are on board with the project. In 2016, I received a letter of support from Jack Young when he was the City Council president. I'm hopeful that he's still in support.

I haven't at this point followed up with Darroll Cribb, Upton's Board President. We met last week, and I shared all the details of the project, including what happened when my team met with Mayor Pugh in that lions' den. Darroll let me know that his absence at that meeting was because he was out of town. He added the fact of how he had neither been informed about the nature of the meeting nor about how it had gone. So essentially, Darroll was saying how all that 2017 news was new news to him.

While all of this was taking place, I was also running around making sure we'd gotten our liquor license in place for this week's concert at The Avenue Bakery. Our popular jazz concert takes place tomorrow, June 1. In that process, I have to get our letter of good standing from the state first. I tried to get all this accomplished last week. But after commandeering a parking spot, which was no small accomplishment, and sinking four dollars' worth of quarters in the parking meter, I discovered the building was closed for the day due to a lack of air conditioning. *It's not even that hot today* was my thought, standing there wearing a hot, frustrated look on my face, reading the unceremonious note on the door. That's how I find myself, today, repeating my mission to obtain our good-standing letter and our liquor license.

I followed up with Rosa Pryor on this month's band, and she indicated that Jim Dow, my board member, was handling the band this month. I gave him a call, and he indicated that *The Guy Curtis Band* would bring eight additional musicians and the singer, Nova. Now I'm excited about the concert because I hired Nova more than twenty-five years ago at UPS. She has now retired. I knew she sang, but I had never gotten the opportunity to hear her perform. This is going to be a treat.

I get so involved with all my initiatives. I don't talk much about the business. Now that Brandon has his driver's license, and until he gets that forty-hour-a-workweek job, I have decided he can come in on Thursdays to give Brenda a break. She doesn't like getting up at 5:00 a.m. to come to The Bakery, three days a week. Yesterday, she enjoyed being home, and she is coming in later today because our plumber, Kenny, will be repairing our water problems at the house. I observed how Brandon did a great job running the place yesterday. He made sure the showcase stayed full as well as keeping the kitchen clean. At the end of the day, he also handled the register closeout, and he shut the place down. I am so proud of him. And although I want him to get that forty-hour job working for someone else, I know I will miss him.

It's now 6:32 a.m., and Lin will be dropping Brandon off. And, together, we will begin the process of opening. I have already made the coffee. Next, the first thing in the oven will be our famous mini sweet potato pies. Sade got in at 5:47 a.m. She's working on decorating the cakes. Yesterday, I made a couple of carrot cakes, so we will have that to sell as well as coconut, chocolate and lemon cakes. Back to the kitchen.

I have been thinking about this historical memoir, *On a Roll*, and how it must be perfect and can't have any mistakes. Like everything I do, I have several people read my work before I send it out. Yvonne Medley is helping put my book together, and she is fantastic. However, I had been thinking of who else I know, owning that supercritical eye when it comes to the written word. The first person to come to mind is John Kyle, who was, and is, the president of the State Center Neighborhood Alliance, of which I am the vice president. We have worked together, leading the group for several years. I will give a little more detail on him later. To make a long story short, I had been thinking of having him lay his eagle-eye on my work, but I hadn't caught up with him.

Well, they say the Lord works in mysterious ways. On Tuesday, while running around getting permits, I drove up Park Avenue, where he lives, and he came to mind. As I drove up to the corner of Park Avenue and Presstman Street, who do I see walking in front of my vehicle. It was Kyle and his spouse, Peter. They didn't recognize my vehicle, so I pressed on my horn like a mad man. First, it startled them, but thankfully only a moment or two passed before they realized who I was. We all had a laugh.

We talked for a while, and John agreed to be a reader for me. I also asked him if he would consider becoming a member of the TRTCHC board. We are trying to diversify it. He agreed to give it some thought. John is great people.

***

It's Sunday 11:15 a.m., June 9, 2019. I have baked everything we need for today. And I've backed up the batters as well—which means I've made multiple buckets of batters for our products in advance. There are items in The Bakery that our customers have to have every day. Several of our high-and-hot-in-demand products, such as our pound cakes, sweet potato pies, and our apple cakes, are time-consuming to prepare. Having those batters at-the-ready ensures that our customers won't be disappointed when they come to see us. So, to keep them fresh and available, I will often make two buckets of batter for both our lemon and butter pound cakes and three buckets of ingredients for our sweet potato pies. There are many staples on The Avenue that folks just don't want to find themselves without.

For once, on a Sunday, I have time to reflect on what's going on in my life. Yesterday, I left The Bakery a little early because the weather was good, and I also needed to replace a couple of boards on our deck. I bought the paint a couple of weeks ago, but I realized that the deck needed a bit more than a few turns of my paintbrush. Evidently, termites wanted to use a few of my boards as their food source. Well, I'm not having that. I hate creepy crawlers, parasites, politicians, and people who feed off helpless targets just because they feel they can. As for my trip to Home Depot, the biggest problem I had was finding the right tools to pull up the damaged boards. When it came to doing the actual work, finding a nice day with no rain had been the issue. Today is a good day for fixing things.

At the beginning of the week, I received a message from Darroll Cribb, the Upton board president, letting me know that he was back from his wedding anniversary vacation. Prior to his leaving, I sent him a draft approval letter at his request, which he, Wanda, and Jules could reference. Darroll promised he would get back to me by the end of the week with a formal letter of support for our project. On Friday, he called me to say that he would be emailing a letter. He asked that I read it and get back to him, and he was sure that we could come to some resolution. He had given me a reason to be hopeful. However, while I wasn't expecting anything earth-shattering positive, I was not expecting what I received.

I opened the email, and its attachment, which turned out to be a letter containing nothing but the same old *BS* that Wanda had given me in the meeting that she and I had a couple of weeks ago. This new letter, which Wanda Best and Jules Dunham constructed, made it seem like Upton had given its approval for the TRTCHC project as far back as 2005. However, it was in 2015 when Wanda presented me with a letter of support—that letter stood firm until the former Mayor Pugh got involved. Not long after Upton's sudden reversal, Jules admitted to me that Upton's or Wanda's actions were merely political. This new letter also falsely alluded to the idea of a new ballfield being a part of Upton's plan, when in fact, it has always been known as Phase I of the TRTCHC project—widely publicized and proven to be sound.

When I previously met with Darroll, he had indicated that he was not opposed to the TRTCHC project—once I gave him all the details, including the economic impact. He also said that he had some influence when it came to Wanda. He assured me that something could be worked out. But instead of a letter expressing approval and support for our efforts, the letter I received held little-to-no value. And absolutely no new news or existing factual news. It is now my view that Wanda and Jules control Upton and that Darroll has no say at all. I also concluded that Upton's board, just as the Pugh mayoral administration, feeds off the work, research, and relationships that I create, with the intention of using that for their source of sustenance.

One of the things I am trying to accomplish besides the project is to keep the community's appearance of unity. I say *appearance* because currently, the community is neither informed about important decisions concerning its fate and well-being nor is it unified. I am sure that if the entire community was aware of the project and its positive impact it could make, economically and socially, it would be in full support of it. At this point, the project has not been brought to the Upton and surrounding communities at large. But I am still hopeful that we can reconcile this and do what is right for our community.

In the back of my mind, I am thinking that something else is going on. I have to admit that it has been a stretch for me to hold on to my positive thoughts in the midst of odd behaviors and turnabouts from these three people. *Maybe they have someone who is planning to build the theater—and it's just that Wanda, Jules, and Darroll lack the testicular fortitude to tell me.* I've hypothesized it, over and over in my head. And if that be the case, I would love it because my bottom-line focus has always been to spearhead the initiative. Yes, I would love to be involved, but if someone else or some other entity accomplishes it—well and good. It's still a win-win for everyone. The endgame is to save and change lives as well as economically redevelop our community. And that would be the perfect ending to this story *On a Roll.*

CHAPTER EIGHTEEN

MOTHER AND MR. JAMES

1950s-Early 1960s

Mr. James Crawford, a.k.a. Mr. James, was the kind of guy who worked all week and liked to go out drinking all weekend. This was something my mother was not going to tolerate. Her view has always been that everyone in the house does what she says. This is the reason she hasn't had a man in her life since 1967. The only lifelong companions she would ever have would be her children and grandchildren.

There were several occasions when he came home after first stopping for a few drinks. And that was when the altercations began. Highly upset that he had spent most of the family's money on drinking, the argument would begin. She would pull at his clothes and sometimes pull and pull until she pulled them off. One of her rituals would be to pull his clothes out of the closet and threaten to toss them out the window. Things would get so bad that sometimes the police would come and threaten to lock up the both of them.

When these wars got started, my task was to keep the kids locked up in the bedroom out of harm's way. Tony and I worked to try to keep

Eldora and Ricky from crying. After the police left, and they quieted down, Tony and I would try to clean up all the broken glass and close all the windows. My mother had a habit of opening all the windows and screaming at the top of her voice to embarrass Mr. James. She'd call him all kinds of m'fs. In fact, to this day, I never knew there were so many kinds. The colorful ways she told him to kiss parts of her body could embarrass Satan. Then Monday came, and things were back to normal.

There were times she would meet him at his job or meet him at his favorite watering hole. On those days, we were left home alone, worrying if we would see her again. Our thought was not that she would get hurt but that she would get arrested for disturbing the peace or killing someone. It was always my duty to maintain the house and protect my siblings from the uncertainties of this stormy life. As I mentioned, my sister, Sandra, was the youngest at this time. There is a difference of ten years between Sandra and me, so I was around ten years old.

If I remember correctly, Mr. James worked at a place called Smelkinson Brothers. My mom started working at the Continental Can. She used to bring home tomatoes all the time. During the week, my job was to babysit the kids during the day. I used to watch all the other kids playing outside, intermittent with changing diapers and cleaning the house. I was also responsible for getting the dinner started before my mom, and Mr. James came home from work. I'd peeled the potatoes or prepared the string beans and get them cooking.

If they came home and I missed one of my tasks, I got a whipping or got punished or both. And that happened whenever I'd lose track of time, staring out the window, watching my schoolmates playing outside. But I do have to say that I often wondered why the kids were so vicious to each other. There was always the one kid, who everyone picked on, but yet he'd still clamor to follow the crowd. That's probably when I made up my mind; I would never follow a crowd. It simply didn't seem worth it. So, to this day, I only have a few good friends. Other than that, I'm basically a loner.

When my mom and Mr. James came home, we would have dinner. After it was over, it was my job, and Tony's to wash the dishes and clean the kitchen. There was a certain amount of time that this was supposed to take. If we finished early, they'd promise, we could go outside to play. But we never made it. Cleaning the kitchen always took us to 10 or 11 p.m.

During this long ritual, Tony and I did everything under the sun. We would spend about an hour fussing about who was going to wash and who was going to dry. One of our other rituals was extermination. We could have put Terminix out of business. He and I used to use rubber bands to kill flies—yes, flies. We were so good at it the flies would leave the kitchen as soon as dinner was over. I tell you—we were so good. If the CIA knew how good we were, it would have contracted us to be snipers. We were so good we could knock them out of the air in mid-flight. That was fun. But these were rocky days for us. It was also during a time when we thought that we would lose our mother to the penal system forever.

***

Today is Sunday, June 18, 1995. I am on vacation in Myrtle Beach with Brenda and Hammy. His special friend, Etoy, and her son, Danté (nicknamed Delo), drove down with us. This vacation is desperately needed. For the past two weeks, I have been working fifteen to sixteen-hour days. Brenda needed this vacation as well. She had been working and running errands for my mother and ten-year-old niece, Ashley.

We had discussed bringing Ashley along, but Brenda needed a break from the responsibility of taking care of my family. I, on the other hand, felt we should have taken her along. But who am I to demand that we bring her when I am not the one who is doing most of the caregiving? I am blessed to have such a caring and understanding wife. So, I did not share my thoughts with Brenda at all.

I meant to give my mother a kiss and hug before I left, but I didn't. I remember saying to myself that I wanted to do that, but in the rush of things … the rush to leave the house, I failed to do so. I remember saying to her, "Take care. Do you think you'll be okay?"

She said, "I'll be fine. We will be fine." She said it in that confident base voice that she has. Deep down inside, I know she was gambling just like I was.

In my heart, I believe she would not have admitted her worry about being without us. In her heart, she knew we needed the time away, and she would not have wanted to do anything to deprive us of that time. Mom is different in her latter days.

I always like to hear her laugh because there is a certain amount of happiness and joy in laughter. At least, that is what I have always believed. To get that laugh out of her, I said, "I left the keys in the little car just in case you decide to take a spin."

She got a big laugh out of that one. She has never been behind the wheel of a car in all her sixty some-odd years on the planet.

There was still some guilt, for me, about going on vacation. Maybe there should not have been. Part of the reason for guilt is that my mother is on dialysis. If something went wrong, it could be extra difficult for her. But since she and Ashley are a pair; I felt it would be okay to leave them home together. Yes, this is all true, but am I trying to convince myself that I'm doing the right thing?

On the other hand, Ashley was not taking it very well. I saw little teardrops affixed to her cheeks like those painted on the ceramic antique doll in the *Women's Home Journal*. I tried to make her feel better by letting her know I was counting on her to take care of her grandmother. It was tough to leave her, but I had no choice. Or did I? Like I often say, whose life is it anyway? How much of it am I supposed to live for myself—how much am I supposed to live for others?

I overheard Brenda talking to Lin, our daughter, over the phone about my oldest sister, Dot. Apparently, she called Donna, Tony's wife, to say that I had said to give her $250. And that I would repay her when I returned from vacation. Certainly, none of this is true. Why would she do something like that when she hadn't talked to me?

On last Thursday, Dot called to say she was going to be evicted, and she needed money. She told Brenda that her friend, Ike was going to pay me back when he received his retirement check. When Brenda told me the part about Ike; I didn't believe it. Dot has lied to me before. Ike is not the kind of person who lives from paycheck to paycheck.

But I had already made up my mind that I was going to loan … or let me correct myself … *give* her the money. Friday morning, she called, but mama did not wake me up. Instead, she told her that I was asleep. Dot never called me back, and she didn't leave a telephone number so that I could call her back. Therefore, the promise was never officially rendered.

I love my sister. She needs help but fails to realize it. Here is a woman who was very attractive, intelligent, and articulate. She has never been able to hold down a job. And she's had a couple of good ones, too. It's always something with her. Either she can't make it to work on time, or someone dislikes her. Whatever the problem is, nothing is ever her fault. Dot's attitude toward life is that her family should take care of her or help support her financially. In her mind, it's her family's obligation.

Somehow, she has missed the point of family. Yes, we all want to try to help our family—when we can. But a family's help and loyalty go both ways. Each one of us owns the responsibility of taking care of ourselves, no one else. We should not expect others to take care of us. Maybe I am confused and missed the boat, here, with my way of thinking. But I doubt it.

There is so much sadness in my family; sometimes, it's hard to even think about it. It's depressing, and I have to keep reaching for pleasant moments to keep from breaking down. I keep telling myself I can't control what my family does or how some of my family members choose to live their lives. It is still sad, though. They are all intelligent, loving, and caring people. The choices they make, I can't control, and my advice is not something they seek. Sometimes I think they envy me, and at times, they despise my way of life. And still, I also know they love and respect me. And that, deep down, they are proud of me.

Getting back to my pleasant moments while on vacation, I plan to introduce my son to golf. I bought a new set of clubs and gave him my old set and bag. Brenda bought him a pair of golf shoes. He and I are close, but somehow, I feel that the game will be something more we can share if he grows to like it. I am always trying to get closer to my kids. Maybe because I love them so much, or it could be that I want so badly to give them what I never had.

I forgot to mention that today is Father's Day. My son bought me a carrying bag for my golf clubs. I guess we're on the same wavelength. I will cherish it as I do all the things my children give me. The card was the tearjerker. It mentioned care and support and love. It appeared the card was made for us and that he had taken such time to make sure it fit our relationship.

Here I am giving him all the tips and coaching. I pay for his first day on the course. I show him how to hold the club and stand. And wouldn't you know it, he gets out there and plays better than I do. For some reason, I couldn't hit the ball straight for anything. My first two balls went into the water, twenty feet from the first tee. I could not believe myself. Hammy thought it was funny. But I have to say that it was fun anyway. I was still proud of my son even though he was able to hit the ball 150 yards on the first four holes. I still think it is a game we can enjoy together for years to come. The fact that Brenda plays also makes it a good family outing. We just have to get Lin involved, and we will have a family foursome.

Well, we just got back home from vacation. I noticed Lin's car outside and another one that I did not recognize. When we pulled up, I was not able to back into the garage because Lin's car was blocking it, and Etoy's car was parked. When I pulled up the street, I also noticed children playing in the backyard. None of them looked familiar to me.

We got out of the car and walked through the garage to enter the house. I had opened it the same as always, on our way up the street. As I walked through, I could hear my mother talking to someone. I opened the door to the back of the garage and saw mom standing, leaning on the rail, and Sandra, my sister, sitting on one of the chairs. Also standing there was my mom's friend, Yvonne. The children in the yard belonged to her. Both Sandra and my mother wore excited expression-filled looks of welcome on their faces.

I, in my calm and unemotional voice, said, "Hello." In fact, my voice was so calm; I was actually not sure if I said anything that was audible. A couple of hours later, I asked Brenda if there is something wrong with me, and I explained my response.

She said that it was not strange; it was understandable. I imagine that though I had worked to enjoy my family time while on vacation, my apprehension over leaving my mother and Ashley behind had left me.

CHAPTER NINETEEN

A TALE OF TWO THEATERS

Today is Sunday, June 9, 2019, my brother Kelly's birthday. I call him my brother, but he was really my cousin. When he was living, and we had gotten back in touch with one another, I would always send him a present on his birthday. And he would do the same on mine. I love and miss his crazy sense of humor and the midnight calls we would have. Up until his passing in 2014, either he would call me, or I would call him when I was on my way to The Bakery in the wee hours of the morning. During our routine conversations, we talked about politics and tried to solve society's issues at least in our heads. I really miss him and think of him often, especially when I walk into my office at the house. His cremated remains sit on the top shelf of my bookcase. That's all I have of him, now. And I have yet to think of the most fitting and proper resting place for him.

This morning, I am beginning to think that he needs to be with my mom at her burial site. He always thought of his Aunt Mattie, my mother, as his mom. Strange bird—he loved but never liked his mother, and he hated his only sister, Rosa. But before he passed, he did get the opportunity to communicate with his nieces. Rosa has five daughters.

"Happy Birthday, Kelly," I look up at him and say, "If not in a heartbeat, then in a minute," I say with a final, "Love you, man." It's funny, but even though he's gone, I still wouldn't dare call him by his first name, Herbert. I bet he still hates it.

I am also trying to plan my trip to Ohio for Ed Reed's induction into the Football Hall of Fame. He and I have been working together at the Booker T. Washington Middle School, Arts Academy. It's been like that from the beginning of his career with the Baltimore Ravens until now. His induction is the first week of August, and Glenn Younes, who coordinates Ed's foundation, sent me my invitation. The only problem I have is that our family's vacation is also the first week of August, and we have planned to be in Myrtle Beach. I have never been to one of these big-time inductions and I would like to attend even though I am not much of a sports guy. Decisions!

I am trying to also determine if Brenda wants to go. I need to order our plane tickets by June 12. If Brenda doesn't want to go, I will ask Hammy if he wants to go. Maybe the grandkids might be interested; who knows. Brenda and I will discuss that sometime today.

***

It's Wednesday, June 10, 2019, late evening hours. Watching TV after my evening nap, I am listening to the report of two shootings today. One, happened in Park Heights, and there were two more over the weekend. I heard a citizen say on the news that the shootings just continue.

Also, on the news, Councilman Eric Costello of the 11th District said, "We will do everything to keep our citizens safe."

The Police Commissioner spoke of safety and that those who drive past the squeegee kids need to stop giving them money. His concern is for their safety and the safety of the public, of course, he states.

I always try to be optimistic, to work to dig out the positive from a negative. The reality in my mind is that when it comes to changing the crime situation in Baltimore, it takes more than policing or discouraging the squeegee kids—enterprising young men, trying to be entrepreneurs, perhaps without even realizing it—because they have no other economic opportunity. They are future businessmen in the making; they just need direction and opportunities.

I think about the approximately three hundred shooting victims in this city during each of the past three years. Why didn't they feel safe? What could have been done to prevent their suffering or deaths? I wonder if anyone has completed a study of the lives of all these people as well as their perpetrators. Has their education, economic status, and mental capacity been looked into? And I am not even talking about the innocent children who have become random victims. But, yes, that is also a lane that needs to be explored.

The question you may be asking is, "James, where are you going with this?" My answer is that something major and positive needs to happen in West Baltimore. The root of the problem needs to be addressed, not just the symptoms that seem to be controlling or not controlling it. The root of the problem, to me, is economics as it was in slavery and in the Civil Rights movement. And it's a lack of pride and respect in our community. We all are a result of what we have been exposed to and the environment from which we come.

A holistic approach to change the environment, economic opportunities, and instilling a sense of pride and dignity in our community are the components of a vital solution. That is what The Royal Theater & Community Heritage Center (TRTCHC) project is all about. I say it, over and over, it's taking advantage of the third-largest industry in Baltimore City at the tune of more than $10 billion. Here we have an opportunity to make a major impact and to be the leaders of positive change—to bring people and organizations together to change lives and outcomes.

It's sad that we have two people standing in the way. Two intelligent, hard-working, community-committed people standing in our way who appear to lack the faith and vision to make the right decision. The other day, my wife, Brenda, mentioned to me how I could be spending my time continuing to complete my education. She shared with me the ten dollars-per-credit available to seniors who enroll at the university. It is times like this that I wonder if I should just ring the bell—and just do *me*. Somehow though, I believe God didn't lead me down this path for me to give up.

Oh, by the way, I was also reflecting on the meeting I had with Danny Henson. I found out that he and I have a lot in common when it comes to retirement and what we do. We both cannot see ourselves just lying around, doing nothing during retirement. Our feelings are the same. We want to remain involved, mind and body because working for the things that mean so much to us gives us a better quality of life. For us, being active keeps us healthier—mind, body, and soul. That was the first time we sat down and sort of got to know one another a little better.

So many things are crossing my mind right now, and I am experiencing a great deal.

***

It's Father's Day, Sunday, June 16, 2019. And the special day has gone well. My son, Hammy, happened to be at our home in Florida, celebrating his wedding anniversary. So, he sent me a text message. And I was fine with that. My daughter wished me a Happy Father's Day yesterday and today. This was an unusual Father's Day because normally, I wake up to my wife, Brenda, fixing me breakfast in bed.

And then I get a couple of gifts, here and there, from my beloved and the kids.

But today, I got up early. Brenda was still asleep. I felt like I wanted to wash my BMW. I guess I could call it my third baby. It's a 1990 525 Series BMW, and I keep it in very good condition. So, I felt like taking it out for a good car wash. To let Brenda enjoy her sleep, I went to McDonald's and got my favorites: sausage, pancakes, and orange juice. When Brenda discovered me gone, she tried to call me on my cell; I found out later. But she couldn't reach me because I'd forgotten my cell phone. I'd left it connected to my charger because the night before, she and I had gone to see that play about Marvin Gaye. It was playing at The Lyric in downtown Baltimore on Mt. Royal Avenue. Our late night out was impromptu because my friend, Wyatt Arrington, arranged for our spouses and us to see the play. And I knew that Brenda loves plays. I love to make sure that she gets to enjoy as much of that as she likes.

Now, I'm sitting back reflecting on our evening. Our night out at The Lyric reflects on what I'm trying to do to rebuild The Royal Theater. Last night, we parked down the street. *Okay*, I thought, *that's one thing to take under advisement*. Then we venture into the auditorium. I'm sitting in my seat. The seats are so tight. I'm getting the feel of being in a sardine can. The floor underneath my feet is concrete. I'm not sure if this theater has ever been renovated or not; I mean really renovated.

The Lyric first opened as a Music Hall on Halloween night in 1895. While not originally intended, during the early part of the 20th Century, it added motion picture showings to beef up attendance whenever times got slow. It was rechristened The Lyric Theatre in October of 1903. Once again, it became a Music Hall when it became the home of the Baltimore Opera Company. In 1986, it earned its protection from demolition when it was placed on the National Register of Historic

Places. The Lyric went out of business in 2009, but it was immediately saved in that same year. To this day, the *Lyric Opera Baltimore* is doing well there. The Lyric, the building, is now referred to as the Modell performing arts center and is also formally billed as The Modell Performing Arts Center at the Lyric.

So, I was looking at the play, which was great, by the way. And I'm saying to myself—these are the plays that we should be having at the new Royal Theater. All the African American plays that are out there that our folks come up with and all—their stories—these should be played on The Avenue at our new Royal Theater.

At the Lyric, premiere vocal performers, Jill Scott and Diana Ross are expected to shine there later this month.

On Friday, June 14, 2019, there was an Upton Community meeting. There were several community-oriented items on the agenda as usual, but a topic concerning *Visit Baltimore*—a nonprofit entity charged to highlight the city's tourism—was on the agenda as well. Prior to this community meeting, Wanda had attended a *Visit Baltimore* meeting. Apparently, she heard about how I had assisted *Visit Baltimore* when it came to me for artwork, artifacts, and pictures highlighting Historic Pennsylvania Avenue. I had put them in touch with graphic artist Stuart Hudgins. As I've mentioned, he has done wonderful work for me, and I wanted to promote and pass on his talent—not only because I knew he would do a good job but also because it would give him new job assignments.

The folks over at *Visit Baltimore* must have said something positive about the TRTCHC project because, during today's community meeting, Wanda pulled me aside to mention her *Visit Baltimore* meeting. *Visit Baltimore's* plan is to move its site, so she asked if we could meet. Something must have happened when she met with *Visit*

Baltimore to make her question the decisions she's been making. Well, that's my take on it, anyway. I'm hopeful.

Also, I had a meeting with Darroll Cribb to share with him my disappointment with the response letter I had received. I let him know how that letter was nothing more than the garbage I had gotten from Wanda previously.

At that point, he said, "Well, yeah. We can work out something."

Today, I'm thinking ... *wait a minute. Wait a minute. The decisions surrounding the support of the project should not be made solely by Darroll, Wanda, or Jules.* The entire Upton Board of Directors needs to weigh in on this subject. Why hasn't it been brought before the entire board? So, I've sent Darroll a text, letting him know that we need to meet, again, immediately to resolve this. Because he seems to believe in what we're trying to do, but it appears that Wanda and Jules continue to sway him in different stagnant directions.

So now I have meetings set up with Wanda and Darroll. I suppose I'd like to meet with Wanda first before I meet with Darroll. It would be nice if one could cancel out the need for the other. But if given the opportunity to address the entire Upton Board, I could present the pros. And Wanda and Jules could present their cons. But the board should make a decision as to whether or not we move forward to support the TRTCHC project. That's my strategy for next week. Boom. That's the bottom line.

***

It's 2:01 p.m., Monday, June 30, 2019, almost closing time at The Avenue Bakery. This has been a slow week for business, although things seem to be heating up.

On Friday, I had a great meeting with Anana Kambon, the CEO of Baltimore Office of Promotion & The Arts (BOPA). About six weeks ago, Lady Brion conducted a tour of Pennsylvania Avenue for a group of agencies that would be instrumental in the determination of whether or not Pennsylvania Avenue would get the coveted designation of Black Arts & Entertainment District. Lady Brion is our lead for this initiative. Anana was part of the group, and when they came by The Bakery, she and I had a homecoming embrace. We hadn't seen each other in years, and it was great to reconnect. I gave her a quick tour of The Bakery on that day. We promised to get back together.

I met Anana back in 2002, when I was the District Community Relations Manager for UPS, and she was the coordinator of the National NAACP ACT-SO Program. We worked together on UPS's commitment to the NAACP program, both financially and logistically. That was when NAACP had its national conference here in Baltimore. As the executive consultant of Kambon Executive Professional Services (KEPS), she has had a thirty-five-year professional career centered on her passion for early childhood education, fine arts, and education advocacy. She also had a heart for political and community activism and government politics.

We caught each other up on what we had been doing since we last worked together. I shared with her our project and the obstacles we have faced as well as the strategy for moving forward. She shared her experience as the national director of the NAACP's ACT-SO Program and the similar obstacles she's faced after becoming the CEO of BOPA. When I spoke of getting Mayor Jack Young and Council President Brandon Scott on board with our project, she invited me to be her guest at a private meeting that will include the Council President. It's set to take place on July 1st. She also mentioned how she wants to introduce me to a gentleman from the organization that built the city of Columbia, Maryland. She was excited about our initiative and felt it was critical in Pennsylvania Avenue's soon-to-be-announced Black

Arts & Entertainment District. Respectfully, I took that as a head's up on good news.

This is all great and certainly a turn of events compared to last year. Still up in the air, as they say, is the result of the possible Weinberg Grant, which is critical. On Thursday, I called Kyle McNair after he had left me a message, saying that he needed our 990 tax filing for 2017. I immediately sent it to him when I got home, but I haven't heard from him since. I had also sent him an email, assuring my compliance, if he needed additional information. I also let him know that we now had an organization willing to be our fiscal agent if needed.

***

It's 5:23 a.m., Tuesday, July 2, 2019. The private group meeting that Anana had invited me to, turned out to be a meeting of supporters for Brandon Scott for Mayor. I don't remember all the names (sorry, remembering names is one of my weaknesses). However, the meeting consisted of a group of African American men that called themselves *Heroes*. I guess I should say led by African American men. And that's because there was a reference to Hebrews and Brothers. I think this is a group of Jewish and African American guys that play golf together and have substantial influence in politics. *How interesting*, I thought *and encouraging*.

I walked into the meeting and was greeted by several gentlemen. All were, of course, very cordial. Even so, I kind of felt a little like Daniel Kaluuya's character in Jordan Peele's 2017 horror movie, *Get Out*. Anana greeted me, and it made me feel a little more comfortable. She introduced me to a lady by the name of Paula, to whom I shared my mission. The meeting was very interesting, and it gave me the opportunity to have a casual face-to-face with Council President Brandon Scott.

Also, on Tuesday, June 2, 2019, this was featured on CBS—Baltimore's WJZ newscast:

BALTIMORE (WJZ) — *Maryland is hoping to revitalize a part of West Baltimore by designating a new arts and entertainment district.*

Pennsylvania Avenue Black Arts & Entertainment District was spurred by a community-led effort to revitalize a part of the city with a rich history as a hub of social, economic and arts for Baltimore's black community.

In its heyday, venues like the Royal and Metropolitan theaters and social venues such as the Arch Social Club, Bamboo Lounge, Club Casino, and Club Tijuana hosted black entertainers and musicians.

"Maryland's Arts and Entertainment Districts serve an important role in revitalizing communities across the state," said Secretary Schulz. "This designation helps attract artists and creative businesses and gives counties and municipalities the ability to develop unique arts experiences that engage residents and attract visitors. I look forward to seeing how these districts utilize the designations for community and economic revitalization."

Another arts and entertainment district was also created in the town of Easton on Maryland's Eastern Shore. These two districts will join 26 existing districts around the state. They benefit from tax-related incentives to attract artists, art organizations and more to encourage community involvement, revitalization and tourism.

Credit: Maryland State Arts Council

A new economic impact study showed that new businesses and events in Maryland Arts and Entertainment Districts support more than $1 billion in state GDP and around $72.1 million in state and local tax revenues. It also created nearly 10,000 jobs.

***

So, it's Monday, July 15, 2019. I was about to go out to start cutting the grass, but I looked over at the kitchen stove clock. It's 11:15 in the morning, it advised me. *It's getting into the hottest part of the day,* was my thought, *so I'll wait until this evening to tackle my weed field.* Redirected, I'm staying indoors to work on all the communications activity that needs to take place.

I have so much on the plate these days. Now that we've been notified that we will receive the Weinberg Foundation grant, the calendar is booked solid. I have been able to confirm a meeting for July 25th with Baltimore City Council President Brandon Scott. Its purpose will be to educate him about the project and to garner his support. Kathleen Sherrill, our architect, and board members will be attending.

On July 29th, I have scheduled a meeting to start working on our professional presentation to obtain significant funding for the project, now that we have obtained the Weinberg grant. Attending the meeting will be Danny Henson, Zed Smith, Kathleen Sherrill, and Dr. Brown, and Brian Grant will attend by conference call. I have also invited members of the TRTCHC board.

On July 30th at 11:30 a.m., I will be at The Center Club to receive our grant. Waiting on whether or not we would receive this significant grant because of the validation it exudes for the project had me a little on edge. Finally, I just had to decide to put it in God's hands. As it's often expressed, God helps those who help themselves. And I knew that I had done all the work within my power to do. I had communicated with the Foundation's Kyle McNair, produced all the documentation that he requested, and I even had a fiscal agent on standby just in case it was needed.

The presentation ceremony will be a small gathering, at which I am allowed to invite two guests. I chose TRTCHC's founding member, Alice Cole, secretary, and Kathleen Sherrill, our architect. Kathleen is perhaps the one person who knows more about the project than anyone else besides me. I also wanted to invite Adrian Johnson, another founding member and our treasurer. Adrian is the vice president and treasurer for the Municipal Employees Credit Union (MECU). Dr. Brown worked her magic to get me an additional invitation. I was grateful.

Because of the Weinberg ceremony, I will not be able to join the family for our annual vacation, scheduled for July 28 through August 4th. I also have plans to attend the Baltimore Ravens' retired All-Pro Safety Ed Reed's induction into the Football Hall of Fame. It takes place in Canton, Ohio, during the weekend of August 1-3, 2019. As some folks know, he and I have been in partnership in a program at Booker T. Washington Middle School, now, Arts Academy. Reed's

L.O.R.D.S. at Booker T. is the name of his program. The acronym stands for Leadership, Order, Respect, Discipline, and Success. He had inherited the program from its founder, former Ravens' Safety James Trapp. Through the Ed Reed Foundation, Ed has committed eighteen years to Booker T. and to our partnership to equip our young people with the tools needed to succeed in life. Our mission is to give our youth what they need to help them overcome the negative elements that they are confronted with every day. Ed's been hands-on via the project and brought all kinds of resources to the school.

On the football field, Ed Reed, a safety for the Baltimore Ravens, wasted no time becoming a formidable landmark for Ravens' fans. His stats are impressive, to say the least. In 2004 he was Defensive Player of the Year. The nine-time Pro Bowler was named All-Pro, six times. And he was also named to the NFL All-Decade Team of the 2000s. While those are just some of the highlights to convey Ed's heart to play hard, his concern for the wellbeing of children and youth conveys Ed's heart to make a difference. And on this, we strongly concur.

Ed Reed is a New Orleans native who began breaking records for the Ravens even in his rookie year in 2003. Though he played briefly for the Houston Texans and the New York Jets, he retired in 2015 as a Baltimore Raven. And Baltimore claims him as its own.

I've decided to bring my grandson, Brandon, with me to the induction to show my appreciation for his hard work at The Bakery. Brandon will travel with the family to Myrtle Beach, and on Thursday, August 1st, he will fly back to Baltimore. So, he'll get the best of both worlds. He and I will then fly out to Canton, Ohio, on August 2nd to attend Ed's private party that Friday night and the parade and induction ceremony on Saturday. We plan to attend the Hall of Fame Museum on Sunday and fly back home on Monday.

With all this happening, we have a group of students from Atlanta coming to visit HBCU colleges and stopping to visit The Avenue

Bakery on Wednesday, July 17th. Also, I have a group of local students coming to visit The Bakery on Thursday, July 18th. In the meantime, I am meeting with Lady Brion to prepare for our press conference on Pennsylvania Avenue's new designation of The Black Arts & Entertainment District, which will take place on Tuesday, July 23rd, at The Avenue Bakery.

***

It's Monday, July 19, 2019; I woke up last night, shaved, showered, and got dressed for work. I went into the kitchen and grabbed my phone to check my messages and any phone calls I might have missed. After all, I do go to bed while my portion of the world is still up and running. I noticed someone had left two messages on my voicemail.

One message said, "I am not going to tell you who this is, but you can't make any money if you don't answer your phone."

The other message said, "Mr. Hamlin, please return my call." And he left his number.

I couldn't recognize the voice, but I decided that I would call the number when I got to work. This morning I called twice and left a message.

It's 11:00 a.m., and I get this call. I looked at the number. Curious, I said to myself, "who is this?"

The man on the line says, "This is James Whitaker. How are you?"

I was so surprised I couldn't believe I was talking to Whitaker. Apparently, Darryl Webster had given him my contact information. I had given it to Darryl when I saw him last week while shopping at Macy's in Security Mall located on Security Blvd. I hadn't seen these two guys in more than twenty years.

Back in the '80s, I was an Operations Center Manager in UPS' Burtonsville Facility in Laurel, Maryland. I was responsible for service to the City of Rockville, the second-largest city in Maryland. I had fifty delivery drivers and two supervisors who reported to me, and I was responsible for millions of dollars of vehicles.

I really enjoyed this assignment and loved the group of drivers who worked with me. We really had a good time working together, and we all respected each other as well. Our operation was always one of the better operations. However, every operation has its problem people. And Whitaker and Webster were my two. As drivers, they did a good job and serviced our customers well. The problem I had with them was getting them to come to work every day. On a couple of occasions, they came to work took their delivery out but called back to be relieved because they were sick—they said.

To make a long story short, they both had substance problems. I tried everything I could to get them to understand what they were doing to their families and to themselves. The company, which was very supportive of its employees, allowed them to get treatment, but it also had to monitor them over time. UPS had to monitor them for the safety of the public and themselves and to meet the Department of Transportation (DOT) requirements. Well, as I have learned from them, and from one of my sisters, who had been plagued with the same types of addictions, one must want to change before he or she can accept the help you're willing to give him or her. But sadly, sometimes that means the person has to hit rock bottom before that happens. Well, they both ended up losing their jobs at UPS. I hadn't heard from these guys in decades. I often wondered what had happened to Darryl and James. After all, I did care for them.

I happened to be walking through Macy's at the Woodlawn Shopping Center, and Darryl and I walked up on each other. It was so pleasant, seeing one another after all these years. Not only did he look great, but also it seemed like he hadn't aged much beyond the last time I saw him at UPS. He shared with me how he had gone back to school.

Now he's a counselor at a drug treatment center, giving back and doing well. He also shared with me that James Whitaker was now living in Texas and doing well.

"Mannnn, I had to get out of town to get my life back on track," James Whitaker said to me during the call. He also said, "My uncle told me to come on down to Texas with him. And I never looked back." He said it to me with confidence. He also remarried and has a new family, all doing well. Whitaker even owns his own car dealership and has numerous rental properties.

It was such a pleasant surprise to hear from these guys and to hear that they are doing well. After the call, Whitaker sent me a few pictures of his family in Texas as well as in Maryland. His mom owns a nursing business in Owings Mills. In one of the pictures at his mom's house, the actress Jada Pinkett Smith was in it. Jada is a native Baltimorean.

There are hundreds of people with whom I have worked, and whether or not they were great workers or individuals who had problems, I made it a point to treat them with the utmost respect. As a manager, these two guys often put me in trying situations, but I understood that they were not in full control of themselves. They knew I genuinely cared about them. However, at that time—as is always, really—they were the decision-makers in their lives. It is so great to know that they were able to find their way to a better life.

Back at the ranch, this has been the hottest week of the summer thus far, and business has been unusually slow. I think it is the heat, and I hope to see my customers again once it cools down. This is also the weekend for Artscape, an annual festival that highlights visual performing, literary, and even culinary arts by way of outdoor venues, exhibits, and stages set up throughout the Mt. Vernon Community, not far from The Avenue Bakery. Even though it's superhot, reaching possible three-digit temperatures, we're hopeful to see a few more customers tomorrow. I have completed all my baking, and the ovens are off. Finally, the heat has convinced Brenda to cut off the kitchen lights. I have been trying to convince her to do that for years to save electricity.

Mother Nature will get you to change your evil ways.

CHAPTER TWENTY

HOT FUN IN THE SUMMERTIME

It's **Sunday, July 21, 2019**, and hot as the unholy place. I got all my baking done early, so I could cut off the ovens. Mother Nature can really make you see things differently when she wants to.

Our kitchen lighting is set up so that we can cut off the lights and turn on the lights along the wall of the lobby where the cash register and showcase sit. For just about eight years, I have been trying to save electricity by operating the lights in this fashion. Now that the temperature has been in the three-digit realm, Brenda likes turning off the bright lights in the kitchen when the baking is done.

Yesterday evening, I was home at the kitchen counter, eating my dinner, when I took a real close look at a picture of Brenda and her crew celebrating her retirement from the Carroll County Public Library System. The framed photograph sits on the counter near the refrigerator, and it was date-stamped. The year was 2011, the same year we opened The Bakery. On August 15, we will hit our eighth year in business. Looking at that picture, looking at that date, it hit me, she retired and immediately started working with me on The Avenue Bakery initiative. It's eye-opening moments like this that I realize how blessed I am and that I am not the only one who is making the sacrifice to bring about positive change in our community. My entire family has been and still is committed to a mission I birthed.

I feel a little guilty, though, because all Brenda's retirement years have been working, here, with me, and at The Bakery. I have assured her, though, that if she ever wants to do something else, or if there's some place she'd like to visit, just plan it—and together, we'll make it happen. A couple of years ago, we did take a trip that encompassed London, Paris, and Rome. We both really enjoyed that. Last year, we took a family vacation to Punta Cana in the Dominican Republic. However, this summer I reduced her workweek from five days to four days. I guess that's something, but thus far, her vacations have been stateside.

As we move forward with the project, my goal is to transition The Bakery into the hands of our kids and grandkids. Perhaps I'll accomplish that by The Bakery's tenth anniversary. At that point, I'm hopeful we will have a shovel in the ground, and The Royal Theater & Community Heritage Center will be on its way to being built. All I can do is work the plan and put it in God's hands.

Well, come Tuesday, those meetings will begin having to do with a press conference to announce the coveted designation of Black Arts and Entertainment District for Pennsylvania Avenue and its surrounding communities. So, at The Bakery, I was out in the heat for about an hour this morning, putting down fresh mulch in the garden and pulling weeds. It was brutally hot. I drank water and orange juice each time I went inside to cool off and hydrate. Outside, I didn't sweat that much but each time I stepped indoors I was sweating like a twenty-mule team.

Between today and Monday, I will try to nail down my welcoming introduction for the press conference. I want to give the purpose of The Avenue Bakery and TRTCHC, but I want to be mindful not to take away from Lady Brion's message. It's her show, and she has done a wonderful job, making the designation happen. The Mayor will be here as well as other politicians, and I want to make sure I follow protocol to make everyone feel comfortable.

***

It's about 10:00 a.m., Monday, July 22, 2019. Today, while I am waiting on the grass to dry before I cut it, I'm also trying to get my speech together for the Pennsylvania Avenue Black Arts and Entertainment designation announcement at The Bakery. And I am working on getting my tickets from the Football Hall of Fame folks because they put the wrong address on the package, and I have not received them. Along with this, I am trying to find out what the attire will be so that my grandson, Brandon, and I can be appropriately dressed for the affair. I also need to get back with my guests, Yvonne Medley, my editor, and her husband, Robert.

I called Courtney Aburn, who is one of the contact persons for The Ed Reed Foundation. I first asked her if she was related to Barney Aburn, who owns a T-shirt company in Baltimore.

"He's my uncle," she said.

Delighted to hear that, I explained that I had done business with him. "He's a great guy," I was happy to say. I then asked if she knew the attire for Ed's private party to be held on Friday, the second of August. We are invited to that, and the actual Enshrinement Ceremony held the day after on the third. She explained that cocktail attire was appropriate for the private party, and for the induction, casual slacks and a jacket would do nicely.

When the dust settled on the proper dress issue, I went on to tell her that I wanted to meet with Ed and Glenn Younes to discuss The Royal Theater project. Ed, Glenn and I had discussed our Phase I, which included the building of the new field and clubhouse. To my surprise, Courtney asked me if the project was related to something the Upton Planning leadership had in mind.

At that moment, I was somewhat taken aback. And I replied, "No."

Now, it is apparent to me that UPC's executive director, during Mayor Pugh's reign, had approached all the people I had brought to the table to support Phase I of the TRTCHC project. That is why I see Upton promoting the new field as its project.

I am shocked and appalled and not sure how to deal with the Upton Planning leadership at this point. However, I will be meeting with Ed and Glenn to get their views on what has taken place. From that, I will chart a course. Out of respect—concerning the Upton Planning leadership—if it's going to do this, I should have been consulted. This is the plan I presented to the Development Committee, and they have identified it as theirs.

***

It's 1:53 a.m., Tuesday, July 23, 2019, and I can't sleep like regular humans. My mind is so busy, thinking about the press conference at 10:00 a.m. today. I have my speech. On Sunday, I mulched the garden in the courtyard. Yesterday, I spoke to Brandon and my son, Ham. They are coming over to help me at The Bakery. James Dow, one of my board members, who also happens to be the uncle of my daughter-in-law, Etoy, had arranged for a musician to come by to perform for about an hour. But last night, he called to say that his backup plan, if the musician didn't show, which was for him and a friend to fill the spot, was not going to work. He informed me that he was in the hospital because doctors discovered he had some plaque in his artery beyond his stint. The doctors are keeping him until they determine the best plan of action. Thankfully, the musician did show, and the backup plan wasn't needed.

I am working in Brenda's office, and all I hear is heavy rain falling outside. Whenever I wake up like this, I always check my emails and text messages. Lo and behold, there is a text message from Lady Brion. I was so busy yesterday; I didn't check or watch the weather report. I sent her a message back, letting her know that we have had press conferences inside The Bakery on many occasions and that that will be the revised plan for today. That means Brandon and I will be hustling to get the room ready later this morning.

Although I have a plan and strategy for moving forward with our project, I am not in a comfortable place. Yes, we have obtained a grant from the Weinberg Foundation, and I am bringing important players back to the table. However, after finding out that the Upton Planning leadership had met with Ed Reed's Foundation and identified the moving of Robert C. Marshall Field as its project instead of what it really is—Phase I of our project—which had already been presented at the Developers Meeting—that fact still amazes me. And the more I think on it, the more I am sure that the Upton Planning leadership was acting on the advice and recommendation of Mayor Pugh. As we move forward, I am sure I will encounter other underhanded activity that has taken place. Although it makes me feel that I need to just ring the bell and go away to enjoy the rest of my life, I must stay the course and keep it in God's hands.

Well, that's what is on my mind at the moment. I guess I will get me some ice cream and cake, flip channels on the TV, hopeful that sleepiness will come to bring me some rest. I need to sleep, at least for a couple of hours, before I have to really get up.

***

It's 5:52 a.m., Saturday, August 3, 2019. My grandson and I are in Canton, Ohio. I just woke up, and as always, I have a thousand things on my mind. We're in the hotel, and Brandon is in the bed next to me, sound asleep even though I have the light on. Writing my thoughts, I am not sure where to start. I could recap the beginning of this fantastic week or relive Ed Reed's party last night and go backward. That said, I am being careful not to get ahead of things and certainly not to lull myself into a celebratory state prematurely. But I must say that compared to 2017 through 2018, so far, 2019 has been fantastic.

Last night Brandon and I arrived at Ed's party just before he did. As a matter of fact, and we didn't know it at that time, we had been driving behind his limo as it traveled down Canton Avenue on its way to the sprawling Brookside Country Club. That's where the party took place. We pulled in the driveway to where there was a bus, offloading guests. While sitting and waiting, I thought for a moment, *I should give Yvonne a call and let her know I'm here.* But she had called me around 9:15 p.m. to let me know she and Robert had arrived at the party. Because she is thorough and detailed about helping me write my memoir, Yvonne planned her trip to meet me here to capture every moment of my journey.

I parked in a lot close to the Country Club entrance, and as we began to walk up the driveway headed to the door, Ed was getting out of his limo. He was sharp, dressed in black, and sporting his gold Football Hall of Fame blazer. We would see those signature blazers being worn by every Football Hall of Famer, past and present, throughout the evening. He also sported a matching fedora, cocked to the side. A group of kids immediately swarmed Ed.

Signature to Ed's character, he began greeting them as if they were celebrities. Another group of folks, whom I assumed comprised his close friends and family, began to greet and hug him as well. Brandon and I stood on the curb, watching instead of going into the party. We patiently waited as Ed made his way through the celebratory crowd. He got to the curb, looked up, saw me, and said, as he always does when we meet, "Mr. Hamlin!" We shared a hearty embrace.

I said to him, "You are so great on the field and even greater in our community. I had to be here."

He looked me in the face and offered a warm and sincere, "Thank you."

As he moved on to greet more of his guests, we then walked into the party room, where I saw Yvonne waving us over to the table that she and Robert had reserved for us. I greeted them both, introduced them to Brandon, and mentioned that Ed had arrived and was on his way in. The place was just about full, the DJ was spinning all kinds of music, and well-dressed people were milling about all over. Surveying the festive room, I also spied a few people who were not so well-dressed. It gave me a chuckle because that's how it is these days.

It's not like back-in-the-day when at evening affairs like this, everybody dressed to make sure they outdid the next person. And if you didn't think you could manage that, well then, you stayed home.

The Medleys and I began to talk about our trip to Ohio for this event. Robert told me the drive from Southern Maryland and the frequent bathroom stops they had to make for their grandsons and their daughter, who also tagged along on the trip. As a family, they have planned to visit the Football Hall of Fame Museum. They also mentioned that their hotel was about fifty miles away from the event. During this time of year, I imagine that hotels fill up quickly in this area.

But boy did I have a story to tell. In Baltimore, Brandon and I got up at 3:30 a.m., left the house in time to check in and board our flight. We arrived at Atlanta International Airport at 8:53 a.m., and our connecting flight to Akron-Canton was scheduled to depart at 9:40 a.m. In order to get to it, we had to take the train. Keep in mind;

you must be at the gate ten minutes before boarding. By the time we got there, after running through the place like O.J.—that's back-in-the-day O.J.—we got there in time to see the flight attendant closing the plane's access door in our faces. I was not a happy camper. At this point, I was thinking; *we're not making the private party.*

We were instructed to see the ticket agent, who put us on stand-by to Pittsburgh. I was not expecting to be able to make that flight, either. However, we did have enough time to get to the appropriate gate. While all of this was happening, I talked to Brandon and demonstrated how not to let unfortunate situations dictate bad behavior. Although I wanted to wring the neck of the lady who closed the door leading to the plane's boarding or yell to the top of my lungs and act a fool like my mom would have done, I remained cool. I also called Brenda to update her about our situation because she did the booking and the itinerary for our trip. She was just as upset. But she immediately started figuring out options.

Canton, Ohio, is only a couple of hours from Pittsburgh. While Brandon and I were making our way to the Pittsburgh gate to see if we could catch our flight, I was also thinking about our luggage that did make the connecting flight from the Atlanta Airport, and I thought about the Alamo rental car we were supposed to pick up at an appoint- ed time in Canton. Now I was gonna have to rent a car in Pittsburgh and speed-race to Canton. And remember, we're not going to Ed Reed's private party unless we're dressed to impress. Not my style. If all went miraculously well, I, too, would be decked out in black—a black tailored suit, outfitted in a pale purple dress shirt. As a further tribute to The Ravens, my bowtie, modest boutonniere, and pocket handkerchief were lavender, which is in the family of purple. Brandon was also decked out in purple and black.

Brenda was aware of all the troubles at hand, and she got right to work doing whatever she could to keep us moving forward. She and her sister, Beverly, managed to call all the car rental places they could to secure a vehicle that we could pick up in Pittsburgh and leave in Canton when we flew back home on Monday. In the moment, though, Monday felt like an eternity away. They were successful and got us a car from Budget Rental Car. Like all couples, occasionally, we have our differences of opinion, and we don't see eye to eye.

However, during times like this I remember what my ninth-grade science teacher would tell the girls in our class.

He said, "No man wants to marry a dumb woman." I thank God I married a smart little cookie.

Brandon and I made our way from the Pittsburgh Airport to the Akron-Canton Airport, picked up our luggage, got to our hotel, had a bite to eat, and even took a nap before party time. My plan is to launch a major complaint with the airline when things slow down this weekend.

This was not my first time attending one of Ed's parties; however, this was the biggest. After my story, Yvonne filled me in on all the goings-on before we arrived. As we sat there, we soon saw Ed come into the room, and a new barrage of people, gravitating toward him like metal to a magnet. Yvonne had her Nikon camera with her, ready to capture every contact I had with him.

After the crowd around him began to thin out a little, I got Brandon to follow me as I made my way to the center of the room to get a picture taken with him. When I greeted him outside, cameras were flashing, but they were not ours. I was able to capture a picture with him. Though I was urging him, my shy, slow-moving Brandon could not get to the middle of the floor in time. However, because Yvonne had gotten his attention for us, she was able to be in the picture with us.

We then faded from the center of the room as more of his many friends, fans, associates, and some of the legendary Hall of Famers also decked out in their gold jackets began to enter Ed's space and focus. Baltimore Ravens player Ray Lewis, Football Hall of Famer, class of 2018, was amongst the mix. One of the Hall of Famers came with a friend to sit down at the two empty seats at our table.

A big burly guy, a Hall of Famer, who reminded me of my grandfather, Burl James Clemons, had planted himself at our table. I decided to introduce myself. I reached out to shake his hand, and we looked each other in the eye while his giant hand swallowed up my skinny little mitten. When he asked me where I was from, and I answered, "Baltimore," he immediately smiled and began to tell his Baltimore story.

He went on to tell me that he was a lineman for the Green Bay Packers, thick rivals of our then Baltimore Colts. He shared with me how, back in his day, he had made the longest interception and run back ever made against the Colts. He shared with me his fondness for Baltimore, and I believe he said he had once lived in Prince George's County for a while. He talked about his experience on Pennsylvania Avenue and having drinks at the Sphinx Club. He said with a fond smile that some of the Colts' players would take him out, drinking to get him drunk before the next day's game. "What they didn't know was," he joked, "holding your liquor was a skill where I came from." This player is from a small town in New Jersey.

He began to talk about some of the Colts' players he had hung out with, such as Lenny Moore and Jim Parker. After his stories, I asked if he would take a picture with us, and he was happy to oblige. Later, when I looked at the picture, I saw me looking like some little kid with this big guy's arm around me.

Somewhat embarrassed, I asked him to repeat his name, confessing that I am terrible with names when I first meet people.

He was not offended and was happy to say, "Dave Robinson like Jackie Robinson, linebacker."

His story was much more than what he shared with me in those fruitful moments. During his linebacker days with the Green Bay Packers, his overall performance helped make the Packers one of the most dominant dynasties in NFL history. Dave was inducted into the Football Hall of Fame in 2013. At the end of our talk, we shook hands again, and he moved on to spend time with the other Hall of Famers.

People were constantly coming, making their way into the party. Some had gold jackets, and some didn't; however, some of the more popular Hall of Famers were very recognizable. We saw, and I walked past, the giant, former Baltimore Ravens player, Johnathan Ogden, who took up the whole doorway. He was also inducted into the Football Hall of Fame in 2013. I got a chance to shake the hand of one of my son's favorite players when he was a kid, Emmitt Smith, Football Hall of Famer, class of 2010.

The one person I was very happy to see besides Ed was Dick Cass, president of The Baltimore Ravens. Back in 2016, I had met and shared our project with him. During the party, once he realized who I was, he indicated how great it was to have Baltimore fans at the induction. I was able to share with him the progress we had in place as well as news of our recent grant from the Weinberg Foundation.

His response was, "Awesome, keep me posted."

The DJ had the music jamming, and I really wanted to get my dance on, but I didn't recognize any of the ladies who could possibly handle my old-school smooth moves. Also, there seemed to be a group of little kids doing their little thing on the dance floor while the adults looked on. I wouldn't dare upstage them or embarrass myself on the floor with any of them.

In the meantime, Yvonne was making her rounds, introducing herself and my book around the room. She and her husband, Robert, were also taking pictures of my mingling with guests and celebrities. I sat down a couple of times, and at one moment, I saw a lady rolling in someone in a fancy wheelchair with a laptop attached. Low and behold, it was O.J. Brigance and his wife, Chanda. O.J. played only one season with the Baltimore Ravens in 2000, during which he played a pivotal role in getting the team to its first Super Bowl. Today, he is still a part of the team's front office in the role of senior advisement to player engagement, and he is beloved by Baltimore fans.

In 2007, O.J. was stricken with amyotrophic lateral sclerosis, or ALS, which is also more commonly known as Lou Gehrig's Disease. I had seen him on TV, but not in person. He seemed to be very comfortable at the party. Nearly every Hall of Famer went to him to embrace, greet, talk, and spend time with him, including Ray Lewis, who wrote the Foreword for O.J.'s memoir, titled *Strength of a Champion: Finding Faith and Fortitude Through Adversity* (2014). It painted a family portrait. It looked like a brotherhood thing to me. I felt honored to have witnessed it.

To date, O.J. has defied the odds on life expectancy for those who have ALS, and through his foundation, aptly called the *Brigance Brigade Foundation*, he and his wife of more than twenty-five years teach and empower those with ALS and caregivers.

In 2019, interviewed by a *Baltimore Sun* reporter, he expressed that he wanted his legacy to be one of, "The spirit of resiliency, no matter what."

Finally, I was standing at the edge of the dance floor, and I noticed a lady casually moving to the music, standing to the left of the dance floor. She seemed to be a prime candidate for the kid to get his dance on with. Just as I was about to make that move, Yvonne walked over with a lady in tow. It was O.J.'s wife, Chanda. Yvonne introduced her to me and mentioned the work I was doing on Pennsylvania Avenue. She then made her exit. It was an opened door to share with Chanda my initiative. We were speaking for a few minutes when someone called her attention. I assumed she was being called to deal with or help with the care of O.J. She said she would be back, but that didn't happen. About an hour later as she passed my table, I assumed leaving the party; she said, "It was great meeting you."

My hope is that she understood the impact of our project I shared with her. I am also hopeful that she could positively influence the outcome when the subject comes up in her presence. You never know the connections that God can make.

Well, we hung out for another hour or so, and I decided to call it a night. Yvonne and I had worked the crowd and spread the word. I was able to see Ed and take another picture with him as well. My plan at this point was to get a good night's sleep to make it to the parade at eight in the morning. Letting Yvonne know that Brandon and I were about to leave, she let me know that she and Robert would stay only as long as I was there.

"I'm working on your behalf," she said with a smile.

Making the executive decision, I told her, "Let's call it a night." After all, they were staying fifty miles away, which was about an hour's drive. Brandon and I were only ten minutes away from our hotel.

I got up in the middle of the night, and as always, I typed a couple of paragraphs. I laid out our tickets for the parade, the induction party, and the Enshrinement evening event, then I went back to sleep. When I awakened around 6:00 a.m., I decided we would skip the parade, aiming to attend the Enshrinement party at 3:00 p.m. along with the ceremony at 7:00 p.m. I worked on my memoir while Brandon slept. I managed to take a nap as well.

Around 9:00 a.m., housekeeping knocked on the door. A little old White lady came in and started cleaning the bathroom. I got back to my typing, and Brandon was looking at something on his phone. I could see her working in the bathroom through the mirror on the wall. When she walked in the room, she was surprised, realizing that we were there—still in the room. She walked over to the desk, picked up the trashcan, walked to the door, and then walked back. At that point, I didn't pay too much attention, yet I was kind of nonchalantly observing her movement.

At 1:00 p.m., we got up to shave, shower, and get dressed for the afternoon and evening events. I walked over to the desk to pick up our tickets, and they were not there. I looked all over the desk. Nothing. Then I second-guessed myself, retraced my movements, and checked my carry-on. Together, Brandon and I searched the entire room. It was apparent at that moment that the housekeeper had either trashed or confiscated our tickets. I went to the front desk, panicking at this point, to make a complaint. The person at the desk said she would try to contact the housekeeper to find out what she knew and where she had placed her trash. But all that was to of no avail. And the clock was ticking.

Now, again, I am so happy I married that smart wife because she put the receipt for my tickets with my itinerary. And that was before she'd taken off for Myrtle Beach with the rest of the family. The Football Hall of Fame festivities fell on our previously planned vacation. Back in Canton, at this point, I determined that I had to drive over to the Hall of Fame office to see if I could I get my tickets replaced. Brandon and I headed over there and found out that we had to drop off our car at the fairgrounds, not far away, and take the shuttle to the stadium. After this hurdle, we had to find the ticket office. Security for the events was high, understandably. Only a precious few could actually drive straight up to the stadium.

Still, in a panic mode, I sent a text to Glenn Younes, Ed Reed's point-person and coordinator of his foundation to explain all that had happened. I asked if he could help in any way. The more I kept asking folks where I should go and who I needed to see, the more frustrated I became. But I kept my cool. The guy at the Will Call counter said he would check into it, and that I should come back later. Brandon and I walked around, got our museum tickets replaced, and decided to shop for memorabilia.

On our way back to Will Call, Glenn called me and said, "Mr. Hamlin, don't worry. I have canceled your old tickets, and new ones are waiting for you at Will Call." At this point, I was relieved as I approached the Will Call window at the stadium with renewed purpose. When I gave the ticket agent my name, he indicated that he'd received a call ten minutes after I had come by earlier. He had the new tickets for me.

Now I had to call Yvonne because the tickets she had were no longer good. So, we were going to have to meet before the Enshrinement Ceremony. We made arrangements to meet at the fairgrounds to make the exchange. She and Robert had their grandsons and daughter with them, and I got to meet them. I introduced myself to the two fine young men, ages ten and twelve. I was so impressed with their firm handshakes and of them looking me in the eye. That is something I always teach kids when I meet them, but these guys were on it. We all took the shuttle back to the stadium, and the ceremony was fantastic. Although the speeches were long, they were so informative, interesting, and inspiring. Of course, Ed Reed's speech was the best. It was emotional, funny, and full of life lessons. He even mentioned Booker T. Washington Middle School and his commitment to the kids in that community of West Baltimore. By the way, the school is in U.S. Representative Elijah Cummings' 7th Congressional District, and he also attended that school as many of us did back in the days of segregation.

We enjoyed our weekend despite the setbacks. "Things happen," I told Brandon, "The key is how you respond to them."

However, as soon as I get a chance, I will be contacting Delta Airlines and The Hampton Inn, which is a part of the Hilton Hotels & Resorts chain, to give them a piece of my mind in a civil manner. Yvonne and her family said their goodbyes as they departed. She and her husband were thankful to have been given an experience that they could share with their little up-and-coming football players. From Canton, they continued on to Chicago to visit old stomping grounds, having once lived in that area.

Now Brandon and I went back to the Hampton Inn to prepare for our Sunday visit to take in the Football Hall of Fame Museum. It was fantastic, and much to see. The history of football is quite a story, and seeing the busts of all the great players was awesome. Of course, we took pictures of the bust of our own Ravens player, Ed Reed—with all his hair standing out. As a matter of fact, his was placed on the top shelf because of his hair. The attendant at the museum said it was put there because every visitor wanted to touch his *bronze* hair.

By the way, as we were touring the museum, people were buzzing and quickly walking because someone said that Ed Reed was at the museum. One lady and her husband came by and said that they saw him. "He tickled our son's tummy in the stroller," the woman said.

I thought for a moment that I should seek him out, but then I told Brandon, "We'll see him when we get back home. He's seen enough of us for this week."

***

It's 3:45, Monday morning, August 5, 2019. Brandon is asleep, and I am here at the desk typing away. I am now in the get-back-home-and-back-to-work mode. I must find the Budget Rental Car so that I can return the vehicle before our flight. We should be checking out around 11:00 a.m. Our task is to pack our bags, brimmed with our souvenirs that we bought for the family. And we're hopeful that our trip home will not be as eventful as the trip has been thus far.

It's now 10:42 a.m., we are at the Akron Airport. We had to check out of the hotel by 10:00 a.m. and have the car back at Budget by 1:00

p.m. Done. All of this has put us at the airport six hours before we need to be here. It makes for a long day but gives me an opportunity to get some of what has gone on and all that's running through my mind on paper.

Earlier, I wrote about the beginning of the week, alluding to the meeting my fellow board members and I had had with our forming development team on Tuesday, the 29th of July at The Bakery. It was attended by Dr. Brenda Brown, Danny Henson, Kathleen Sherrill, and board members Alice Cole, Adrian Johnson, and Rev. Arnold Howard. Zed Smith and Brian Grant had conferenced in. Everyone introduced themselves around the room. Brenda Brown and Alice had never met but seemed to connect very well. After the meeting was over, we found out that both were members of the Delta Sigma Theta Sorority.

The meeting seemed to go very well. It opened with the purpose and stated goals of the meeting. Rev. Arnold Howard opened the meeting with prayer. After everyone chimed in with questions and concerns, we addressed the next steps. It is at this time that Danny Henson, the most experienced developer at the table, suggested that we schedule a meeting with Ben Siegal of BDC and the Opportunity Zone Fund (OZF) expert. The reasoning was that we are looking at the project to be funded by an OZF, and we wanted to make sure our pro forma meets the requirements.

Immediately after Danny recommended that next step, I called Ben on my cell. I had met him during the July 12th Upton Developers' meeting, during which he had given a presentation on the Opportunity Zone Initiative. Much to my surprise, he answered the phone and seemed happy and excited to hear from me.

I explained that we would like to schedule a meeting to move our project forward, and he seemed happy to attend. In the room with Ben on the line, everyone agreed we would meet on the 14th of August at 10:00 a.m. Looking at the faces in the room, I think everyone was surprised and impressed at the speed at which I was able to get our next meeting scheduled and how quickly I was able to get Ben on board.

Although the meeting was on the calendar, emails were sent out to confirm. A couple of days later, Ben emailed to ask if he could bring a couple of Opportunity Zone Funders with him. I put the question out to the team, and the response was, yes, he could bring a guest; however, we want to keep the meeting small. But all agreed that having Zone Funders at the meeting was a positive.

The hour and a half meeting ended with everyone feeling good about the outcome and the next step. After Danny left and Brian and Zed hung up from the conference, I took the time to meet with our board members who were present. I addressed my question to Alice because her background is with the Baltimore City Department of Education. My question was, "How do we best include the school system in our project so that we can plan space in the design and construction?" We were fortunate that Brenda Brown and Kathleen had not left yet and could weigh in as well. It was determined that Alice would reach out to Baltimore City Schools' Superintendent Dr. Sonya Santelises and whomever else she feels is appropriate staff to work with us to bring this idea to fruition. Rev. Howard closed the meeting with prayer.

Tuesday, July 30, 2019, was Weinberg Grant receipt day. I didn't sleep much, but I had all my clothes and speech ready for the 11:30 a.m. presentation at The Center Club. The plan was for me to pick up Alice at her house on the way in town. Kathleen, my second guest, would meet me at The Bakery so that we would take only one car downtown. Before I left home, Kathleen called me to say that she was already downtown, and she would stay there and come over to The Center Club. That worked well for me because it allowed me to take my two-seat convertible for a needed spin.

I got to Alice's house earlier than what we had agreed; however, she came out right away. She was prepared and ready because she is well familiar with how I operate. I like to be early. She and I worked closely together during the mayors' O'Malley and Dixon administrations when I chaired Baltimore's Youthworks Summer Job Program. Together we developed a media campaign to attract businesses to provide funds and job opportunities for youth during the summer. Whenever we had a TV or radio appearance, I was always there early, waiting for her.

Whenever I would give Alice a time and date for an appearance, she would always ask me, "What's the real time?" That's because whenever I schedule a meeting, I give my guests and participants a time that's a half-hour earlier than the actual meeting time.

We waited in the lobby for Kathleen to arrive. The three of us were escorted to the elevator by security. When the elevator door opened, the first person we saw was Kyle McNair. He was so excited to see us; you would think we were rock stars. When we got to the sixteenth floor of The Center Club, we checked in and were seated at table number two, close to the podium. In the process, Kyle introduced us to several people. We got to our table, Alice and Kathleen were seated to my left, and Kyle was seated next to them. To my right was an older White woman who introduced herself to me and ended up being one of the trustees of The Harry and Jeanette Weinberg Foundation.

As I looked around the room, there were several people whom I knew. One of the persons I recognized was Rasheed Tawheed, who heads up a youth manufacturing program. Recently, he had a ribbon-cutting ceremony at his North Avenue factory location.

I enjoyed sharing about the TRTCHC and its major focus with other guests. During the ceremony, there had to have been at least twenty-five organizations that were being presented with grant awards.

And I think we were at least five or six from the end of presentations, so I got to take in all the good that's been going on around me.

Sitting at the table, Alice, who was sitting next to me, asked, "Do you want us to go up with you?"

I whispered back a resounding, "Yes! You go up with me. You're with me." As I approached the podium, I noticed how Alice and Kathleen seemed to be about three or four feet away. With the crowd looking, I offered a hearty smile and said, "Come on over here." It tickled the crowd. I then pulled out my speech and shared with everyone TRTCHC's focus, and more specifically, our project—about how it's a holistic approach to changing Baltimore, changing lives, and changing the vision of our young people and the atmosphere in which they live. There were those in the audience who felt moved to give us a standing ovation. After my speech, our pictures were taken.

Each table was garnished with huge, beautiful flower arrangements, planted in heavy, fancy vases. At the ceremony's end, the organizers made gifts of each arrangement to anyone who wanted to take one home. I was glad that both Alice and Kathleen got to take advantage of that.

During the ceremony, I got the opportunity to talk to a couple of notables. One of the persons was the new CEO of the Greater Baltimore Urban League, Tiffany Majors. The previous CEO was Howard Henderson. He and I had an excellent relationship. Often, we would sit down and talk about the community and the changes that were occurring during any given time. Certainly, when I was at UPS, we supported the Urban League. But I had not met its new CEO. And so, I got to meet her. She was very receptive, and I'm looking forward to sitting down to talk with her in the future. All of us, Kathleen, Alice, and myself, left the event, feeling very encouraged.

For our nonprofit, TRTCHC, this was history. It was our first time ever receiving a grant. It warmed my heart and further fueled my resolve to make positive change in West Baltimore. Kyle was so excited about the speech and about us being there. His enthusiasm over how the foundation gives back, coupled with his opportunity to present grant awards on the foundation's behalf, was very evident and contagious. I believe he told me it had been his third year serving in that capacity. His work, coordinating and guiding us through the overall process, was priceless.

Here's my Weinberg Grant acceptance speech, in full:

In 2005, The Royal Theater & Community Heritage Corporation was founded. Its purpose was and has been to address the negative perceptions and realities of Historic West Baltimore and Pennsylvania Avenue, part of the 7th Congressional District. We realized that if we are going to change and enhance Baltimore's future, we need to address the root cause of its problems.

Our focus has been to create a positive environment, economic opportunities, and to change the negative outlook of our future leaders.

As a result of our mission and investment, 2229 Pennsylvania Avenue has become a positive Oasis in this community that has been neglected for over 50 years. There, we have been able to attract visitors from all over the country and beyond to come and learn of the great history of this community. We have been able to host student visitors from schools and community organizations. Here, they learn about great leaders such as Thurgood Marshall, Parren J. Mitchell and entertainers like Billie Holiday and Cab Calloway.

Our goal is to build The Royal Theater & Community Heritage Center. This holistic development project consisting of a new Royal Theater, Jazz Center, retail shops and restaurants. As part of the project, we are investing in outdoor recreational space that our seniors and youth can enjoy together. This new recreational space and clubhouse will become a safe place for our youth and something they can be proud of. This project allows us to take advantage of Baltimore's third-largest 5.7 billion-dollar-tourist industry while creating jobs and careers in our community.

We have the history and legacy. People are coming. We want to build the infrastructure for economic and social change.

We thank The Weinberg Foundation for supporting us in our efforts to bring about positive change and outcomes for Baltimore and for our future leaders.

***

It's 10:29 a.m., Wednesday, August 7, 2019. I have not been able to sleep. This was the first day back at The Bakery. Things were a little slow, but I was able to get the sweet potato pie mix done. What got me up and unable to sleep was a voicemail that Courtney Aburn had left me. As I mentioned before, she is the point-person for the Ed Reed Foundation, whose uncle I know. I saw her the weekend of the Enshrinement Ceremony. Her message was that the meeting went well with the Upton Planning leadership concerning an initiative with Wells Fargo and that she had heard about how I had some funding for the project.

I assume Ed must have mentioned to Courtney and Glenn that I told him I had funding and that she should reach out to me. However, what alarmed me was the news about the Upton Planning leadership having some sort of agreement with Wells Fargo—I was thinking—pertaining to the field. This could be good or bad because TRTCHC and our development team already have the field in our development package. It has been there for four years now and makes for a holistic initiative.

The Upton Planning leadership has been keeping their actions off my radar. Now I realize why. Last year, when there was a meeting at Shake and Bake, they were having a pre-meeting with not only Courtney, but also a representative of Wells Fargo; and told me that I was not to be included. At this point, I have decided to find out the details of what they have done.

I asked Courtney if she could meet with me for an hour. She said she was out of town and would be back next week. We are meeting next Tuesday at The Bakery. I also called that representative of Wells Fargo to schedule a meeting for Monday at 1 p.m. My plan is to individually share our entire project with all the details, including its first phase, which includes the field. I plan to have hard copies along with the former mayors, O'Malley, and Stephanie Rawlings-Blake's financial commitment. I will let them determine if they were given all the correct details.

Now that we have The Weinberg Foundation on board and we have a development team, things are moving fast. We also have Baltimore Development and significant Opportunity Zone Fund managers coming to the table. I have reached out to Joe Haskins, President of Harbor Bank; we will be setting up our development account there, beginning with our Weinberg grant money. Next week is going to be very busy and interesting.

It is sad that I can't get the Upton Planning leadership to be honest and upfront. It gives me no pleasure to do what I am about to do next week. It's terrible when community people can't come together for the sake of changing lives for the future.

CHAPTER TWENTY-ONE

THE TIES THAT BIND

It's still Monday, August 26, 2019, and I had a hectic day today trying to get the yard and gazebo ready for our annual family cookout. We have been doing this for forty-three years now. Over the years, the house has gotten bigger, and although we have lost family members, we still have a big crowd every year. Brandon drove up to help me, and the two of us were able to get all the limbs and leaves cleaned up from recent windstorms. I asked Brenda to come out to supervise the cleaning of the gazebo. She had been working inside the house. I also cut the grass and trimmed up around in the yard. It took me about two and a half hours on my John Deere.

While going about my tasks, I received a few calls, one of which was from Harbor Bank. The executive assistant of its president, Joe Haskins, called me to ask if I would be available on Wednesday around 2:00 p.m. Apparently, Joe is giving a group of possible investors and members of his staff a tour. He wants to bring them by The Bakery to have me share our project. When Joe and I met last week, he had shared with me that he wanted to bring a cherry-picked group by The Bakery. Certainly, my response to her was yes.

I also received a call from Wanda Watts, who used to work for Sheila Dixon when she was mayor. Wanda has her own marketing business and is the coordinator of The Cadillac Parade & Billie Holiday Festival that will take place this weekend. She called to let me know that Fox45 would be at Billie Holiday Park, Friday, doing interviews pertaining to the festival. I have been designated as the spokesperson for the business district. "You need to be there at 7 a.m.," she let me know.

One of the calls I missed was from Wanda Best. But she left me a voicemail. Apparently, the festival volunteers and managers will be using golf carts to get around, and there is a need for a secure location to leave them overnight. My parking lot at The Bakery is gated and locked when not in use. Wanda asked me if I would allow them to park the golf carts on my parking lot Friday night. They would be picked up on Saturday before the parade begins. It's 9:53 p.m., I haven't had time to get back to her to say yes. I am always willing to do what I can to help our community.

Saturday was my birthday. And the only surprise I received was a visit by former Mayor Kurt L. Schmoke and his wife at The Bakery. I assume their visit came by the encouragement of Professor Teno Pearl of Coppin State University. She came by The Bakery about a year ago. The professor was so impressed; she wants to help us change the community. I had once asked her to invite the Schmokes because I wanted Kurt to see the picture of him featured in our Civil Rights photomontage that's very visible when you travel down Pennsylvania Avenue. His picture is there because he is the first African American elected mayor of Baltimore City. As the former Mayor, I'm hopeful that he can, and will want to, bring resources to the project.

We didn't get a chance to really talk because he had just come from having eye surgery. During his visit, though, he did ask for me. But I was in the garden with a group of young ladies from New York who were interested in investing in our community. Brenda rushed to get me, letting me know that he was there, asking for me. He and I spoke, shook hands, and he promised to come back. I gave him a copy of our project handout and my card, and he gave me his. Today, I sent him an email asking about his opinion of what I gave him and his experience at The Bakery. I am looking forward to his response.

After I completed my chores, I called Kathleen to inform her of the meeting with Joe Haskins. I'd like her to attend the meeting. Because she is the architect for the project, I always like having her by my side. We talked for a couple of minutes about our working birthdays. We both were born on August 24th. She said she worked all day, and I worked at The Bakery. I also hauled countertops so that my son could remodel his kitchen. Brenda did take me out to Tony's Restaurant, though. The kids and grandkids were invited; my sister, Sandra, and my niece, Ashley, were invited as well. Dinner was nice, and afterward, I washed my truck, went home, and went to bed. Getting myself to sleep, I spent about an hour reading all the Facebook posts and text birthday wishes I received.

I forgot to mention that my brother, Tony, was in town. He drives for a motorcoach company in Georgia and was on assignment in D.C. Tony has never been a suit-wearing kind of guy. While he was here, he mentioned how he and a friend had been invited to a wedding coming up in Atlanta. He asked me where I purchased my suits because he had checked into Men's Warehouse and found that their suits were somewhat expensive. Okay, please know that nobody's hating on the Men's Warehouse. But I shared with him that K&G had a sale going on. And I had recently purchased three suits from them; I let him know. He took my advice and purchased a couple of suits, shirts, and ties. Tony sent me, by text, a couple of pictures of his newly purchased suits. Then he called me to say that he was going to stop by The Bakery to get me to refresh his memory about how to tie his ties. And that's when the déjà vu streamed in.

Me, being the oldest of my mother's sons, I was the only one interested in suits and ties. When I was a little boy, my fondness was seeded, gazing out my living room window, studying all those smartly dressed professionals walk to and from work in our neighborhood. Growing up, an interest in coordinating colors and patterns and how to make them look sharp was stitched into the lining of wanting to grow up to be somebody. I admired the professional look, and I wanted to look professional as well. It's possible that this trait was inherited from my father because whenever his name was mentioned, remarks about how well-dressed he was always came into play. As a matter of fact, when I attended Booker T. Washington Junior High School, and Brenda and I were in the same class, I was voted as the best-dressed classmate. But my brothers and sisters weren't always interested in that. Even so, still, on occasion, if we had to be somewhere, formal-like, my younger brothers and I were called to wear a suit and a tie. It fast became my responsibility to tie all the ties—to make sure the small part of the tie didn't pass the big part of the tie—so that they didn't have to tuck the tie's end down into their pants. And there were different types of ties: you had the three-point diamond tie, and certainly, you had the slanted-knot tie. But I always liked the three-point diamond tie. It was my job to make sure their outfits matched up; their sport coats and pants, suits, and such.

Back in those days, my goal was to take care of my brothers and to teach. But what ended up happening was I would tie all the ties, and my brothers would slip them over their heads then pull them tight. So, when Tony stopped by The Bakery with all his outfits in tow, my intention was to help him coordinate and to teach. However, I'm pretty sure that once he got back to Atlanta, dressing for his special event, that he slipped his selected tie—diamond-knotted by me—over his head and pulled it tight. I'm also pretty sure that when he got to where he was going, he looked sharp. I was glad to do it, and it felt good helping my little brother—at our golden ages. He's sixty-seven, and as of Saturday, I'm seventy-one.

Well, it's bedtime.

***

It's 6:00 a.m., Tuesday, September 3, 2019. As always, I have a lot on my mind. The Labor Day weekend was busy and laborious as well. Even though we had a four-day week, which meant an extra day off, it was quite tiring. Yesterday, on Labor Day, we did the final cleanup from our annual family cookout. It's been our Hamlin tradition for more than forty years. Over that period of time, the older generation has passed on, but we always have a pretty big crowd of fifty to seventy-five people. This year was no exception. In the midst of my running around, getting things done, and again, right now, the reality sinks in. Wow, *we* have become the older generation.

Nowadays it's a little different because of The Bakery and always having to work on the Saturday before our Sunday gathering. The cookout always takes place on the Sunday before Labor Day. While we work on getting the house and the yard ready, the week before, we also start preparing our food. Brenda makes her homemade burgers, and they are wrapped and placed in the freezer. My task, as always, is to prepare the baby back ribs for the event. As I normally do, I purchased my ribs when they are on sale and place them in the freezer. I start preparing them the night before, taking out the membrane, cutting them into small sections, and applying rub. I then place them in the fridge to marinate overnight. I won't give up all my secrets about how I prepare my fall-off-the-bone ribs; however, I have been using my Bone Sucking Sauce for fifteen years. Yes, that's the actual name of the sauce.

Ham takes care of frying the fish and sometimes chicken, and Lin creates all kinds of salads and deviled eggs. She also brings all kinds of mixed drinks and stuff that will never pass these lips of mine. Every extended family member will bring something such as drinks and their favorite dish that they like to prepare.

I am not sure, but I think God favors our family because, in all these more than forty years that we have been doing this, it has never rained on us. This year, the weatherman called for showers, but only a few drizzles managed to materialize. It might have lasted for about ten minutes, tops. All in all, it was a perfect day.

Brenda's older brother, Larry Taylor, constantly thanks us for hosting the family every year. He spoke of how important it is for family to come together and to know each other. There were many times over the years, Larry and his family couldn't make it to the event because of his work schedule. He worked nights. Now that he has retired, he comes all the time. He was pleased yesterday because both of his sons were able to make it as well. One of his sons, Craig, lives in Connecticut. His other son, Brandon, recently moved to California. Larry is the only one of Brenda's siblings who doesn't have grandkids. If you'll recall, his wife passed away some years ago, and he's now dating Wanda Best.

My brother, Tony, didn't make it this year due to his schedule down in Atlanta. Of course, I understood and was grateful to see him the previous month when his job brought him to D.C., and we had our special time together. There are times when we have to grab and appreciate our special moments whenever we can get them. I was disappointed that my granddaughter, Bria, did not come. She decided to spend her time with others. I have been disappointed for years that my favorite nephew, David Knight, doesn't come as well. His dad, my ex-brother-in-law Joe, seems to think David's religion is the reason he never shows. He's Seventh Day Adventist. I believe he doesn't come to family events because his second wife doesn't feel comfortable around his family. The reason for that is because, as a family, we still have a positive relationship with David's first wife, Robin. She's the mother of his three sons. I call him occasionally to see how he's doing, and occasionally, I get a callback. The last time I spoke to him, I promised Brenda, and I would take him and his wife out to dinner. I must get on that real soon.

I really miss my mom, brothers, Harold and Carl, and my sister, Eldora, who have all passed. Each of them had their unique personalities and made family get-togethers fun. They always had stories about the crazy and funny things they did or took place at mom's house. For years they all lived in the same house together in the 1800 block of East Fayette Street. It was once a neighborhood where all the families got along, and everybody knew Miss Mattie. That community was torn down to make way for the Johns Hopkins' expansion. Little did my mom, brothers, or sister know that the place where they worked would take over their community. Johns Hopkins' focus was expanding its empire and providing housing for the professionals it attracted. In other words, the name of the game was gentrification.

Well, back to 2019, our event was great. Everybody did their part, and Brandon even cooked on the charcoal grill for the first time during our annual family event. I stood watch, proud and cognizant of this modest historical marker in the making for the next generation of Hamlins.

CHAPTER TWENTY-TWO

FAMILY JOY AND PAIN

First, The Pain

Today is the Fourth of July, 1997. I decided to write my brother, Carl, who was in jail for doing something against the law. I never asked him what he did. I wasn't interested in that.

He had written me twice, asking for money, and until now I hadn't responded. In my letter, I explained to him how the only time I hear from most of my family members, it's when one of them needs something. Tony, Gertrude, and Eldora are the only ones who call to say, hello, without expecting a handout.

I tried to let Carl know that I love him, and I worry about him. He is an intelligent person and could be doing so much better. My concern is that he will never get any better if I keep supporting him. I'd just become one of his enablers. Somehow, I think we do that to our people. Instead of forcing them to take charge of their lives, we make them dependent on us.

***

I thought I was being strong by my actions, writing what I saw as the truth in a letter. But I am not sure I made the right decision. You see, Carl is out of jail now, and he has disappeared. No one has seen him in months. It is now October 11, 1997. And for all we know, he could be dead. The last indication of him being alive is a report from a homeless shelter that he had applied for assistance in June. And someone told Tony that they had seen Carl in June.

Tony had also said that Carl had visited him last in December of 1996. At the time, we thought it strange that he had not contacted anyone during Christmas. Donna, Tony's wife, encouraged us to try to find out where he was.

***

We drug our feet for months, well into 1998, hopeful he would finally contact someone. At the same time, we were afraid of what we might find out if we intentionally searched. I was especially afraid because after I wrote him that letter about getting his life together, he stopped calling or writing me. I don't know if it was because he felt bad that I had to resort to tough love or if he felt mad that I was not going to continue to enable him. Maybe he felt I was no longer there for him. This is something, a possible fact, I will never know and with which I will have to live.

Donna gave me the name of a private detective she knew, who felt assured that he could help us locate Carl without going through the usual channels. I called him to give him the information we had. A few days later, he paged me. I was at work at the time but knew I had to answer the page. Yet, I didn't want to answer for fear of my suspicions being true. I called the detective.

His words to me were, "I'm sorry."

I knew what he was going to say after that. A knot began to form in the middle of my chest, and I wanted to hang up the phone. I listened to the story and maintained my composure until he finished.

He explained that in December of 1996, three days after Carl had visited Tony, he had been placed in a taxicab at Broadway and North Avenue. The cab driver took him to the drug rehab center on Charles Street, where no one could identify him. The cab driver then took him to Johns Hopkins Hospital Emergency. According to the hospital's report and the investigator's report, Carl died of narcotic intoxication. The hospital then sent his remains to the morgue and gave their report to a police officer. The police officer said that she would notify the family. She never did. After his body remained at the morgue for three weeks, his remains were cremated.

This was the hardest thing I've had to deal with. We would never see his face to know for sure if that body *was* indeed Carl's, as they claimed, or we would never be able to say goodbye. The detective went on to say that we should have been notified, and someone failed to do their job. He also mentioned that no law had been violated because Carl was an adult. He wondered why we had not filed a missing person's report. I explained about Carl's lifestyle of drug abuse and of being in-and-out of penal institutions.

"We just always took for granted that he would show up at one time or another," I said. When Carl was bad off, he didn't want any of us to see him that way. I thanked the detective for his help, and he agreed to fax me the documents he had obtained.

I knew he was faxing documents to me at work, and it is the company's policy not to use company equipment for personal use. I always go that extra step to follow the rules and protect my back just in case someone wants to take my job away. I notified my manager that I would be receiving a fax and what it was all about. Under the circumstances, my manager understood.

We finally were able to get together to have a formal symbolic goodbye in 1998.

Family Joy

Today, Hammy, Lin, their spouses, and kids are coming for dinner. Ham and Etoy married in 1997. It feels a little weird to say that—*my children and their families*. I am happy for them, of course. We often talk of them being on their own with their family concerns, not ours. In reality, that is what we expect, and we're hopeful that our kids understand that as well. Every parent's dream is for their children to grow up, get an education and a job, whichever comes first, have kids, and enjoy the same pains and worries we experienced while rearing them.

Brenda and I consider ourselves blessed. We have two wonderful children. Neither finished college, but they work hard and are good people. Neither of them is on drugs nor alcohol. Neither have criminal records (as long as we don't count traffic tickets). When I look at them and reflect, back in time, I don't remember them coming with a tag that brandished *a good person*. We didn't even get a warranty. But somehow, I knew they would be good kids.

The years 1997 and 1998 have been good and bad years for us. Of all things, they have been quite busy.

CHAPTER TWENTY-THREE

SHARING FAVOR, FITNESS, AND THE ROARING '20s

It's **Tuesday, September 17, 2019**. And the weekend, prior to, was a full one, to say the least. Friday morning was filled with fruitful, impactful deeds led by The Ed Reed Foundation. Its special program, *Fitness Day*, for Booker T. Washington Arts Academy students got underway around 10 a.m. on Friday, September 13. Glenn Younces, executive director, Courtney Aburn, point-person for the Foundation, and Booker T.'s principal, Mrs. Misha Scott, and I looked on and shepherded the event. And, yes, at times, all of us took a brave crack at the athletic obstacle courses that Ed had set up. Ed, who now lives in Atlanta, did not come alone. He brought his former trainer, Monte Sanders, and one of his close friends, former Kansas City Chief's wide receiver player, Eddie Kennison, III. Together they all electrified the students and encouraged them by also offering life-changing talking points between the physical fitness sessions of the day. Booker T.'s teachers were no slouches, either. They joined in the fun and instructed all the while.

As usual whenever visitors come into my sphere, we all rounded up the day at The Avenue Bakery. Everyone took home generous amounts of sweet treats. Each one signed our guest book that's posted up in our lobby, and I was able to share the historic glory days of Pennsylvania Avenue and share more about the TRTCHC's project and goals.

Back on the field of Booker T. Washington, immediately after the *Fitness Day* came to a close, Wanda and Jules moved into action. They were there, set to present Booker T. with the Wells Fargo donation check of $100,000. The donation would be made on behalf of The Upton Planning Committee. Accruing the check had been the result of their secret grant-seeking project that they had worked so hard to keep me out of. However, on the day of, when it was time to make the presentation, take pictures, and all of that; the school officials, Ed Reed, Wells Fargo, and Ed's Foundation representatives, not only included me but thanked me for all my years of dedication to Booker T. They thanked me, both as a Pennsylvania Avenue businessman and as a former UPS executive. Our State Senator Antonio Hayes's representative brought with her citations for Wanda and Jules, and she brought one for me as well. I had no idea such was coming. I was stunned, and my heart was filled.

These are the remarks that Glenn Younces made:

[Thank you to] the community of Upton and the Booker T. children. I won't be very longwinded but we couldn't do any of this without, of course, our founder, Ed Reed, who is a Hall of Famer, not only on the field but off the field. And we are lucky to be in this community, and to give back. And thank you also to Wells Fargo and all the politicians, and folks in the neighborhood. Also, I have to mention Mr. Hamlin, who's been in this community long before we ever got here. He was a graduate and alumnus of Booker T. Washington Middle School. He made it well in the corporate world and has given back for nearly fifty years. So,

thank you, everyone: Mr. Hamlin; our founder, Ed Reed; Wells Fargo and UPC. We're excited for this opportunity.

These are the remarks that Ed Reed made:

I didn't prepare a speech. [Laughter] I really want to thank Wells Fargo for this lending hand. It's definitely needed. We also need more corporate sponsors, any, anybody who wants to donate and help us out in this community. We more than need it. We ask that you come out and support and help these kids in this community. And also, Booker T. Washington, you are always opening your doors and letting us come—to all the volunteers who came out today to just help the kids, just try to plant these nuggets and these seeds to make our kids better. They're our future. I used to be one of those kids, that's why it's easy for me to come back and do things like this. We want to do more. So, we need more help. I want to thank everybody for coming out.

Mr. Hamlin, you know that you're like my dad. [We're] honoring and recognizing what you do—what you've done for so many years. Thank you, Mr. Hamlin, and UPS, for what they've done over the years. I won't be longwinded but thank you all. And like I said, we need your help. We need your support. So, lend a hand, Baltimore.

My admiration for Ed's continued long-term commitment to our children is simply over-the-top. To say that the sentiments of both Ed and Glenn merely warmed my heart would be an understatement. Their words energized me as well. I was surprised and grateful at those turn of events beyond words. In the aftermath of those moments, though, I couldn't help but wonder what Wanda and Jules were feeling.

Friday evening held the promise of more, resulting in another wonderful event. Set to take place was the Ed Reed Foundation's Roaring '20s Gala, held at Baltimore's Four Seasons Hotel. I was excited about it from the minute I received the invitation to attend. Brenda is not much for those kinds of festivities, so I decided to take my niece, Ashley Crawford, along. An avid fan of The Baltimore Ravens, she's earned it. In fact, that week, prior, she had just come from Miami, attending a Ravens-Dolphins' game.

For years, for the Booker T. kids, I have hosted tailgate parties at the Ravens' home games. When I got too busy with the TRTCHC project and around The Bakery, Ham took it over. And when he got too busy with his sons' organized athletic participation and his home projects, Ashely gladly picked up the mantle. So, attending the gala was a real treat.

As I mentioned, the theme was the roaring '20s, and everyone was to arrive dressed in the era. The first thing I did was to take to the Internet to find a suitable outfit. And I thought I'd managed it—until what I ordered arrived in the mail. It turned out to be terrible. Standing in our kitchen holding that thing up to the light, I told Brenda, who had gotten quite a chuckle out of my surprise package, "It ain't no way in the world, I'm gonna wear this thing. It looks like something that a clown would wear at the circus."

This unfortunate turn of events sent me scrambling to my closet—to the very back of my closet—wondering, *now just what am I going to wear*. I dug in and found I had a double-breasted suit. It was a dark gray pinstripe with a vest like back in those days. I hadn't worn it much, so it looked like new. For the gala, I wore the suit with a combination red and black tie. I had also pulled out my Bostonian shoes. I hadn't worn them in God-knows-when, either. They were so polished; they shined like patent leather. For the finishing touch, I went back in that circus outfit I'd gotten online and pulled out the spats. My newly improvised ensemble worked. Brenda approved. My only problem, now, was that I didn't have a fedora. I have big brim hats and short brim hats, but I don't have a fedora. The search for one sent me all over, hours before the gala. But God was on my side. I ended up finding just the right fedora in a beautiful hat shop in Fells Point. God was on my side, but He didn't make it cheap. It cost me a hundred and twenty dollars. But I'll get to wear it again. I was grateful and set.

Ashley looked perfectly themed, beautiful, and she had a good time. It made my heart glad. She also got to meet one of her favorite Ravens players, Torrey Smith, a retired wide receiver. Torrey had played for the Ravens, the San Francisco 49ers, the Philadelphia Eagles, and the Carolina Panthers. Ashley got to take pictures with both Ed Reed and Torrey Smith.

I also got to talk with Ed about the project. He let me know that he would reintroduce the project to Dick Cass and would get back to me about it.

Everyone came decked out and looked great—including Ed, Courtney, Glenn, and Booker T. Washington's Principal Scott. Ms. Jones was there; also, she's Booker T.'s vice-principal. Ashley and I joined Principal Scott at her table. It was definitely a party atmosphere. Jules walked up, and we all started talking about one thing, then another, and then we hashed over some of the occurrences of the Foundation's *Fitness Day* at Booker T. That's when I got in, "Where's Wanda?"

Looking a bit vague, in my estimation, Jules responded, "Wanda had something she had to do."

While the odd explanation hovered in the air, I left it there. Eventually, Jules and I began talking about how much we both loved to dance. The music was jumping, and lo and behold, she and I found ourselves on the dance floor, showin' the young folk how it's done. I felt it loosened the tensions of our past, mightily.

I've mentioned this before, and I'll mention it again; I have the utmost respect for Wanda and Jules, and I realize that they're doing what they feel is good for the community that they both love. I also realize that they're trying to make the right decisions. However, just because they don't see the light the way that I see it, and how so many others see it as well—it doesn't make them bad people or anything close to that. It's just that I happen to strongly feel that the decisions they make aren't always wise. That said, every day, I work to recognize their right to have different opinions and to acknowledge their honest effort to try to do what's right in their eyes.

In 2018, our country's former First Lady Michelle Obama's memoir was published. It was simply titled *Becoming*. In it, she chronicles her life's journey from birth to profession, to love, marriage and motherhood, to her experiences and treatment while becoming—and being our First Lady.

During President Barack Obama's second term, she visited her hometown of Chicago, spoke at a high school in Englewood's neighborhood, and interacted with its students. Over the decades, Englewood, a neighborhood she knew well from her growing-up days on the Southside of Chicago, had become a dangerous part of town. "In the previous year, twenty-nine of the school's current and recent students had been shot, eight of them fatally," Mrs. Obama penned in her book. About this subject, there were more points shared. But respectfully, from her memoir, *Becoming*, this is what I want to share about her visit, about her accrued political perspective since her husband had become president of the United States and the hard, cold truth that she felt she had to share with children, living with life-altering challenges. Its message knitted a kinship with the children and community; I fight so hard to serve, protect and improve.

Believe me; there was a lot to glean from Michelle Obama's memoir, *Becoming*. She made the point that *"Politics was a mess."* And she felt terrible to be the bearer of such reality. Still, she did manage to leave the students with the heartfelt advice to use school, i.e., getting an education and putting their knowledge into action, as a formidable path to freedom and achievement.

While I'm hoping to be successful at getting across my overall message about being thankful and remaining positive—even when I may struggle—I don't want to make Jules or Wanda, or anyone else, trying to do good for West Baltimore, villains in my Baltimore Story or my mission. I don't always feel that their decisions are right; I've said that, but more importantly, there is much more at stake. I do want us to recognize the fact that we have to be careful not to always rely on politicians to do the right thing all the time. We cannot allow them to influence or change what we know, what we believe, and/or the realities of what we need. Some of the political moves that had been made, including those made decades ago, should have never happened. And we as a community should have stood up and voiced our opinions and fought for ourselves—our rights. We should have made clear what we wanted. That's what we, the TRTCHC and its supporters, have been working on for quite some time.

I'm prayerful that the Foundation's gala has worked to soften the ground, enough for new seeds to be sown between Jules, Wanda, and me. Well, we all know that the Lord works in mysterious ways.

Backtracking to earlier on Friday, I had an encounter at The Bakery with two inspectors from the Health Department. They had contacted us previously, but apparently, they kept making their surprise visits at the wrong times—when we were closed. Eventually, they wanted to know whether or not we were in business anymore. Of course, we were. So, I had to call them to tell them what times to come—for their surprise visits. Lo and behold, Friday, here they come.

The inspector happened to be of Asian descent. Ms. Lew barely spoke English. She had another young lady with her, also of Asian descent, who helped her by pretty much typing all the information into her phone. They walked through the place, but they couldn't find anything wrong, so they checked my refrigerator. The temperature in my refrigerator is supposed to be forty-one degrees or below. When Ms. Lew and her assistant inspector checked it, it was forty-three degrees. So, she started inspecting its contents and saying things like—through her young associate, of course, "Oh, you have to throw your milk away." And saying, "You have to throw this away and that away." Now my pressure is getting up a few degrees as well. So, we got into it for just a bit—as much as the language barrier would let us.

One of the things that I had just done before her arrival was that I had just gotten through preparing my sweet potato pie mix, and I had not long put it away in the refrigerator. I had failed, or perhaps, my pressure was too high to even bother to disclose that, mainly because I strongly sensed that she wasn't looking for any viable answers to anything. Any explanation I could offer was going to be lost in translation—inspector-speech or otherwise.

I boil my sweet potatoes. I do not use canned sweet potatoes. So, they are still hot when I mixed them up. I then pour them into buckets so that the mixture is ready whenever I need to meet customer demand. Those buckets are warm when I store them in the refrigerator, which was probably why the inside temperature was up a degree or two. I did try to explain to Ms. Lew that we had been going in and out of the fridge, which can also drive the temperature up.

"Ahhh, that happens to everybody," she managed to retort in suspect English.

I just stopped trying to convince her of anything. I called the refrigerator repair guy, requesting that he come out as soon as possible. The quickest he could schedule was for the coming Monday morning. I had no choice but to accept it. And come Monday, which was yesterday, my industrial refrigerator was set at thirty-five degrees to ensure that neither buckets filled with fresh sweet potato pie mix nor the opening and closing of its doors by busy staff could drive the temperature up more than forty-one degrees. I like to keep everything in order to not have to worry about inspectors or anything else. That's the life I've led during my thirty-five-year career at UPS and the life I lead now.

My next bump in the inspector-road was the news that a license, of which I was told, years ago, I didn't need—somehow, now, I needed. I was given twenty-four hours to correct it. It was rectified by close-of-business that Friday. I like to stay on top of everything. And I try to impart the way one should do business to my grandsons, even though they are just teenagers. I share the ups and the downs and the situations that one just has to deal with to remain on the right side of things.

My profession and my family are important to me. Having to wait until Monday for the refrigerator repairman meant that Brenda and I could not go to Petersburg, Virginia, as we planned on Sunday. Gert has been in the hospital. She had not been feeling well, but this time was a little bit different. She was eventually diagnosed with having a stomach blockage and would need to have surgery. Once her doctors started the surgery, they decided to remove her gallbladder. I've been calling her every day while she's been in the hospital, expecting her to be released. But when Friday came, and she was still there, Brenda and I had made plans to take a drive on Sunday. It was a disappointment to realize that we wouldn't be able to leave until Monday night.

So, yesterday, we came down here, and it was a tough ride because I had so much stuff to do. Waiting on the repairman, waiting for him to get finished, two o'clock rolled around fast. We didn't get on the road until about three o'clock, in time to catch rush hour traffic in D.C. and Virginia. The traffic just got heavier and heavier, so instead of the ride taking us three hours, it took us five. But I slept most of the way because Brenda drove. Thank God for helpmates. She got me back, though. Because today, on the drive back, I did the driving.

This entire past week has been very, very interesting. Earlier in the week, I was trying to tackle a faulty icemaker at The Bakery. It's been leaking for about a week and a half now. I'd been trying to figure out the problem. I bought a part for it from the manufacturer. I installed this brand-new tube I'd gotten, and the next morning had me mopping up water for about an hour. So, needless to say, that didn't solve the problem. However, Ham's been helping me. And one of the things about my son is that I can plainly track the traits he's gotten from his mother and the traits that come directly from me, his dad.

There are exceptions, but for most repair problems, the Hamlin motto has been—if someone else can fix it, that means we can too. We just have to crack the code. As long as we can figure out the *how,* then we can make it *happen.* And that's the kind of thinking that my son gets from me. So, Ham gets another part for the icemaker, and he starts in. We were trying to figure out how to take it apart, researching techniques online and everything, when somewhere along the journey, I lost my patience. But Ham's mama-trait kicked in, and he refused to quit. On his mama's side, he's persistent. Brenda is like a Pitbull when it comes to tackling a problem. Ham figured it out and figured out which part that truly needed replacing.

We were going to order it from the manufacturer, but that was going to cost us 300-and-some dollars. Nowadays, we've learned, like with most anything else we buy, to comparison shop. Eventually, we were able to find it $100 cheaper on Amazon. So, we've ordered it, and we're waiting on that part. So, trying to keep up with that and keep up with The Bakery and our customers have kept me busy. The children are back at school; vacations are over. Customer traffic is growing steadily, and that's a good thing.

As far as the project is concerned, things are working. I'm moving. So, I'm working with Kathleen and Brian, who is the engineer.

They presented some work that they had completed on Friday. And between that and trying to study their proposals and how to get them paid are front-burner tasks that need to get done.

Danny Henson, on the other hand, reached out to the Housing Commissioner, Michael Braverman. However, when Danny reached out to him about the project, he didn't seem to have a clue. And that's sort of interesting because Braverman was a part of the Housing Department back when I was revealing the project to the previous mayors. Perhaps it's because he wasn't directly involved; maybe that's why he wasn't familiar with the project. Still, that fact raises my eyebrow. Danny, right now, is working on us setting up a meeting with Braverman. We also want to give him a tour of the community to get him further familiarized with the project.

Braverman is the guy who replaced Paul Graziano, so we're looking at that and trying to pull all those pieces together. I did have a meeting with Leon Pinkett. As a matter of fact, on late Sunday, I stopped by his house, and we sat on his steps in Reservoir Hill to talk about the project. I went over it, again, with him, and he understood it, he said. I asked him for his full support and asked, outright, for his updated letter of support.

He responded, "The project is in Eric Costello's District [which is the 11th District]. I'm waiting for him to pull the trigger first." Leon also indicated that he likes the plan and that it's a good project.

Pennsylvania Avenue covers both their districts, but the project is in the 11th District. So, I called on him too.

I also want to ensure that our state delegates are aware and on board before they all get started in Annapolis for its 2020 legislative session. I had talked to State Senator Antonio Hayes in June. On July 13, he had gotten married; in fact, that happens to be mine and Brenda's wedding anniversary date. So, his focus might have been diverted a bit. It was good to talk with him briefly when he stopped by the Ed Reed Foundation's *Fitness Day* at Booker T.

As mentioned before, Alice Cole is the secretary for the TRTCHC. She used to work for former State Senator Nathaniel J. McFadden, who is still a powerhouse down in Annapolis. He reached out to me. And I sent him information on the project. And he sent the information to the point-person for Lt. Governor Boyd K. Rutherford. McFadden is saying that this project should have happened long ago. So, he wants to help in any way that he can. As I mentioned, he doesn't work down there anymore, but his influence and respect remain intact. And he wants me to reach out to Don Fry, who is a part of the Greater Baltimore Committee (GBC). McFadden also advised me to set up a meeting with Cory Dennis, the Lt. Governor's point-person. So, I'm trying to get that done.

Well, we're home now. It's about 1 p.m. I'm a bit tired from the Petersburg drive, but it's time to pick up the dogs and then give the grass a good cut.

CHAPTER TWENTY-FOUR

TREASURED FRIENDS

It's Tuesday, September 24, 2019. As usual, I am up with a lot on my mind. This morning, my body is talking to me, too. Yesterday, as promised, Wyatt Arrington, my friend who retired from UPS as well, came out to help me work on my shed. As a matter of fact, as I mentioned earlier, I was his first supervisor at UPS. The shed is out back behind the house and where I keep my lawnmower and all my tools. I need to take care of our little acre of land the best way I can. For the past three years, the field mice have made a cozy little home out of my shed, and they've made quite a few meals out of the wires of my lawnmower, evidenced by their chewed-up status. Inspecting the shed, I can see that the field mice, or other little critters, have managed a host of things to keep themselves nice and warm during the frigid months or the unforgivable heat. And of course, where there are field mice, there are also black snakes on the lookout for a nice meal and a comfy living as well.

Finally, after years of providing a home for the wildlife and allowing the termites and other insects to eat away at my belongings, I decided to rehab the shed. We were able to take off the roof to replace it with plywood instead of particleboard. The task of taking off the roof was very challenging—and probably deserves its own chapter. There were no nails or screws lurking about but giant staples. If it wasn't for Wyatt's out-of-the-box idea, we would still be trying to get the old particle board to loose itself from my shed. He suggested we get a jack of some kind and a two-by-four to force the roof up off the trust. I was skeptical at first. However, we made our trip to Home Depot, and we picked up a car jack and two-by-fours. And during our determined stroll through the aisles, I was a silent partner in the venture. But what seemed to be a crazy idea worked.

When we got the job done, some five and a half hours later, having left our blood, sweat, and tears in the wake of the job, we managed enough gumption to share a meal that Brenda had prepared for us. After our dinner together, before he left, he indicated how sore he was after our arduous and adventurous workout.

"I haven't worked this hard in over fifteen years," he said, attempting a stretch-out of our kitchen chair.

And oh, by the way, Wyatt always makes sure I pay him for the work that he does for me. And I had to pay him in advance for helping with the shed, too. He charged me five dollars. I also had to pay him for looking out for the house in Florida during the recent hurricane, threatening to reach land. It just so happened; he was traveling around Florida fulfilling his bucket list, visiting, fishing, waterskiing, etc. And he ended up close to our home in Kissimmee during the storm threat. He volunteered to take a look at our house to make sure everything was tied down for the potential storm. He stacked our furniture in the lanai, got my neighbor, Krystoff, to put our trash cans in his garage before the heavy winds came. That task cost me two dollars, but I gave him an extra dollar as a bonus.

Later today, I will be out here putting on the roof shingles and working on the shed's back wall with my faithful, reliable companion, Brandon. He came over to help, and he promises to be back tomorrow after he visits his grandmother, Betty. Wyatt, on the other hand, said to call him if I need him. However, I couldn't put him through another grueling day. Besides, I am sure he will be going fishing with Leon Funderburk, another fellow UPSer, not retired. Fishing is his newest adventure on his bucket list.

Much to my surprise, I came to the house from the shed to pick up some more tools, and lo and behold, Wyatt was parked in my driveway. I was pleasantly surprised but couldn't believe that he came back for more torture. He spoke of how stiff and sore he was but that he just couldn't leave me hanging the next day—this kind of friendship I treasure. When I see family and friends, whether it's my siblings, my children, and so on, my last words to them are always; I love you. Due to the friendship and relationship that Wyatt and I have, I want to address him the same way. But for some reason, I don't know why—maybe it's a man thing or something—I just can't seem to get myself to do that. To just say, "I love you, man." It's strange and funny.

This past Sunday was Bria's twenty-third birthday, which means I have been *Poppay* for exactly that period of time. I texted her at 1:20 a.m. on Sunday to say happy birthday and to say that I love her. Brenda stopped by Ham's house to say happy birthday to Bria and drop off our birthday present. While that was going on, I was at The Bakery, waiting on Rock, who has experience repairing appliances. Rock is John's friend, and John is my brother-in-law. Rock was going to help with The Bakery's icemaker that Ham and I have been trying to fix. The timing of Brenda's arrival was perfect because she, Ashley and my sister, Sandra, were getting ready for their vacation trip to Jamaica.

I also called my sister, Dot, to wish her a happy birthday on Sunday as well. September 22nd is her birthday as well. She didn't pick up the phone, so I left her a message. In recent years it has been a pleasure to speak with her and see her and Paul at family events as well as the Jazz events at The Bakery. Every time we talk, we joke around a lot. We're always able to find something to make us laugh. It gives me that warm-and-fuzzy feeling for us to communicate the way we did as teenagers. We could always come up with something to smile and laugh about regardless of the hard times and the negative things that were always impacting our lives.

Certainly, our TRTCHC project is on my mind, and I am constantly working toward the day that we break ground. Last week, I was able to meet with Lt. Governor Boyd Rutherford. I was able to meet with Councilman Leon Pinkett as well. However, Eric Costello, the Councilman whose District is where we plan to build the project is missing in action. Although I have seen him at events and says to reach out to him, he does not return emails, text messages, or phone messages. I am also concerned that we still haven't been able to meet with Mayor Young as well. Also, although State Senator Antonio Hayes said he would be willing to pull together a meeting with the delegates so that we could update them before their new session in Annapolis, he isn't responding to emails, either.

To add to my discomfort about all this, Darroll Cribb, President of Upton Planning, is trying to desperately schedule an Upton Board meeting. To his *sent* emails, he's gotten little response. He's now resorted to personal phone calls. When he called me, he asked if I could meet this Friday or Saturday, which is the same request made in his emails. I indicated that Saturday would be the better day. In his voicemail, and when he reached me, he indicated there were a lot of things happening in Upton and that we need to meet. With all of this going on, I have a host of concerns, placing me out of a comfort zone about things.

We—all those working to see this project through—are still working on the mission. I received the proposals from Brian and Kathleen and shared them with our board. They have both completed the first installment of their deliverables as promised, even though they have neither received signed agreements nor the first payment installment. I sent a copy of the proposals to my Board for review and only received a response from Alice. I have communicated to Adrian and Alice that we would make the final decisions on the proposals. I am trying to be as transparent as possible.

Another thing that troubles me is that Danny Henson had committed to schedule a meeting and a community walkthrough with Commissioner Michael Braverman of Baltimore's Department of Housing & Community Development. Kathleen was able to send him everything he needed to identify the site and plan. These were the items for which he indicated a need prior to meeting and taking an informational tour. Even though we have communicated, he has not come up with a date.

Now let me see if I can get some sleep. I have a big day tomorrow, working on the shed.

CHAPTER TWENTY-FIVE

IS IT HIGH NOON, YET?

It's **Tuesday, October 1, 2019.** Well, the body clock is at work and I am up 3:55 a.m.

Yesterday did not work out as planned. It was my goal to work on getting the roof shingles on the shed, but that didn't happen. I wasn't surprised because I knew it would be a cloudy day, threatening rain. I mowed the lawn first thing in the morning. Brandon had called to see whether we had rain. He came up to help with the shed, anyway. While whacking the weeds and cleaning up I thought I felt a few raindrops. As I finished cleaning up the lawn job, I decided I had enough of work, and I needed some escapism. When Brandon finished putting the outdoor furniture in the gazebo for the winter, I asked him to get with Brenda to schedule us for a movie. The last installment of the *Rambo* series was out, and we wanted to see it. As we finished getting ready for our movie trip, I noticed that the clouds had made good on its promised moisture. At that point I was glad that I had at least gotten the lawn done, especially since I hadn't cut it last week.

We were on our way to the movie at Gary Cooper time. That's a saying we use, referring to the Western film classic, starring actor Gary Cooper, titled *High Noon*. If you haven't seen it, or better yet, studied it, you ought to add it to your bucket list. *High Noon* doubles as a morality play, a study on human behavior—especially when one must step out of the crowd to stand up for what's right. Just before leaving, at high noon, I got a call from Manete Smith, a broker for the Propel Opportunity Fund, LLC, which is recognized as a 2019 top twenty-five national opportunity zone fund/manager/developer. He contacted me earlier this year, interested in funding our project. He's been constantly following up trying to facilitate a meeting with myself and other projects along with city officials. Anyway, I let my cell phone ring to keep us moving. I decided to call him back when we got to the movie, thirty-five minutes early.

During the call, Manete explained he was following up on the emails he had sent to Councilman Eric Costello wanting to schedule a conference meeting with him and Councilman Leon Pickett. The purpose of the meeting would be to discuss the Propel Opportunity Fund plans to fund our project in Costello's 11th District and the Madison Park Development in Pinkett's 7th District. Manete shared an email he had received from Councilman Costello indicating he would be reaching out to Councilmen Pinkett to make that happen.

Manete also wanted to make sure I received the email he sent referencing the New Yorkshire Comprehensive Community Safety Initiative to address the issues of crime that investors may have concerns about. He suggested that we adopt the plan and make it part of our presentation so that investors will feel more comfortable investing in the community and in our project. I had already shared it with Alice and asked her to translate the plan into our language for our project. At the end of our conversation, we both agreed to keep moving together to bring the Propel Opportunity Fund and TRTCHC together to change Baltimore.

I also had to reach out to Brian Grant to respond to his proposal and layout for the first phase of the project, which is the new athletic field. I apologized for the slow response, which was due to sending it to our board for possible questions and suggestions. Alice was the only one who had responded with questions. As a result, I decided that these types of time-sensitive issues, Alice, Adrian and I would handle and report back to the board. I also explained to Brian that we are in the process of drawing down the money from the $300,000 for the project that former Governor O'Malley had provided in his last budget. Those funds had been set aside for TRTCHC and placed under Baltimore's Recreation & Parks. Utilizing that funding rather than drawing from the $20,000 we received from the Weinberg Foundation was a better option. The Weinberg grant is unrestricted and can be used for whatever the nonprofit needs or determines. On the other hand, the $300,000 that Recreation & Parks is holding for us is specifically allocated to the acquisition and design of the new field. To make this happen, Alice has reached out to Recreation & Parks as well as Mayor Jack Young to make sure we have the access to the funds designated for our project.

On Friday I attended an Upton Board meeting that was called by Darroll Cribb. The purpose of the meeting was to address the MOU that The Black Arts & Entertainment District had submitted but was not signed in a reasonable timeframe. Lady Brion, the coordinator, had been frustrated how over a month had passed and Upton had not signed it. Darroll also had a list of things he wanted to update the board on as well.

***

It's Tuesday, October 8, 2019 at 1:30 a.m., and as usual I am up, and I can't sleep. Last night, I laid down after dinner, and fell asleep as I usually do on a workday. But this is my day off. So, I wish I could have slept a little longer. I got up early, yesterday, to go to the Department of Motor Vehicle (DMV) to get my new driver's license that Maryland, or perhaps the nation calls Real ID. It requires you to have your birth certificate or passport, social security card and proof of residence. I got there and the information officer convinced me to wait until six months before my driver license expires to update my license.

"It will cost twenty dollars, less, if you do," she said.

Well, I couldn't argue with that logic, so I went back home, mulling over the options of taking a nap. However, when I got home, I glanced out the window at the shed that I know I need to complete. I hadn't planned to work on it because Marty Bass, the weatherman on Channel 13 said it would be raining. Well, I hadn't seen a drop of rain all that morning. It looked like a cloudy and potentially rainy day, but there was no rain. So rather than relaxing in bed, I put on my work-around-the-house jeans and T-shirt, and I started working on the shed.

I was able to complete putting the shingles on the front of the A-Frame roof. I had just enough of the old shingles that had been stored in the shed for more than twenty years to get half the roof done. I also put metal sheathing around the back of the shed, so the critters couldn't dig their way in. I knew I didn't have enough shingles to do the back, so I decided it was time to move to my next day-off task, cutting the grass. It's fall and the grass is no longer growing fast. I'm glad to only have a few more cuts left on my to-do list this season.

In the back of my mind, I am thinking about our vacation which starts on October 18th. Normally, I am not too anxious to go on vacation, but this time, I am really ready for a break. I mentioned to Brenda, the other day, that I was getting tired. Part of my fatigue comes from the mental strain of trying to get our project to the groundbreaking stage. The other part is the grueling schedule of running The Bakery, scheduling meetings for the project with Upton, the TRTCHC board, and with the Pennsylvania Avenue Black Arts District. I am also fielding the growing list of organizations that are requesting to bring youth to The Bakery for a history lesson.

I have about fifteen things going on, including repairs that are needed at The Bakery, and at our apartment building on St. Paul Street. I always make a point not to think about all the things I have on the table at once. I just take one day at a time, and tackle what is needed, one by one. However, lately, I have been feeling a little tired, and I think I need to take a little break. I'm hopeful our vacation will do the trick. My heart and my head are busy self-talking, though, because I just can't give up on trying to get that Royal Theater rebuilt. But I'm tired, and I'm fighting the feeling of wanting to simply ring the bell. These are the times when I know that God's footprints are the only ones marching forward in the sand. He's carrying me, totally.

Also, on my mind is my sister, Gert, and her recent stomach surgery. At the age of seventy-nine, she has not quite fully recovered. In a couple of days, she will be going to get the stitches removed. Her energy level is low, but she fights to keep her body moving by walking up and down her long driveway for exercise. I'm proud of her. But we're so close. When she's down, I'm down. I try not to worry about her, and I also take my concerns for her one day at a time, just as she does. We both find that that's the best way to handle it. To not get overwhelmed about matters we cannot control.

Well, as the saying goes, we do not live in a vacuum. So, it's also alarming to hear about all of the entertainment icons, including Diahann Carroll, passing in their seventies and eighties—around the same age as Brenda and me. At each patch of news, I find myself digging a little further to find the root cause of their demise. To add to the list, my one-and-only best friend, Thomas Lewis, has a problem with his energy level. I'm praying for him not to ring the bell, either.

***

It's Tuesday, October 15, 2019, Brenda and I are preparing to get away for about a week, but my mind is still heavily on preparations for a big meeting set for Tuesday, October 29th. I've called on Stuart Hudgins again to put together a dynamic visual presentation, highlighting the historical events of The Pennsylvania Corridor, and what the future could be like if we get the victory on completing TRTCHC's project. The piece he's put together, thus far, is sharp. It will also include bios and pics of TRTCHC's ten board members as well as our development partners.

Stuart is a graphic artist and an historian, and he is the gentleman to whom I go whenever I need a presentation of this type. When you come to The Bakery, you can see all kinds of videos and photomontages, displayed in the lobby for our customers to enjoy. We work well together. I give him the materials and the concepts, we discuss and tweak arrangements, and then he works his skills to make it all tangible.

Well, vacation week is soon upon us, and Brenda usually has to drag me away from all the West Baltimore action, kicking and screaming. But this time, I had settled a new notion in my mind. Just the other day, I simply told Brenda, "I'm getting tired." And, oh yes, I did notice the shocked look on her face. It tickled me a bit, but with a straight face, I kept talking. "I'm ready for a vacation," I said. And then I waited to pick her up from the floor.

Of late, whenever I feel that way, when I walk into The Bakery, usually during the wee hours of the next day, I catch its aroma. Nothing will have been baking at that moment, of course, but the lingering aromatic smells are still there. Breathing them in is the same as breathing in my accomplishments and love for West Baltimore. It's like receiving a shot of adrenaline in my arm. And, yeah, my soul is back on automatic pilot, trying to make changes and improvements to the community. But I'd be lying if I didn't admit that sometimes I get a little tired.

Reflecting back, this past Thursday, I attended an Upton meeting. My plan was to really put Wanda and Jules on the spot when they started talking about projects because out of everything, I've heard them talk about—even though there has been an indication of them meeting with some delegates and various city officials—I had not seen any reports or proof of specific details or progress. And so, at this community meeting when Jules stepped up to talk about the development in the area, I had documentation and papers with me, declaring the TRTCHC project, and I was all set to ask questions about what's going on with the Robert C. Marshall Field? My readiness, and my goal, was to put the eyes of the community on Upton's plans.

But when I looked at the agenda for the meeting, it appeared that Jules, once again, was not giving a report on development, which meant that all my plans went straight out the window. And so, I backed off. There was, however, quite a bit of conversation about crime in the community. At these meetings, there is always a crime report rendered by the police department.

Later, Bronwyn Mayden, who's with Promise Heights, asked me a question about Booker T. She wanted my help to get the Booker T. students an opportunity to go to The Castle. The Castle is the training facility for The Ravens. It's located in Owings Mills, Maryland. I told her that I would look into it.

At the end of the community meeting, I approached Wanda. I just wanted to clear the air. I said to her, "look, I'm still trying to work on this project. What are you guys doing? Are you guys planning on building the new field that I'm trying to build? We're trying to move the project forward."

And her comment to me, which was quite cavalier, was, "Go ahead and do what you guys are doing. We're not doing anything with that."

I was surprised to hear it.

She added, "By the way, I'm not the point-person for that." And then she gave me the name of the treasurer for Upton, who is a gentleman by the name of Preston Harry. I've seen him at the Upton meetings. But we really haven't had a talk, face-to-face. I assume he knows what I'm trying to do and all that—that Wanda and Jules have briefed him. Wanda gave me Preston Harry's telephone number. I haven't called him yet. I'm not planning on engaging him at this point. I do want to keep moving on with what we're trying to do with the project. At least, now, I feel more comfortable that Upton is not doing anything with the project—with Robert C. Marshall Field. *But can I trust that*—is my thought._

From emails, it appears that Recreation and Parks is putting together a plan having to do with the present Robert C. Marshall Field—to do some renovations on it. And somehow or another the department feels that what we're doing is not important. And that Mrs. McGuire, the point-person for Recreation and Parks, has been trying to convince us that the money former Mayor O'Malley put in the budget—the $300,000—such should have been spent already within five years. So therefore, it has been forfeited. Her inference has been that *We should have started on the project.*

But when Alice, my secretary, did the research, she found that the viable span is seven years, not five years. All of this has been playing out in our email correspondence between Mrs. McGuire, myself, my architect, Kathleen; and Brian Grant, our engineer. I'd like to get them paid for their work. Mrs. McGuire's next point of opposition was that the site for the field had to be consolidated before we could get the money. However, that's not accurate either. Because the money that was allocated was for the acquisition of the property and for the design of the field. All this leaves us trying to get the allocated funding honored and realized. We have also cc'ed our emails to Mayor Young.

This morning, I cc'ed— the correspondence to Councilman Eric Costello. He had been eluding me. However, last week, he finally acknowledged me, and set up a schedule for a meeting with myself and Manete Smith, the gentleman from the Propel Opportunity Fund. It's set for next Tuesday, October 29th.

About our redevelopment project earmarked for the Pennsylvania Avenue Corridor, it stands in Councilman Eric Costello's 11th District. I have gone to Councilman Leon Pinkett (in the 7th District) for added support because he is probably more familiar with the project. He supported the project back when he was a part of former Mayor Stephanie Rawlings Blake's administration. And he has worked on Pennsylvania Avenue under The Main Street Program. I've been working every angle I can to garner success.

This has been a very, very positive year. Things seem to be moving quickly. Or at least, I should say that it's been a 190 degree turn from 2017 and 2018. But it's been grueling and tiresome, and it's taken up a lot of my energy.

So back to my confession to my Brenda. Watching the frozen expression on her face, I added, "I just need a vacation. I need some time off. What time do we leave?"

"Whaaaaat?" was her response.

And I had to laugh. To say that she was surprised that I actually said, out loud, that I wanted to take a break coated the space between us with a strange thickness. But like I said, I've been feeling a little bit tired.

Still, I'll also tell you that, I don't look in the mirror and think about my age. Age doesn't bother me. I do what I do. And I am who I am. Yet lately the news has been showered with the passing of various notables. Folks are passing away at the age of seventy-one, seventy-six, seventy-nine and seventy, and it's forced me to say to myself, *How long do I have? Am I going to get this done or what?* That said, I feel good, physically. Everything is where it should be. Most of the things that others my age say they feel, I don't feel. However, like I said, seeing so many around my age kick the bucket for whatever reason, sometimes creeps into my *what-if* zone. I try not to think about it. And I work to keep it positive and moving.

CHAPTER TWENTY-SIX

LEGACY MATTERS

It's October 25, 2019, at 1:51 a.m. It's Friday morning, and I am up as though I have to go into The Bakery. But this is our vacation week, our rest-up week before the Thanksgiving holiday rush. You might say that The Bakery is to Thanksgiving Day like what Black Friday and Cyber Monday is to Christmas Morning. So, typically, this week, I sleep for a couple of days as if I could store it up for what's coming. Then I'm bright-eyed and ready to enjoy the rest of the week with the family. We're at our home in Florida.

This week started off quite differently from previous years. When we landed on Sunday, October 20, I tried to book a Lyft ride using my cell phone, but that met technical difficulties. I was unsuccessful. However, Brenda was able to get us alternate transportation. When we got to the house and opened the door, a puddle of water was waiting to greet us. It had the nerve to be waiting right in the middle of the hallway just at the entrance to the kitchen. We would soon find out that it was being fed from an air vent above. The temperature in the house was eighty-four degrees. I knew, immediately, that accruing my first night of rest-up sleep was going to be a challenge. It was going to be a hot night in the Florida house.

Both air conditioners were off, and like the film, *The Hunt for Red October*, I went on a journey to find the problem. After checking the circuit breaker and checking the upstairs unit, I called the 24-hour A/C service. The lady on the other end of the phone took me through some diagnostic procedures. It was determined that the condensation line was backed up. She scheduled a service person come out to fix it, but not until Monday morning. While I was on the phone, Brenda was busy opening windows to coax some of the less-warm outside air to flow inside the hot house.

As we laid there, sweating and trying to get some sleep, I was formulating a plan to fix it myself. My plan, which I executed the next day (Monday), was to take my shop vac outside and suck out the blockage in the condensation line. I also sucked out the water from the inside unit, upstairs. I then put the float back in the line so that the system would start back up. It worked for about an hour or so. Then the water gushed out of the ceiling vent faster than it did the previous night. I shut the system down and waited for the repairman.

While waiting for the serviceman's 9:30 a.m. committed arrival, I decided that I would clear the weeds out of the front yard's flower bed. Estevez Lawn Care, a landscaping company that takes care of our lawn while we're away, sends us updated pictures of its work throughout the year. We had noticed in Estevez's latest pictures the flower bed was looking a little shabby. It was a lot worse in person. So, I got to work on it. After a couple of hours of struggling with stubborn weeds, the A/C repairman showed up. He was a nice African American gentleman with a foreign accent that made it a little difficult to understand him. However, he had a good sense of humor. His funny statements that came naturally off his cuff made a bad situation feel less hopeless. Making lemonade out of lemons, I threw in a few humorous quips as well. And then, somewhere in the midst, he blew the crap out of the line and got the system back up and running. A good man.

He left and I went back at pulling weeds, not the kind you can smoke. Committed to finishing the job, and plenty sweaty, I was trying to get it completed before I had to pick up my brother, Waymon, and a friend from the airport at 5:50 p.m. It turned out to be such a massive undertaking; I was barely half done before having to shower and pick them up.

Brenda and I met Waymon-Teddy-Monk-or-Tony, whatever name he is identifying with these days, and his new love, at the Frontier Airlines gate. Basking in smiles, hugs, and catch-up conversations, we got to the house, only for pit stops and to drop off bags. We were headed to the Outback Steakhouse for dinner—our treat. There, Waymon formally introduced us to Michelle Jones, his new love.

My brother has been married three times and has had a string of relationships. Like most of his love interests, Michelle is a very nice person who seems so in love with my brother.

He introduced her as, "The special person in my life." And he beamed.

Michelle is a college counselor, and they met when she took a group of students on a field trip. Waymon has been working as a motorcoach driver for a company in Atlanta for eight years now. Besides driving for the company, he is a trainer as well. Michelle is the most educated of all his past loves, meaning that she has her master's degree. My brother also bragged that she doesn't have any kids and that there is no drama in their lives together. Over dinner, Michelle talked about how her nieces liked him. He went on to talk about how he shared with Michelle, nuances of our mother's wisdom and her colorful use of language. We all shared a good chuckle over that one. Observing the two of them together, they seemed to be very much into one another. I never judge my brother or question his relationships. However, whenever his relationships go south, his women tend to call me to share what they are going through and ask if I can help. So, during dinner, my thoughts were, *let's just see where this goes.*

After dinner, we returned to the house and enjoyed a little more conversation before retiring. Waymon announced to me that he was going to prepare breakfast Tuesday morning, and he seemed excited about doing so. Now, this is something new for him. I can't remember him ever cooking. But perhaps, he's been getting a little practice and was proud of it. He shared the fact that Michelle does not cook and that he's the food preparer in their relationship.

His pancake-and-bacon breakfast was very good for him. And for all of us, it was okay. It did the job. Afterward, I went outside to continue tackling the flower bed. Waymon, Michelle, and Brenda were busy in light conversation before migrating onto their phones. I came in after about a half-hour and handed Waymon a pair of gloves, which was my way of saying, "come on outside and help me." I really didn't need the help, but I knew it would give us an opportunity to do something together. We also made a trip to Home Depot to pick up mulch. He and Michelle also made a couple of runs back to *HD* to get additional supplies.

We finally got the victory on the flower bed. Waymon and Michelle retired to their room. I took a shower and began preparing my pepper steak, rice, and salad dinner. I can show off in the kitchen, and I was kind of waiting for Waymon's critique during dinner. I did make the comment with a smile, "This is not Mattie's pepper steak." Still, no comments came, but they must have enjoyed it because they had seconds. As with most everything, actions speak louder than words. We all went to bed early because I had to get them to the airport at 5:30 a.m. that next morning to catch their flight. This part of our vacation was positive and enjoyable.

After dropping them off, Brenda and I were the first customers at one of our favorite spots, The International House of Pancakes

(IHOP). When we returned home, I began my next chore, which was to power wash our driveway and sidewalk. I also started working on our huge back patio, consisting of pavers that now had mold in the cracks. This ended up being a two-and-a-half-day job, which pushed me into Thursday of our rest-up week. I also had the task of installing our doorbell alarm system as well.

Rounding back to today, October 25, 2019, Friday, I felt a little lazy and decided to do nothing. Brenda went out to do some shopping while I took naps and ate snacks. At least that was the plan. However, also on my mind was the homegoing ceremony for The Honorable Elijah Cummings, who represented Maryland's 7th Congressional District. My congressional District. He died on Thursday, October 17th, at age sixty-eight. And I thought about how much I really wanted to be there at his service, held at New Psalmist Baptist Church where he was a member.

For decades, he had been a shining light and consummate champion for Baltimore. Even in his last days. He never shied away from taking on the Trump Administration, declaring truth and integrity to power. In February, as the ranking Democrat and chairman of The House Oversight and Reform Committee, Rep. Cummings presided over the hearing of Trump's former attorney Michael Cohen. In his closing statement, Rep. Cummings put to his congressional colleagues, and really, to Americans alike, a poignant question.

With fervor, he asked, "When we're dancing with the angels, the question we'll be asked: In 2019, what did we do to make sure we kept our democracy intact? Did we stand on the sidelines and say nothing?"

When I heard that, it stuck to my ribs. After his passing, I essentially said to myself, "He preached his own eulogy with that weighty question he posed.

The late Rep. Elijah Cummings had become the first African American lawmaker to lie in state at the U.S. Capitol. It is still hard to believe he is gone.

Working at The Bakery when most folks are asleep, I listen to the news all night. When his passing was reported, I first wasn't sure of what I heard. I was in the middle of calculating ingredients for my peach cobbler when the words invaded the newscast. I was stunned. As newscasts do, the awful news repeated itself, again and again. I had to stop and reflect for a moment.

Just last week, Vernon Simms, who served as Chief of Staff for Cummings, had made his monthly stop at The Bakery. I asked Simms, as I always do, "How's my friend coming along? Tell him I said hello."

My relationship with Congressman Cummings had evolved over the years. I had met with him in the early years, representing UPS as the Congressional Coordinator. After retirement, our meetings had also centered on community issues and our project. When we opened The Bakery, he often came by to purchase sweet potato pies for his mom. After she passed, he would stop by occasionally for himself. The last time we spoke was at an event for the then-candidate for governor, Benjamin "Ben" Jealous.

I just can't seem to wrap my head around the fact he has passed.

I wanted to be there for his homegoing ceremony; however, I did call Vernon to ask where I could send a card, and he gave me the Park Avenue office address. I have been searching my computer files for the picture I took of Congress Cummings and Brandon, who was ten years old at that time. I want to put that in the card as well. Cummings was an inspiration and a role model for Brandon just as he was to so many. His commitment to community and the future of our young people cannot be matched. There are politicians, and although he was our congressman, he was different; he was Elijah E. Cummings.

I am also focusing on and thinking about, the project. I'm not feeling very optimistic at this point. It concerns me that Danny Henson has not scheduled the meeting with Braverman, who is the

Commissioner for the Department of Housing & Community Development (DHCD). He has also not responded to my inquiries. Also, Mrs. McGuire seems to be putting up resistance to our trying to access the $300,000 that former Governor O' Malley put in his last budget for the acquisition and design of the new field. Brian and Kathleen have almost completed the rendition, and Stuart Hudgins has almost completed the impact statement portion.

When my plane lands in Baltimore on Tuesday, October 29th, at 10:30 a.m., I must drop Brenda off at Lin's so that Brandon will bring her and the dogs home. I'll drive directly home so I can get suited up to attend a two o'clock meeting with Councilmen Costello and Pinkett to discuss moving forward. Also attending the meeting will be Manete Smith, the representative for the Propel Opportunity Zone Fund. He and I are hopeful to meet—and walk the site at noon before the meeting.

On Wednesday, the following day, Alice and I will meet with Johns W. Hopkins, the executive director of Baltimore Heritage, a nonprofit organization dedicated to saving historic buildings and revitalizing neighborhoods. His organization may be able to assist us with resources to renovate the Harriet Beecher Stowe House. Our strategy is to gain site control of the building and work on it, while the city finishes putting together the site for the new field. And for us to have the stabilization of promised allocated funding.

***

Today, it's Monday, October 28, 2019, at 1:58 a.m., and I am braced in my work mode although this is my regular day off, although it's—well, technically, the last day of my rest-up vacation. That's because tomorrow is the big meet day—and I cannot take my mind off it. Yesterday, Kathleen and I went over the presentation for the meeting and our visual selections for the presentation via phone. We decided on showing what the theater and clubhouse will possibly look like. We also went over the impact statement. My hope is that she can make the meeting on Tuesday. If she can't, the plan will be is to make sure I have all the details I need.

We have all the components of the project except Danny Henson's housing piece. As a partner of the project, he has ownership of that piece. However, at this point, we have no details from him. I will be calling him today, attempting to get the facts, hopeful that he is still on board and still working to get Braverman, of HCD, on board.

The overall plan is to utilize some of the acquisition funds for moving forward. Once we have the acquisition funding in place and the Harriet Beecher Stowe House project moving forward, it will be easier to get The Ravens, Ed Reed, and Under Armour on board. It also enhances the possibility of getting the Weinberg Foundation to give us another grant. Again, I am not overly optimistic—but this is my plan.

God has blessed me so far, and He has opened so many doors. I just pray that I am doing the right thing and not wasting my time and resources. I truly believe this holistic project will change Baltimore for the better. As Police Commissioner Michael Harrison stated in a recent press conference, Baltimore's crime and gun violence is a culture that must change. I believe this project is just what the City and community need to change that culture. It spans generations and stands to make both a social and economic positive impact that can be a model for the redevelopment of urban communities. I just must keep pushing to get the people with the resources to see the light. Although I am down and sometimes depressed about things not moving, I refuse to ring the bell.

Brenda and I are so comfortable, relaxing here in the house in Kissimmee—puddle-free, flower-bed-pretty, and air conditioning working. I know she would be so happy if I suddenly made the decision to give up the Baltimore mission and transform us into snowbirds to enjoy the fruits of our labor for the rest of our days. Such a notion glows in a special spotlight of so many of our peers, famous and not, passing on around us. The loss of Congressman Cummings is on my mind.

Let me stop this—and get the job done. I thank God for today and for allowing me to share my thoughts, hopes, and dreams. Even if, sometimes, the *share* is only with Him. Because I truly believe, "Whatever the mind can conceive and believe, it can be achieved." That's my quote for today.

***

It's Monday, November 4, 2019, at 9:48 a.m., our first day off after our rest-up week, October vacation. I got up early, took out Roc and Bruno for a walk, and gauge the weather. It's cold. The grass is wet and crunchy and blanketed by frost. And so is the pavement, glistening under a new sun. My plans for today consist of a host of outside tasks such as the final cutting of the grass, raking up leaves and pine needles, and bringing up the snowblower to the house from the shed. I'm a proponent of planning and being prepared. The weather folks say that we may have some snow flurries by Friday.

The week prior was a busy one, beginning with me hopping off the plane last Tuesday, rushing home, and preparing for my big meeting set for that same day. Well, I did meet with Manete Smith and his friend, Kaheed, who had driven him down from New Jersey. I was hoping to meet them at 12 noon, but because of a tight scheduling window, we met at 12:40 p.m. at The Bakery. I drove them on a tour of the project site before we proceeded to make our way to our 2:00 p.m. meeting with Councilmen Eric Costello and Leon Pinkett at City Hall. I dropped them curb-side-service-like, then searched for a parking spot. God was on my side. I was able to join them five minutes ahead of meeting time.

In addition to the two councilmen, the attendees were Ira Kowler, representing BDC; Ben Seigel, Baltimore's Opportunity Zone Coordinator; Manete Smith, representing Propel Opportunity Fund and Kaheed. Frank Auston, the founder of Propel Opportunity Fund, joined us via a conference call. Also in the room were the councilmen's aides, Justin Lane and Monique Marshall.

Councilman Costello officially opened the meeting. Then he turned it over to me since it was myself and Manete who scheduled the meeting. Sometimes when you are in a situation where you have forced people to the table, you can sense their displeasure and lack of desire to be there. That was the nonverbal feedback and body language I observed from the Councilman's opening. He also made the statement that everyone was aware of our project. Yes, Costello, Councilman Pinkett, and Ben Seigel were familiar with the project, but Ira Kowler of BDC was not. I decided not to address the inaccuracy of his statement, choosing, instead, to move forward by explaining where we were with the project. I also made clear that the Propel Opportunity Fund was interested in financing it. At that point, I turned the meeting over to Manete and Frank.

Ben Seigel questioned Frank and Manete on whether Propel had the funding or was seeking the funds to invest in Baltimore's Opportunity Zones. I was happy to hear them say they had the funds because when Ben and I rode up in the elevator on our way to the meeting room, he mentioned to me Propel was trying to acquire the funds. Eric Costello also had some questions about Propel's financial capabilities. During the meeting, Ben mentioned that only the east side of Pennsylvania Avenue was a part of the Opportunity Zone, and our project spans both sides. I am still concerned by what he said and the distinction he made. I hadn't heard that before, and it sounded like a newly-composed glitch to us moving forward.

Costello did mention that two million dollars are being invested in Robert C. Marshall field. I explained to him that that had nothing to do with our project at this point. I also shared with him that back in 2004, the NFL was thinking of putting in a field at the Robert C. Marshall site; however, it had been determined and/or discovered that it was prohibited due to the huge grade between Lafayette Avenue and Dolphin Street. He came out and said that the two million dollars investment was for nothing more than moving dirt. Councilman Pinkett alluded to the fact the two million dollars could be better used in supporting the new field we are working on.

As the meeting ended, everyone shook hands, and Costello asked me what Wanda Best's feelings about the project were. I repeated what she mentioned to me at a community meeting two weeks ago, and that was, "No, we are not building a new field. Go ahead and do your thing; I am not dealing with that."

What I didn't mention to him was that she had also said, "Our Treasurer Preston Harry, is dealing with that. He is over there."

I assumed she was saying that he lived near the proposed new field. At this point, I have not reached out to talk to him.

Again, I am very concerned about Councilman Costello, especially when he seems to be reluctant to look me in the eye and seems to avoid my communications. I am not sure if Wanda is the problem or if it's because an election year is coming up. It may be because I have not supported any of his fundraising campaigns, although I have been solicited. I have also received solicitations from Councilman Pinkett as well. However, when we met last month, I explained that I don't do that because TRTCHC is a nonprofit, and I don't make contributions because of that.

God is so great. While I have been working on funding sources, councilmen, and community awareness, our secretary and TRTCHC founding member, Alice Cole, has been working on making sure we get an extension on the $300,000 that O'Malley granted. She is also seeking the procedures to draw down on the funds to pay for design and acquisition of which Brian and Kathleen are doing. I am so fortunate that she has retired from the school system and owns the expertise to deal with the state issues we face. Her experiences come from the years she spent with the Baltimore Workforce Investment Board (BWIB) and the years she spent assisting former State Senator Nathaniel McFadden.

She has been pursuing a meeting with State Senator Antonio Hayes to this end, her notes:

TRTCHC

The Royal Theatre & Community Heritage Corporation
Meeting Notes
Honorable Senator Antonio Hayes
12 Madison Avenue, Baltimore, Maryland 21217
October 30, 2019
1:00-1:30 p.m.

Attendance: Senator Antonio Hayes, Rahwa Andemichael, Chief of Staff and Alice Cole, TRTCHC Board Secretary.

The meeting was requested to discuss an extension for SB171—$300,000 restricted grant awarded to the Board of Directors of The Royal Theatre and Community Heritage Corporation Board in FY 2015.

Senator Hayes shared his concern that the funding has been in place for so long and, according to his most recent update, that there has been no expenditure of funds for any of this money—the entire $18,872.000. He inquired if the funds had been released to the City. We discussed that the City requested that the funding be moved to the

Robert C. Marshall Field for development. I shared that based on our preliminary design work this land was not conducive for the type of athletic field that TRTCHC is planning.

In an effort to learn the city's process for accessing the funds awarded to TRTCHC, I shared my research with the Senator. Funding was sent from the State to the Department of Natural Resources (DNR) to Baltimore City Department of Recreation and Parks. The City needed to submit a grant application for the funds that met the tenets stipulated in the State award. It was my understanding that all paperwork was completed, and the funding was sent to the Baltimore City Department of Recreation and Parks.

The Senator reminded me that we are required to have a match for the $300,000. I was aware of this grant stipulation. He indicated that according to the information he received from Recreation & Parks, TRTCHC funds were to be used for the Robert C. Marshall Field per the previous Mayor's administration. TRTCHC was not aware of any changes in the funding awarded to its Board.

We discussed the stipulation in SB171 that the $300,000 was restricted to the *TRTCHC Board of Directors for the acquisition, clearance and site preparation of land and design of an athletic field and open space uses.* He stated that design was not usually an allowable expense for this type of State funding; however, the Senator acknowledged this is what the bill indicated. I explained to him that we have spent some of the funds on the design component and we have invoices in hand waiting to be paid. We have been trying to obtain the draw down process from Rec. & Parks since July, 2019.

He wanted to know if the project was shovel ready. I shared we cannot be shovel ready until we have site control of the land and the Harriet Beecher Stowe House that is on the property. He wanted to know the connection between The Royal Theatre and the field project. I gave him a copy of the three-phase revitalization plan. The plan explained the connections and footprint for each component. Additionally, we discussed that this property was City owned and that the building on the site to be developed was listed on the Vacant to Value listing by the Housing Authority of Baltimore City.

In conclusion, Senator Hayes sent an email to Mayor Bernard "Jack" Young's Chief of Staff Carolyn Mozell to gauge the level of knowledge that the current administration has on this issue and what they were planning. Furthermore, I shared that I too was in contact with Carolyn and that she is arranging a meeting with the Mayor within the next couple of weeks.

Action Items

Send to Senator Hayes

- **The projected date when the design work will be completed.**
- **Date when the Vacant to Value Application will be completed and submitted.**
- **Information on our Developers. Where are they in this process?**
- **Projections on when we will be ready to begin this project.**

Senator Hayes shared that he has a large number of funding requests, including Orchard Street Church. If we were not ready to begin, he wants to repurpose these funds and perhaps re-award when we are ready. I stated not acceptable. These funds are off the table and as soon as we can get the City to release the property, we are ready to start.

We never got to the process for extension as the Senator was not interested in extensions. Too many organizations have received funding and are not using it.

Respectfully Submitted,
Alice Cole

At this point, I'll be sharing her notes with the development team, especially Kathleen, Brian, Danny, and Brenda Brown, so that we can schedule a conference call to discuss how to respond to the state senator. I plan to also submit our Vacant to Value application to Baltimore Housing this week as well. I am not sure how to handle that application because it is handled by Teresa Stephens, who was the President of Upton Planning and has a dislike for me and the project. Somehow, I must figure out a way to get it to her boss as well as to her. I have a feeling that she will do everything in her power to delay and stand in the way.

Last Sunday morning, this scripture came before me: "Therefore, as we have opportunity, let us do good to all people, especially to those who belong to the family of believers." Galatians 6:10 (NIV)

I was in The Bakery, enjoying this sermon by Rev. P.M. Smith, the senior pastor of Huber Memorial Church in Baltimore while preparing the sweet potato pies and pound cake for our Sunday customers. When that Bible scripture was shared, it dawned on me that this work that I am doing to change our community is my opportunity to *do good to all people*. And as complicated as this effort has been, the mission itself is as simple as that.

We are coming to the end of 2019, and I am playing that old television game show, created in 1950 by Mark Goodson-Bill Todman Productions. It was called *Beat the Clock*. I am trying to get this project financed and a shovel in the ground so that we can change lives and outcomes. Unlike the *Beat the Clock* prizes, that's the prize on which my eyes are affixed. I turned seventy-one this year, and I am watching friends, celebrities, associates, and great people that I know, respect, and look up to, like Baltimore's beloved Elijah E. Cummings, pass on. The more I move forward, the more obstacles step in the way. Lord knows I am not trying to ring the bell.

CHAPTER TWENTY-SEVEN

THE 2019 WRAP UP, HOPEFUL FOR 2020

It's **Monday, December 30, 2019, 5:53 a.m.**; I just woke up with 3,000 things on my mind. My plan is to try to sort them out and put them on paper. Yesterday was the last open day of the year for The Bakery. It has been a great year in many respects. Our peak season, November and Thanksgiving holiday, went exceptionally well and was more profitable than last year. However, the ice machine went up, and the freezer compressor went bad, and the entire freezer had to be replaced, which ate up the profits. I still feel as though we have been blessed.

I so enjoyed the time spent with the family, working together to satisfy our many customers who have made The Avenue Bakery offerings part of their holiday seasons. Lin and Hammy both plan their time off from their regular jobs so that they can be there to help us through the super busy times. I can sometimes get a little emotional and even drop a few tears when I think about how close we are; and when I think about how they don't even think twice to sacrifice and pitch in. I fought to keep my eyes dry as I occasionally looked across the kitchen at my two kids, working at getting Poppay's Rolls made for our customers.

Well, that's over and done, now—for this season. And Brenda and I are getting ready for our trip to Florida to get some rest before starting the new year. Today, Brandon and I will be going into The Bakery to give it a cleaning. I must clean out the grease trap, which is the worst job of the business. We will clean all the equipment walls and polish the floors. Brandon has become my right hand, and I am not sure what I will do next year when he pursues that regular forty-hour job in his field of auto repair. I won't hold him back, though, and I will survive.

As we wrap up 2019 at The Bakery, so do we wrap up the year working on The Royal Theater & Community Heritage Center project. Our momentum this year increased after the change in city administration took place. Thanks to Dr. Brenda Brown, one of our development partners, we were able to obtain a grant from the Weinberg Foundation and craft our impact statement and plans.

We are now in the process of overcoming the setback to access the funds that former Governor Martin O'Malley put in his final budget before he left office. It appears the previous City administration may have illegally decided to use the funds for purposes other than what was designated. Alice was able to force the City to schedule a meeting to reconcile the matter. She has been trying to make this happen for six months. And after getting State Senator Antonio Hayes involved, we have a meeting scheduled for 1:00 p.m. on Wednesday, January 22, 2020, at the Department of Planning. We sent a message to Chad Hayes, the West Baltimore Planner, thanking him for the meeting to reconcile issues and move our project forward.

Also, on my mind is my brother, Waymon, Monk, Teddy, Tony, whatever name or alias he is using at the moment. It appears he has had headaches and blood pressure problems. He went to the Emergency Room twice. The second time it appeared that everything is okay.

However, he has an appointment with his primary care physician to adjust his medication for high blood pressure. Living in Atlanta with no family down there, he keeps me updated on his condition. And I appreciate that his new love, Michelle, whom we met back in October, keeps me informed as well. That's a good thing.

During our peak season, I have also been working with The Roots of Scouting, Inc., a scouting initiative dedicated to addressing the particular needs of African American youth through leadership activities, life skills, and mentoring. Its president is Mr. Leo Boroughs, Jr. The nonprofit's goal is to partner with The Bakery to produce cookies that its Scouters can sell to raise money. I have been meeting with its 1st Vice President, Melaughn Butler, who coordinates the fundraising initiative. So far, the nonprofit has been able to provide us with molds for their cookies. Last month, we donated cookies for an event they held at the Shake & Bake Family Fun Center located on Pennsylvania Avenue. It was a little difficult because of our busy schedule, but we were able to bake twenty-five dozen cookies for their Kwanzaa event the day after Christmas. We are looking forward to also getting some of their Scouters in the kitchen to learn how to bake. I'm looking forward to this partnership in 2020.

With all that's going on, the battery in my computer went bad. And we, meaning mostly Brenda, could not find a replacement. She searched Hewlett-Packard (HP) and Amazon, and it could not be found. That meant I had to buy a new laptop. We ordered one online, got a great deal, but were told it wouldn't be delivered until sometime in January. To our surprise, however, it was delivered a day before Christmas. While that was a blessing, as everyone knows, next comes the task of transferring all the programs and files from one computer to another. After having a laptop for four years, the task of remembering all the passwords and where we kept them was daunting.

I was somewhat fortunate to be signed up with The Geek Squad at Best Buy. Those techies can figure out almost anything. I was relieved that they were able to help me. On one of my visits there, the young lady who helped me gave me some instructions on what to do. After I followed her instruction and got some things done, I still needed help. I went back to the location in Owings Mills, Maryland, and a tall, slender African American young man, by the name of Nathan, spent about a half-hour with me, getting my new laptop set up just the way I wanted it, even better than the last laptop I had. God is so good to me.

I also have been contacted by Ethan McLeod, associate editor of *The Baltimore Business Journal.* He wants to interview me for a section of the paper called, *The Takeaway.* It's a weekly column that highlights local small businesses or an entrepreneur's journey, the challenges they've faced, and how they're working to keep growing their businesses—amid a recent shift change. I agreed to meet with him at noon today.

***

Wednesday, December 31, 2019, the last day of the year, and it's moving along in great fashion. Ethan McLeod had to reschedule our interview for today. He confessed to me that, while he had passed by The Bakery on several occasions, he had never stopped in. So, this would be his first visit.

Normally, when folks come for the first time, I give a brief tour. Ethan was very impressed with The Bakery as a whole, especially the courtyard and the artwork—the photomontages—that are beautiful and informative. I shared with him our summer Jazz Courtyard series and its popularity. His drive-bys, perhaps, had piqued his curiosity about us, but they hadn't afforded him a glimpse of all that.

During our time together, he wanted to make sure that he captured all the details he needed. So, he asked very specific questions such as: How long had the business been around; What are the changes, in both our business and in the area that we are seeing; How is the business growing; And what was my motivation to create The Avenue Bakery?

I made it clear to him that the business was a means to an end and not an end goal. I explained how the business was there to certainly bring fresh products to the community and to other businesses, but also it was to prove the point that we, as African Americans, can bring our businesses back to our community and be successful. We can do that—and educate folks on the history and the legacy of The Avenue. Ethan McLeod listened, intently, when I explained to him how I wanted our young people to know more about this community—more than the negative images the television series, *The Wire*, gave us, nationwide; or what the Freddie Gray tragedy wrought—when the wounds of frustration and sadness about our economic and cultural setbacks were ripped open, misrepresented over the airwaves and newspapers, but not resolved. I told him I want our young people to know more about The Avenue than its drug activity, which is a symptom of much deeper and complicated issues. These are the reasons why The Avenue Bakery is here.

The interview moved forward, and we then talked about the fact that now that Pennsylvania Avenue has the title of *Black Arts and Entertainment District*, it can positively impact the totality of the area, its residents and businesses, and my dream. Along with a significant few, the dream is to see this area economically and culturally revitalized. The designation sheds a new light and a new view of Historic Pennsylvania Avenue.

Ethan promised to reach out to me when *The Baltimore Business Journal* was going to publish the story. And, as is customary with first-time visitors, I sent him away with a sample of *Poppay's Rolls*. The Bakery was shut down on that day, but I was able to find a half dozen of rolls in the freezer. I stuck them in a bag and gave them to him, saying, "Be sure to share them with your family." Later, I sent him an email, asking how he and his family liked them.

On Thursday, January 2, 2020, this was his response, "Morning James, they paired perfectly with the meal my mother-in-law made—pasta, roasted chicken, some buffalo cauliflower, and rolls. Thanks again—will come by again to have them fresh!"

And when he comes, we'll be ready.

***

It's the first Saturday of the year, January 4, 2020, at 10:00 a.m.; I just finished eating breakfast after my four-mile bike ride this morning. For the first four days of the year, I have been relaxing, resting, and napping. And it's great. But it seems that there is always some issue to deal with when we get to our home-away-from-home in Florida. Last time it was the air conditioning system. This time it's the Kia.

I connected the battery as I always do and tried to start it up. I got nothing. No big deal, though. I keep a battery hotshot power bank charger in the back. Before long, I was able to get it started. I let it run for about an hour and a half. Brenda and I jumped in it and drove over to Sam's Club to check on some things. When we got back in it, the car would not start. I was about to jump-start it with the charger I had when Brenda intervened with her wisdom.

"Why don't we just get a new battery from Sam's," she suggested, simply.

What would I do without the love of my life? Who knows?! I purchased it, and the gentleman in the shop came out to help me install it because I hadn't brought any tools with me. He was having problems taking the old battery out because he wasn't familiar with the Kia. I told him that I could handle it and decided to call AAA. While we were waiting, I realized the faulty battery was one we had purchased from AAA a couple of years ago. Long-story-short, AAA replaced the battery at no cost, and I returned the one I bought from Sam's, saving me $109. I love it when a story ends well. But the stakes got higher.

Brenda has been bugging me for a while, telling me that we needed to get rid of that 1999 Suzuki, our second car down here. She had been looking online and saw a Hyundai she liked. So off to the dealership we went. After much hesitation and procrastination on my part, we purchased a replacement vehicle. We decided we would give the old vehicle away to a charity. It still runs well but gives off fumes. And you must drive with the windows down. I never took the time to take it to the dealer to correct the problem.

The new year is starting off positively. I have my new laptop, and it works so much better than my old one, and now we have a new second vehicle. This also means when we come down next month to attend Super Bowl 2020, we'll drive down to Miami in a newer vehicle. Yes, we decided that for once, we would see what it is like to go to a Super Bowl. It would be great if The Ravens make it there, but we will be there either way. This has been a great year for The Ravens and Lamar Jackson, and we have our fingers crossed that they will make it. Our plan is to fly to Kissimmee to the house, drive to Miami, spend the night there, and drive back to our place in Kissimmee. We will then fly from Orlando back home to Baltimore. I am looking forward to it. However, in the back of my mind, I am thinking about this Iran situation and that country's plans to retaliate. I am sure that the United States will have available all the security that's needed. At least, let's say, I'm hopeful that is the case. That said, we are going to enjoy ourselves and not worry. It's in God's hands.

Yes, I have been resting, but also thinking and communicating to our board and development team. I am looking forward to the two meetings scheduled for January 21 and 22, 2020. Chad Hayes, West Baltimore Planner, will be hosting both meetings. The one on the twenty-first of January will be a follow-up of the Leveraging Investments in Neighborhood Corridors (LINCS) initiative. This initiative supports our project and was formulated during the Stephanie Rawlings-Blake Administration. However, the Pugh Administration ignored it, and convinced Upton, specifically Wanda Best and Jules Dunam, to abandon it. Our development group will be attending the meeting to determine if Planning and the Young Administration *are* wise enough to reverse that decision.

The meeting on the twenty-second of January is critical because it will bring to the surface exactly what took place during the previous administration and how it handled the funds O'Malley put in his budget for our project. It will also reveal what was done with the funds that Stephanie Rawlings-Blake put in her last budget to support the project. I'm hopeful that the Young Administration realizes we are at a unique situation and threshold. Working together, we can bring together the community, the City, our sports teams, and investors to bring about a renaissance in Baltimore. Enough of my preaching.

Brenda and I are now watching the playoff games, and I am also baking my rice pudding—my favorite. Most of the day, I slept and spent time flipping channels on the TV. It has been so relaxing I am not sure what to do with myself. And I am so happy that Brenda is relaxed and enjoying her time here as well.

***

It's 11:22 a.m., Sunday, January 5, 2020. I prepared pancakes for breakfast, Brenda's request. I was thinking of taking a trial run to Miami to be better prepared for Super Bowl Sunday. Brenda seems to be reluctant. So, I guess we will relax and stay put.

I'm hopeful that Brenda and I will have a great positive experience at the Super Bowl this year and that The Ravens will be there. Today has been great, Brenda watched The Saints & The Vikings, and I watched the inside of my eyelids. I got up, we ate the dinner she prepared, we watched The Eagles and The Seahawks. Now we are watching the Golden Globes; I have no idea who more than half of the people are and programs getting awards. I watch very little TV, maybe that's it. Or maybe not. I am trying to stay awake long enough to finish watching it. But I'm proud of myself, accomplishing another quiet day, doing what my mind and body need most: a restful time of doing *nothing*.

Still, this morning as we sat here, watching *Face the Nation*, my hope is that Iran has not targeted its retaliation on American soil. When I think about the direction our country is going in, I have many concerns. With all the turmoil in the Middle East, will the need for additional troops mean we will have to, one day, reinstate the draft of our young men and women to meet the needs of war? Our country, internally, has grown to be so violent, not just in Baltimore. Attacks by our citizens and/or homegrown residents on churches, schools, businesses, and other places of worship have occurred. It's White supremacy groups implementing most of the terrorism and hate.

Yes, my focus is on our community and trying to positively impact our young people's future and set an example of how we need to structure our communities. However, we can't be blind to those things that threaten our very existence.

Periodically, though, throughout the day, I still read, answer and send emails. For the last two years or so, I've gotten emails from someone by the name of *aaparker2*. Sometimes he or she gives messages of wisdom. He or she sent me one today that I felt was so appropriate when it comes to the work we are trying to get done in our historic community. The message was, "*'Throughout history, it has been the inaction of those who could have acted; the indifference of those who should have known better; the silence of the voice of justice when it mattered most, that has made it possible for evil to triumph,' Emperor Hailie Selassie.*"

I felt this was appropriate because there are many people who could have acted, but they were silent when our Historic Pennsylvania Avenue was destroyed. Word has it that Mayor William Donald Schaefer told the community that it could have saved The Royal, but community leaders told him at that time to tear it down. In 1971, there were many African American politicians and community leaders who were indifferent, fell silent, and failed to act in our best interest. However, it is our responsibility at this juncture to make sure history does not repeat itself.

***

Today, Monday, January 6, 2020, Brenda and I got out of the house. Today, our task was to go to the Department of Motor Vehicles to get the title for the 1999 Suzuki that we plan to give away to charity. Although the miles are low, the car is twenty years old, and it has some problems not worth us spending the money to fix, but we think that those problems could be conquered in the right hands, and it could become a gem to someone in need. We got our task completed, and now Brenda has gone out to get our E-ZPass for the new vehicle.

As usual, when I got back, I checked my emails and noticed an email from Chad Hayes of Planning. It was a report on Baltimore City's Six-Year Capital Program. It is the Ordinance of Estimates Recommendation for each City agency and/or department. After going through the report for about a half-hour, I came across the one for Baltimore City Recreation & Parks. I found its request for funding and scrolled down to item 474-123 Robert C. Marshall Field. The description read, *Create regulation multi-purpose field for football, soccer, lacross, and youth baseball. The Field is currently sloped and too small to play league games. Location 1201 Pennsylvania Avenue.* (City of Baltimore - Six Year Capital Program Ordinance of Estimates Recommendation for: Dept. of Recreation & Parks, P. 66 [FY2020])

This request stated, "... sloped and too small for league play." However, it did not reveal *The Paul Harvey* of it all, which is that the slope and size of the land make it neither feasible nor cost-effective to put a regulation football field there. This has been determined by architects, engineers and revealed in the letter that former Mayor Stephanie Rawlings-Blake sent to us. Certainly, this request by Recreation and Parks brings up integrity issues as well as the poor utilization of taxpayer dollars. The request also states that $1.5 million for the project was coming from State Open Space Matching Grants, of which we know contains $300,000 that Mayor Martin O' Malley put in his last budget for TRTCHC.

I am somewhat sure that Jack Young is not aware of all these facts, although there are people, he inherited from the previous administration who are aware of these facts. I am sure that Mayor Young will do the right thing for Baltimore City and its taxpayers. He is a man of integrity who loves Baltimore and wants to see it move on to greatness.

We, as an organization, must determine how we will handle this situation on January 22, 2020. I have forwarded my findings to our team members for their review.

***

It's 2:08 a.m., Tuesday, January 7, 2020, and I am up, as I would be if I were working at The Bakery. I flipped channels on the TV for a while, and now I am working on my memoir. Brenda had asked me if we were going to make our trial run to Miami, but I think I will spend some time with Yvonne on my book. We will also clean up the Suzuki. I am still waiting on Pastor Rafy Fuentes to forward me all the details of his ministry that I need so that I can donate the vehicle. He is our next-door neighbor, down here, in Kissimmee. He and his wife, Mary, seem to be very nice people.

My plan is to make the trip to Miami on Wednesday, check out the Hard Rock Stadium where the Super Bowl will be played, and the hotel where we will be staying for that night. It will make for a long travel day, but it will be an adventure, and I am sure there will be memorable moments made as well. Life and God have been so good to us, and I am so grateful. The year seems to be getting off to a good start; my hope is that it will continue. I know, as life goes, there will be ups and downs, but we will deal with life—one day at a time.

CHAPTER TWENTY-EIGHT

WHEN IS ENOUGH LIVING, ENOUGH?

It's **Monday, April 13, 1998**, and I feel sort of neither here nor there. I am not sure what that means, except I can't describe how I feel or why I feel this way. Let me stop this before I turn into some sort of nut case and prick my finger to commit suicide.

I came home early today because Brenda called me while I was at work with some not-so-pleasant information. She received a call from the dialysis center that my mom had a mild seizure. I called home several times before leaving work, but mama did not pick up either phone line. I began to get a little worried, but I worked to keep hopeful for the best. But instead, for some reason, my mind kept wandering and thinking about the worst. I sometimes do that, think of the worst and what I would do in such an instance. And I rehearsed the possibility of her having a seizure and how I would hurry to call 911 to get instructions on how to handle her. If she passes away, yes, I let my mind go there on the way home, I don't know how I am going to tell the rest of the family—after burying the remains of my younger brother, Carl Crawford, this past Saturday, which was long after we discovered him missing, long after he died and long after the private detective uncovered the sordid grim facts.

Adding the fact that a month ago, Aunt Beula passed away, mom will be the third person in the family to pass. *Where in the world did that come from?* was the thought that popped in my head; the fact that people die in threes. And when I think of that, I realize that three people on Brenda's side of the family have recently died. Aunt Gladys and Uncle Norman, husband and wife, died within three months of one another. Then Aunt Midge, the sister of Brenda's stepmother, passed.

I am trying to get home as quickly as I can. And it seems traffic is ridiculous. Everybody, and his brother, wants to pull in front of me—and then drive like they're in a funeral procession. I finally get to my street and pull up to my driveway. As I back into the garage, I want, and I don't want, to play out this scene. I walk from the garage into the kitchen. The first thing I notice is cake crumbs all over the floor. The counter looks as though some wild animal ripped open a baggy container of cake and shook it with its teeth. I was not alarmed at the mess because messy was my mom's normal M.O. But I thought I heard some feet shuffling, which told me that if she had had a seizure, at least she was still on her feet. As I walked down the hall and looked into the bathroom, I thought I was having a flashback. Mom was bent over with her back to me. She had on a long T-shirt that hung about three inches below her butt cheeks—had she been standing up.

Even though she was bent over and displaying her backside cheeks, I could see this huge stain on her T-shirt. Immediately, it reminded me of that long underwear my grandfather used to wear with the brown décor in the back. As a matter of fact, my mother's rear was looking identical to my grandfather's. I guess that's because my mom is built like and looks like her father. She even has a bass voice as he had.

Well, needless to say, I was happy. The worst had not happened. I asked my mom a stupid question. I see her bent over trying to clean up this stuff that I very well know is not melted Hershey bars. "Did you mess yourself?" I asked her. I was surprised by her soft answer.

Somewhat startled, she just simply confirmed, "I messed myself."

Recalling the colorful mother of my youth, I expected her to say, "I shit all over the place." But when I said, messed, she picked up my word and dropped her usual colorful vocabulary.

Occasionally I look at my watch, or the time will come up on my phone, and the time, 5:11, will pop up. And immediately, I think of Mattie. I should also mention here that 511 is also our street address. May 11th is Mom's birthday. It's a day after her father's birthday, Burl James Clemons, which was May 10th. Occasionally, certain life instances will arise, such as how kids of today behave. And that's when my siblings and I will look at one another to say, "Mattie would not put up with that." We delight ourselves, reminiscing about the colorful response she'd give to the current events and the characters of today in the news and in our White House. When the number, five-eleven, pops up, I think to myself she is looking down on me with pride.

I have always believed that there comes a point in our lives when we decide that we've had enough, and it is time to move on. Other than accidents that can take place and/or sudden death situations, which can occur, most of us will die of some type of illness—even if it's simply old, old age. If it's an illness, we go through all kinds of treatments, hopeful to get back to normal. If we're fighting it, we decide to deal with our illnesses and grueling treatments, one day at a time. But then there will come a time when we will say, "we've had enough."

Occasionally when five-eleven (511) pops up, I think of my mom's final days. I assume most people do not forget a parent's final days. Mom passed on January 5, 1999, a day I will never forget. Her health had deteriorated to the point that we had no choice but to move her to a nursing home. We searched and researched until we had found one that seemed to take good care of its patients. Irvington Knolls was located on Athol Avenue, down the street from Edmondson High

School, from which I graduated. Most importantly, it was not far from my UPS job location on Joh Avenue in a Baltimore County community named Arbutus, about seven miles southwest of Baltimore. This meant I could stop by, daily, unannounced to check on her treatment and to visit with her.

In hindsight, we realized she was trying to tell us something back at Christmas. We picked her up on Christmas Eve from the nursing home and took her over to Sandra's to spend the night with Ashley and Sandra. The plan was for us to take mom back to the nursing home after they had all spent Christmas together. Sandra was living in an apartment complex on a second-floor level. When we got there, with our help, mom slowly made her way up the stairs. However, when it was time to get her back to the nursing home that Christmas night, she seemed not to be able to walk. Getting her down the stairs and into our vehicle was a struggle—to say the least. When we finally got her back to the nursing home, we could not get her out of the car. We had to get one of the caretakers at the nursing home to help us.

On New Year's Day, we all visited mom at the nursing home. She seemed to be in and out of it, although she did recognize us. Our thought at that time was that she was tired or perhaps it was her string of medications affecting her cognitive ability. Physically, we knew she was feeble. Mom was on dialysis, and she had been recently diagnosed with breast cancer. I had Power of Attorney, and as a family, we decided, along with her doctor, that keeping her comfortable rather than surgery was the best option.

It was Tuesday, January 5, 1999, and I was returning to work after the New Year's holiday off. I had stopped by the nursing home that morning, and mom seemed to be out of it when I stopped by. *I'll come back by after work*, was my thought. But I was only at work for a couple of hours when I got a phone call from the nursing home. On the other end of the call, the nurse informed me that my mother had been taken to St. Agnes Hospital in Baltimore City, which was down the street from my job. The short drive was quick but a blur. When I got there, to the nurses' station, the nurse informed me that she had passed. Following her to Mattie's room was an out-of-body experience. I kissed her for the last time.

My mother was seventy-one years old when she passed. Although a person knows that the experience of losing a parent or grandparent will most assuredly come, it seems unavoidable to escape the pain and the sense of great loss that it brings. At this point, I had to gather my strength to take care of the family. I knew Ashley and Sandra would take mom's passing harder than anyone. Ashley had been with mama all her life and Sandra as well. Eldora would also be hard hit. With her bad heart, I needed to be strong for her. Dot and Tony were as strong as I was, and they could take care of themselves. Tony has always been a little emotional, but he has his mechanism for dealing with life's tragedies.

Rev. Edward R. McClurkin of Mt. Carmel C.C. Church presided over Mattie Virginia Clemons Waymon's homegoing ceremony. He had presided over my brothers' services as well. Ed was my first supervisor at UPS, and over the years, we have become friends. His wife, Ada, gave birth to their daughter the same year my son, Ham, was born. When we moved to Carroll County, Brenda and Ada would run into each other at the market in Randallstown. Ed has always been a distant older brother figure. The brothers at UPS looked up to Ed. Although he was a tough manager, he was always fair and had earned our trust. As a man of the cloth, Ed was always there whenever any of us needed someone to talk to about the job or our personal issues.

CHAPTER TWENTY-NINE

LOYALTY, LOVE AND HARD-LISTENING

It's **Saturday, January 11, 2020, 2:32 a.m.,** and I am up as I would be on a workday at The Bakery. Yesterday, I had mentioned to Brenda that I slept all night, like a regular person, for three nights this week. As a matter of fact, yesterday, after going to the movies to see the film, *Just Mercy*, we watched TV together until 11:00 p.m. It's something I can't remember the last time we did. However, it did make her happy, and she went to bed before I did for a change.

I awaken tonight, or should I say, in the wee hours of this morning, because I had a dream that we were digging the foundation for the new Royal Theater. There was a line drawn across The Avenue, and a three-foot path was marked off. I didn't see who all were there, but there were a couple of shovels, and people were putting soil in little plastic bags for souvenirs. Suddenly I woke up sweating, and it just so happened that Brenda woke up as well. I shared my dream with her.

I got up to head to the bathroom because part of the reason for waking up was my bladder, which has been my alarm clock for more than nine years now. As I was making my way, it dawned upon me that Wanda Best had deceived me once again.

Back in November, when I asked her if they were building a regulation football field on the Robert C. Marshall field, she said, "No." And for me to "do what you want."

Well, based on Baltimore City's Six-Year Capital Program, Ordinance of Estimates Recommendation for Department of Recreation and Parks that Chad Hayes shared this week, there is a plan to put a field on the site of Robert C. Marshall field.

That is what bothers me most—the dishonesty and mistrust that takes place. Before we went on vacation, I sent Wanda a text message to ask that she and I meet. She indicated she had scheduled a meeting with my development team and me. When I asked her if she had a date for the meeting, she replied, "no." The next day, she stopped by The Bakery for rolls. I mentioned the meeting, and she indicated that the date was set for the twenty-second of January. However, that is the meeting Alice forced the City to hold after getting Senator Antonio Hayes involved to determine the whereabouts of the State funds allocated to TRTCHC. We are looking forward to that meeting. And another thought: just thinking, *why didn't Chad Hayes make all this information—the plans for Robert C. Marshall Field—public in 2018 or in June of 2019?* So many questions and a lack of transparency or integrity with the City government. Hopefully, the mud clears soon.

Our vacation is just about over. Today we will be cleaning up the house and getting ready for our trip back home. We are looking forward to watching the Baltimore Ravens playoff game tonight. And maybe we'll get to watch The Houston Texans' playoff game on Sunday. We are hoping The Ravens win because, as one of the items on our bucket list, we have tickets for the Super Bowl. On Wednesday, we had our dry run to the hotel where we will be staying as well as the Hard

Rock Stadium where the game will be played. It was an all-day trip down and back, but we enjoyed it.

Sunday morning, we will be heading back to Maryland to get back to work in 2020. Lin and Brandon are working Saturday preparing cookie dough and bean pie mix as they always do on Saturdays. With their help, we should have plenty of product when we open on Wednesday.

I got a call from Lady Brion, reminding me that the Pennsylvania Avenue Black Arts and Entertainment District retreat is Sunday. She wanted to order sweet potato pies, but I explained that we were out of town. I mentioned to her that I might be able to get Lin to make them for her and that I would let her know Saturday morning. She also asked me if I would serve as one of the five interim board members. I said yes. It will be this board that will put together all the documents and procedures for developing the regular board necessary to apply for its 501(c)(3) nonprofit status.

Well, it is Sunday, January 12, 2020, and the fantastic Ravens Football season is over. However, we are still proud of our team, and we love Lamar Jackson. Yes, Brenda and I will be going to the Super Bowl, but at this point, we don't know what team we'll be rooting for. I watched the first quarter of the game between The Kansas City Chiefs and The Houston Texans. I watched The Seattle Seahawks and The Green Bay Packers last night and was so disappointed and sensed they were not at their usual performance level. I watched intermittently as I went about completing Brenda's honey-do list, which was repairing the toilet paper holder in the guest bathroom. After that, I gathered everything I needed for our trip back to Baltimore. I shaved and showered, after which I saw the score. I then went into the bedroom and did my usual, flipped channels until I got sleepy. I turned off the TV and went to sleep.

Now it is 2:31 in the morning, and I am wide awake. As I woke up, I thought about the fact that our Super Bowl adventure next month will be the completion of one of the items on my Bucket List. The next item on my list is to complete a college degree. I promised LJ that when he graduated from high school, he and I would attend college to both graduate at the same time. He is fifteen and has two years to go in high school. However, I think I need to get a head start on him. I also blame myself for the fact that I allowed Hammy and Lin to choose not to get their degrees. Both are very intelligent, hard-working people. I feel that had I pursued my education to set the example for them, it might have motivated them to do so as well.

So, within the next few weeks, my plan is to gather all my experiences over the years to see how much credit I can get for it. I, and the higher education institution I choose, will calculate what I need to do to earn my degree. My thought process is that with more than thirty-five years with UPS, gaining experience as an operations manager, personnel management, training & development, Safety Manager, as well as community relations manager and publications editor—all that should earn me a few credits. Then there are the nine years of running The Avenue Bakery, which required all the skillsets to include marketing and business development.

Yes, this is on my Bucket List for many reasons. I am not pursuing a degree for monetary reasons or for the pursuit of a career. It's about finishing something I started. When I graduated from Edmondson High School in 1968, I immediately attended Coppin State College. I didn't finish because working and providing for my wife and son was a priority. So, I pursued that with every fiber of my being. Yes, concerning my career, I took courses in personnel and business management, and I even took Dale Carnegie courses. It is not that I didn't continue my education; I just didn't pursue a degree.

Yes, I want to do this for me, but I also want to see that framed degree on a wall someday. At this point in my life, I have received hundreds of awards and citations for my work in the community, none of which I pursued. I am grateful that others have recognized my efforts to make life better for others; however, that is our responsibility—to do God's work. Well, I guess I will figure out how to get it done. I know Brenda will say I am trying to do too much, but I think I must have Attention Deficit Disorder and must have many things going on in my life.

Well, late today, we will be making the trip back home. I figured Sunday would be less traffic, and it will give us time to get ready for our workweek. I am up, but most likely, I will start off driving, and Brenda will take over when I get sleepy. We will stop by Gert's for a break when we get to Petersburg, Virginia. We may stay for a few hours, and I know she will want us to eat before we get back on the road. We will probably get back home late in the night.

We got up around 6:30 a.m., showered, and did the walk-through of the house to make sure everything was straight, and we loaded the truck and headed out. On the way, I stopped by the gas station to put a little air in the right rear tire. It had a very slow leak. It gave me no problem on the way down, but it had lost quite a bit of air after sitting for about nine days. It was early Sunday morning, and there was very little traffic on the road. On the way, we made a couple of stops. One was for lunch in Georgia at Sonny's Barbecue. One of Brenda's favorites is pulled pork with coleslaw, a dish she's enjoyed since childhood. Her dad, Johnnie Taylor, would take Brenda and her brother, John, to North Carolina to spend the summers with their grandmother, Betty Brown, whom they called Nanny, and her sister, Lena. Over the years, we would bring Nanny down to North Carolina to visit her sister and stop at different barbecue places along the way. It became a ritual.

We got to Gert's around 7:45 p.m., and of course, she had prepared dinner for us. Brenda ate the bean soup and rice that Gert had prepared. I was not quite hungry because I still had some of that pulled pork in the tank. But I was happy that Gert had baked a pudding pound cake, so a hunk of that and a tall glass of ice water was my choice.

I sat and talked with Bob, discussing the disappointing Ravens' game on Saturday. We both felt they had too much time off and had lost their momentum. I think that Lamar Jackson was doing his part, but with all the missed catches, penalties, and turnovers, the rest of the team wasn't stepping up. Brenda and Gert were back in the bedroom conducting girl talk, which for them meant not football, and discussing the work Gert had completed in her bathroom. She recently renovated it herself, and I must say, it looked like a design from a Good Housekeeping Magazine.

Gert is a self-taught interior designer who does everything from window treatments, painting, furniture refurbishing, and upholstery. She has all kinds of sewing equipment and a She-Shed out back where she does a lot of her work. Like me, and it must be in our blood, she is always busy and has a project that she is working on. Her business is called *Eye For Color*, and she is still working at the age of eighty. By the time she retired from the nursing profession back in New York and had moved to Petersburg, Virginia, about fifteen years ago, she honed in on her passion in retirement life. Like the Hamlin genes we possess, she looks as though she is in her late fifties or early sixties, and she works as though she's in her twenties.

We left Gert's around 10:00 a.m. After we said our goodbyes and had gotten our hugs, I headed to the gas station to fill the tank. The ride home was steady, and the traffic moved well. We always leave after the morning rush hour to avoid delays and traffic jams. All went well except the occasional knucklehead determined to creep in the fast lane. We got to Lin's house around noon, picked up Rock and Bruno, our two Miniature Pinschers, and headed home. After unloading luggage and dogs, I began collecting the Christmas decorations outside and gathering the containers so that Brenda could undress the tree.

After that was done, I began the task of getting ready for the workweek. The first thing I needed to do was to go to Mr. Tire and get that slow leak fixed. When I got there, the customer parking lot was nearly full. So, I assumed that Mr. Tire must have had a busy Tuesday schedule. But much to my surprise, they were able to get me in and out in about forty-five minutes. While waiting, I asked the manager if they were hiring, thinking about Brandon's desire to get a regular forty-hour job this year. He graduated from Lincoln Tech's Automotive Program, and he loves cars.

The manager said, "Yes. If you have a possible candidate, give me his name, and I will call him now."

I mentioned Brandon and gave him Brandon's phone number. And, as Brandon always does, he didn't pick up the phone, not recognizing the number. So, I called Brandon and explained the opportunity. However, I could tell he was very apprehensive. At this point, I knew I was getting him out of his comfort zone. I asked him, "Do you have time to come up to the shop today?"

"No," he responded back and started in, trying to come up with excuses.

But I kept pushing because sometimes that's just what you have to do. "Standby," I said to Brandon, "I'm giving my phone to the manager. You talk to him."

They talked, and an interview was scheduled for 10 a.m., Tuesday, which is tomorrow. After the call, Brandon called me back to ask for directions to the shop. I told him that he and I could meet at 9:00 a.m. at the McDonald's down the road to discuss the job and make sure he gets there by 9:30. As the time ticks by, I think he is getting a little excited because he called his mother, Lin, to let her know about the job interview.

I called Brenda to let her know what I did and to get her feedback. She was pleased. However, we now must figure out how to fill the possible void at The Bakery. Brandon has been such an anchor and a critical component to our success. But a constructive dream, realized, is a dream worth the sacrifice. Brandon got the job.

***

It's Monday, February 24, 2020, at 3:42 a.m. As usual, I am awake with a thousand things on my mind. Yesterday Brenda and I completed an eight-hour training for our Carry Permit license. Lin ran The Bakery with LJ and Susie (Ham's mother-in-law) by her side. Ham came at the end to help shut it down. They did a fantastic job, and I am so blessed. I mentioned to Brenda how pleased I was that our family is beginning to really learn the business. This is the second time they took care of it for us. And that's when Brenda quickly shared with me the hard, cold facts.

With her signature directness, coded with a little sugar in her eyes, Brenda looked at me and said, "Lin is tired." She paused a bit to let me take it in before continuing on, "and helping with the business like this is a little much."

I was silent, still hard-listening to the echo of the words that had already been said. Brenda stood close to me, ready to undergird my feelings. What I felt was disappointment in my daughter's response. But I do understand. Lin loves me so much she will do anything I ask of her. She always wants to show her love. That said, I must be careful not to take advantage of that. More importantly, perhaps, I must not mistake her loyalty, love, and tangible hard work to help me for a genuine interest in the business.

That revelation leads me to this point—I need to develop a phase-out plan. I love The Bakery and what we have been able to build. The dream is that my children and grandchildren will carry on from here. But I can't count on that. And it is not fair to expect them to do it. One thing for sure, I refuse to sell the property. I remain hopeful that they will be wise enough to hold on to it when I am gone.

On a same note, I believe I need to allow Brenda more time to enjoy her retirement years. Although she does everything she can, to support The Bakery and the work that I am doing in the community, she is getting tired. Even though it keeps her mind and body moving, she wants to move less or at least activate the well-earned luxury to move only when she feels like it. I can't help but feel guilty, and that I am not fair to her when it comes to this mission I am on. I often tell her, "Whenever you want to do something or go anywhere just plan it. And we will work out the details." She knows that I have been, and I still am, a man of my word. We've been to some great places and enjoyed some great things. However, in my mind, the battle to give my family what it needs and desires: peace, a healthy rest, and stability while trying to bring about change in our community continues to loom.

I must admit that on occasion, I feel a little tired from my rigorous schedule and inability to relax and enjoy life. I battle with trying to get community leadership to see and to grasp a bigger picture of what we can do together. I repeatedly question myself, "Why am I agonizing over a group of people who appear to repeat the poor decisions of the past?" They allowed The Royal Theater to be the only venue of the Chitlin' Circuit to be torn down, and now they are standing in the way of its rebuilding on the original site.

Then it comes to me that my quest—it's not for me, it's for the future generations of our community. It's about changing the environment our children are living in, right here, right now, and providing a better economic and social community of which they can be proud. The battle, inside and out, rages on.

From November 17, 2018 to December of 2019, my heart for The Pennsylvania Avenue Corridor and TRTCHC's mission had been a part of an exhibition featured at the National Building Museum in Washington, DC. *Flickering Treasures* was created by Amy Davis, an award-winning photojournalist for the *Baltimore Sun,* based on her book, *Flickering Treasures: Rediscovering Baltimore's Forgotten Movie Theaters* [Johns Hopkins University Press, 2017]. In it, Amy celebrates the history of The Royal and seventeen other theaters that once graced the Pennsylvania Avenue commercial district, dating back to the early 1900s. While researching the history of The Arch Social Club, once a white-owned theater from the early 1900s that later catered to Black audiences, she stumbled upon The Avenue Bakery. As its aromas drew her in, she was nearly floored to find all the historic tributes The Bakery also offered. Including it in the exhibition became an instant no-brainer. Later, Amy donated to us the exhibition's panels that celebrate The Royal Theater and The Pennsylvania Avenue Corridor.

On February 15, 2020, at The Bakery, we held an official ceremony for the unveiling of the exhibition's panels, titled *The Avenue and Beyond.* We had a crowd of community notables, neighbors, and press members joyfully squeezed into our conference room where the panels are now mounted. Of course, Amy was on hand to make a wonderful presentation.

In a Facebook post, this is some of what Amy shared about the lively celebration, "The whiff of Poppay's rolls wafted into the back room of the bakery, where a jazz group led by James Dow set the mood. Owner Jim Hamlin and his wife, Brenda, did a fantastic job arranging the movie theater history panels that were originally displayed in the recent *Flickering Treasures* exhibition at the National Building Museum. This permanent installation [now at The Bakery] tells the story of

The Royal and more than a baker's dozen movie theaters that thrived in the Pennsylvania Avenue corridor from 1907 to 1986."

I haven't thought about my adventure of being led to the lions in a while but considering how we must all be careful of the legacy we leave, especially those in government, at every level, I spied an interesting headline. It stated that Baltimore's former mayor, Ms. Pugh has been sentenced to three years in prison.

Evidently, in her brief heyday, she may have been the mother of all deals. Not only was she good at breaking my deal with the city to revitalize Historic Pennsylvania Avenue, but also, she made a dream deal with several entities and nonprofits. NPR's report, dated, February 27, 2020, sums up the details. This excerpt taken from the full story is some of what it revealed:

Pugh resigned as mayor in May 2019 as allegations of "self-dealing" in connection with the sale of thousands of copies of her Healthy Holly children's books engulfed her administration.

Prior to her resignation, federal investigators were looking into the book sales, many of which went to entities she had influence over or businesses that hoped to do business with the city and the state.

Prosecutors had accused Pugh of earning approximately $800,000 from the Healthy Holly book series, about an African American girl who promotes exercise and nutritious eating habits.

"But the problem was thousands of books that nonprofits and foundations ordered to distribute in schools and day cares to promote healthy choices and combat obesity were never delivered to the city's children," as *NPR* reported in November.

"Instead, authorities say she took books that were already purchased and resold them. Pugh then funneled those proceeds into her own political campaigns and used the cash to purchase and renovate a house in Baltimore."

In early April, Pugh took an "indefinite leave of absence" as mayor, citing health challenges as the reason. By then, the book scandal had already jeopardized her term in office.

That same month, federal agents with the FBI and Internal Revenue Service raided Pugh's home and offices at City Hall in connection with their investigation into the fraudulent book scheme. Hours after the raids, Republican Gov. Larry Hogan called for Pugh's resignation.

He said at the time: "Now more than ever, Baltimore City needs strong and responsible leadership. Mayor Pugh has lost the public trust. She is clearly not fit to lead."

It should be noted that the newsroom staff at The Baltimore Sun (including Amy Davis) won the Pulitzer Prize for the investigation that brought down Ms. Pugh. *The Sun* broke the story thanks to the investigation begun by reporter Luke Broadwater.

***

It's March 9, 2020, my day off, and around 1:25 p.m. I am sitting at Boney's Auto Enhancement Center on East 25th Street, needing to get my 1990 BMW tinted windows. I came here because I think this is where Brandon got the windows of his vehicle done. At 10:00 a.m., I attended the ribbon-cutting ceremony for the Bakersview Development project next to The Bakery. Although I opposed the Druid Heights CDC building houses that took up valuable commercial development space on Pennsylvania Avenue, I had to congratulate the CDC on its success.

I had hoped, Mayor Jack Young would be there, so that I could confront him on the support of our project. While he was present at the event, I decided, instead, to offer my greetings. The Baltimore City Housing Commissioner Michael Braverman also attended the event. Prior to today, Danny Henson had committed to reach out to

Commissioner Braverman to familiarize him with our project. Here, I had an opportunity to talk to him about it. The housing commissioner has a critical role in the implementation of our TRTCHC project.

Commissioner Braverman at the event, and he formally addressed the crowd as well. I introduced myself to him and invited him to join me at The Bakery after the ceremony. He said that he was pleased to finally meet me as if I was some sort of celebrity. He mentioned that he had stopped into The Bakery to grab some rolls before a meeting and was especially happy to get them hot out of the oven.

I shared with him the recent exhibit we had unveiled in the conference room. One of the components of the exhibit featured a poster of Louis Armstrong. Braverman marveled at it. "I was just listening to a recording of his," he shared, commenting on how much he enjoyed it.

Giving him a tour of The Bakery, we moved from the conference room's exhibits to the main lobby area. There is much history to see there as well. I opened the door leading into the lobby where The Pennsylvania Avenue Heritage Trail panels are on the wall and propped the door open with a doorstop—something I do a thousand times. I have a problem with opening that door whether I'm coming from the conference room or leaving out of the lobby, but I have been reluctant to pay a locksmith $200 to come out to repair it. Braverman and I walked through it, entering the customer area. We were busy talking when suddenly the door bullied the doorstop, pushed it out of its way, and slammed itself shut.

And here's a moment to contemplate one of life's little funnies. Why is it that down through the annals of time, when a first-time dinner guest is given a choice of seats in the dining room, he or she will choose to sit in the chair with the wobbly leg? And so, why, when the Baltimore City Housing Commissioner and I were engaging in a fruitful, impromptu conversation about the history of The Pennsylvania

Avenue Corridor and the prospect of changing the lives around it, were we about to get locked inside The Bakery's lobby?

We were talking, and the door slams shut, but besides hearing the abrupt noise of the slam, Commissioner Braverman didn't appear to be moved. My innards moved; however, my outer shell played it cool—even when I realized that The Bakery's front parking lot gate was still down and locked. In my mind, I shouted, *Oh sh_t, we are locked in the lobby. I'm gonna have to call somebody to get us out.*

While the Commissioner studied our historical panels, artifacts, and literature, I—dressed in my event-going attire—accomplished a few quick assessments and even quicker moves. I was praying that the customer window was not also locked, which it mostly is when not in use; I checked, and it wasn't. Next, I backed up to the customer window—which resembles a bank teller's counter—gracefully lifted myself up and swung my legs around to land into the kitchen. From there, I walked to the other side of the locked door and opened it. In my mind, my sigh of relief was thundering. My next thought was, *Thank God, I'm still wiry and agile.* At seventy, that's a blessing.

Braverman was very impressed with the garden—the artwork and photomontages. I asked him if he was aware of our project. Curiously, it seemed that he wasn't. During our conversation, he talked about the development of the Avenue Market, Sphinx Club, and the Lenox Theater. He indicated he would like to know more, which opened the door for me to give him a copy of our project's Impact Statement. Finally, he left to go to another meeting, looking very pleased about what he had learned. As he left our parking lot, he admired my 1990 BMW and the fact it was a stick shift and still has the big handheld telephone in it.

After he left, I closed The Bakery and decided that finally, I was going to get the windows of my BMW tinted. I called Brandon to find out where he had gotten his done, kind of remembering that he'd shared how it was at a shop on 25th Street—just around the corner from his

Grandma Betty's house. Grandma Betty is his father's mother. While I had spoken with him earlier, right then, he wasn't answering his phone. I assumed he probably didn't want to be bothered, so I tried to find the place myself. The odds were somewhat stacked against me since I didn't have the name of the place or the exact address. But stacked-up odds have rarely halted my quest to do something I need to get done.

I ended up at Boney's Auto Enhancement Center, located in a building that appears to have once been a car dealership service garage. Although it looked as though it could use some cosmetic repairs, it was functional. I didn't meet Boney but was approached by Roslyn, who seemed to be in charge. I explained what I needed to have done.

Without batting an eyelid, she said, "that will be $125. It will take two hours to complete." To soften the abruptness, she seasoned it with a smile. So, I went ahead and scratched that off my list of things to get done.

***

Tuesday, March 9, 2020 an 8:00 p.m. roundup

My next appointment on my day-off list was at 6:00 p.m. with TRT-CHC's founding board member, Adrian Johnson. He and I have been trying to meet for some time to catch up. He has been very busy as a VP at Municipal Employees Credit Union (MECU), teaching and dealing with his wife's health issues. We had decided on Ruth's Chris Steak House as a good place to meet and have dinner. The restaurant is not far off the beaten path to his home in Pennsylvania.

Our meeting happened to take place in perfect timing because I had heard there was a major accident on I-83, the road he had to take home. He would have been sitting in traffic for possibly hours. Instead, he was sitting in a great restaurant, valuing our catch-up time.

He and I have a long history that goes back to the late '90s, when I was the UPS District Community Relations Manager and the 2nd Vice President of The NAACP's Baltimore Branch, under GI Johnson. We met when I was chairing the Branch's Business Breakfast years before forming TRTCHC. I used to attend the functions of an organization of Black bank professionals called Urban Bankers, of which he was an officer.

Our meeting went well, and we talked about our lives and the direction we are going in to get this project done. I had a nice steak sandwich with sweet potato fries, and he had a salad. We decided that we would schedule a presentation to his board on the project and a meeting with Joe Haskins of Harbor Bank. We both enjoyed having the meeting of the minds and a bite to eat together, after which we each parted for home.

***

It's Monday, March 16, 2020. And, yes, I was up at 11:30 p.m. last night, as though I was going to work. But like I said, it is Monday, our off day. Last week I was contacted by Kali-Ahset Amen Ph.D. of Johns Hopkins University wanting to meet today or Tuesday, which are my days off. It seems I find myself meeting on days I should be spending doing what I want to do. She has come to the community to conduct a study with her class on urban businesses. I am one of the four business owners who were selected. I had two students who were assigned to report to me once a week. Their names are Maggie and Caroline. However, because of the coronavirus situation, the students have gone home and are now working online. As a result, she wants to interview me for about forty-five minutes to an hour. I was able to schedule the meeting for Wednesday when we're open rather than scheduling it on my day off.

Sitting up at 11:30 p.m., as soon as the sleepiness vacated and clarity moved in, my thought was *Wow, two days off and no meetings*. It had to be a first for some time.

Sunday was normal, except when I returned from going to get supplies, Brenda met me in the conference room while I was off-loading packages of sugar, eggs, milk, sweet potatoes, and some other items.

"There's a man waiting for you in the lobby," she said.

I entered the lobby to see a casually dressed, medium-height man, nearing my complexion, standing there waiting for me.

"Hello, my name is Michael Tisdale," he said.

Normally when I meet someone for the first time, it's second nature to offer a welcoming and hearty handshake. But due to the Coronavirus outbreak, neither of us made such a move. Instead, we gave each other a nod.

He wanted to discuss the possibility of having Mrs. Lena Boone's picture or image included on one of my murals or photomontages. "She's done a lot for the community and Pennsylvania Avenue," was his reasoning. "When former Mayor Schaefer gave The Royal Theater to her and Willie Adams," he said, giving a slight pause before continuing, "she said tear it down."

I stood there taking in every word he was saying, at first wondering—or should I say studying him and what I heard to see—where all this was going. When he uttered the words *tear it down,* I fought not to show any emotion, but I could feel my eyes widen. And if he was waiting to get a premature comment out of me, he wasn't getting it. I make a habit of not making premature comments.

Michael continued, "That was a major mistake," he conceded, "but she did a lot of good in the community."

I shared with him that my focus has been on its rebuilding, "but I've been having some difficulties in the process."

He indicated how he thought that the project was well on its way. He asked, "How much is needed to get it rebuilt?"

"The theater cost is about seventy-five million dollars," I answered. I watched him look at me, talk, and take in all the history and interactive mementos like our signing book in the lobby. A steady stream of customers flowed in and out around us. And now, he had the poker face.

"That is not much," he said, looking me directly in the eye, now. "I could raise that in a short amount of time."

Okay, now the conversation was on, officially. I told him that the entire project would be around one hundred twenty-five million dollars because the project included retail and restaurant space and parking. We ended up in the conference room, where I gave him a copy of our Impact Statement and our 501 (c)(3) certification. He asked would we be willing to pay him a two percent fee to raise the money for the project. My response was, "That sounds reasonable."

After sharing with him that we are trying to get site control from the City so that we can move forward with seemingly no concern on his face, he said, "I can reach out to Mayor Young and get that done." He went on to share his relationship with former Mayor Pugh after I shared with him her opposition to us moving the project forward.

Michael seemed to be very excited about the opportunity to help with getting the project moving and raising the money to get it done. He also expressed an interest in the housing component of the project.

He shared with me that he already happened to have a meeting scheduled with Mayor Young for tomorrow, which was Monday. He asked if I could put together a letter that spelled out exactly what we needed from the City. I agreed to do so, and he left as we were beginning to close The Bakery.

I sat in the conference room after he left to work on the letter he had requested. He later called me to let me know he would be willing to stop back by to pick up the letter. I shared with him that I was working on it and would get back to him as soon as I had it done, which I did after completing it and having Alice and Brenda read it and make corrections. When I notified him that it was done, he returned to The Bakery with his wife. They got to our back door as I requested and called me to let me know they had arrived. This was because we had closed, and the front entrance gates were locked.

At this point, I gave him a copy of our request letter for Mayor Young. I asked him if it was what he needed. He took a quick peruse, and he stated, yes. He also asked me if I would send him a copy and a copy of our Pro-forma, and I did so. Michael went on to express his interest in the housing component of the project. He expressed an interest in raising money for that as well.

His wife interjected, "What school did you attend?"

"Edmondson Class of 1968," I answered with a smile.

"I'm a member of that class," she said warmly.

Glad to find that we had something in common, but questioning still, I said, "Oh, but I haven't seen you at any of our class reunions."

"Oh, I don't attend any of those," she finalized with a gentle laugh. And the side conversation was over.

In the short time that we were apart, Michael emailed me a contract agreement that he wanted me to sign. But face-to-face, I shared with Michael that I could not sign an agreement without legal counsel and board approval. He was somewhat concerned that if he met with the Mayor on behalf of the project, he might not be compensated if there was no signed agreement. I shared with him how without site control of the project, nothing would happen. I also let him know that we have not contracted anyone at this point to do what he proposes, but that if the agreement made sense, I could not see why our attorney and board would not support it. He repeated what I said and looked at his wife for a sign of approval, and she seemed to gesture an *okay.*

At this point, as they were leaving, we had a conversation about some of the people who ran in the circle as his wife did at Edmondson High School. I recognized some of the names, but because I worked a full-time night job during my high school years, I didn't have time to hang out with classmates.

I received a call from Michael about twenty minutes later after they had left, asking if I had a contract with Danny Henson to do the housing component of our project, and I responded, no, which was accurate. However, to make sure I was upfront with Michael, I sent him the following email:

"Michael, I make a point to be honest and upfront with everyone I work and/or deal with. You asked me a question about Danny Henson and our housing component. My answer was no we don't have a contract. However, when Danny came aboard as a member of the development team it was because of his interest in the housing component of the project. I know that you are interested in that as well and raising money for the project.

Let me be clear, I try to be honest and upfront with everyone and to be a man of my word. As much as we need and could use your help to get Mayor Young to come aboard, I am sending you this email in advance of you doing anything. Certainly, I welcome your offer to help raise money for the project and will work diligently to get my board and attorney to agree. Our meeting in my mind is God's work, however integrity is key to every relationship.

You can email and or text me with your intentions at this point. My hope is that we can work together to change lives and outcomes in our community. God bless. By the way, what is the name of the fund that Mayor Pugh indicated was available?"

Well, perhaps it was the fact that my board and my legal counsel would be involved or perhaps it was something else that spooked Michael. I may never know. However, again, it was like the lyrics of The Temptations' song, titled, Fading Away, *Like smoke from a cigarette …* [and] *dreams that you soon forget…* that fella simply faded away.

CHAPTER THIRTY

The COVID-19 GLOBAL PANDEMIC HITS

Mid-March of 2020. We are also trying to run the business and deal with the Coronavirus situation. We are feverishly using our sanitizing wipes at The Bakery to keep the customer contact areas clean, and we're making sure we are doing what we can. Brenda was concerned that we might have to close the business even though all we do is carryout. Even on a regular basis, we never have more than six or eight people in our customer area at any given time—except for the Thanksgiving Holiday. We make a point to service our customers promptly. The virus is beginning to really hit at home. After this week, Lin will be laid off because the Hilton Hotel where she works is closing.

Because of the escalation of the Coronavirus and all the new restrictions, and the fact that they talk about it not being especially safe for folks who are over the age of sixty-five and seventy, I've decided that this is not a safe environment for Susie and it's not a safe environment for Brenda. So, they are no longer working at The Bakery. Instead, my grandson, Brandon, is working at The Bakery, and because my other grandson, fifteen-year-old LJ, is out of school because of COVID-19, after his homeschooling sessions, he's now at The Bakery, too. I've got those two guys working hard at helping. They also have been trained to maintain their mask-wearing while serving customers, sanitizing the work area on a constant basis and making sure they operate in their gloves appropriately.

Now, customers are no longer allowed in our lobby. All business is handled through our walk-up service window that we use during Thanksgiving. We have made a conscientious effort to adjust and comply with the Governor's stipulations so that everyone, our customers and personnel, will be safe during this extraordinarily challenging time.

***

Tuesday, March 17, 2020 around 2 p.m., this message was sent through The Bakery's online ordering feature by way of our website: *I'm writing a story about how black business have been impacted by the current coronavirus crisis. Would like to speak to the owner if there's any interest in talking. Thank you.*

It was a surprising and welcoming message to receive. But I was so busy working and revamping; it took me a couple of days to get back to him.

***

It's about 1:30 p.m., Tuesday, March 24, 2020, and I need to stop writing now. Jerry Bembry, a reporter from *ESPN's Undefeated*—I guess news assignments are becoming more diverse these days—has set up the interview for 2 p.m.

***

It's July 2020 and a hot summer in Baltimore. And we continue to work to stay healthy, keep our customers healthy, and maintain social distancing. But that doesn't mean we've halted our mission to join with others to make a difference. We finalized The Bakery's partnership with The Roots of Scouting, Inc., the scouting initiative. It's dedicated to addressing the particular needs of African American youth of all genders through leadership activities, life skills, and mentoring. Its president Mr. Leo Boroughs, Jr., and I managed to get together to iron out our plan for The Bakery to produce cookies that its Scouters can sell to raise money. I finally met with its 1st Vice President, Melaughn Butler, the organization's coordinator of the fundraising initiative. And as soon as we can, we will get moving and baking and fundraising for the scouts.

We took July fourth, Independence Day off, from The Bakery. And a couple of days later, I had kind of a health scare. I wasn't feeling well, but I didn't want to go to the hospital because during these Coronavirus days, who knows what I would catch there. Instead, I decided that I was going to Patient First. Brenda was concerned about me and urged me to go get checked out. All this happened at around 8 a.m. I asked Brenda to find out what time Patient First opened. She did and found out that it wasn't until 10 a.m., which was perfect, I told her. It gave her time to go do her morning walk, an exercising ritual that she does with Lin, Etoy, and Etoy's mother, Susie, about three times a week.

I woke up this morning feeling lightheaded, a little dizzy, and weak. And that's happened to me before when I'm dehydrated. But yesterday was an uneventful day for me. I had not spent it out in the heat or working in the yard, perspiring. All that said, I knew that I needed to get checked out. And I found that my blood sugar was low. It was at sixty-seven, and it's supposed to be at one hundred. Also, I was, indeed, a bit dehydrated.

After my visit to Patient First, I scheduled a visit with my primary doctor, Jacob Levine. Dr. Levine has been my doctor for about fifteen years now. He and I have an excellent relationship—to the point that I have his cell number. I had texted him about what was going on and even gave him my blood pressure numbers for that morning. The appointment was set up for the following day. And as a result, he recommended that, number one, I stop taking my blood pressure medicine, and number 2, he wanted me to monitor my blood pressure to make sure that it doesn't go above 140, which is the higher number, and that the lower number doesn't go above 90.

I'm thankful that the basic to-do list from my doctor was to watch my diet, drink plenty of water, and sometimes mix it with Gatorade. Lastly, he scheduled my annual physical for August, during which he'll do a complete work-up on me. Of course, I'm already pretty active, and I'm thankful to be in pretty good shape for a man who is going to be seventy-two years old in August of this year.

But I'd be lying if I didn't admit to the fact that I find it quite alarming seeing so many others dying around me, who are much younger than I. I found out later in life that my father had an enlarged heart and that he died of a massive heart attack at age fifty. My sister, Gert, is eighty and in the best of health. Next week, Brenda and I will head down to Petersburg, VA, to visit her on July 13, which happens to be our wedding anniversary. Brenda and I will be married for fifty-two years. For someone that's two-and-a-half lifetimes. If you're an adult and commit a crime, the system could give you twenty years in jail. So, fifty-two years of marriage is equivalent to more than two-and-a-half lifetime sentences. I do have a big backyard, but I don't have a doghouse. But when Brenda reads this, I may have to build one.

I still feel that I have so much to do in my life. I just can't let go of the fact that I want to do all that I can to build a legacy for my family and the community of my birth—and for my people.

TRTCHC remains hard on its mission. Alice Cole just sent letters and emails to various elected officials, including State Senator Antonio Hayes, to solicit his support in obtaining a reimbursement of funds spent by The Royal Theater & Community Heritage Corporation on the project design plans that remain in the City's Recreation and Parks budget. These funds were restricted to TRTCHC. Additionally, she reached out to the President of Baltimore City Council, President Brandon Scott, who is familiar with and supportive of the project. He has attended our events and has written a letter of support. The Senator immediately sent an email of inquiry to the Mayor's Office. TRTCHC received a letter in response to our Board's letter informing us of a new contact person and that they are in the process of preparing the necessary documents for the reimbursement of funds to be placed on a Board of Estimate agenda for approval.

Mayor Pugh blatantly and unceremoniously ditched the project in 2017 without explanation. But before she could devote the time to deliver the last rites to our efforts to revitalize The Pennsylvania Avenue Corridor, she herself went down in flames. Next, we could not get substantive cooperation from her successor, Mayor Bernard "Jack" Young. He seemed to understand the mission. But then, without warning, his administration wanted to change the location of the project. The news came during our meeting in January of 2020, during which Mayor Young sent his point-person, Carolyn Mozell, and representative, Chad Hayes of the Department of Planning, to make the argument that perhaps TRTCHC—still unpaid—was taking too long to get the project off the ground; and for that reason, it had come up with a new location. That very action—perhaps, we could call it a tactic—would delay the project further. It was the same tactic used back in the Graziano days in 2006.

On Tuesday, June 9, 2020, *The Baltimore Sun* reported, "Brandon Scott has won the crowded Democratic primary for Baltimore mayor, making good on his campaign to 'change the guard' at City Hall and usher in a new generation of leadership."

Let's see.

***

It's Wednesday, July 8, 2020, at 3:30 a.m., and yes, I'm up. Day after day, we constantly hear the state of our nation during this COVID-19 Global Pandemic. I even hear it in my sleep. We are constantly reminded of all the lives that could have been saved if our country's leadership had the capacity to lead. It reminds me of the same strategy that has been used against the Black communities in Baltimore—divide and conquer.

For years, the powers-that-be have pitted Black communities against one another by creating minimal grants for which they have to compete, only for it to create more division than economic assistance. Urban renewal plans that destroy our communities are disguised as missions meant to invest in our communities when it's really all about the scavengers that pool their capital together in the name of building housing projects that either turn out to be substandard, far too few for any perceived or needed demand, or too expensive for local residents to afford—and that's when gentrification moves in, instead of the underserved and/or the low-to-middle income residents that the project was purported to serve. Every election year, these housing project boons arrive christened with a different name. The builders recoup their investments, take Baltimore's tax dollars, and run back to their rich worlds—until another crop of politicians arrives afoot, to which they can entice with the same old dried-up message. For them, this is the only time Black communities matter.

This pandemic, the *Black Lives Matter* Movement, and modern technology have worked together to draw back the curtain and truly unveil what we, as African Americans, have been saying all the time. Nobody believed us! The thought has been that we just do not want to do the work to achieve the American dream. And systemic racism is merely a figment of our imagination—or an excuse to allow legacy wealth and equal opportunity to escape us.

We have struggled for generations to lead our children in the directions of preparing them for this cruel, unjust world that they must deal with while giving them hope. The hope that there is an American dream for them as well as for others.

I applaud our young people of today for their relentless efforts to accrue success and take a stand to tell it like it is—before the world and in the light of day. They have been unveiling that which society has kept away from the direct sunlight for decades: The true America that our ancestors warned us about, but kept it undercover, fearing it would erase our hope, ambitions and lead us to failure. As the *Black Lives Matter* Movement gains momentum and positive changes in policing and glimpses of social equality emerge, there needs to be another movement—*Black Communities Matter.*

There needs to be an economic rebuilding and renaissance in our Black Communities. We must have a plan to invest in our communities much like the Black Wall Street that had sprung up out of the collective perseverance, sweat, and ingenuity of an oppressed people in Tulsa, Oklahoma, in the 1920s as well as in other thriving Black communities in America that hateful racism destroyed or imploded in order to keep that knee on our neck.

We must make sure those political leaders who look like us understand when they are being played and when that knee is on their neck to inaction or indifference to the plight of Black Americans and businesses. Our community leaders need to understand that building a community is not just about housing. It is about building an economic engine that fuels the community and allows it to grow and feed the needs of its people. Creating jobs, careers, and entrepreneurial opportunities instill a sense of pride and dignity—as well as that all too elusive legacy-building wealth. This is what community building is about. It's nothing new; we have done this before in this country.

As the old folks used to tell us, God works in mysterious ways. It is God's gift of the creative mind and spirit that has given us today's technology and the benefit of technology that is yet to come. It was His gift of choice that allowed us to choose to be complacent during the 2016 election. What a teachable moment that was. He has allowed us to see where we have been and where we are going in this country. He has blessed us with our children, asking the pertinent questions, *why*, and making the statement—No, this will not continue to happen in our country. So, you see, we are working God's plan.

Therefore, I have been and will continue to pursue the revitalization of our Historic West Baltimore and Pennsylvania Avenue. *Black Communities Matter*. As I have said so many times, "With this rich cultural area, being one of the most historic African American communities in the country—we need to set the example.

***

It's Tuesday, July 14, 2020, at 4:00 a.m., the day after our fifty-second wedding anniversary. Last week, I told Brenda that I needed to go see Gert the following week, not thinking of our anniversary.

For months, Gert and I have been talking over the phone, at least on a weekly basis. Again, not thinking of our anniversary, I had planned the week out in detail so that I would be free to make the trip. And mostly, that meant that I fulfilled all my father-to-do list for both Lin and Ham. I made sure I completed Lin's assignment to put her new kitchen cabinet in over her refrigerator. And I had committed to Etoy that I would help Ham put in a door that would lead out to their deck so that they didn't have to go out the front door to walk around the house to enjoy it. I had been trying to get them to make the decision to do this for years. So last week, I helped him take down the mirror, posted up on the wall where a new patio door should have been. We worked together to cut into the wall to make space for the new door. We soon discovered that there were electrical wires in the way, so he scheduled an electrician to remove them by last Saturday, which meant the Sunday after I closed The Bakery, I had to stop by his house to finish the demolition and get the new door installed.

Getting my father-to-do list done meant that if I was going to make the trip to Gert's on Monday, July 13, I was going to have to get my chores done, which meant cutting my acre of grass on Saturday after work. Needless to say, this task had to be completed after coming to work the previous day, Friday, at 3:00 a.m.

Well, as "John Hannibal" Smith, played by George Peppard, in the 1983 action TV show, *The A-Team*, would say after a mission, "I love it when a plan comes together."

Monday morning came, and we were free to make the trip. The night before on Sunday, after Brenda had gone to bed, I placed roses and a card on our kitchen's island. She was delighted by the surprise. Continuing my plan, I decided we would get up early to take the dogs, Rock and Bruno, to Lin's so that they could spend the night there. I also had to drop off some documents to Arnold Williams, our accountant. Arnold needed them to complete our 2019 taxes, and next, I needed to drop by The Bakery to pick up some pies and rolls to take to Gert. I also decided to stop by the G&M Restaurant to pick up a crab cake for her as well. This visit was a total surprise to her.

On the way, Brenda and I stopped by the National Harbor, located in Prince George's County, MD, minutes away from Washington, D.C., It sits on the banks of the Potomac River. It was a nice place to have lunch. Our experience there was the total opposite of what we went through last year. Then the place was bustling. We had to drive around, searching for a parking garage with space. Lines to do everything and anything were long. But this time, none of that was a problem. We did not go into the casino this time but walked around and saw that most of the restaurants were closed. There was hardly anyone on the streets. However, we found two of our favorite places open—a crab cake restaurant and another place called *Honey's Fried Chicken & Donuts*. With no lines, our food was prepared quickly. Finding a table was not an issue because there were only about twenty people in the area. The only people we encountered were the vendors. We sat down and enjoyed ourselves, then went back to our vehicle, sanitized ourselves, and continued our journey.

When we got to Gert's, she was busy painting her spare bedroom, which is our room, whenever we come to visit. Bob was outside, sitting in his vehicle when we pulled up, and it took him a few minutes to realize who we were. Greeting us warmly, he led us to the front door and pointed to the room where she was painting. I opened the door, and she looked over at me and almost dropped her paint roller.

Joyfully, Gert said, "I was just thinking that I needed to FaceTime you because I hadn't seen you in a while."

We haven't visited one another in a while due to the COVID-19 challenge. She just could not believe I was really there. We hugged for a minute or so, and she hugged Brenda as well.

We talked for a while, and she decided to bake a cake. Since we could not go out to dinner, I decided I was going to prepare a steak dinner for us. After her cake came out of the oven, Gert drove me over to Sam's Club, where we picked up steaks, the ingredients to make a salad and sweet potatoes for our dinner. I prepared the steaks; Brenda prepared the salad, and Gert took care of baking the sweet potatoes. So, we all enjoyed a great dinner, great conversation, and Gert's rum cake was fantastic.

Because of the rum in the cake, my first thought was to skip it. Plus, since everyone knows that I do not consume alcohol, Brenda chimed in and said that I could not have any. But heck, it was our anniversary. I snuck a small piece, and I was happy that I did not pass out from the rum. If I had, Brenda was gonna kill me.

***

It's Tuesday, July 28, 2020. After 2020, God must have some great things planned for the world, this country, and for our people. Sunday was not a bad day at The Bakery. We were able to capture more revenue in the four and a half hours than we made in the seven hours we worked on last Friday. Additional good news came from a visit I got from Father Meadows of St. James' Episcopal Church. The church is located on 1020 West Lafayette Avenue, steps away from The Lafayette Market, or some call it The Avenue Market, and it's a five-minute drive from The Bakery. Father Meadows, Jr. is the Priest in charge there. A while back, I had received a call from a lady parishioner of his church who had asked if we would be interested in preparing products for their food giveaway.

She said to me that, "The Bakery was recommended to me by Joseph Haskins of Harbor Bank, and [he said that] it was a way of helping Black businesses."

Soon after, I sent her a proposal but had not heard from her in nearly two weeks.

Saturday's visit from Father Meadows was promising. Actually, I had missed his visit because I was out getting lunch for my crew. When I returned, I called him. And he informed me that the former president of the NAACP, Ben Jealous, recommended that the parish, in its mission to support its food drive, should support Black businesses to accomplish its goal. Jealous' NAACP five-year tenure was from 2008 to 2013. At age thirty-five, he had become NAACP's youngest president. Jealous, a Columbia University and Oxford graduate, was elected as the 2018 Democratic nominee in the political race for Maryland's governor but lost to the incumbent, Republican Gov. Larry Hogan.

After we closed on Sunday, I delivered a sympathy card to a friend I have been knowing for years, Ronald Goodridge, who lost his fifty-year-old son to colon cancer. The viewing was taking place at Williams Funeral home on Monroe Street, also close to The Bakery. I had LJ with me because I usually take him home after we close. I wanted to make sure he was protecting himself from COVID-19, so I left him in the truck and made my way through the crowd outside of the funeral home. I made sure I wore my mask and only stayed long enough to extend my condolences and to deliver the card. The same family also has a fifty-year-old family member who has just died in his sleep while on a honeymoon in Las Vegas.

Life is so short these days, and from celebrities to great leaders, it appears people are dropping like flies. One cannot help but try to make the best of every day. With that in mind, next week we plan to take a trip to our home in Florida. We were last there when Brenda and I attended the Super Bowl back in February, pre-pandemic. We normally go down Easter week, but we did not due to the pandemic. We had booked a flight, but we decided to drive. Knowing that Florida is now a COVID-19 hotspot, and, for right now, among the twenty-seven U.S. states listed as such, Brenda and Lin are shopping for everything we need for the stay so that we will not have to leave the house when we get there. Our dining room is beginning to look like a food pantry.

Over the years, as I have pursued the rebuilding of The Royal Theater and the revitalization of Historic West Baltimore, I have received calls from strangers all over the country and Europe as well. All the calls have been questions about The Royal. I received another one yesterday from a lady by the name of Alice Bernstein, who identified herself as a journalist. She spoke of *Aesthetic Realism* and its founder Eli Siegel. She sent me an attachment by email, information from The Library of Congress about *The Force of Ethics in Civil Rights Oral History Project* that her late husband, David Bernstein, and she began fifteen years ago, and it continues. We spoke on the phone for forty minutes, and I shared with her all I knew about The Royal and our mission to rebuild it. I sent her a copy of the video that UMBC did on me and the project, as well as a copy of our impact statement. We said we would keep in touch.

Speaking of the project, for the past seven years, we have held *our Concert Music Series* at The Avenue Bakery, and we had planned it this year as well. Back in February, I applied for our city permits and paid the application fees. Due to the pandemic, we cannot have our event, which is a fundraiser and education campaign on the project, titled *The Royal Theater & Community Heritage Center*. We decided that on September 5th, which had been pre-slated for the last concert of our Summer 2020 season, we will do a live stream concert at The Bakery.

***

It's Saturday night, August 8, 2020, at 10:58. I had a busy day. I waxed the two cars and my truck. I helped Brenda with the hot tub so that she and Lin could enjoy it. It took some coaxing for Lin to get Brenda to join her, though. For some reason, the geckos find their way into the screened-in backyard, where the hot tub is. Usually, *hate* is a strong word for Brenda, and she avoids such a notion at all costs. But Brenda hates geckos. I spent part of my time yesterday cleaning out the moss in the backyard as well. I think geckos love moss.

I was busy spraying and scrubbing the backyard's pavers when the little older lady—well, older than me—who lives in the house at the end of the street came to the door of our screened-in yard. We often see her working in her garden. Her backyard is beautifully landscaped with all kinds of plants and interestingly arranged shrubs. Italian is her native language, I believe. And it is often difficult to understand what she's saying. She had seen me working on the pavers and came up to give me some advice.

"You should work in your yard early in the morning to avoid the heat," she said, looking seriously helpful. "Like I do. When I lived in New York," she shared, "I used bleach to get the moss and fungus out." Pointing all around the yard to give her words an added visual, she finalized, "I use bleach rather than those expensive chemicals you're using."

I listened intently to her sturdy advice. Initially, she had introduced herself, but somehow, I missed it. So, I asked her for her name. And she said, Rosario, so fast that I had to get her to repeat it. I then told her my name. Then an idea popped into my head. Abruptly, I asked her to, "Please wait a minute while I run in the house?" And she did. I felt that she was very thoughtful. I returned to the backyard with a couple of slices of apple cake that I had brought down to Florida from The Bakery. Our apple cakes are favorites in Baltimore. And looking at the smile on my Floridian neighbor's face, it was about to be a big hit here in Kissimmee.

Later in the evening, we heard our doorbell ring, which was unusual. I opened the door, and it was Rosario there with her walker. She explained to me that she really enjoyed the apple cake that she shared with someone at her house; I could not make out who.

"How can I order a whole one?" she asked.

Thoroughly delighted and grateful, I replied, "I'll figure out how to ship one to you."

"How much?" she asked, and she was making her way to hand me some money.

I refused to take any money from her and told her that I would get back to her on the price. While we stood there, talking some more, she began checking out our shrubs. She asked if she could take care of them. I did not know what to say, but I ended up saying, "Yes, if you would like to." At this point, I decided I would send her an apple cake and some other goodies from The Bakery to thank her for taking care of our shrubs. At that point, I had her hold on for another minute so that I could run into the house to put three more slices of apple cake into a bag to give to her.

One of the things I've always understood about older people is that they like to stay busy and they love to do things for others. She reminded me of Nanny, Betty Brown, Brenda's grandmother, who loved to sew. Even though I could afford new dress shirts, she'd take off the worn-out collars of my dress shirts, turn them around and resew them to make my shirts look new again. It made her feel useful, and it made me feel good to make her happy.

While doing a few other maintenance chores around the house, I was still working on and thinking of ways to keep moving on our project. For the past seven years, we have hosted a concert series in our garden, The Avenue Bakery courtyard. But because of the pandemic, we are hosting a live stream concert on September 5th, which would have been our last concert of the 2020 season. Alice and I have been diligently trying to work out the agenda—and figure out how we can make this fundraising event work during this COVID-19 Global Pandemic. We are working with Calvin Watkins of Chosen Media for the streaming and Rosa Pryor Trusty for the band selection. James Dow, one of our board members, is helping by putting together a band for the event. We are also working with Rick Lamonica, who is upgrading our website. My mind is busy while taking this quarantined vacation here in Florida. When we get back to Maryland, we expect to quarantine for fourteen days as the State mandates.

***

It's 1:41 p.m., Tuesday, August 18, 2020. My first task was to call the second air conditioning repairman to get a second opinion on my first-floor apartment unit that had gone up. The first repairman is saying I will need a new unit which will cost around $10,000. That is not in my budget. The second guy will meet me at the apartment, 5:00 p.m. today. I spent the early morning trimming the hedges and bushes around the house. I did that while I was waiting for the dew to burn off so I could cut the grass. After I finished, I hauled away all the clippings and proceeded to cut the grass. I have an acre, and for some people, I assume this would be a task. But for me, it is therapy. It gives me time to be alone riding my John Deere and letting my mind wander.

The first thing that came to my mind was the visit I received from my sister, Dot. Two weeks ago, she and her husband, Paul, moved back to the city from Chase, Maryland. That's about twenty miles north of Baltimore. She moved about ten blocks from The Bakery in the 1600 block of McCulloh Street. When I was in high school, we lived the block above where she now lives. I didn't ask why they decided to move back in town but just accepted the fact and figured I would see her more often. Anyway, she came to The Bakery to purchase a dozen and a half of Poppay's rolls and insisted on paying for it. In her younger adult years, she would have expected me to give them to her whenever she asked.

The past few years, when she comes to mind, it has been a pleasure to call Dot to say I love her and check on her. She has really changed over the years. And she seems to be back to the supporting-big-sister I grew up with. Dot and I used to be close, and we shared everything.

We could always find something to laugh about and trusted one another with our most personal secrets. As a matter of fact, she is the person who taught me to hand dance when I was around fourteen. And I am good at it, too. I may have mentioned it before, but when I go to a party all I need is some good music and someone to dance with.

The next thing that popped up in my head was the live stream concert we are planning on September 5, our fundraiser. The first Saturday of September is always the last concert of the season for TRTCHC. I had been hopeful, we would be marketing and raising money by now, but we are just about ready to start promoting it on social media.

Then came the TRTCHC project itself, that popped into my head. Arnold Williams, my accountant, had suggested that I reach out to Colin Talbert, President of the Baltimore Development Corporation (BDC), which is the development arm of Baltimore City, and I did. It has been a week since I left a message for him. As of yet, I have gotten no response. I am not sure, but he may have attended the meeting that Mayor Pugh held to shut down our efforts. As a follow-up, I will share the results with Arnold to see what he suggests.

For the past forty years, we have held our family cookout at our house on Labor Day. In past years, we have had close to a hundred people—family and friends here. We normally have served hamburgers, hot dogs, and I prepare my fall-off-the-bone ribs, dripping with the Bone Sucking sauce that I doctor up for the occasion. Family members make their favorite dishes and bring beverages and snacks as well. With everyone bringing something, we never run out of food, and some have take-home plates as well. Needless to say, with this Pandemic going on, we have a decision to make. Brenda and I went back and forth with our discussions, and I came up with an idea. We decided we would have an Over Fifty-five or Sixty Labor Day Cookout and call to see who wants to attend. Our thoughts are that our generation is the smallest group and that the younger folks will understand.

***

It's Monday, August 24, 2020. I woke up at four o'clock this morning, and I sent the pictures of Brandon's accident to our Triple-A insurance agent. Yes, Brandon had his first car accident. He and the other driver, seventy-six-year-old Mrs. Johnson from Georgia, were uninjured but slightly shaken. Brandon and I had just finished up at The Bakery. He had left about five minutes before me. As I was locking the parking lot's gate, he called me to say he was involved in an accident. It happened just that quickly. "Is anyone hurt?" I rushed to say, "Are you okay?"

"No," he answered back and explained that he was at Gwynns Falls Parkway near the Mondawmin Mall Shopping Center across the street from Coppin State University.

"Stay calm," I said, "and make sure you and the other driver exchange information."

When I got there, Brandon got out of his vehicle and began explaining what happened. It was clear to me that it was not his fault. He explained how he tried to avoid hitting Mrs. Johnson's car. I then went over to her car to make sure she was okay. She was and confirmed that, yes, she was a little shaken up. When I asked her for her insurance information, she was reluctant to share it. I asked her if she had something I could write on to give her Brandon's insurance information, and she gave me an envelope. I stepped aside and explained to Brandon, in detail, how to handle this type of situation. I had him dial 911 to get a Baltimore police officer there.

I was glad I had the opportunity to be there for his first accident. Let's face it; I believe ninety-nine percent of us have had at least one car accident. Being there for his first one sort of rounds out the driver education I have given him. He was nervous, understandably, but settled enough to understand what needed to happen. And now that I think of it, I remember Mrs. Johnson mentioning that she was having problems seeing the text message on her phone that her daughter was sending her. Now I'm wondering whether she had an issue with her vision that caused her to proceed past the stop sign into moving traffic. Well, that was yesterday, and today, which happens to be my birthday, I had to wrap up the next steps to get this accident resolved and Brandon's car repaired.

Yes, today, I'm seventy-two years old. And as I have mentioned when sharing the details of my birth, the first decision of my life, well—pre-birth, really—was deciding that the home-visiting doctor was taking too long. So, I brought myself into the world. I had to get out of that cramped space I was in. Thinking about that, I'm also remembering how my mom never told me what time I was born. Since I have always had trouble sleeping all night, I assume it must have been a late-night journey.

Anyway, after getting up 4:00 a.m. and sending the information to Triple A, I went back to bed. When I woke up again, Brenda had already left for her morning walk with the girls, Lin, Etoy, and Susan. I went into the kitchen and noticed a blue gift bag on the kitchen island with a card sticking out. That is what Brenda does for all my special occasions, now that I think about it. I read the beautiful card she created; she never buys cards off the shelf. I opened the bag and unwrapped the contents, and yes, she got me just what I needed. Whenever we go to our house in Florida, I get up in the morning to ride my bike for about three miles. I enjoy this; however, there is pain to be had in the rear. It takes me about three days for my backside and backbone to get readjusted after riding on that hard seat. You see, both a blessing and in this instance, a curse, I have truly little cushion back there. Lately, it seems my rear never gets readjusted. Brenda has been noticing me complaining about it. True to form, she's a woman of few words but loads of action—and she loves to problem-solve. So, in that bag, I pulled out two pairs of bike shorts with the cushion in the seat. Now I am looking forward to our Florida trip in October so that I can see how they work. I am sure my buns, to be more exact; my boney butt will feel much better.

I prepared my breakfast, an egg bagel, and chocolate milk. Chocolate milk has been my favorite beverage since my first day of school. I mentioned, previously, about how on that day, my mother took me to school to show me the way, and said to me, "Now you know how to get home."

But after school, I got lost. And an older girl noticed my fear and predicament. She took me to her house. Her mother greeted us and fed me a bologna sandwich. To wash it down, she gave me chocolate milk. Later the older girl helped me find my way home. Neither had I forgotten that experience nor did I forget that nice cold glass of chocolate milk.

Back to today, I went outside to see if the grass was dry enough to cut. It wasn't. Next, I went to the shed to get the hedge trimmers so that I had something to do until the grass was ready. And I went about the three-hour task of cutting the grass and trimming up. It took me a little longer than usual because I was repeatedly answering my phone, accepting all the birthday wishes coming in from family and friends. After that, I was on my computer taking care of something. Then I ate lunch and took my evening birthday nap. I got up to find that Brenda had ordered dinner from one of my favorite restaurants, *Texas Roadhouse*. I love its ribeye steak, green beans, and loaded sweet potatoes. I could only eat my way through half of that as always.

I will end my birthday by searching for and watching movies on Netflix. I am so blessed and happy to be alive and in decent health, especially during our nation's handling of this COVID-19 Global Pandemic. God has blessed me so much. I do not need a lot of fanfare on my birthday. It feels so good to just be alive and able to function.

CHAPTER THIRTY-ONE

THE BURNING QUESTIONS, AT LARGE

It's Tuesday, September 22, 2020, at 6:30 a.m. Today is my Sister Dot's birthday. It's also my granddaughter Bria's birthday as well. Bria is the one who named me, Poppay. They are both on my mind, front and center. However, the end of this memoir is beginning to take over for a moment. The question of just how I end my story when life keeps moving on, and so many life issues continue to manifest daily is not an easy question to answer. This is what I was thinking, but somehow as I woke up this morning, I realized we are at a breaking point in this country. And let me take the time to say, here, that I offer my heartfelt condolences to the late Supreme Court Justice Ruth Bader Ginsburg's family and to our country at this time of her passing.

We have come to a point where Murphy has taken over this country, our city, and our community. As Murphy's Law goes, A*nything that can go wrong will go wrong*; and by the way, I have no idea who in the heck Murphy is. I'll leave that up to you to google. But just the same, here we are with the worst leader of the most powerful country in the world. We are experiencing a pandemic, and people are dying. We have a Congress that has lost its way—proudly exhibiting no ethics, with no respect for our governing principles or our Constitution. We have leadership that is divided with no sense of working together to make decisions that are good for the country. We are held hostage by leaders like Mitch McConnell and Lindsay Graham, who are more concerned about power and control than working together for the country's good. And, by the way, what is good for the country is plain to see, but their choices are power, absolute control, and no compromise.

We are experiencing much of the same here, in Baltimore, and more. The trickle-down effect from this country's lack of responsible leadership, and the mishandling of a pandemic response as well as the economic fallout that followed. But even before the COVID-19 Global Pandemic, we, the City of Baltimore, were already suffering from the economic disparity that has existed since the riots of 1968.

With assets of monumental proportion, the most historic African American community in the country could be activated and enjoyed if only our divisive community and city leaders could see it. Instead, we have leaders who divide us rather than unite us. We have, and have had, city leaders who have cared more about control, power, and self-satisfaction. Much like Congress, we have our *Lindsey Grahams* and *Mitch McConnells* who refuse to see and do what will bring unity and economic prosperity to our community and to Baltimore City as a whole. Worse than that, we have had City leadership that did not have the testicle fortitude to take on a leadership role to bring everyone together and to say that, "This is what we are going to do for the good of the City and its people."

As a result, we have a city, divided, with no positive economic opportunity for sixty percent of its population. We have people who are either dying due to poverty or shackled due to a drug trade that has been allowed to be the economic engine of our city.

So here we are at the dawn of a new day, heading to the year 2021. This is the most critical election year in the history of this country and our city. There are many questions that will need to be answered for this country, our city, and our African American community. Will there be new leadership that brings people together and begins our healing process—both for America and Baltimore? Will there be leadership that is willing to bring us together and make good decisions for the people, void of an insatiable thirst for power and control? Will we come together to ensure there are no haves and have nots in the country and Baltimore City? Will there be leadership that has the fortitude to make the right decisions for the good of the people and not individuals, political parties, or shortsighted community leaders?

On a Roll is about a life struggle, not just for me. It's sharing a vision and commitment to doing God's work. This is about a vision of a better community, a better Baltimore, and having faith that, one day, people will see the light. It is about making sacrifices to make life better for our young people and providing them with the economic opportunities they deserve. It is a call to put aside our differences to have the gumption to do what is good for our people, our community. It is about making the drug trade and its economy, along with the death and destruction that goes with it, a minor issue rather than a controlling factor. We must give our community alternative economic opportunities. I keep repeating: We have the assets; we need to build the infrastructure.

***

It's Wednesday, December 2, 2020, at 2:02 a.m. The first day of December, Tuesday had been a busy day. The day began with preparing for Greg, the handyman's arrival to repair the sheetrock in the bedroom, downstairs. A week ago, Brenda went down to the room to store her stash of paper towels and toilet paper and found a puddle of water on the floor. To make a story short, the copper water line to our ice maker had sprung a leak that must have gone on for months. It took Ham and me quite some time to find the source of the leak that had damaged the ceiling and back wall of the room. I replaced the copper line with an insulated one; however, sheetrock, I leave to the pros. When I completed the additions to the house years ago, my father-in-law Otto Finnick handled that for me. That was his profession.

After Greg was settled in at work, I worked on my memoir with Yvonne. Skype was not working well, and we went to Zoom, which was a little tricky since it was the first time, I had used it with her. After about two hours working with her, I had to get Brenda to take me to the dealer to pick up my truck. I have had problems getting it to start for the last month. I thought that either the connection to the key or the battery might be the problem. But after replacing the truck and key batteries, the problem still existed. It turned out that the ignition switch was the culprit. I have an extended warranty on my truck with a $100 deductible. Of course, the dealer's mechanics came up with a list of things they suggested needed attention. Of course, I said no thanks.

After picking up my truck, I headed to Sam's Club to pick up the supplies I ordered. I have been trying to get The Bakery ready for opening back up on Thursday. Since the day before Thanksgiving, we have been closed when my customers purchased everything, I had but the kitchen sink. After picking up my supplies, I had to stop at Lin's to drop off a blender. And I decided to participate in our 6:00 p.m. TRT-CHC remote board meeting while at Lin's. After the meeting, I headed to The Bakery to offload. By the time I finished and got back home, it was 9:00 p.m.

This Thanksgiving for us as a family was a little different. However, The Bakery was just as busy as last year, though most of our customers shared that they were not having large gatherings. I must say that this was the smoothest Thanksgiving we've ever had. Yes, we processed 649 dozen of Poppay's Rolls, but the demand for our sweet potato pies was off the charts. We sold 325 sweet potato pies to our customers for the holiday season.

***

It's Monday, December 28, 2020, 4:30 a.m. At this moment, there are a lot of things on my mind. Today would be my younger brother Rick's birthday. I believe he would be sixty-five years old had he not been killed. Tony and I often talk about his sense of humor and how he used to keep us laughing. I can still visualize that big smile of his and that very muscular physique he had. I remember when we were kids, he would talk us to sleep.

Also, on my mind, of course, is the prostate biopsy I must have done. It is not so much the procedure that I am concerned about. My concern is making sure the anesthesiologist understands it does not take much to put me to sleep. The last time I was put under, it was hard to wake me up. I had this procedure done twice, about four years ago. The first time, it was uncomfortable, but the second time it was extremely painful. That is why I asked to be put to sleep when they do it this time around. I am not having any prostate issues, but my PSA jumped up, and Dr. Sigmon wants the biopsy done as a precaution. Two weeks ago, I had a CT scan (a computerized tomography scan) of my prostate, and it was normal.

It is not out of fear that I have concerns; it is more about the family and the work in the community I am trying to get done. These comprise all the questions that come to mind and trying to beat the clock—as they say. I'm trying to get my bucket list completed before God says, "You've done enough. It's time to rest."

As I get older and go through my daily routines, I sometimes think of each task and wonder, *Is this the last time I'm going to perform this?*

It is weird; other than this situation, I feel healthier than I've ever been. I do not seem to get bronchitis and colds like I used to. My weight is just where it should be, and my BMI is perfect. I exercise three days a week, and I even compete with LJ on our six-packs. My mind is working, and most of the time, it's overactive. I guess life is like a baseball game; occasionally, you are thrown a curveball.

At The Bakery, Lin hugged me a couple of times, and it reminded me of the hug she would give me as a little girl. It made me feel so blessed and fortunate. When I look at my life and where I am today, I say, "God has been good to me."

Well, Brenda will be taking me to get the procedure done, and it will be a three-hour process. The instructions were not to eat anything after midnight. The procedure begins later this morning at 11:00 and it will take three hours. That means when it is over; I will be so hungry, I could eat a cow. I must make sure she has something in the car for me to eat when she picks me up.

***

This has been an exceedingly difficult year with the COVID crisis and this dysfunctional Trump Administration. It has torn our country apart and caused thousands of deaths due to the poor handling of a deadly virus. Now that the election is over, there is light at the end of the tunnel. It is so refreshing to see the Biden-Harris team diligently lining up all the components and diverse professionals to get our country in order and moving in the right direction.

I am looking forward to 2021. Effective Tuesday, December 8, Baltimore City came under new leadership. And the questions are: Will Mayor Brandon Scott and Baltimore City Council President

Nick Mosby see the light? Will they understand that the root of our problem in our City is economics? Will they realize that the key to changing Baltimore is to bring its people together and to pursue an economic agenda and development plan for Historic West Baltimore and Pennsylvania Avenue? Will they understand that this is a critical component of positive change? Do they have the testicular fortitude?

And here are a few more pertinent questions:

Stated quite simply, we have not let two important facts fall off the radar of Baltimore City's administrations: Fact #1. We will not stop fighting for the TRTCHC project to be implemented for the good of West Baltimore and beyond; and Fact #2. That $300,000 was provided by former Governor O'Malley in his last budget expressly for the TRTCHC project to proceed. Yet, down through the years, these two facts have been consistently dishonored and derailed.

Recently, $300,000 in fines have been levied upon a developer involved in an unsanctioned 2018 demolition as reported in the *Baltimore Business Journal* [December 11, 2020]. The *BBJ* news goes on to state that the city will use the funds "toward the redevelopment of Robert C. Marshall Park in Upton."

We've kept up our fight throughout the mayoral administrations of Rawlings-Blake (that was supportive), Pugh, and Young. The question: Will Baltimore's newest administration recognize the funds, long-designated for the long-recognized feasible plan for Robert C. Marshall Field, i.e., the long-presented TRTCHC plan? Will this finally end the bait-and-switch tactics regarding the city's proposed physical sites for the project?

Will this group see the light to enact a plan that will strategically reconstruct historic West Baltimore and Pennsylvania Avenue, its commercial district? Will the powers-that-be, newly put in place, work to bring the communities' stakeholders, along with State representatives, to create real communities owning a vibrant economic business district? Will they understand that the key is to utilize every block and acre of land on our commercial district to bring about economic opportunities?

We have acres of land to build homes and to preserve our open spaces without inundating or threatening our valuable commercial core. The City's Planning Department needs to be strategic and visionary in its urban development plans. This group of politicians must be boldly aggressive and held accountable when it comes to economic development and changing Baltimore for the better. To sit in a seat and govern the status quo means nothing. The late former Mayor William Donald Schaefer was the architect and visionary for the Inner Harbor, once a filthy dirty place overrun with weeds and trash. We have Historic West Baltimore, Pennsylvania Avenue, and a long history of art, entertainment, and political legacy that is more valuable today than ever. We are sitting on a gold mine—and suffering—rather than developing our assets and creating a new Wall Street. The Avenue Bakery has overwhelmingly proved the point that we can attract people from all over the country and beyond. Imagine how self-sufficient and engaging to the world we would be, owning a vibrant commercial corridor that included arts and entertainment and history to enhance what is already the third-largest industry in our City—tourism, which is (under normal conditions) at the tune of more than $10 billion annually.

***

A Baltimore Story—*On a Roll* — Reflections

It is 12:44 a.m. on Wednesday April 21, 2021. Normally I would be getting out the shower and dressing for work. However, we are on vacation at home here in Florida. We picked up Gert in Virginia as we drove down. Waymon, Tony, Teddy and his fiancée Michele are on their way down from Georgia, and Lin will be flying in on Thursday. It will be an interesting and unusual week.

Yesterday we were glued to the TV waiting on the verdict for Derek Chauvin the police officer who killed George Floyd. The verdict that was the obvious was not expected because so many police officers have gotten away with murdering Black men. For once there is a glimmering light that justice for all might become a reality, along with addressing the issue of bad cops—so that good cops can get the respect they deserve.

I'm reflecting on this year that is moving so fast, knowing that our focus on Pennsylvania Avenue and its revitalization is still very much on the agenda. As we reach out to Mayor Brandon Scott to determine if he still supports our efforts as he did when he was Council President and running for the higher leadership of our city, we're hopeful that his commitment has not changed.

Also on my mind is the fact that August 15th will be the 10th Anniversary of The Avenue Bakery, *Home of Poppay's Rolls.* We have not decided how we are going to celebrate this milestone. We are sure, however, that we need to keep in mind COVID-19 precautions to keep the celebration safe.

My thoughts journeyed to how, years ago, I started testing the waters so to speak. I began baking and selling my rolls, that had long been family favorites, to friends and former co-workers to get their opinion. And orders started coming in. I then decided to participate in a baking orientation at a culinary school to get a feel and advice on the idea. The instructor discouraged me about my silly venture, and to help me, he indicated his desire for me to abandon the idea of building a bakery. I nearly moved on to my other dream to become a teacher, hoping to teach at my Junior High School alma mater, Booker T. Washington, which still is not a bad idea. Shortly after his advice, he stopped responding to my calls or emails. But the more enthusiasm and requests for rolls I received, the more I felt like I could make it happen.

We are extremely fortunate that in these ten years, The Bakery is still standing and thriving, while in the midst of seeing quite a few businesses come and go—especially during the pandemic. The Avenue Bakery has attracted busloads of tourists from across the country and internationally. Our local clientele extends from Virginia to Pennsylvania. Pre-pandemic, we even accommodated visits from some of Maryland's elite schools.

During 2020, the busloads halted, but our local clientele kept us busy. Folks come not only for the baked goods, but also for the vibrant tributes The Bakery offers to showcase and educate about this community's rich African American history.

The first outdoor piece was The Royal Theater painting in our courtyard by artist Cisco Davis. I believe he visited The Bakery one day and we had and enlightening conversation. He and I seemed to have the same mindset when it came to the legacy of our people and communities. We talked extensively about the history of The Royal; me, from personal experience, and him from what he heard and learned from his family. Cisco is originally from the Dominican Republic and traveled a lot while in the military. He agreed to create a mural of The Royal and convinced me not to put it on a wall because, "if you move," he said, "you cannot take it with you." He shared with me his experience of creating a mural while in the military and soon after, the Air Force shut down the base.

I bought all the materials he needed, and he created our fantastic center piece of The Royal in our Courtyard—created on a moveable wall. The following year he created the adjacent pieces that depict many of the great churches and images that trigger memories about what is great about our community.

The next year, Stuart Hudgins and I began planning the huge civil rights photomontage that people cannot miss when they travel, walking or driving, south on Pennsylvania Avenue. When I purchased the Bakers Hardware property in 2004, I vowed that one day I would replace that liquor signage plastered there about twelve feet from the ground. So, our photomontage is twenty-eight by sixteen feet. It tells the civil rights story here in Maryland, our northern most southern state. It highlights the segregation, lynching and mob violence against us as well as the great leaders in the movement to bring about equality in our country not just our city and state. It gives visuals of the fact that the heart of the movement was here in Baltimore, the protests, and the fact that Reverend, Dr. King Jr. came here to council with Reverend Woods and pastors with whom he attended seminary.

Then came the Billie Holiday photomontages that we unveiled to showcase her life and the bandleaders with whom she performed. We unveiled this one celebrating the one hundred years of her birth. Next was the Thurgood Marshall piece that we unveiled the year after Law Professor Larry Gibson published the book, titled *Young Thurgood: Making of a Supreme Court Justice*. For this unveiling event we invited him to give a presentation to our students of Booker T. Washington Arts Academy at the ceremony. From Theater to sports, politics, and entertainment we have images of our great African American legacy of Pennsylvania Avenue and Historic West Baltimore. We have almost run out of space to put more images, but we continue to seek out more that can create that since of community pride and dignity.

Every year, we have had unveilings that give us opportunities to increase our market and provide positive media coverage for our community, which is rare.

Over the years our days of operation process and procedure have changed as well as our menu, which has expanded since our opening in August of 2011. I remember the hustle and bustle, and the excited chatter of that first opening day. Five people milled about in the kitchen setting things in order, rolling dough, filling the pans to process the rolls, and praying that because we built it, the people would come. Today, Lin and I process rolls with the help of our dough rounder machine, Erika. Back in 2011, we did not have pecan pies, brownies, apple cake or carrot cake on the menu. After a couple of weeks in business, Lin came up with making bread pudding out of the rolls we did not sell. It became a hit with our customers.

When I think of The Bakery family, I must mention Sade Robinson, whom we met, interviewed, and hired as our cake decorator. After a year in operation, we realized our customers wanted cakes as well as pies and rolls. Even though we could bake our cakes, none of us were able to decorate cakes professionally. So, I reached out to Edmondson High School, my alma mater, because of its culinary program and bakery. I wanted to hire one of its baking program students, possessing decorating skills.

I learned that Edmondson did not have any students whom we could hire; however, one of the teachers introduced us to a former student, Sade. Long story short, today, I call her an artist, not a cake decorator. She is so talented that she can make a cake look like anything the mind can imagine. More than that, she has become family. I attended her wedding, and we celebrated the birth of the couple's son, Jay. Her family also attends our annual family Labor Day cookout.

Hundreds of our customers depend on us to make their Thanksgiving and their other special occasions enjoyable. Our upcoming celebration will center around thanking our customers for their support.

I remember back in January of 2011 when the family and I had a meeting in the clubroom in our home to discuss the birth of The Bakery. We talked about who would do what and the hours of operation. As I mentioned earlier, thanks to Omar Mohammad, an instructor at Morgan State University, we recruited students from Morgan's Earl G. Graves School of Business and Management (SBM) to help develop our business and marketing plan. Brad Redd, who worked with me when I was the 2nd Vice President of the Baltimore Branch NAACP helped with the business plan as well. We used the plan to acquire the loan to renovate the old Bakers Hardware. Kathleen, our architect, got right to work. Over the years, she's become like a daughter to me.

We acquired a loan from SBA to renovate the building and purchased the equipment we needed. In 2010, I almost made the decision to finance it myself because the bank was requiring me to use everything I had for collateral. It was not enough that I owned the property on Pennsylvania Avenue, the steely bank representative looked me dead in my eye, directing me to put up my home rental property as well as my stocks. While she was very nice and cordial to me, her job was to adhere to the demands she was given. And so, she steadily interviewed me and reinterviewed me in a quest to make sure I put everything on the line for *my quest* to own a business to prove that establishments on the Pennsylvania Avenue Corridor could indeed translate into economic success and feed its residents. Of course, outwardly during each visit Brenda and I made, I remained calm, cool and collected, while I studied every word and every inflection of the words, the banker uttered. I studied her demeanor and her thinly veiled incredulousness, which perhaps was in innocence, at my nerve to want what I wanted, and to have owned the collateral that I had owned. I also observed how during our meetings, she had to continuously dip out to the office of her a higher boss, unseen, who was the hierarchical source of inventive hurdles to my accruing the loan.

Society paints African Americans with a broad brush of anger. We are branded with, among other negative connotations, as angry men and angry women. So, was my assessment that Ms. Banker was doing a bit too much in my case, requiring me to jump extra hurdles to acquire the American Dream of legacy-building wealth, at best or ending a negative cycle of economic dependency, at the least, on point? Was my gall an overreaction?

In January 2020, reporter Gene Marks writes the following in *The Guardian. According to data recently made available from the US Federal Reserve, more than half of companies that have black owners were turned down for loans, a rate twice as high as white business owners. The report found that while black-owned firms were the most likely to have applied for bank financing, less than 47% of these applications were fully funded. Even when black business owners get approved, their rate of failure to receive full financing is the highest among all categories by more than 10%.*

The story, which puts forth the question, *Is this discrimination?* And highlights additional factors, and the struggles, of other minorities is titled *Black-owned firms are twice as likely to be rejected for loans.*

In 2011, it came to my mind, *what about those who did not have the assets that I had?* They would have no chance of getting a business loan. That still concerns me today—the fact that African American entrepreneurs have less of a chance to get a loan as whites.

Well, the last ten years has been rewarding and exciting to say the least. We have been covered by just about every newspaper, magazine and TV station in Baltimore. We have been defined as a mini-museum, and you can find us in a book published in 2019, titled *111 Places in Baltimore That You Must Not Miss*, by Allison Robicelli.

***

It's Monday, May 3, 2021 at 3:00 a.m. As I think about The Bakery and the journey to today, many things come to mind. Yes, I have been baking my rolls for years, but I only baked white rolls. However, now I bake wheat as well. The beginning of the wheat roll came about because of a question by Mayor Sheila Dixon when she visited us. One thing about her is that she is very health conscious, and she has a regular exercise regimen. As I remember it, on her visit, she got a taste of our rolls and loved them. Her question to me was, "Do you make these in wheat?" Thanks to her, we offer them in wheat and white.

Recently, the former Baltimore City mayor, Ms. Dixon, did some reflecting of her own that made me smile with gratefulness. She shared, "I watched you leave UPS, which is where I met you, to take on this dream of opening a bakery—because of your passion to please others through baking and showing Black people that they could accomplish success and create a business that would have a tremendous impact on the community!"

I cannot find the business card or remember the name of the gentleman who made the large 2229 purple and orange address sign on our building for the life of me. I just remember the fact that shortly after we opened, he came by, asked us for the address, and a week later, he came by and installed it. I believe he owned a printing company and that creating a sign for us was meant to be his quite effective calling card. It was. But we never got around to doing business with him.

As we began developing our menu, one of our customers, René Wartman, worked for the Baltimore Police Department. On her visit, she mentioned that one of her aunts, who used to make a fantastic coconut cake, had a recipe that she was willing to share. Although we didn't end up using her aunt's recipe, we have to have coconut cake for our customers.

Another visitor who comes to mind who impressed me was Dr. Keiffer Mitchell of the political family by that name. I believe it was a few years before he passed. We have a podium in our lobby with an autograph book for our customers to comment on their experience with us. Dr. Mitchell sat in our lobby and completed an entire page reflecting on his family.

About two years ago, Sandra Banks, one of our customers asked me, "Do you bake Jewish Apple Cake?"

To which I replied, "no." However, that same year, Brenda and I took a weekend vacation to Philadelphia. She wanted to visit the Liberty Bell and other historical Philly sites. We visited the Reading Terminal Market downtown. We encountered a bakery booth and happened to see apple cake, and we bought a couple of pieces. We did not taste them until after dinner that night in our hotel room. It was fantastic. When we got back home, I looked up a recipe online and tweaked it. Soon after, apple cake became a huge hit with our customers.

As we celebrate our tenth anniversary, I'm reflecting on so many people who have helped make our business what it is today.

***

When I think of Baltimore and our presently divided city, I think of the classic and timeless film, *The Color Purple*. I will never forget what Whoopi Goldberg's character, *Celie*, in the 1985 film said to Danny Glover's character, *Mister*, which was, "until you do right by me, everything you think about is going to crumble." So goes the same for Baltimore City. Until this city and Baltimore City's Leadership do what's right for the Historic Pennsylvania Avenue Corridor and its residents, the whole of Baltimore will never change for the better. And we will continue to lose valuable lives to the current illegal trades and lack of economic parity.

So, I end this historical memoir as we—together—live the next chapter of our country's history and legacy. God has brought all of us to this point. It is up to us to make the decisions that will change the outcomes in our Country, City, and Community. As Michael Jackson pointed out, "If you want to make the world a better place, take a look at yourself, and then make a change."

God Bless.

The End — For Now

THE BIRTH OF A MISSION —AND BEYOND

Back in 2005, *The Royal Theater & Community Heritage Corporation* (TRTCHC) was founded by James Hamlin, Alice Cole, Adrian Johnson and the late Raymond V. Haysbert, one of the original Tuskegee Airmen. Haysbert, through his relationship with Little Willie Adams, was able to bring *Parks Sausage* to Baltimore. These founders and its members had banded together to make a difference.

Still today, TRTCHC's purpose is to address the negative perceptions and realities of Historic West Baltimore and Pennsylvania Avenue—vital parts of the 7th Congressional District. Long ago, we realized that if we were going to change and enhance Baltimore's future, then we needed to address the root cause of its problems. Our focus has been to create a positive environment to develop economic opportunities, and to change the negative outlook of our future leaders. We are dedicated to creating a model for urban revitalization for cities across the country that will create jobs; develop an environment that will bring together multi-generational populations to instill pride and dignity in our community as well as attract tourists, globally, and reduce poverty and crime in Baltimore.

TRTCHC MISSION STATEMENT

Our goal is to build The Royal Theater & Community Heritage Center. This holistic development project consists of a new Royal Theater, Jazz Center, retail shops and restaurants. We are also investing in an outdoor recreational space that our senior citizens and youth can enjoy together. This new recreational space, including a clubhouse, will become a safe place for our youth, and something of which they can be proud. This project allows us to take advantage of Baltimore's third largest 5.7 billion dollar-tourist industry, while creating jobs and careers in our community.

TRTCHC'S IMPACT STATEMENT FOR THE ROYAL THEATER & COMMUNITY HERITAGE CENTER

The Past is the Future...

"Pennsylvania Avenue was once the beating heart of Baltimore's African-American community. It was the city's premier cultural and entertainment district, featuring famed nightclubs, bars, and restaurants. At a time when black performers were not allowed in white venues, the Royal Theatre showcased an astonishing array of brilliant and now-legendary talents: Louis Armstrong, Charlie Parker, Ray Charles, Sarah Vaughan, Mahalia Jackson, James Brown, and many others. Forged within the cruel crucible of segregation, the Pennsylvania Avenue corridor was a vibrant place of commerce, community, and culture and the adjacent neighborhoods were home to many of Baltimore's greatest figures, from Thurgood Marshall and Cab Calloway to Billie Holliday and Kweisi Mfume." - *ULI Baltimore Pennsylvania Avenue Technical Assistance Panel 09/14/16-*

TRTCHC

Impact Statement

In 2005 The Royal Theater & Community Heritage Corporation (TRTCHC) was founded by James Hamlin, Alice Cole, Adrian Johnson and 9 other members. Its purpose was and has been to address the negative perceptions and realities of Historic West Baltimore and Pennsylvania Avenue, part of the 7th Congressional District. We realized that if we are going to change and enhance Baltimore's future, we need to address the root cause of its problems. Our focus has been to create a positive environment, economic opportunities, and to change the negative outlook of our future leaders. We are dedicated to creating a model for urban revitalization for cities across the country that will create jobs, an environment that will bring together multi-generational populations that will instill pride and dignity in our community; attract tourist globally and reduce poverty and crime in Baltimore.

2

Our goal is to build The Royal Theater & Community Heritage Center. This holistic development project consists of a new Royal Theater, Jazz Center, retail shops and restaurants. As part of the project, we are investing in an outdoor recreational space that our senior citizens and youth can enjoy together. This new recreational space, including a clubhouse, will become a safe place for our youth, and something of which they can be proud. This project allows us to take advantage of Baltimore's third largest 5.7 billion dollar-tourist industry, while creating jobs and careers in our community.

3

Economic Impact

As Maryland's top destination, tourism drives Baltimore's economy and quality of life in a number of ways – visitor spending, job creation and tax generation.

In Calendar Year 2017, Baltimore welcomed 26.2 million domestic person trips, growth resulting from a 1% increase in day trips over the prior year .Thanks to gains driven by increased day visitation in the food & beverage and recreational activities categories, overall visitor spending rose 2.5% to $5.7 billion in direct sales. In total, Baltimore area tourism spending generated $717 million in local City and State taxes, saving each Baltimore area household $685 in personal income tax contributions. *–Visit Baltimore-*

The Arts & Entrainment (A&E) districts supported an estimated 7,049 direct, 1,313 indirect, and 1,626 induced jobs (total of 9,987 jobs) during FY 2018. This is an increase from the total employment impact of 8,594 jobs in FY 2016. Of these jobs, 1,753 (1,083 direct, 312 indirect, and 358 induced) were supported by new businesses formed within A&E districts' boundaries. The other 8,234 jobs (5,966 direct, 1,001 indirect, and 1,268 induced) were supported by visitor spending at events and festivals supported by the A&E districts.

Estimated projections, the $49 million Royal Theatre & Community Heritage Center will generate $6 - 8 million in annual revenue, approximately $2 million in state tax revenue, an estimated $5 million in tax revenue for Baltimore City and more than 1000 new jobs.

4

EPILOGUE

THE PRODUCT OF LIFE EXPERIENCES

It's Saturday,_March 20, 2004, I'm ready and set to make my second UPS retirement speech in front of a brand-new dining hall filled with family, colleagues, mentors and friends. This event has the dual purpose of being a fundraiser for Coppin State College. My family gave me a surprise retirement party, about a week ago. But an opportunity for this second event came around to celebrate my retirement as a fundraiser and to inspire others to volunteer their time and to donate to community causes. With gratefulness in my heart, I took it. My speech:

Summing up Thirty-five Years of Service—and A Thousand Thank Yous!

First, I would like for our political leaders who have blessed Coppin and me with their support to stand and be recognized.

My 35-year career with UPS has been a rewarding and educational experience. It has afforded me the opportunity to provide for my family, meet and work with a host of fine people. I have enjoyed the challenges that I faced, each and every one of the 10,900 days at UPS—and the lives I have had the opportunity to impact. For that, I thank UPS.

At this point I would like to thank many of the people who have played a part in developing the man you see standing before you. We are a product of our experiences in life, and the decisions we make. This evening is not just about Jim Hamlin.

God, for guiding me and placing so many wonderful people in my life. And this room is filled with many of them.

James W. Hamlin, my dad, although he was not able to play the role in my life that he and I would have liked, thank you dad. I possess many of his traits especially his enterprising and entrepreneurial spirit.

Mattie Virginia Waymon, a single mom for most of her life, did all she could to rear her ten children. And she gave them all of her love. She taught me responsibility and did an excellent job of holding me accountable for my actions. She taught me how to burp babies, change diapers, clean house, and prepare meals and shop for women's clothes. More than that she taught me that no matter how little you have—you have something to give. It was not unusual for us to share a meal with someone less fortunate in the community.

Berl James Clemons, my grandfather who worked for Bethlehem Steel for 45 years. He was a very strong, positive role model and the first person in my family to own a car.

Mother Hamlin, who spent her life in the church, loved me unconditionally and was an excellent entrepreneur.

Mr. Archie Laden, the grocery store owner at the corner of Druid Hill Avenue and Preston Streets who gave me my first job working every day after school and all day on Saturday for $7.00 a week. There I learned how to clean fish, cut up chickens, wait on customers and deliver groceries. It is here that a gentleman, by the name of Henry, taught me the sense of urgency.

My Science Teacher, Mr. Harris, at Booker T. Washington Middle School who preached respect and what it means to be a man. He also made the point to share with the class what it means to be a woman.

My Art Teacher, Mr. Apple, who taught me Good, Better, Best, Never Let it Rest until The Good is Better and The Better is the Best.

Mr. Eddy, a home improvement painter, who taught me that I could reach any heights. I was the one, at age 14, who would do all the painting when the ladder had to be extended beyond 25 feet.

Thomas Lewis, my closest friend. He was the person who called me up in 1968 to tell me about a job that was paying $3.35 an hour, and the rest is history.

Rev. Edward R. McClurkin was my first supervisor when I began this 35-year journey. He has always been a role model and a valued friend. He has always answered my call for support and words of wisdom.

I thank my wife, Brenda, for helping to rear our two beautiful children, James and Belinda, and filling in when I couldn't be there. My fellow UPSers know what that is all about. I thank my children for understanding and for being the wonderful people they are. I thank them for D'Angelo, Bria, Brandon and James Hamlin the IV who will soon be here. I love them with all my heart—for my family is of the utmost importance in my life.

Managers and Supervisors at UPS, past and present, whom I have had the opportunity to hire, train, work for and with. I have learned and grown so much as a result of these relationships. I could not begin to name them all. But here's a few:

Jerry Mc Allister	*Warren Wilson*	*Ed McClurkin*
Mike Stokes	*Cal Tyler*	*Willie McDuffie*
Bill McCoy	*Wyatt Arrington*	*Mel Smith*
Greg Myer	*Roy Brown*	*Jack Nice*
Jim Hanley	*Mike Hewson*	

There is a point to all of this. I am a product of my environment and the decisions I have made. I continue to meet role models and develop valuable relationships. There are so many people who have influenced my life and continue to do so. God and you have blessed me.

My point. Friends, there are thousands of Jim Hamlins in our City who need our help, whether it is a kind word, a meal, tutoring, mentoring or setting an example. God will bless them in many ways. I ask that you pass on the blessing you have given to me, on to them, as so many of you do.

I again thank you, and those who could not be here, but who sent contributions, for the wonderful part you have played in my life and for supporting Coppin State College. There are young people in our community who will become great leaders as a result of your action.

ABOUT THE AUTHOR

James W. Hamlin is the Owner and Operator of The Avenue Bakery, *Home of Poppay's Rolls*!

Hamlin's passion has been chronicled in *The Baltimore Sun*, *The Baltimore Afro*, *Baltimore Magazine*, *Baltimore Business Journal* and elsewhere. During his more than 35 years at the United Parcel Service (UPS), he excelled at fostering its mission to empower local communities. Hamlin galvanized his UPS troops to teach/mentor students of all ages. Post retirement, in 2003, he became even more active in community organizations and civic duty. And in 2005, he founded *The Royal Theater & Community Heritage Corporation* (TRTCHC) to rebuild The Royal Theater. Its demolition in 1971 is considered an affront to the communities it served.

Also, via TRTCHC, Hamlin is building an economic engine to fuel stability and awareness in West Baltimore—a region of great divide between blacks and whites in median household income/jobs, quality of education, healthcare, the receipt of city resources, and much more.

The Avenue Bakery is a tour stop for visitors, nationwide and internationally. The Avenue Bakery is famous for its courtyard mural, depicting historic icons, and its summer Courtyard Music Series, featuring live entertainment and plenty of good food to eat.